The European Radical Left

The European Radical Left

Movements and Parties
since the 1960s

Giorgos Charalambous

PLUTO  PRESS

First published 2022 by Pluto Press
New Wing, Somerset House, Strand, London WC2R 1LA

www.plutobooks.com

Copyright © Giorgos Charalambous 2022

The right of Giorgos Charalambous to be identified as the author of this work has been asserted in accordance with the Copyright, Designs and Patents Act 1988.

British Library Cataloguing in Publication Data
A catalogue record for this book is available from the British Library

ISBN   978 0 7453 4051 7   Hardback
ISBN   978 0 7453 4052 4   Paperback
ISBN   978 1 78680 795 3   PDF
ISBN   978 1 78680 796 0   EPUB

Typeset by Stanford DTP Services, Northampton, England

Simultaneously printed in the United Kingdom and United States of America

Via and for
Haris and Nestoras

Contents

Contents

Tables

Figures

Abbreviations

15M	*indignados* movement
AKEL	Ανορθωτικό Κόμμα Εργαζομένου Λαού (Progressive Party of Working People)
ANTARSYA	Αντικαπιταλιστική, Αριστερή Συνεργασία για την Ανατροπή (Anticapitalist Left Cooperation for the Overthrow)
Attac	Association pour la Taxation des Transactions financières et pour l'Action Citoyenne (Association for the Taxation of financial Transactions and Citizen's Action)
CND	Campaign for Nuclear Disarmament
CPs	Communist Parties
DC	Democrazia Cristiana (Christian Democracy)
DiEM25	Democracy in Europe Movement 2025
EACL	European Anti-Capitalist Left
EEC	European Economic Community
ELP	European Left Party
EP	European Parliament
ESF	European Social Forum
EU	European Union
FI	France Insoumise (Unbowed France)
G7	Group of Seven
G8	Group of Eight
G20	Group of Twenty
GJM	Global Justice Movement
GPs	Green parties
GUE/NGL	Gauche unitaire européenne/Gauche verte nordique (European United Left/Nordic Green Left)
IMF	International Monetary Fund
INITIATIVE	Initiative of Communist and Workers' Parties
IRA	Irish Republican Army

IU	Izquierda Unita (United Left)
KKE	Κουμουνιστικό Κόμμα Ελλάδας (Communist Party of Greece)
KKE Interior	Κομουνιστικό Κόμμα Ελλάδας – Εσωτερικού
LGBTQ	lesbian, gay, bisexual, transsexual, queer
M5S	Five Star Movement
MEP	Member of the European Parliament
NATO	North Atlantic Treaty Organization
NGO	non-governmental organisation
NPA	Nouveau Parti Anticapitaliste (New Anti-capitalist Party)
NSMs	new social movements
PAH	Plataforma de Afectados por la Hipoteca (Platform for People Affected by Mortgages)
PASOK	Πανελλήνιο Σοσιαλιστικό Κόμμα (Panhellenic Socialist Party)
PCE	Partido Communista de Espagna (Communist Party of Spain)
PCI	Partito Comunista Italiano (Communist Party of Italy)
PCF	Parti Communiste Français (Communist Party of France)
PCP	Partido Comunista Português (Portuguese Communist Party)
PS	Parti Socialiste (Socialist Party)
RAF	Rote Armee Fraktion (Red Army Fraction)
Rifondazione	Partito della Rifondazione Comunista (Party of Communist Refoundation)
RLPs	Radical Left parties
SDPs	social democratic parties
SMO	social movement organisation
SP	Socialistische Partij (Socialist Party)
SPD	Sozialdemokratische Partei Deutschlands (Social Democratic Party of Germany)
STWC	Stop the War Coalition
SV	Sosialistisk Venstreparti (Socialist Left)

SYRIZA	Συνασπισμός της Ριζοσπαστικής Αριστεράς (Coalition of the Radical Left)
TINA	'There Is No Alternative'
UN	United Nations
USSR	Союз Советских Социалистических Республик (Union of Soviet Socialist Republics/Soviet Union)
WSF	World Social Forum
WTO	World Trade Organization

Preface

Discussion about European politics has changed in the past decade or so, in turn inviting, among other things, several inquiries into the Radical Left and altering the terms on which decisions are made as to what to research and publish. Correspondingly, the trend of the 1990s, which saw a large downsizing in academic research about the Left and a large rise in the volume of literature about the far right, which continues until today, has shifted dramatically. A large number of articles and books employing rigorous analysis about the European Radical Left and the politics of contention and resistance have been produced. Writing about the Left, be it about partisans or activists, elections, governments, strikes or the occupation of public squares, is a new norm that for many years was not as common. So, why write yet another book? What has prompted it?

In an attempt to make a modest contribution to this flourishing literature, both academic and political, two points of departure were taken in the broader scene of a dialogue on the prospects and challenges of alternative futures. First, plenty is being said about the contemporary Radical Left from the past to the present, but little about the past *in* the present. For this author, it often felt that in socialist strategy and or the study of radical politics, the historical benchmark is not properly set or understood when a discovery, a novelty, a fundamental change, a critical juncture or a breakthrough are claimed or implied. To understand the evolution of politics entails asking if and how politics 'recur' – is there historical 'recurrence', analogy or parallel – not in what concerns events, of course, but in terms of the forms political conflict and within it the Radical Left take. An attempt to capture long-term development and place the contemporary within a complex sequence of events also opens up space for tracing cross-national as well as country-specific legacies, which often determine whether the Radical Left moves backwards or forwards.

Second, to say the least, there is still meagre discussion about the diversity of actorness on the European Radical Left and the dynamics between different ways of mobilising in opposition to capitalism and neoliberalism. Indicatively, while the New Left of the 1960s constituted above all a constellation of New Social Movements, an authoritative voice in this domain, Donatella della Porta, recently lamented that the Radical Left has so far largely received 'a silence in social movement studies'. If anything, an understanding of the Radical Left today requires above all a (re)interpretation of the political itself, including the most subtle forms of engaging with socialist and progressive politics. It thus seemed important to zoom out and consider both institutional and electoral affairs and the politics of activism, including relations between the relevant forces. Given its comparative purview, a fair warning about the book at hand is that it encourages more a rethinking of the Radical Left in Europe since the 1960s rather than aspiring to a proper, start-to-finish historical reconstruction.

Largely the product of a longer period of gestation, the book was written during the past four years or so, and during this time a number of individuals have provided me with ideas and critical comments on chapters and parts of the manuscript in development. Elin Haugsgjerd Allern, David Bailey, Ioannis Balampanidis, Amieke Bouma, Paolo Chiocchetti, Leandros Fischer, Loukia Kotronaki, Christos Mais, Kevin Morgan, Andreas Panayiotou, Serafim Sepheriades, Yiannis Stavrakakis and Aimilia Vilou each offered constructive feedback. Costas Eleftheriou and Gregoris Ioannou read the whole of the draft manuscript and provided meticulous comments, with both conceptual and empirical insights. Pluto's three anonymous reviewers suggested very sharp improvements and David Castle as the editor has been, to these final moments, very supportive and incisive. Alexandros Gregoriou and Panos Panagiotopoulos offered valuable research assistance with data collection. Christophoros Christophorou and Andrea Pedrazzani assisted me with survey data analysis. Informal discussions with Charis Psaltis, Orestis Antonas, Andreas Panayiotou, Stergios Mitas, Nicos Trimikliniotis, Kleitos Papastylianou, Maria Hadjimichael and Giorgos Tsiakalos opened avenues for analytic treatment.

Drafts of different chapters of the book were presented at the Annual Conference of the Italian Political Science Association in September 2018 in Urbino, Italy; the European Sociological Association Annual Conference in August 2019, in Manchester; and the seminar series of the Laboratory of Contentious Politics, Panteion University, Athens in November 2020. Thanks, therefore, are also due to the discussants and participants of the relevant audiences. Some of the arguments were also presented at a seminar presentation on the Radical Left at the 2019 European Elections organised by the Institute of Alternative Politics in Athens; and at the seminar series of the University of Glasgow's Sociology Group. Sharp remarks on these occasions have helped to refine the thinking behind the book's story.

All these individuals, although bearing no responsibility for the interpretations advanced and any errors in the book, which are fully the author's own, have infused the materialisation and shape of the research and writing phases. This is greatly appreciated. Finally, small parts of text in Chapters 4, 5 and 7 are reproduced by permission of Christian Fuchs and *tripleC: Communication, Capitalism and Critique*, from the article 'Reclaiming Radicalism: Discursive Wars and the Left'.[1]

G. C.
Nicosia, June 2021

PART I

Mobilisation, Resistance and the European Radical Left

1
Introducing the Approach

Since the global financial crisis of 2008, western Europe, like many other regions, has witnessed large-scale social and political upheaval. A significant part of this has been resistance from radicals and progressives to neoliberal governance. Initially, mobilisation focused on support of better democracy and against the implementation of aggressive austerity measures, and subsequently on many other frontages. Many scholars and commentators have treated this phase stretching into 2020 as signalling at least a redefinition of progressive politics and at most a dramatic increase in the mobilisation of anti-establishment forces, responding to a post-democratic capitalist crisis through polymorphous dissent.[1] In this light novelty on the Radical Left has been announced aplenty during recent years.

Social movement studies research highlights novelty, adaptation and learning. The apparent ubiquity of upheaval in the wake of the crisis has generated talk of its divergence from previous episodes of intensified mobilisation. Activists and scholars alike spoke of 'new' or 'third wave' anarchism,[2] and post-anarchism,[3] blending with citizenship claims into 'anarchocitizenism'.[4] More broadly, the most recently emerging social movement actors have been identified as a new global movement phenomenon,[5] as 'occupy social movements',[6] 'populist social movements',[7] 'new social movements'[8] and 'new new social movements'.[9] The Radical Left now also includes the 'digital party',[10] the 'new left populist parties'[11] and reradicalised social democracy as in the phase under Jeremy Corbyn's leadership of the British Labour Party. More generally, historical sociology has suggested relative novelty in the contemporary period[12] to which one would expect the Radical Left to logically respond by adapting. Yet it is not clear what this adaptation has entailed, how far it has gone and what it looks like today in the third decade of the twenty-first century.

3

Does the frequent invocation of radical reinvigoration as something which discontinues the old underestimate the socialist lineage? In what sense is the new a misused or misunderstood term, amid a broader mania of neologisms, including the ones about the 'New Right', the 'New Centre', 'the populist radical right', the 'Alt Right', the 'new extremism' and so on? What can unravelling this definitional issue teach us about the Radical Left in general, and about radical left parties (RLPs) and movements in particular? The task at hand is to historicise the Radical Left of today, to bring into the light continuities and discontinuities between different historical instances of radical left politics in western Europe. In order to achieve this purpose the book analyses and explains parallels and distinctions between and across three periods of time in the twentieth and twenty-first centuries during which the western European Radical Left has been conventionally understood as 'new'. These periods include:

- The main developments around radical mobilisation after the mid-1960s and into the late 1970s (what we will call the Long '68, symbolised by the May 1968 uprisings in France and considered as the temporal high ground of the New Left).
- The period between the mid-1990s and mid-2000s, during which the Global Justice Movement (GJM) was a central figure of radical politics and many RLPs supported it.
- The post-2008 movements and parties until today and into the global Covid-19 pandemic (alternatively, we refer to this period also as the 2010s).

The relevance of left radicalism has been acknowledged in much of the literature on the 1960s/1970s.[13] It is also to be found in work on the GJM and anti-austerity protests in Europe.[14] The three decades considered here include what have come to be known as protest 'waves', part of broader and longer periods that resemble 'cycles of contention', or in the language here: mobilisation and resistance. While these 'waves' are taken into consideration the perspective on 'newness' does not look at waves of contention but at the Radical Left during (and beyond) these waves, out of which 'newness' emerges, or to which 'newness' gradually comes to belong. Via a comparison between the Radical Left during these time spans, the book aims at interrogating patterns of evolution since the 1960s and offers an interpretation which rationalises them. The motive of our intended scrutiny is that 'newness' has been repeatedly pointed out for the Radical Left in scholarly research[15] without offering the appropriate comparative analysis that would qualify and nuance the term across multiple alleged episodes.

THE EUROPEAN RADICAL LEFT AND 'NEWNESS'

The three periods of 'newness' taken up have been reflected upon as distinct epochs for the Left as a whole. They have also been endowed, at least in the eyes of their protagonists, with the symbolic significance of a key and global 'moment' in the struggle for a better world. The post-2008 period in Europe has been unfolding within the context of a global wave of dissent since 2008.[16] The Long '68 was also the 'Global '68', the result of three geographically defined mobilisation cycles, which in coinciding and influencing each other gave rise to 'a globality': student and worker protests in the West; anti-bureaucratic dissidents in the Soviet bloc; and national liberation movements in the so-called Third World.[17] In this sense, 1968, like the end of World War II in 1945 and the fall of the Berlin Wall up to the Soviet Union's (USSR) disintegration in 1989–91, has been seen as a 'transnational moment of change'.[18] Post-2008 seems to fit into this category as well, as do the events surrounding the GJM from the mid-1990s to approximately the mid-2000s.

More specifically, in the Long '68, students, workers and others fuelled partisan trajectories, produced intellectual openings and challenged entrenched cultural values and social behaviour. Starting in 1968 and lasting for about three years, demonstrations, social and political disorder and violence were a global phenomenon that was sufficient for the period to be understood as revolutionary. Over the decade, between the late 1960s and the late 1970s, with stretching back and forth in some countries, material and non-material grievances mobilised extensively, both in the electoral and the non-electoral realm. The truly massive bibliography that exists about the political and (indeed) cultural subversions and openings during these two decades itself testifies to how they reverberate in historical terms. The wake of '68 received not only observations about 'newness' but a whole strain of research into 'new social movements' (NSMs). Among scholars contributing to this tradition of investigation, itself signalling a renewal of academic reflection on social movements, there has been strong agreement that the social forces of the 1960s and 1970s reconceived political participation, and in doing so ultimately blurred conflict over wealth distribution.[19]

In the second half of the 1990s and until the mid-2000s, western Europe was host to a left radicalism that criticised neoliberal globalisation and its private and public international institutions on multiple policy dimensions. This period had a strong anti-European Union (EU) and anti-war element, channelled into protest in western Europe but paralleled with crises in Asia and Latin America, followed by extensive grassroots mobilisation. Likewise, post-2008, the ten years or so after the explosion of the global financial bust which severely affected the eurozone and especially Europe's southern periphery, have seen an unparalleled series of crises, from austerity, authoritarianism and anti-immigrant sentiment, to climate discussions, and by the end of 2020 the Covid-19 pandemic and a refuelled economic crisis.[20] Global protests have been rising dramatically, increasing worldwide by more than 10 per cent annually between 2009 and 2019.[21]

In the book, under discussion is above all a broader comparative historical sociology of the European Radical Left. The question of the new is not merely a lexicological issue; by incorporating the past into our interpretative grid we can better appreciate and understand the current state of affairs on the European Radical Left, as well as evaluate its future challenges and assess its moves forward.[22] In this light it becomes a meaningful task to discern the old and the new in historical time, since the scrutiny of 'newness' in a macro-historical comparative fashion can in turn clarify the following: how 'newness' and thus change has been perhaps, or not, overstated for the socialist politics of today or before, or not sufficiently contextualised in cross-country terms; the connections of left radicalism with macro-level changes such as large-scale shifts in technology, economics and politics; and the prospects of contemporary left radicalism in Europe based on its precedents.

Our analytical choice of looking at 'newness' concerns significations of change, such as adaptation, rupture and transformation, or gradual, incremental evolution. These notions lie at the core of both sociology and political science, more specifically the study of systems and conflict within and between institutions.[23] Among radical intellectuals, there is a long-lasting debate about what constitutes the new socio-economic transformation. Historical materialism as developed by Karl Marx and Friedrich Engels was an explanation of historical evolution from one economic system to another, each time with the same reason – class conflict, an ingrained antithesis – producing the subsequent one. Cornelius Castoriades wrote about the 'unconditioned new', the new emerging 'out of nothing', continuing with theorists such as Alain Badiou and Slavoj Žižek. From the post-Marxist perspective, 'radically new inventions' are seen as 'neither already available in prior circumstances nor causally preordained by antecedent conditions'.[24] Possibilities for radical system change can in this sense lie in 'emergent publics', which cannot be foretold.[25] Our pursuit is to turn the radical preoccupation with the historically new and historical change on its head, applying it to socialist politics itself. On the Radical Left, what are the emergent publics across time and how new are they? To what extent have today's inventions emerged out of nothing?

To be useful, 'newness' can be a non-dichotomous variable, a spectrum with dimensions along which institutional and non-institutional actors can be gauged and compared. To simply choose to describe a party or group of political actors as new or not new is to miss the more fine-grained question of how and in terms of which of its manifestations the European Radical Left has changed or transformed, or simply demonstrated a situation of historical recurrence or inertia between key phases of mobilisation and resistance. A new phenomenon is not necessarily something recently discovered or exhibited which has not existed before. In the case of social and political forces, where the prefix 'new' is added to collective actors, 'newness' may denote the revival of another or others of the same kind. In this book, we set the benchmark somewhat higher, since radical revival is, as we already know, present across all periods of 'newness', which effectively legitimises announcing a 'New Left' every time this space intensifies its mobilisation. Rather, here we define the 'new' and 'newness' relatively – 'for something to be new it must be other than the old, it must be different'.[26] But difference itself needs to be operationalised through theoretical notions. Our conceptual grid is elaborated in the rest of this chapter, which presents an actor-centred framework of analysis, aiming to go beyond an either/or understanding of 'newness'.

PARTIES, MOVEMENTS, HISTORY

The actors are multiple on the Radical Left, so when it is addressed, distinct means and agents of mobilisation and resistance are at stake. The Radical Left has been researched predominantly from the 'party's viewpoint', that is, with an emphasis on party calculations, strategies, electoral tactics and institutional dilemmas. This angle has its usefulness and as a disciplinary strain it has generated rich party theory about left radicalism. But it cannot hide what is clearly implied: that parties (and institutional politics) are the natural locus of power and thus have the most endemic significance on the Radical Left, among the different types of actors and mobilisation formats employed in socialist resistance. This is of course, in part at least, a normative assessment, as the progressive impact of left radicalism in parliament or the state, as opposed to the streets, cannot be accurately operationalised and measured, even if they can be distinguished.

Filtering left radicalism through party politics and social movement studies, each domain broadens and contextualises the other, and together they enable a macro-historical view at the level of the Radical Left in western Europe in its (near) totality. The analysis also addresses other organised or quasi-organised actors of left radicalism – such as left-wing trade unions, the left wings of social democratic parties and Green parties (SDPs and GPs), subcultures within the left, intellectual activity and protest participation, wider community action and other campaigns. Because this is for the most part currently missing, and is employed mainly in case study research, three gaps remain unfilled in our collective wisdom about mobilisation and resistance by radicals. What does a two-level assessment of radical politics looks like? More specifically, in what fashion do RLPs evolve as compared to more loosely structured social movements (or the interest-based trade union bodies)? And how has the interaction or, as conceptualised in this book, linkage between these two types of entities developed across time and countries? The first question is about the multifold conjunction between and across different types of radical collective action at any given point, which can be simultaneous or asynchronous. The second speaks to the viewpoints of both social movements and activists on one level and political parties and politicians on another. Together, they allow us to consider both social and institutional politics on the Radical Left as theoretically equivalent versions of system critical mobilisation.

Next is how to connect our actor-centred framework with historical evolution. A comparison, or rather juxtaposition, of three historical instances of radical left politics, as is the approach of this book, lies within the analytical search for 'generalisations about common properties and principles of variation among instances across time and space'.[27] Having periods of 'newness' as cases can facilitate the revelation of key differences while at the same time cater for capturing those phenomena that hold across temporal settings and thus suggest historical resonance and political continuity.[28] Following the paradigm of causal stories, we need to unpack aggregated variables through a comparative historical inquiry.[29] At one and the same time two tasks are pertinent: to juxtapose across time the indirect manifestations of historical contexts on radical identities, rhetoric and organisation, while searching for variation across countries and accounting for it. A delicate balance needs to be pursued between 'individualising and generalising comparisons'; between capturing idiosyncrasies and cultural nuances on the one hand and illuminating trends of universal applicability on the other; and between descriptive accuracy and general 'causal laws'.[30]

Hence the tone of any generalisations of the argument has to take into account the complexities that inevitably arise within the large scope adapted in the book; more specifically, the national variation across countries. The national political system generates and responds to protest, movement and party dynamics, influencing parameters such as the salience of issues in the public sphere, insurgent consciousness and broader constraints and opportunities. It also conditions what is generally acceptable, hostile, unconventional or mainstream in terms of language, ideas, institutions or historical legacies. The narrative proceeds and the book concludes with four criteria in mind: what the predominant and most visible trend is inside the political family in each of the periods considered and across them; which the 'exceptions' are and why; how variable the situation is across countries; and how the western European left has evolved in itself but also in relation to its globality.

To provide the ground for associating actor 'newness' with their changing setting, it is necessary to identify the main objects (phenomena): the observed processes (towards a series of outcomes) and events (landmark occurrences) during particular periods. The distinct parameters of the historical context since the 1960s are extensively integrated into the rest of the book and summarised in Chapter 9. In Appendix 1, these are outlined for each decade considered and the periods between them as concerns Europe-wide and global trends. Moreover, to associate structure with agency, social processes with political actorness, the analysis requires not only a delineation of different histories but also their in-between times. Events and developments such as the onset of neoliberal globalisation after the 1970s, or the financial crisis of 2008 several years after the peak of the GJM, or the events of 1989–1991 leading to the USSR's fall and the dissolution of the international socialist bloc, or technological advances like the social media, need to be brought in. We ought to suggest that features and moments of social life have facilitated or inhibited a particular evolution in actor characteristics. The narrative must be wed to the identification of causal mechanisms and sequential processes across periods and over time. It must also retain sensitivity for the long-term development perspective: slow outcomes and thus underlying factors of change which become visible over the very long term,[31] or ones catalysed by certain events but preceded by earlier conditioning factors.

OVERVIEW OF THE BOOK

The book is divided into three parts. In the rest of Part I, Chapter 2 is devoted to introducing and elaborating the main concepts guiding the empirical focus. It outlines a comparative approach towards the study of the Radical Left, centring on mobilisation by several types of individual and collective agents, chiefly parties and movements, as constituent parts of a political space *qua* family, navigating the friction between resistance and co-optation and/or demobilisation. Distinguishing between group ideas and ideologies, rhetoric and communication, and organisation, including composition and linkage, the framework examines analytically distinct but interrelated aspects of mobilisation and resistance. Chapter 2 also provides a working definition of the Radical Left that brings in its universe of collective forces.

Part II and III proceed on the basis of the taxonomical approach, drawing out the chief similarities and differences between the three periods of 'newness' in question, considering in turn identities, rhetoric and organisation as actor dimensions of comparative analysis. While Part II concentrates on social movements (and activism), Part III deals with political parties and electoral competition. In each chapter, sections reflect key ideas, rhetorical patterns and organisational tendencies within the Left, asking how these have changed (or not) until today. Chapters 3 and 6 deal with democracy and opposition to prevailing economic processes and doctrines, solidarity, immigration and internationalism. In this perspective attitudes towards European integration are a key part of the story. Chapter 4 and 7 are about the rigidity or by contrast the universality of radical left rhetoric, revolution and utopia, and populism and nationalism, as signifiers of left-wing identity in the communicative sphere. Chapters 5 and 8 engage with the radical politics of space, the tension between horizontal and vertical (hierarchical) organisation, democracy as a procedural form of organising the party or movement, state legality, civil resistance and violence, and the constituencies of left radicalism. Within the chapters of Parts II and III, each section follows a broadly (although not very strict) chronological order.

In all, each dimension of analysis is structured on key, selected topics, which although they do not exhaust what one could ask and say about the Radical Left, nevertheless they respond to circulating claims about 'newness' and reference themes that are both topical and historical; core themes of diachronic intellectual debate so to allow a long-term evaluation. They also incorporate overarching sub-issues, and this allows us to expose various other more specific, relevant discussion points about left radicalism. Empirically, the book is argument-driven and methodologically it relies on: (1) a synthetic view and critical discussion of the existing literatures focusing on anti-systemic mobilisation and resistance across disciplines, namely political science, political sociology, political economy, history and social theory; and (2) the analysis of aggregate and country-level data from rigorous surveys and other primary sources, which include websites, online archives, interventions by activists and politicians, and other communication material. Not all of these sources are used directly in the text.

As ideas are transposed into actions, social movements and parties in Europe, the main mobilisers of left radicalism share a number of similarities as well as differences with the radical mobilisers of the 1960s/1970s and the GJM. Which ones they are and why things have evolved in this way is what the conclusions try to synthesise through summarising and accounting for the Radical Left's life-course over the past six decades.

2

Analytical Framework

A time-honoured instrument of political analysis is the notion of party families. These are groupings of political parties across countries, sharing common features and often connected through transnational political networks. A number of indicators are used to capture the perimeters of party families, including ideology and policy, origins, labels and international affiliations. Out of these indicators, the most important one is the first concerning parties' links, and by extension parties' links to cleavages, which often albeit not always capture the other three indicators as well.[1] Party system studies based on cleavage theory probe the idea that the structuration of political conflict is a function of the number, nature and dynamics between distinct social divides based on class, religion, ethnicity, geographical periphery and values.[2] Although, in terms of cleavage and party system alignment patterns, European countries show considerable variation, political conflict is considered to be cross-nationally structured and characterised by similar divides across western Europe.[3]

It would of course be restrictive to consider parties as the only available medium of being or becoming a political subject and actor on the Radical Left, or otherwise enacting a political identity or ritualising a power struggle. Particularly at a time of a historical low in party membership, deidentification with parties and widespread disaffection with institutional politics, being political is not only nor mainly being partisan. Taking as a hint that party ideologies are the most commonly used tool of deciding which parties belong to one or another family, normative political ideas as a source of antagonism are the starting point for elucidating the separating lines between political spaces. Given that political actors are of diverse ideological types, one can speak more broadly of political families occupying a range of space on the political spectrum and its axes of conflict, and within them families of parties, trade unions, social movement organisations and other sectional and value groups.

POLITICAL FAMILIES: HOW TO STUDY THEM?

Taking one step back on the conceptual ladder towards higher levels of abstraction allows us to obtain a larger selection of political actor types than that permitted by the notion of the party family. It is therefore a more appropriate theoretical format for understanding how political ideas are channelled into activity, in parallel and intersecting processes of human interaction, which include but are not limited to party systems. In turn, our investigation must be broader than what politics is often taken to mean, as the study of the Radical Left, like that of any other actors or families of actors in social and political space, is a phenomenon at the crossroads of political science, sociology and anthropology. It is an inherently multi-disciplinary subject of study and its routinisation by human beings is an individual and social as well as political praxis.[4]

A political family is a group of actors with common ideological references and policy preferences engaged in social and political conflict within and also outside of state institutions. Enacting a system of ideas in everyday society and politics, a political family draws from proximate historical ideologies or ideological traditions, in essence combining them in envisioning a series of goals. The word as used in this book assumes the possibility of different organisational types and ideological mixes coexisting within the same broad arrangement of ideas, which has existed as a historical social force since the French Revolution. The Left is in a sense a constituent part of organising around a systemic contradiction between oppressors and oppressed. Political families denote political activity that is often diverse in nature and purpose, driven and inspired from within the same system of thought. Their function is the embodiment and performance of systematised values, principles and beliefs that defend popular grievances. These ideas denote a political space, which becomes a family when it is collectively engaged in social and political conflict; theoretically speaking this collective engagement ranges from full fragmentation to organic unity. Strictly speaking, political families are spaces *qua* families because to constitute themselves as a family with common denominators and little internal conflict is itself variable across country and historical contexts. After all, in party family theory, because the concept is deductively derived, fragmentation within historical, political groupings can be low or high, at the national or the transnational level, affecting the family's cohesion but not the very notion of family as reflective of the social origins of issue conflict. But we can still broadly transpose the configurations of European party families onto their broader, political space. We can thus continue to speak of the Radical Left and (also extreme) Right, the mainstream or centre-left and its historical or contemporary variants (social democrats, most Greens/liberal environmentalists and others) and the mainstream or centre-right and its variants (Christian Democrats, Conservatives and Liberals).[5]

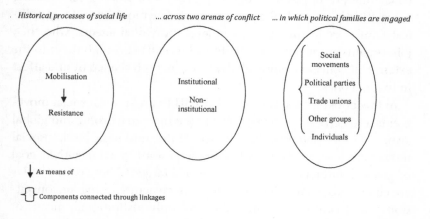

Figure 2.1 Delimiting the study of political families

On the whole, political families denote the ideational proximities and concrete relations between distinct types of mobilisers within a political space. Figure 2.1 illustrates the conceptual architecture of political families. They are composed of actors connected through a network-like structure, which engage in institutional and non-institutional mobilisation. Since the mid-nineteenth century, the Radical Left specifically, has mobilised through trade unions or trade union fractions; anti-fascist militia groups in 1920s Italy; political clubs during the period of the French Revolution; ethical socialist charities in the UK; agrarian associations in late nineteenth-century Russia; freedom or independence movements in Latin America, Africa and Asia; social bandits, indigenous populations and local churches in various Latin American countries and elsewhere; or academics, public intellectuals and artists.

In this historical sense we can speak of several types of mobilisers or components of a political space, acting (not merely thinking about how to act) to achieve certain objectives on the basis of shared principles. This can happen either in an organised or unorganised fashion, collectively or individually, to different degrees of intensity and antagonism. The transposition of ideas into discourse and behaviour presupposes a cognitive process of ideological thinking whose starting place is the human mind. The mobilisers of any political family are at the most basic level individual agents, who then join organisations and coordinate and mobilise through them to the extent that collective political identities are both shaped by and affect individual ones.

In this book, we focus primarily on RLPs and radical social movements and activism because they are the most diachronic and global agents of mobilisation and resistance. At the most basic level, 'a social movement is a collectivity of actors who want to achieve their goal or goals by influencing the decisions of a target'.[6] These collectivities are commonly seen as having a network structure, using 'unconventional', that is, non-institutional or not only institutional, means of political action, espousing shared beliefs, practising solidarity and pursuing conflictual aims.[7] Networks translate into loose associations, which involve informal interactions between individuals, groups and organisations.[8] Social movements as understood here are engaged in 'sequences of contentious politics',[9] have change-oriented goals and a degree of organisation and exhibit more or less temporal continuity, even when they mutate compositionally or adapt organisationally.[10]

The term social movement encompasses both what has come to be called social movement organisations (SMOs)[11] and relatively unorganised turmoil or protest activity expressing discontent without clearly defined proposals and a prescribed structure. The distinction between the individual and the collective level is a crucial one in mobilisation studies.[12] Given that any political family entails agents acting in an organised fashion, or individual or informal group action without regular affiliation to a larger crowd, it must also encompass the mass trends through and around organised forces which channel themselves in activity, agitation and protest. These are wider than the range of participants identifying with specific organised groups. Here there is also a role for intellectuals (high-skilled opinion leaders, experts or other personas) intervening in the public sphere, who link movements as audiences and are recruited for electoral purposes by parties, sign petitions, organise nationally and transnationally, but are foremost defined by their individual capacities, actions, scholarly work or militancy.

The social and political arenas of mobilisation host different actors, endowed with distinctive capacities in relation to political power strictly defined as lying within the ambit of the institutions of governance. Parties are stable political entities that have regular access to the media, the state and political institutions, and they are legally bound to follow electoral rules that in turn shape the nature of party competition. The fact that parliamentary parties have a formal role in organising legislation impacts on their strategic calculus, organisational structure and programmatic positions in ways which, unlike in social movements, concern the 'uneasy relationship between participation, competition and representation'.[13] Co-optation in institutional arenas, such as the party system or government, is of course more likely than in extra-institutional or less formal and binding settings, which are further away from the corridors of public decision-making power. On the other hand, proximity to power may fuel partisan life, something which remains a void in social movements, especially loose and prefigurative ones that are almost never exposed to power motives.

What are regularly referred to as movement cycles with syncopated mobilisation waves do not always coincide with the electoral cycles of their ideologically proximate parties, especially if transnational mobilisation is taken under consideration. Movements, after all, emerge partly to claim social space that lies unoccupied by parties and perform functions that parties do not pursue to the fullest.[14] When parties are busy remaking themselves into electoral machines, movements (and interest groups) fill the role previously and partially played by the mass party on the ground.[15] As social movements and parties are not substitutable, on the Left, especially where extra-institutional action was the way into politics, movements (starting with trade unions) have often injected party systems with dynamism, innovation and debate. Systematically, as we will see, party formation on the Left and electoral realignment towards the Left have been the outcome of mobilisation by organised actors outside or against the state.

Mobilisation is a historical process employed as a means to resist, among other things, securing interests, defending dominant practices, creating art, feeling good or accumulating social capital. Resistance – literally the refusal to accept or comply with something and the display of opposition to it – is endogenously a political concept as it relates directly to the contestation of power and signals dissent from a dominant narrative, an imposed series of 'universal truths', which in the times of neoliberalism have been summed up by TINA ('There Is No Alternative'). Adam Roberts, referring to resistance, wrote of 'activities against a particular power, force, policy or regime'.[16] Vinthagen and Lilja suggested that 'resistance is a subaltern response to power; a practice that challenges and which might undermine power'.[17] In this sense, an act of resistance is undertaken by someone subordinate, as a response and challenge to power, and 'contains at least the possibility that power gets undermined by the act'.[18] Paul Routledge defined resistance as 'any action imbued with intent that attempts to challenge, change or retain particular circumstances relating to societal relations, processes and/or institutions ... [which] imply some form of contestation ... [and] cannot be separated from practices of domination'.[19] This last point of the de facto inseparability of resistance and domination is expressed by Michel Foucault's analysis which transformed orthodox understandings of power, shifting concern from abolishing power altogether to 'what forms of power do we want to live with and which forms do we wish to limit or prevent?'[20]

Indeed, a common point in the above (as well as other) definitions is that although resistance constitutes a counterpoint to global power, it can theoretically be performed inside as well as outside of state institutions and it can be effective or co-opted. In other words, it can either reinforce or reverse the usual direction of co-optation by the magnetic forces of the power being challenged. The history of resistance is full of temporal and spatial variations. As a politics which predates democratic practice, it has been evolving on the basis of centuries-old elaborations of how to respond to oppression, ranging from being aggressive and transformative to being defensive and limited. The form of resistance is determined at the same time by the meaning and pervasiveness of the act of oppression itself.[21]

Focusing on the European continent, resistance is connected to the Radical Left as long as it translates into a vocal opposition to the reproduction or infusion of perceived socially unjust power relations and structures. Resistance can theoretically be practised by all political and party families, yet the history of the Radical Left is more closely tied to the collective interests of the oppressed, subordinate and subaltern sections of society, and thus those most likely to resist systemic forces. Therefore, not all political families resist; some rather dominate by pursuing or negotiating the interests of the dominators.

Yet resistance can be co-opted. Co-optation is equivalent to 'the de-subjectification of a subjectivity initially fabricated under relations of domination'.[22] It can include the process through which an anti-attitude towards the dominant practices, whose criticism renders resistance to what it is, becomes a pro-attitude in declaration and in practice. That is, when there is positional – ideological or programmatic – change that clearly violates policy pledges or ideational principles that are employed in the critique of that notion of the good society, which is embodied by those exercising or attempting to exercise domination. Co-optation will thus naturally lead to deradicalisation.[23] Importantly, the history of the Left is full of instances of 'compromise', 'moderation' and 'defeat'. A number of dilemmas have been pointed out between consistency and co-optation, which have often constituted important sources of tensions within the Radical Left. These tensions were on many occasions resolved in favour of co-optation, as concerns, for example, the EU,[24] the pursuit of executive office[25] or electoralism.[26]

Co-optation can also concern the teleological dimension of ideology (the long-term vision of society by a particular family of political actors), generic rhetorical schemas which avoid revealing one's true credentials or organisational practice which diverges from ideological principles. For social movements, co-optation might mean a number of things: either inflow into parties compromising in parliament or being defeated electorally; or movement demobilisation, that is, social implications analogous to the electoral desubjectification of parties. For party leaderships, unlike for activists, electoral defeat, analogous to social movement demobilisation, does not mean co-optation; often, electoral defeat might be the product of appearing 'too radical'. Co-optation and resistance are temporal, dynamic, intermingled processes, which actors and collectivities navigate through crafting a more or less successful strategy on the basis of specific goals.

Any actor engaged in political conflict and in mobilisation thinks, speaks and organises, thus a collective action framework can both capture and compare movements and parties across their key functions. Analytically distinguishing between the ideational, the rhetorical and the organisational elements allows us to address all and any political actors in processes of mobilisation and resistance without narrowing down the scope of analysis appropriate at the level of political families to more specialist concepts. More field-specific conceptualisations will provide useful analytical tools in the book when it comes to examining each of the three dimensions of analysis consulted here. Indeed, the main point of scrutinising identities, rhetoric and organisation is not that more detailed tools of investigation cannot be employed depending on whether it is movements or parties or other actors under discussion. It is that one can also fall back on categories providing the possibility for generalisations across collective action types (and including individual agents) at the level of the political family: the European Radical Left.

IDENTITY, RHETORIC, ORGANISATION

First, the Radical Left like any other political space is intrinsically connected to systems of thought. Accordingly, as we know from the work of Michael Freeden, ideational morphologies include central, adjacent and peripheral ideas.[27] Studying the morphology of ideologies allows one to consider each value, principle, theme or belief by itself as well as in relation to the others, to approach its content and significance, or put differently, its salience. This is what determines its relational weight within a political family. The salience of currents within a political family can change as there is no particular reason as to why one should exclude the presumption of a dynamic nature between the centre and the periphery of an ideational system.[28] Ideas and often the visions to which these lead can be added, abandoned or modified. They can also move from the centre to the periphery and vice versa, in this way obtaining more or less *salience*. Theoretically, both the centre and the periphery can enlarge, simply incorporating more ideas as social forces on the ground find ways to accommodate them systemically. This is a plausible assumption as long as it is taken into account that change in one concept, whether its addition, abandonment or modification, generates further ideational realignment within the ideological system, because the latter's essence is above all relational.[29]

The morphological perspective is important because it reveals the central and less central variants of ideologies and by extension the constellations of agents expressing these variants. By itself, though, it is still insufficient for our task. Political families reveal the assumption that ideas can only be understood in terms of mobilisation, as 'manifestation[s] of a particular being-in-the-world of conscious actors; of human subjects'.[30] Ideologies and systems of ideas are thus understood here in the sense used within the Gramscian tradition that sees ideology as an action-oriented system of values and beliefs that allow different groups to make sense of the world. Social linguistics, for example, remind us that knowledge, values, intentions and goals of actions are properties of mental representations, themselves generated by the human mind.[31] In turn, the mind is often driven by interests that ideas rationalise, although not necessarily the material interests of all groups espousing these ideas.[32]

This experiential dimension – the connection of the realm of ideas with the condition of human existence – entails that only through their enactment can we understand ideas, by tracing the processes in which their exponents apply them.[33] The assumption here is that ideologies and systems of ideas are not composed of concepts with strictly given meanings, hence we cannot explain their development without tracing how they are practised, reflected upon and contested by people or organisations.[34] We have to accept that the location of ideas is to be found in thought, behaviour and discourse. It is impossible to study ideological phenomena as purely ideational since ideologies influence both language and political behaviour.[35] The ideational morphology of political families is thus only one dimension of analysis that concerns the interrelations between different ideas within the confines of the family's actual political action.

John Schwartzmantel clarified aptly the role of social and political organisation in understanding ideas: 'so ideologies cannot be divorced from movements, whether political parties or broader social movements, which move in the "real world" of politics, and require a certain constituency and social base'.[36] An ideology is thereby not reducible to a system of ideas in a vacuum; ideas are the driving forces of the human agency that allows them to materialise into social and political activity. Political families are constituted through the very act of mobilisation in favour of systematised and contextualised ideas. Out of this mobilisation approach to ideas and the subsequent focus on social movements and parties, three analytical categories are addressed (Figure 2.2). The book considers central ideas and programmatic positions, as the key identity features and ideological referents of actors. At large, ideologies develop a worldview premised on three main axes: how the past has evolved and what this entailed; what the present looks like; and what the future should look like and how to get there.[37] Programmatic positioning cannot capture by itself the radicalism or broader identity of the European Radical Left. As in the 'European tradition' of social movement theory, different kinds of mobiliser bear meanings and axioms that reflect their historical positioning and can thus be ideologically and politically situated.

Collective identities are not only pre-existing givens; most importantly, they form and are negotiated through and during collective action.[38]

Identity ⟷	Rhetoric ⟷	Organisation
Ideas	Self-description	Structures and procedures
(principles/values/beliefs)	*(casting left radicalism)*	*(including linkages with society and other groups)*
Programmatic positions	Predominant schemas	Synthesis/composition
(against/for/policy proposals)	*(frames of language/narratives)*	*(social bases of mobilisation)*

⟷ Direction of influence

Figure 2.2   Matrix of comparing political families

For parties, examining policies often assumes that in different countries the same policy means the same thing;[39] this is certainly not the case given that radicalism as a relational property can easily vary according to the national 'superstructure'. Additionally, party ideology signifies more than programmatic positioning as it goes beyond the characterisation of parties simply by the policy dimensions on which they compete and into their domains of identification.[40] Social movements and party ideology or identity are thus blends of programmatic positions and ideas, deriving from an organisation's origins and the social fault lines which produced it. They also evolve through processes of micro-interaction within the confines of mobilisation and resistance. Therefore, to understand radical identities, one must focus on what form they take, when projected to the outside and debated within the political family itself.

While ideas about the past, present or future (whether values such as freedom, equality and community, or principles such as democracy, sovereignty and solidarity) denote the founding stones of an actor's identity, programmatic positions reveal the objectives of actors in terms of concrete policy measures. This is so in what concerns demands upon governance for the immediate short term and in relation to the long-term, more teleological dimension of a good society. Teleology is about attention to and preoccupation with ideal-type social systems and a plan to attain a better future. Utopian thinking, whether revolutionary planning or prefiguring ideal societies, can form a strong bind among radicals, while its absence, beyond conducing division, can damage legitimacy. If anti-establishment forces present no feasible alternative proposal, then the view that they are merely blame shifters provoking with easy promises prevails more easily.

The book also examines rhetoric in mobilisation and resistance on the western European Radical Left, that is, 'the choice of words (diction), the figures and forms of speech and the overall tone of a discourse'.[41] Rhetoric refers to spoken or written language and is the sum of and interaction between the rhetorical components or frames employed in communication. Framing refers to 'the conscious, strategic efforts by groups of people to fashion shared understandings of the world and of them that legitimate and motivate collective action'.[42] In Benford and Snow's words, a frame is 'an interpretive schema that simplifies and condenses "the world out there" by selectively punctuating and encoding objects, situations, events, experiences, and sequences of actions within one's present or past environments'.[43]

How do social movements and parties articulate discursively their opposition to entrenched politics, communicating their profile to society at large? In what ways do they codify a political synthesis through the signals of their collective language? According to the classic study by James March and Jonah Olsen on the 'new institutionalism(s)', all institutions have a formative culture, and historical antecedents inform rhetorical tradition in particular spaces.[44] Hence, there is the oft-used distinction for casting the broad socialist movement between 'the Left' and 'the progressives', or 'the progressive space'. The former uses 'a capitalised, collective singular', which invokes a unified or rigid bloc, while the latter ('progressives') 'retain their individuality while happening to share certain values'.[45] Given that their symbolisms differ as to the invocation of the collective as opposed to the individual, these terms can be assumed to reflect or wish to emphasise where one stands as to negative liberty, or as to their proximity to the centre.

Rhetoric operates as the storyline contextualising ideas and programmatic positions. It simultaneously seeks to ingrain convictions and shape fertile grievances.[46] Positions arrived at in movement assemblies or party congresses are framed and performed through the means and tricks of language, speech, art, design and culture, in the process triggering emotions, realisations or rationalistic appeal. One element of political communication and thus rhetoric is casting oneself, projecting the movement's or party's image and circumscribing left radicalism more generally. Slogans, leadership speeches, manifestos and the organisation's or action's name, as the very punchlines of mobilising under a political banner, provide crucial information in this respect.

A second element of political rhetoric is how some terms, concepts and schemas of discourse unpack an ideological principle or political message. Terms and concepts, as well as labels, are employed to serve political narratives. Discourse is thus important; the common circulating concepts within academia, politics and activism inform militant ways of perceiving and saying things and update theoretical and argumentative debates. In this sense, book titles, scholarly strains or theories, intellectual figures and pamphlets can all tell us something about radical left rhetoric, where the intellectual and the political coincide, especially among movements. Schemas can be characterisations, narratives, binaries or trichotomies. Is an actor exclusive or inclusive? Which category of the population is she addressing the most? Against which opponents? How is the hardliner/moderate divide in politics at large played out in the radical left space? More generally, how are ideological messages packaged into discourse through communicative framing? Two labels often ascribed to the Left, nationalism and populism, are by and large rhetorical schemas. Framing something in nationalist and populist terms certainly engenders ideas and positions – such as national self-determination, a particular approach to ethnic conflict or an end to elite corruption – although it is not defined by them. Nationalism and populism do not offer the complexity of ideational systems, while they constitute performances centred primarily, although not entirely, on rhetoric and discourse. Their main difference is whether a binary or schema works vertically in casting a hierarchy (as in populism) or horizontally (as in nationalism).[47]

The third dimension of analysis is organisation, by which we mean how mobilisation and resistance are 'administered': their structures and procedures through which leaders, members and sympathisers organise and practice their politics. The structural aspects of a party or movement organisation concern the delimited settings through which individuals engage in politics. These organisational formats include: party or group offices and bodies, more generally patterns of hierarchy and internal procedures, and the 'party models' in use;[48] physical space and how it is associated with political purposes; and existing technological resources and communication channels of mobilisation upon which actors capitalise, such as the internet and social media. In addition, for parties, the occupation of executive and parliamentary office means operating within the structures of the capitalist state.

Incumbency may trigger the redistribution of power towards one of the party's three organisational faces, the party in public office, as distinct from the party in central office and on the ground (membership). This entails institutionalised encroachment into the state by parties, for example, their public financing.[49] Procedures determine how mobilisation unfolds, the processes of decision-making and the forms resistance takes. Movement tactics or 'repertoires of action', for example, can be less or more uncivil, passive or confrontational, violent or peaceful. Decision-making processes can be more or less vertical and horizontal, and more or less participatory, representative, efficient or alternative to the broader political space.

Mobilisation and resistance (or the opposite, co-optation) can both be linked and unconnected to the state, both street based and parliament based, both in the presence of the subaltern or that of political elites. To organise includes networking and cooperation with others and thus provokes the notion of societal (also called organisational) linkage between different types of organisations such as social movements, unions and parties. This concerns, among other things, the role of individuals in the connective chains of mobilisation and resistance. Linkage as a broader concept of democratic theory, as per aggregating ideas and interests in opposition to and via the state, can be specified in the relations between different types of democratic actors.[50] We are thus concerned with common strategies to achieve shared goals and possible interorganisational penetration between collective actors. In the entire history of communist and social-ist parties, linkage with social forces, both interest based and value based, was from the very process of party formation a paramount feature of mobilisation. Speaking of this, Hilary Wainwright suggested that there might be 'a *permanent* tension, inherent in the very nature of political organisations whose source of radicalism rests on the knowledge and power of grass roots movements but whose stability and lasting, cumulative political impact requires at least a foothold within the existing political system'.[51]

At the most basic level, members of parties often engage with movements, thus prompting changes in partisan attitudes.[52] Party-movement linkages can be very loose and informal, as civil society organisations want to stress their autonomy and non-partisan character, and political parties do not wish to give the impression of wanting to hegemonise social movements so as not to alienate them.[53] In fact, movements can only hope to achieve significantly compromised policy change: 'a movement's demands are not only filtered through partisan politicisation processes; they also acquire further mediation and compromise within parliaments'.[54] For a social movement's demand to become a policy pledge within the party manifesto and from there law is a long process ridden with conflict and the politics of sectional and popular pressure opposite electoral incentive and public office. Yet the boundaries between institutionalised and extra-institutional politics have been 'fuzzy and permeable'.[55] State institutions, parties and social movements are interpenetrated, the last two of these developing out of institutions, responding to their pressures or acting as allies in parallel arenas of mobilisation.[56]

Social movements and parties with common values and interests do not necessarily compete – for attention, resources or political influence. They also interact, and this interaction varies in both strength and form. The conditions and factors driving organisational ties are telling as to the nature of democracy. For example, whether party–group linkages act as a counterweight to the deficiencies of programmatic party competition or conversely constitute its mirror, thereby reproducing its logic of antagonism and democratic deficits. Reflecting on the broader literature, some argue that it is shared basic policy views that decide interaction and its strength, while others argue that it is non-ideological factors and more specifically the exchange of tangible resources– such as money, campaigning for parties and favourable legislation for groups.[57] Political exchange models seem to provide much explanatory capacity, although a historical institutionalist eye has also emphasised that organic and close arrangements between trade unions and parties last over the long term through changes in their environment.[58] Early on, French political scientist Maurice Duverger explained that because of their lack of state and business resources, more broadly their lack of higher-class support, parties which form outside the legislative arena will be more likely to develop networks for mass support to counteract their institutional weakness.[59]

Organisational linkage is also informed by ideology, orienting the organisations across existing possibilities of social groups and how top down, or conversely bottom up, linkage is. Overall, both in terms of direction and strength, linkage is pursued in line with each side's needs and interests, their organisational autonomy, ideological orientation and the historical association between them. Hence, the realities of party–movement linkage vary across time, countries, social movement types, party systems, party families, parties and the dynamics between the tendencies inside them. All of these variables, we seek to show, can influence linkage on the Radical Left. External linkage also interacts within internal linkages between a group's organisational components – for example, leaders, activists and members.[60] Competing factions, or when leaders seek to consolidate their power, may also condition a party's environmental linkage.[61] Conversely, movements might induce intra-party polarisation.[62] New member or voter inflow can alter power dynamics and drive organisational change in order to accommodate newly acquired constituency profiles or utilise recently formed associations with sections of society previously detached from the party.

When deeply entrenched in the organisational culture of parties, centralism and leadership power grabs may alienate movements. As an indication, where the membership base is not effectively autonomous, linkage will likewise resemble a top-down process, where it is sought to control and guide outside forces rather than engage in a more open process of mutual learning and adaptation with them. Office seeking may also work towards disrupting linkages. As Hutter et al. explain, in seeking office parties turn to movements; however, once inside the government they turn towards the median voter and away from radical commitments, while movements who chose to align with, or helped to propel, the new incumbent party to power tend to remain fixed to their radical positions.[63]

Social movements are, it should be maintained, different from the typical professional group because they are more ephemeral, that is, they last less in time almost by definition.[64] They also have a loose organisational structure that makes formal interaction with institutional actors rather complex. Thus parties are less incentivised to maintain a close association with them.[65] The terms of leadership strategy and whether the party organisation seeks the upper hand by way of enjoying political capital and power resources is associated with how top down the linkage is. Yet parties with ancillary structures (like the archetypical Communist Party, see Chapter 8) are not necessarily less oriented towards linkage with society. Rather, it is their conception of the Left, and how its social unity should be forged in society, which differs from the more autonomist perspectives and libertarian approaches to party and alliance building. Bottom-up linkage in its ideal type, in other words, corresponds more to the claim of a 'progressive space', which underlines above all individuality and heterogeneity.

Beyond linkages and other structures and procedures, the very process of mobilisation and resistance, whether in elections or protest, rests upon social subjects, the micro-agency driving either societal currents or formalised groups. Thus our dimension of organisation, finally, also concerns the composition of radical movements and parties, their social roots or absence thereof. Composition reflects the collective interests, demographics, classes and generations a group attracts or claims to represent, seeks to mobilise and identifies as political allies, key historical subjects or newly emerging forces to be approached or confronted. Sectional, demographic and class sections of society, themselves, alter or fluctuate in relevance across time. Which classes and sections of society are prioritised for representation by parties determine the core organisation – party models of organisation have centred on the elites (caucus party), masses (mass party), cadres (cadre party), median voter (catch-all party, business party), working class (Leninist party), or state (cartel party).[66] Indeed, organisational and other features of parties depend strongly on their positions in the national party system, and on relations with state institutions and voters.[67] Developments which affect party systems, the state and voters have incapacitated the mass model in so far it is no longer adequate for optimal electoral competition.[68] Party decline in Western democracies has meant organisational decline in particular, that is, erosion in the links tying parties to their electors.[69] More specifically, the near universal collapse of party memberships across the board translates into a crisis of partisan voluntarism.[70]

Analytically distinguishing between the ideational, the rhetorical and the organisational elements allows us to address all and any political actors in processes of mobilisation and resistance, without narrowing down the scope of analysis appropriate at the level of political families to more specialist concepts. More field-specific conceptualisations will provide useful analytical tools in the book when it comes to examining each of the three dimensions of analysis consulted here. Indeed, the main point of scrutinising identities, rhetoric and organisation is not that more detailed tools of investigation cannot be employed depending on whether it is movements, parties or other actors under discussion. It is that one can also fall back on categories providing the possibility for generalisations across collective action types (and including individual agents) at the level of the political family: the European Radical Left.

THE RADICAL LEFT: WHAT'S IN THIS POLITICAL FAMILY?

The fundamental characteristics highlighted for contemporary RLPs and movements by Luke March and Cas Mudde offer a useful depiction of the Radical Left's ideational and policy core, its internal (re) configuration partly withstanding. It is therefore a solid first step in our definition of the Radical Left as a political space or family through time.[71] This particular political family is today said to either reject consumerism and neoliberalism, or even fundamentally oppose capitalist profit; it advocates for extensive redistribution and the establishment of alternative institutions and structures of political and economic governance that reinforce social justice; it identifies economic inequality as the basis of existing arrangements and espouses its elimination through the establishment of collective economic and social rights; it is more anti-capitalist and less anti-democratic while it does articulate a critique of capitalist democracy and offers its own democratic alternative; it embraces international solidarity and asserts that national and regional socio-political issues reflect global dynamics. The first two characteristics denote radicalism and the last four a left-wing identity according to the definition's authors.[72]

Radicalism means advocating root-and-branch, systemic change which doesn't merely change policy and reaches into the rules of governance. Left radicalism in the current conjuncture signals a vision of redistribution of economic and political power towards the marginalised, the exploited and the excluded, actively performing repertoires of resistance to one or more out of a number of identified and interrelated enemies: inequality, exploitation, elitism, neoliberalism, exclusion, authoritarianism, racism, xenophobia, chauvinism, fascism and so on. To use customary labels assigned to political traditions to define its ideational composition, the Radical Left includes anarchism and various forms of libertarianism, Trotskyism, Maoism, radical ecology, old fashioned social democracy, communism in its Marxist-Leninist and Stalinist strains and even some currents of social liberalism; their cross-fertilisation within the human mind, in parties and in movements; and their reciprocal influences. The prime goals or principles and the strategy of fulfilling them may vary spatially and temporally and across types of organisation. The value substance remains a (contested) combination of freedom, equality and fraternity, ranging between a radical libertarian and a radical egalitarian perspective; involving a wide horizon of institutional and non-institutional policy and strategic options; and that can take varying organisational shapes when enacted in practice.

At the most abstract level, and in the tradition Norberto Bobbio, social egalitarianism is always a key component of this political family even in its libertarian varieties ('egalibertarianism'). It is a necessary as well as a sufficient condition for the family coming into shape,

the family's *sine qua non*. More specifically, inequality is a derivative social problem that arises from exploitation: the exercise of one's
capital over other people's needs and wants. Then come freedom and
fraternity. As a tool for the historical analysis of the European Radical
Left as a political family, the triptych of freedom, equality and fraternity may seem reductionist. Yet, when isolating the core of the
family's ideational morphology, the triptych is useful to illustrate that
historical change may not concern the range and nature of principles. Rather, it might affect their strategic combination and each one's
salience during the process and in the opportunity structure of particular mobilisation waves.

To assess evolution and dissect change, we need to further specify
left radicalism in terms of the actors we shall engage with. Mobilisation and resistance by radical left movements as central actors denote
collectivities that have 'a firm base in ideologically driven left-wing
groups and have tended to predominantly mobilise left-wing-ori-
ented activists'.[73] A note of caution is, however, due, since radical
left movements often operate in large protests, occupations or other
widespread demonstrations of resistance. Within them, colourations of radicalism differ across the boundaries of the smaller groups
inside. In the grounds of mass mobilisation, multiple organisations,
campaigns, initiatives and networks within networks coexist, and so
do multiple shades and magnitudes of radicalism.

When it comes to the study of political parties, with focus placed
chiefly on the party system and the electoral arena, the idea that the
Radical Left is located to the left (and not simply on the left) of contemporary or mainstream social democracy has been unquestioned
in recent literature. Hence the popular use of the term 'far left' interchangeably with RLPs. There is a problem with this assertion, making
it in part ahistorical and rendering the concept of left radicalism
applicable only to the contemporary period once social democracy
completed its shift to the right. Further, the positional conceptualisation of the Radical Left applies only to the party system – there is no
use of this approach for social movements. It also excludes radicals
who (have) mobilise(d) from within SDPs and GPs. Overall, this is
a restrictive view for macro-historical endeavours and raises a point
made by Chiocchetti, who argued that 'the adjective "radical" is not

to be understood as a substantive but as a predominantly relational qualifier'.[74]

Approaching the Left relationally would of course first have to establish the point of comparison, that is, against which 'others' one is radical? There is an inherent temporal dimension to considering what constitutes left radicalism on the ground at any given point in time. In this book the others against which one is radical are the centre; a Radical Left is thus left of the centre at a distance approaching more the extreme end of the spectrum rather than the centre. Yet, to define the centre and in turn radicalism is a substantive exercise. If the centre denotes mainstream ideas and practices influencing society, and radicalism means root-and-branch change, which both the communists and social democrats celebrated in earlier times and which gives an empirical face to the positional distance between a centrist and a Radical Left.[75] What constitutes root-and-branch change in given contexts must be understood in the spirit of Bobbio, whereby '[l]eft and right do not represent two sets of fixed ideas, but rather an axis which shifts considerably from one generation to the next'.[76] The significations of root-and-branch change obviously vary across time and space, hence radicalism has taken up meanings and associations which differ across countries and evolve through history.[77] The term is also clearly ideologically charged and contested in politics itself, and used communicatively to elevate oneself or undermine others. This explains why 'there is no universal accepted definition of radicalism, and, by implication, radical attitudes'.[78]

To reduce the ambiguity, substantive metrics can inform positional understandings of dichotomies such as left–right and by extension Radical Left and centre-left. Accordingly, the Radical Left rests on a series of theoretical choices. These primarily include:

- A specific conception of equality, initially social above all, then also national, cultural and political, which is tampered by exploitation.
- The relation between equality and liberty is such that both are centrally present – the former engenders the latter – while liberty must never be allowed to harm equality.

- The level of commitment to rectifying inequality and liberty is intense, immediate and often militant.
- A positive conception of human nature which casts it as adaptable and by extension improvable.
- A forward-looking attitude towards historical change, with progress signalling a decrease in oppression, either its intensity or the brutality of its form, or both.
- A more generally progressive view of history wherein the role of human agency is structurally situated, as constantly striving for a better future, as a result of the antithesis which inevitably arises out of oppression or inequality.[79]

Any kind of historical approach to left radicalism which includes political parties must consider that during a long period of time, SDPs and their ancillary organisations were substantively radical, even if in terms of position they were that time's centre-left.[80] From there, a rightward transition unfolded with the espousal of neoliberalism in the 1980s, 1990s and thereafter.[81] When taking the party family as a whole in Europe, SDPs and their organisations may still host radicals and sometimes differentiate themselves from the centre-right. However, in reflection of the progressive exodus of the working class and the youth from social democratic ranks, they project neither radical policy visions of left-wing principles nor a rhetoric that diverges from the neoliberal mainstream.[82] When social democracy shifted from radical to mainstream in a substantive manner was the time, to paraphrase Gerassimos Moschonas, of 'mutation' in the historical movement, out of socialism and into the centre-left.[83]

Nevertheless, if the threshold between a radical and a centre-left is 'to radically transform, not just reform contemporary capitalism',[84] then social democracy's policies of internationalism, welfare and democracy did transform contemporary capitalism after World War II, before succumbing to the undoing of its glorious past achievements. In the decades before the 1980s, and in part depending on the case, the distinctions were not always clear between the centre-left and Radical Left. Three points are worth highlighting here. First, in terms of economic and social policy positions only a handful of communist parties (CPs) were revolutionary after the 1930s, in the

sense of arguing for the subversion of the state or excluding on principle participation in the branches of government. This is a point
made well by Carl Boggs, who explains that once the Popular Front
strategy materialised on the ground, the Leninist party effectively
disappeared, in so far as insurrectionary hopes and goals were being
progressively abandoned.[85]

Second, CPs and SDPs converged somewhere around Keynesianism on economic policy, often making their actual incongruity when
negotiating programmatic agreements a matter of degree of redistribution and state intervention, or in reverse material compromise in
terms of pre-established demands. The 1960s and early 1970s social
democratic governments in the UK (Harold Wilson's cabinet), West
Germany (under the chancellorship of Willy Brandt) and Sweden
(with Olof Palme as prime minister) all operated in defence of trade
unions, investing in industries under state control and a universal
welfare state. These policy axes are more or less what today's Radical
Left strives to promote. Third, both the communists and the social
democrats had and some of them still have 'orthodox' and 'reformist'
or 'radical' and 'moderate' sections. Until today most of the SDPs host
a number of left-wing tendencies or dissenters, 'the usual suspects'
who are significantly more radical than the party's politics, advocating a less consensual labourism and being more involved with social
movements.

Who would dare question then or today that many students supporting or mobilising within the same Labour Party that Ralph
Miliband[86] was famously accusing of trumping socialism with parliamentarism and electoralism espoused a radical policy agenda, or at
least a more radical one than the party leadership majority? Or that
they understood themselves as anti-capitalist? How can we doubt
the historical presence of radical left militants in the British Labour
Party within the context of the UK's two-party system? Or that Olof
Palme, the social democratic leader and Sweden's premier in the
1970s, inspired socialist students and introduced policy measures
which compare as much more radical than the policy demands of
today's European RLPs?[87] Is it at all possible to draw clear ideological
lines today between the militant parts of the left wing of the German
Social Democratic Party (SPD) and various sections of *Die Linke*?

Haven't activists on the radical left space turned to pirate parties in certain northern European countries? Additionally, aren't there some GPs which are oriented towards the left, such as in the UK?

We can argue that the institutional lines of differentiation across political space are not fixed in time and across place. Yesterday's RLPs have not remained such until today, but they could once be reasonably classified as advocating a radical egalitarianism in the form of systematic redistribution, underlined by a commitment to a socialist state of affairs, a hostile stance to NATO (the North Atlantic Treaty Organization) and the EU, internationalist solidarity and social militancy. Consider the belief that state institutions regulate the conflict between labour and capital, or the claim by social democrats to represent the working class and by extension the people as a whole. Consider the political ties between SDPs and labour unions, as well as the teleological dimension of social democracy, which was officially socialism as an advanced democracy. In fact, all of the axes sketched by March and Mudde as defining the Radical Left after the USSR's fall once applied to the SDPs as well,[88] although the dichotomies between communism and social democracy structured socialist movements for much of the last century. While SDPs since about the 1980s–1990s (depending on the case) became increasingly centrist, a part of them at least, if not whole parties in many cases, satisfied fully the ideological criteria of the Radical Left, while not being strictly anti-capitalist or with revolutionary credentials. In deeply polarised issues or contexts this radicalism showed clearly in SDPs or their cadres.

Given that a Radical Left can be identified as such first and foremost at the individual level and across organisations, and also across the institutional–non-institutional nexus, the notion of a social and political space must transcend the formal boundaries of parties and social movements and must include the social democrats or their affiliated organisations as potential returnees to their older self.

PART II

'Newness' across Movement Waves and through Time

3

Social Movement Identities and Left Radicalism

INTRODUCTION

Many movements emerged in western Europe once the effects of the 2008 global financial crash were felt: the Austurvöllur, the *indignados* (or 15M movement) and Platform for People Affected by Mortgages (PAH) in Spain, the Syntagma Square 'aganaktismenoi' in Greece, Blockupy in Germany, UK Uncut, Occupy London and the campaigns against tuition fees, the People before Profit in Ireland, the 'Screw the Troika' movement and the Citizens' Debt Audit Group in Portugal and the Living in the Crisis network and various activist networks behind the Five Star Movement in Italy (M5S). Through the 2010s many other movements sprung up, among them the Gilet Jaunes in France exploding against the government; Momentum in the UK, which managed to make the Labour Party under Jeremy Corbyn the largest membership party in Europe; and the climate movements, Extinction Rebellion or the global Fridays for the Future school strikes in 2018, inspired by Swedish teenager activist Greta Thunberg.

Given that all the above movements and organisations have been much wider than the Radical Left strictly speaking, and that many other more strictly radical organisations exist on a more systematic basis, it is not clear whether they should be labelled 'anti-capitalist', 'anti-neoliberal', 'anti-austerity' or 'pro-democracy', 'progressive movements' or 'counter-movements'. They have been called all of these names.[1] The literature on the GJM also used different labels for the movements: 'alter-globalisation movement(s)', 'anti-globalisation movement(s)', 'anti-neoliberal globalisation movements', 'global justice movement(s)', 'anti-systemic movements' or 'anti-establishment movements'.[2] Out of the Long '68, the mobilisers included anarchism and autonomism, radical ecology, anti-fascism, the peace movements, second-wave feminism and revolutionary organisations. Having these labels as a background, our task here is to decode the ideas and positions of radical left movements and draw out their ideational trajectories between the Long '68, the GJM years and post-2008. In order to facilitate a broad discussion in this direction, we grapple with the Radical Left's key diachronic ideas.

This chapter starts with equality and freedom, two of the elements that constitute the triptych of left radicalism. First, we delve into the historicity of a term popular in the 2010s, 'radical democracy', before turning to the meaning of anti-capitalism, with reference to the old divides – between reforming capitalism and revolutionary outlooks envisioning its overthrow, between statism and extra-institutional struggles – that have existed since the organised Left's inception in the nineteenth century. The chapter then examines how internationalism and solidarity, which complete the triptych, have been understood and projected. The anti-war movement is treated in a distinct section, and subsequently the EU (and before it the European Economic Community, EEC) as a social movement target is discussed – how has the regionalisation of politics affected left radicalism through movements?

SOCIAL MOVEMENTS AND DEMOCRACY'S RADICAL VERSIONS

The self-organisation, direct action, enhanced deliberation and shift to multiple leaders, a critique of elections, plus the experience of the anti-war, feminist, anti-racist and other movements focusing on the commodification of social and public goods, all have roots in the 1960s and 1970s. As Marianne Maeckelbergh sums up, 'the *political* legacy of the 1960s lies in the lasting significance of movement experiments with democracy as part of a prefigurative strategy for social change that is still relevant today because it is *still in practice today*'.[3] Democratisation was a key issue for left-wing students in eastern central Europe too. Here a contradiction arose between the notion of democracy and the realities of communism. In Belgrade, protests called for freedom of speech, freedom of assembly and the right to demonstrate, occupying the city's university. In Czechoslovakia, the democratisation of the political and economic system itself was at stake; 'socialism with a human face' was the opposition.[4] Although not so much the case in eastern Europe, in the West the 'legacy of 1968' is represented by democratic participation in the society's and the polity's affairs, which was both demanded and won.[5] In southern Europe, the Left's democracy was mostly a response to the dictatorial past. Parliamentary democracy was new, it signalled progress away from fascism, it had to be consolidated and defended, and nothing short of it would ever be acceptable.

A key part of the New Left was the direct democracy of anarchists and second-wave feminism. In exposing patriarchy, it often took as its starting point the patriarchal obstacles to true democratic participation, which women had not really experienced in the various movements of the New Left. Some of the other key issues upon which feminist protests in the USA and Europe mobilised included equal opportunities in the workplace and 'reproductive rights', especially access to the contraceptive pill and abortion rights, the point being that women's emancipation could arrive only through better democracy.[6] The organisational spirit of feminist movements would translate into a democratic imprint, thoroughly pervading their disseminated discourse and above all their organisations – whether journals and magazines, the very popular consciousness-raising groups or even parties. For the feminists, the struggle against patriarchy could only be anti-hierarchical.

The left-wing milieu of the 1960s and 1970s was appealed to by western European Marxism, the 'heterodox kind', more democratic and open to cultural imaginaries than its eastern European variant; more critical of deterministic tendencies in the name of historical materialism; and refusing to silence its critique of the patriarchal and authoritarian elements inscribed in Soviet politics.[7] The theoretical drive of participatory, direct and alternative ideas of democracy flows through elaborations of 'radical democracy' as a long-term goal as well as an everyday social and political custom. Theories of radical democracy have been consolidated by the ontological turn in political theory most notably with Laclau's post-Marxist approach to social antagonism.[8] However, in terms of normative substance they date back to Rousseau and Marx, and in terms of political symbolism they are most connected to the contentious acts of the 1960s and 1970s that sought emancipation without identifying this process exclusively with either class or representation.[9]

During the GJM years, the amalgam of forces driving the movement was initially concerned with the structural adjustment programmes in indebted, less developed countries in the early 1990s, emphasising transnational solidarity over the formed gap between the 'Global North' and the 'Global South'. Protests and mobilisation against transnational financial institutions, trade agreements and corporations took place first in Central and South America and Africa. Focused on the transnational and international arenas of policymaking a key demand was for the hegemonic countries to acknowledge the debts and damages in various directions that the Global North and its hegemonic powers imposed on the underdeveloped world of the Global South.[10] Common to all of the campaigns in the GJM was the critique of understanding market deregulation as a positive effect of technological advance. A neo-imperialist strategy adopted and defended by international financial institutions drove this naturalisation. It was argued that the World Bank, the International Monetary Fund (IMF) and the World Trade Organisation (WTO), aligning with the Group of Seven (G7) and the Group of Eight (G8) (and the EU), benefited multinational corporations and international elite networks in finance.

Concerning the GJM in particular, the question of internal democracy was of the highest importance, not only because of the social context in which it emerged and the technological means available, but because among the objectives of the GJM, democratic participation and the democratisation of the institutions and mechanisms of globalisation were key objectives. The WTO protests in Seattle in 1999 and the G8 demonstrations in Genoa in 2001 signalled the GJM's explosion to prominence. The GJM would more generally meet on the occasions of the European and World Social Forums (ESFs and WSFs). Some of the large organisations that gave stability to the European parts of the GJM at the national level were the Association pour la Taxation des Transactions financières et pour l'Action Citoyenne (Association for the Taxation of financial Transactions and Citizen's Action, Attac), the emerging Solidaires, Unitaires, Démocratiques trade unions and Confédération Paysanne in France, Attac in Germany, Spain and the Scandinavian countries, Associazione Ricreativa Culturale Italiana, La Rete di Lilliput and Dissobedienti in Italy, which also influenced the Spanish autonomist currents, black blocks and anti-fascists across nearly all countries, and feminist and radical ecological groups, as well as several trade unions (radical as well as mainstream) which interacted with these organisations in the context of the ESFs and beyond.

Democracy was also important because anarchism played an important part in the GJM. Its logic was 'that no one will ever convert anyone else entirely to their point of view', following 'the motto, if you are willing to act like an anarchist now, your long-term vision is pretty much your own business'.[11] In fact, during the three periods examined in the book there has been a renewed interest in anarchist theory because radical politics and movements have often been 'anarchist' in organisational form.[12] To a great extent anarchism and autonomism in the 1970s lent its aims, lifestyles and tactics to the 1990s social movement wave on the Left. Autonomism is multifaceted, and since the 1960s has cut across ideas and forms of activism, feminism, squatting movements, disarmament campaigns, the rock and punk music scenes and anti-fascist street fighting.[13] Inside the GJM, the 'new anarchism' and its driving force has been more a sensibility or methodology rather than a dogma or an abstract radical theory.[14] From this perspective, the breakthroughs or novelties of the GJM's 'new anarchism' amount to multiple, often disjointed retheorisations of violence, political power, the state and democracy.[15] Their commonality was the articulation of a non-sectarian and inclusive conception of anarchist thinking focused on process and experimentation rather than the vindication of an ideology. While other contemporary theories of democracy are concerned with the ways in which identities and interests are aggregated or accommodated, radical democrats emphasise how what is elsewhere conceived as the rules of the game – such as citizen participation in political decision-making and the limits of representation as necessary evils – are themselves effectively under dispute, without 'preordained content'.[16] In this sense radical democracy is always a 'work in progress'.[17]

More recently, neoliberal management transformed the global crash of 2008 from a financial crisis into a fiscal crisis through the massive rescue of banks. For western Europe it all begins in Iceland. When at the end of 2008 Icelandic banks defaulted and material crises ensued, struggle unfolded at multiple levels: the social, legal, political and economic. Social movements, civic groups and campaigns, and other collectives in Iceland demanded alternative structures and processes, called for social and economic justice, encouraged participation and demanded transparency. From web-based participatory budgeting to direct democracy experiments with deliberative assemblies, the 'Pots and Pans Revolution' (*Bïsahaldabyltingin*) was the first case of intense and mass grassroots mobilisation in Europe after the financial crash. Iceland dealt with the crisis if not in a truly radical manner, then in an unconventional fashion that differed from elsewhere in that it didn't save its banks in which there was substantial foreign capital, in this way resisting powerful EU member states. Effectively, this meant that both company and household loans were given a write-down, which was quite extensive in most cases. Civil society was a key player in the process of drafting a new constitution through crowdsourcing, which translated for Iceland into a novel experiment with statehood, and in securing a 'No' in the two referendums on the Icesave debts (to the UK and the Netherlands).[18] In this sense, Iceland has been a case of a clear impact of contentious politics on governance.[19]

In the square occupations of 2010 in Spain and Greece as well, the economic crisis in Europe was quickly labelled political: neoliberal mentalities were deemed responsible for democratic deficits and distortions. Economics and its cultural manifestations were seen as inevitably affecting the scope and quality of politics while existing modes of governance seen as limiting the potential for economic justice. Because neoliberalism is a global system, European pro-democracy mobilisation can be seen as part of a global current for 'real democracy'.[20] The very idea of political representation as practised in the West was fundamentally challenged by the Occupy movements.[21] In the midst of large-scale and cross-country political fluidity, and the public's decreasing levels of institutional trust and incumbent punishment, the promotion of democracy became a second 'master frame' or 'master signifier' for tens of mobilisations in Europe.[22] In identifying an enemy, many of the activists were driven by the notion of 'post-democracy' that has neo-Marxist roots, and connected the process of democratic erosion to neoliberal economic practice.[23] The movements' criticism of national, and secondarily transnational and intergovernmental, institutions was projected onto a vision for a more decentralised, autonomous, participatory and deliberative politics, reflected in self-organisation and cooperative association. The movements questioned the viability and justice of existing representative political structures, and promoted democracy outside of its liberal format and beyond constitutionalism as the mode of governance for a sovereign people.

The term 'pro-democracy movements' that accompanies many radical left groups emerging in post-2008 Europe too often implies that today's European Radical Left is more democratic than before. It is not really the extent to which democratic practice has been a feature of mobilisation and debate that differs between the post-2008 movements and those of previous epochs but instead the historically specific understanding and actualisation of democracy. If in the 1960s radical conceptions of democracy aimed to enhance participation, enrich deliberation, challenge the USSR and so on, today's radical democracy is a method of accommodating and appropriating multiplicity in the context of distinct but also shared social struggles. In retrospect, however, by adding radical democracy to anti-austerity the post-2008 movements in Europe did not call for alternative forms of political participation that were wholly new in spirit.

There is no doubt that recent movements have placed a great rhetorical emphasis on radical democracy, both as a goal and as an everyday experience; and that their repertoires of decision-making expanded innovatively, as we discuss later. That said, history is replete with democratic concerns within both the revolutionary and reformist left. Lenin's *The State and Revolution* (1917) is entirely devoted to this, in an attempt to deconstruct bourgeois democracy (and social democratic support for it) and accentuate the class basis of seemingly democratic political institutions. After 1935 and the inauguration of the Popular Front strategy by the Third International amid concerns regarding the dramatic rise of historical fascism, communists gradually abandoned the advocacy of Soviet democracy but constantly talked of 'democratisation', 'progressive democracy' and 'popular democracy'. In the junta regimes of southern Europe during the 1960s and 1970s, being democratic was one of the key identifiers of left-wing and progressive citizens, who were persecuted by the dictatorial regimes and fought against the supporters of monarchies. Moreover, Eurocommunists, as we discuss later, saw their central task in democratising the state and society.

To recapitulate, hitherto, democratic practice and its conceptualisation are what change in the eyes of activists who mobilise more or less around its various manifestations. 'The meaning of self-government and democracy in society changes over time, with social movements often playing an active role in that change.'[24] First, diverse, radical movements exercise informal control of institutions and elites, enlarge the scope of politic debate and cultivate citizen participation and associative (rather than competitive) practices. Radical movements also fight an evolving type of hegemonic democracy, as perceived to be imposed and managed by the elites through the lens of critiques and principles. In the 1960s and 1970s, the enemy was corrupt democracy on the Left and Right and Stalinist authoritarianism, thus it was also identified in the socialist camp. The critical imaginary argued that established democratic practice mediated the materiality of alienation, produced unresponsive behemoths in the party system and excluded various sections of the population by not acknowledging their rights.

In the 1990s and 2000s, the criticism was on the elitist democracy of the neoliberal and impersonal international organisations, the hegemonic states and their disrespect for human rights, social equality and dignity. In the 2010s, the enemy has been that of 'legal democracy' or 'technocratic democracy', testified by the technocratic governments of Greece (led by Lucas Papademos) and Italy (led by Mario Monti) in 2011–12 and 2011–13, respectively. The Radical Left's movements and parties vehemently opposed these. Technocratic democracy restricts political power to unelected 'enlightened elites' and is a key feature of 'authoritarian neoliberalism' whereby the capitalist state has turned into a less democratic entity insulated from social and political conflict.[25] Government and public office becomes 'technocratic' in an attempt to depoliticise authority and shift responsibility away from politics.[26] In addition, the enemy of movements in the early 2010s was representative but corrupt and shallow democracy.

As 2020 was progressing and a second phase of lockdowns across Europe set in, anti-authoritarianism and civil liberties became a more apparent front of struggle in which many unions, student groups and movements from the Radical Left, among other sections of civil society, participated. Many governments across the world and within Europe have violated 'rights-protective democratic ideals and institutions' to an extent 'beyond that which has been strictly demanded by the exigencies of the pandemic'.[27] A look at almost any radical left website or publication shows that authoritarianism takes central stage in the positions of radical left movements and groups. Liberal democratic institutions are being reclaimed this time round rather than rejected, as at the beginning of the previous decade.

Across the whole spectrum of radical mobilisers, democracy has been a central idea and position, in opposition to authoritarian measures implemented in the name of containing Covid-19 and public safety. Social scientists on the Radical Left have already began seeking ways to understand this 'new crisis of democracy', which can awaken anti-authoritarian sensitivities. What is required is essentially to dissect what caused governments in Europe, mostly but not only those on the right wing, to slip into democratic backsliding in the face of the pandemic. A discursive battle has ensued in various countries broadly structured along the main areas affected by authoritarianism – executive orders versus required legislation, the right to gather and to protest, authoritarianism as a response of governments with inadequate health care systems, the constitutionality of restrictive measures (everywhere) or police violence.

In retrospect, we see a qualitative shift after 2008 and then again in 2020 regarding the question of democracy, rather than one of size, similar to both the GJM and the Long '68, while there is a thoroughly historic character to the democracy debate within the Radical Left.

THE FIRE ONCE AGAIN? BETWEEN ANTI-CAPITALISM AND ANTI-NEOLIBERALISM

To get a fuller picture of radical movement identity, let us recall the dialectical drift between democratic and economic claims, democracy and capitalism, or more generically political procedure and economic structure.[28] Herein lies the old divide of the Left between root-and-branch change, understood as reforming the system in a perpetually progressive direction until it is transformed, and overthrowing it, through frontal opposition and utter rejection of activity through its structures and institutions, and of the capacity to develop out of itself and into a different system.

The prevalence of revolutionary spirits and confrontational dissent, and the broader revolutionary left internationally, emerged in the years 1967–9 and was a sizeable force. Its social milieu bore a conviction that revolution was around the corner.[29] Slogans such as 'smash capitalism' or 'smash the system' became commonplace in the UK. 'Everything, now' by the Vive Revolution group in France expressed the development of utopian notions of unlimited growth. The Il Manifesto group in Italy spoke of the immediate fulfilment of communism premised upon the conviction that abundance was to be imminently achieved,[30] hence also the slogan, 'We want everything', through which Nani Ballestrini's classic biographical 1971 novel came to symbolise the years of revolution in Italy.[31] In 1968 the global roar of conflict and resistance was unique. Chris Harman wrote about it succinctly:

> Every so often there is a year which casts a spell on a generation … 1968 was such a year. 1968 was a year in which revolt shook at least three major governments and produced a wave of hope among young people living under many others. It was the year the peasant guerrillas of one of the world's smaller nations stood up to the mightiest power in human history. It was the year the Black ghettos of the United States rose in revolt to protest at the murder of the leader of non-violence, Martin Luther King. It was the year the city of Berlin suddenly became the international focus for a student movement that challenged the power of the blocs that divided it.

It was the year tear gas and billy clubs were used to make sure the US Democratic Party convention would select a presidential candidate who had been rejected by voters in every primary. It was the year the Mexican government massacred more than 100 demonstrators in order to ensure that the Olympic Games could take place under 'peaceful' conditions. It was, above all, the year that the biggest general strike to that point in history paralysed France and caused its government to panic.[32]

Revolutionary ideas were effectively a counter-force on the Left after almost three decades of reformism by the established communist and socialist parties. They gained momentum by the generational gap between pre- and post-war radicals, extreme right violence and the international situation of counter-insurgencies. There was major impact of new Third World ideologies on western Europe, profoundly so in terms of revolutionary cultures.[33] Direct, ideological-cultural influences pervaded not only constitutional democracies but also affected, although in a more nuanced manner, southern European societies under dictatorship, mostly in the 1970s.[34] Intellectual searches into revolutionary politics flourished and various radical academics were in contact with counter-insurgencies. Slogans of revolt echoed the words of the Third World's heroes, such as most famously Che Guevara ('Two, Three, Many Vietnams'). The tactics of guerrilla warfare were often the result of training abroad and helping with revolutions where they had started.

After the conservatives taking hold of France and restoring order and favourable opinion, the Left losing the elections of 1969, the communists still excluded from power in Italy and the oil crises of 1973 and 1974 which paralysed production in many countries, neither 'abundance' nor 'everything' could be perceived as possible. The defeat of the revolutionary left was clear a few years after the French May of '68 – the historiographical consensus indicating between about 1973 and 1976 – and it occurred both in the ballot box and by force.[35] Political defeat meant a particular social climate. Public opinion data from the 1970s in France indicate that the majoritarian position supported gradual reform and only a small percentage (about 5 to 10 per cent maximum) revolution. This was even lower in other western European countries.[36] In terms of an orientation towards socio-economic issues and by extension radicalism itself, there is indeed a discontinuity between the 1960s and the post-2008 movements, but continuity between the latter and the GJM. The radicalism of the 1960s and 1970s as expressed in the public sphere entails all the richness of the 'silent revolution' of ecology, sexual liberation, communitarianism, broadening the spectrum of civil rights and cultural critique.[37]

It is still clear in the historiographical consensus that confidence in visions of large-scale transformation from below was declining, and by the end of the 1970s it was marginal and stigmatised. 'A more conservative trend in thought became predominant', resting on post-structuralist and post-modernist readings of both the 1968 events and ideas in general.[38] Post-structuralism bred reformism because it fundamentally challenged the Marxist 'notion that social hierarchies of various kinds are essentially immovable until inequalities within production relations are removed'.[39] Thereby, there can be no theoretically justified need to displace capitalism. The complex interaction of 'economic structure' and 'historical agency' were underplayed in such a way that politics was no longer understood as arising out of historical and material realities.[40] At its worst, post-structuralism engaged in what Tony Judt called 'verbal gymnastics'.[41] Similarly, Perry Anderson observed a 'veritable *débandade* of so many leading French thinkers of the Left since 1976'.[42] Beyond and above broadening the scope of left radicalism as a historical social force, identity politics as the decentring of class and the politics of recognition and inclusivity also confronted, challenged and often replaced Marxism.

To specify further the dialectic between reformism and revolutionary visions, the question of attitudes towards the state is a central one. Radical left opinion has veered between a 'state-centric' perspective and those that viewed the state as an intrinsic enemy and pursued instead civil transformation and individual emancipation. The state-centric perspective has diachronically proved triumphant within the European Radical Left, arguing that the immediate source of power and influence is located in the apparatus of governance. Therefore, the most appropriate way forward has been a 'two-step strategy', first gaining power and then using it to 'transform the world'.[43] Any sort of anti-systemic activity could thus only be attained through political mediation and the eventual control of state power, which in turn suggested a centralised direction of the movement and hence the creation of permanent, professional political organisations, that as we will see later have been joined by activists from all three waves of mobilisation under question. The anarcho-syndicalist position was repeatedly marginalised upon the conviction that given the social context and the distribution of political power in capitalism, spontaneity would both heighten the internal divisions of wage labour and maintain insufficient political capacity when opposing its enemies.[44]

This crisis of Marxism was situated in an economic crisis. Before the 1970s, neoliberalism in western Europe was chiefly an intellectual project which launched a critique of the post-war Keynesian orthodoxy, subsequently promoting austerity and monetarism as a 'solution' to a stagflation crisis. The first practices of neoliberal policies were undertaken in the 1970s outside of Europe, notably in Salvador Allende's Chile under the auspices of the 1973 USA-backed military coup. Soon after, there followed the governments of Margaret Thatcher and Ronald Reagan. According to hegemonic forces the crisis could not be resolved by means of macroeconomics, state intervention and the orchestration of the world economy by the World Bank through the gold–dollar standard. Hence, on America's initiative, there came the collapse of the post-war Bretton Woods monetary arrangements of the previous 25 years. Yet the various emancipatory movements of the 1960s framed the economic situation in accordance to their sectionalised goals and in contrast to the largely pro-Keynesian stance of communists and social democrats who focused more on redistribution than recognition. Theirs was a critique of a failing system not due to strictly economic factors but rather developmental strategy more broadly. Various non-communist groups criticised the institutionalised social protection embedded in Europe's welfare states of the post-war era. Nancy Fraser's succinct account is worth quoting at length:

> For example, New Leftists exposed the oppressive character of bureaucratically organised social protections, which disempowered

their beneficiaries, turning citizens into clients. Anti-imperialist and anti-war activists criticised the national framing of first-world social protections, which were financed on the backs of postcolonial peoples whom they excluded. ... Meanwhile, feminists revealed the oppressive character of protections premised on the 'family wage' and on androcentric views of 'work' and 'contribution', showing that what was protected was less 'society' per se than male domination. LGBT activists unmasked the invidious character of public provision premised on restrictive, hetero-normative definitions of family. Disability rights activists exposed the exclusionary character of built environments that encoded able-ist views of mobility and ability. Multiculturalists disclosed the oppressive character of social protections premised on majority religious or ethnocultural self-understandings, which penalise members of minority groups. And on and on.[45]

For the emerging social movement critics looking into rights beyond the sphere of production there was often little worthwhile to defend. Hence, there arose a revolutionary response to crisis that was not limited to sustaining the welfare arrangements of the post-war boom. There also emerged a conflict line between intersectionality and classical Marxism, about the relative significance of class as opposed to ethnicity, gender and sexuality. By extension, the notion of crisis was not, either in the 1960s and 1970s nor subsequently, understood exclusively in economic terms. In the 1960s, a literature appeared that was more aware and more critical of the many 'contradictions in social development'.[46] Crisis was a buzzword for many academics writing in the 1970s, and it was not always or not only conceived as unfolding exclusively in the labour market in terms of conflict; it expanded to the crisis of the university, society, politics and international relations.[47] According to Habermas, it was a 'legitimation crisis'.[48]

Student revolts led to analyses of the oppressive and non-egalitarian functions of mass education in capitalist society, out of which emanated rhetoric about social control. During the 1960s, universities were changing across western Europe. Students numbers nearly doubled in various countries and this generated pressure on the system through organised student unions and groups. This, among other manifestations of student and academic turmoil, is captured by a book written at the time by Wallerstein and Starr, titled *The University Crisis Reader: The Liberal University under Attack*.[49] Growth in the number of technocrats and the cultural intelligentsia, as well as the development of subjects such as sociology and subsequently the field of cultural studies, opened up multiple questions for discussion about the foundations and social purpose of mass education.

During the GJM, academic debate about the centrality of structural conflict re-emerged. Such conflict was not or no longer pacified, as argued by frameworks of 'post-industrial society', 'relative affluence' and 'post-materialist values'. The Giddenian suggestion that 'We are middle classes now' soon found its opposite thesis. The limitations of neoliberal policies were clear in terms of environmental sustainability, social and global equality, and economic growth. Activist analyses, such as those by Attac, identified instabilities in the supposed self-regulation of the global and EU market, detecting emerging pathologies in neoliberalism and financial economic realities. A series of economic and financial crises broke out in countries which eventually adopted neoliberal policies – Mexico (1994), Turkey (2001), Argentina (2001–2), and the Asian crisis of 1997 – against which one of Attac's founding slogans was produced: 'Disarm the Markets'. The crash in Argentina was also an issue taken on passionately by European party and social movement activists, pointing to how neoliberal policies were malignant and ineffective, namely, the IMF's recommendations for Argentina to open its economy, liberalise labour relations and privatise public capital. A first quasi-obituary emerged out of the intellectual fuel that drove the GJM. For several social scientists from various disciplines, neoliberalism in the 2000s was no longer a hegemonic force because it proved to be too problematic in too many countries as well as on a transnational scale.[50]

Though anarchism, horizontal politics, anti-capitalism and a critique of representation lay at the core of widespread protest and activism, GJM organisations put forward a number of objectives suggesting their institutional orientation: the Tobin tax; taxation of the rich; debt relief; changing international trade rules and barriers, and fair trade; the implementation of a universal basic income; the reduction of the working week; the defence of the public sector and democratically renationalising privatised services; the introduction of ecological measures that discourage extractivism, avoid climate change, protect the environment and are universally binding; the end of the military-industrial complex, including the demise of NATO; universal nuclear disarmament; and support of civil liberties. With the GJM, the NSMs' policy repertoires re-emerge through a combinational whole to a significant extent.

The claims of the chief global pro-democracy events of 2010 were mass, direct democracy, occupation and provocation. But like the GJM, anarchism was only part of the mix. 'Autonomous spaces' in society or the Occupiers' 'politics of exodus' did not characterise the movements throughout the 2010s, which instead projected a more populist and statist image geared towards making neo-Keynesian demands. Indeed, all post-2008 movements sought to reappropriate the municipal, regional, national and supranational institutions of the state. The positions of organisations of the Occupy assemblies, Real Democrazia Ya!, UK Uncut, the Screw the Troika movement in Portugal, Gilets Jaunes and Noit Debut in France and many others have been explicitly anti-austerity and welfarist rather than anti-capitalist.[51]

Through state intervention, the overall exemplar has been to reverse the logic of austerity back to a more anthropocentric capitalism: shift back from finance domination to wage-led growth; redistribute income from capital back to wage earners; undo precarity as a tool reinforcing the financialisation of everyday life; reduce inequality and stratification, poverty and exclusion; deactivate the penetration of state institutions by big corporations and thus redemocratise the economy; return from a coercive workfare back to citizenship rights shared through welfare provisions and empowering society; and deconstruct the values of hierarchy and competitiveness, so as to foster a communitarian and cooperative spirit. The anti-austerity movement, in being reformist and statist, as a whole exhibited two interlinked discourses: a politics of redistribution and a real (primarily more participatory and horizontal) democracy, the latter facilitating or its absence impeding the former.[52] This very sequence of real democracy as necessary for anti-austerity, and thus a better, fairer capitalism, carries forward a historical combination of the Long '68: Bernsteinian social democratic discourse of post-World War II Keynesian welfare state expansion and the rise of new democratic spirits through the New Left.[53]

'Degrowth' constituted an axis of positions, emerging through activist scholarship in the 2000s. This happened at a time of vibrant debate over the meaning of development and the increase of human well-being, at one and the same time as gross domestic product (GDP) came to be regarded as at best a partial measure of happiness. The term has existed since the 1970s but became prominent in the 2000s, especially after the first international degrowth conference in Paris in 2008. Connecting multiple prefigurative social movements, degrowth has animated a variety of 'nowtopias' in the context of anti-globalisation and climate justice struggles. These, for example, include ideas about production for users rather than exchange, the decommodification of labour through its partial substitution with political participation and the rejection of utilitarian thinking in arranging for the circulation of goods.[54] Degrowth evoked opposition to neoliberalism's guiding principle – that growth was the solution to all ills and benefited everyone. Underpinning the term is a radical rejection of eco-modernism and specifically growth as the driver of human and social development, extractivism as necessary and inevitable for human flourishing and industrialism as naturally progressive. Degrowth informs multiple types of groups, especially in France, Italy and Spain, but also in continental and northern Europe – from *buen vivir* to ecovillages, to institutes for new economic ideas, to anti-advertising movements, solidarity economies and food sovereignty, among others.[55] As the concept, which appears quite transformative opposite mainstream economics, still suffers from conceptual and policy ambiguity, degrowth has remained a marginal, decentred and variegated social movement in western Europe, not seriously taken up by RLPs and unions.[56]

All in all, the post-2008 crisis period has not radically changed the programmatic direction of social movements into an explicitly anti-capitalist direction. The social movements of the 2010s have stimulated the same type of RLPs (the reformist, democratic socialist parties) as during the GJM years. In addition, the demands of the movements themselves are anti-neoliberal, although driven by 'composite identities' as in the GJM and by more or less radical (or more or less well informed) reformism. In a sense, the GJM was a bridge between the 1960s and the 2010s, because as a protest wave it attracted the participation of traditional left-wing militants, which in turn legitimated the lingo and political turn to a more classless civil society that continues today. While the 1960s had a clear revolutionary, anti-capitalist and anti-imperialist content and form, which faded during the 1970s, the GJM and the post-2008 movements have not reignited the flames. It seems that Chris Harman remains correct in declaring that the Long '68 was *The Fire Last Time*.

Neither did the climate change movements exploding in 2018 change the social democratic profile of radical struggles, in spite of their easy popularisation of 'System Change, Not Climate Change'. For groups such as Extinction Rebellion, known for sabotaging commuter trains in the UK and civil disobedience, they stretch back in time to participant sections of Global Climate Summits; engagement with anti-capitalism does not describe the majorities therein. What characterises them the most is that their cause is 'beyond politics'. This means a lack of articulate strategy, as they on the one hand advocate for radical proposals – decarbonisation by 2025, nuclear disarmament etc. – but on the other hand are far from suggesting a programme to do so. This is the most common criticism by radical activists of Greta Thunberg and the Fridays for the Future school strikes as well.

A resulting line of division has been between system critical framings and those oriented around individual (including leadership) action.[57] Radical constructions of the climate crisis utilise the climate (or environmental) justice frame, pointing to the problem being capitalism and consequently the solution being its dismantling, which contrasts with the climate change paradigm of organisations such as Greenpeace and Friends of the Earth, which aim to raise awareness, change habits and bridge climate struggles with frames of human rights, thus widely promoting 'environmental rights' (see also Chapter 4).[58] The radicalisation of the 'climate justice paradigm' has meant shifting action repertoires of campaign initiatives and gatherings such as the Camps for Climate Action towards more civil disobedience and confrontational tactics. In this manner, they resemble the urgent and self-legitimated spirit of the anti-nuclear movements of earlier decades, which raised nuclear energy as the biggest emergency for human civilisation to justify much of their interruptive and destructive action.[59] The justice frame is nevertheless explicitly a multi-issue one, encompassing climate in a wider referent to justice, which ranges from indigenous populations to food sovereignty, austerity and many other issues. Contemporary climate justice movements are best understood as entrenched in cross-cutting struggles and in this sense also (although not totally) differentiated from the more single-issue orientations of the past anti-nuclear movements.[60]

Radical discourses, even the justice frame which is effectively a bridge between distinct currents, diverge from most climate change policy currently following market-based and utilitarian approaches to 'sustainable governance'. Prevalent thinking combines the approach of 'green governmentality' (obviously a capitalist one) and the discourse of ecological modernisation, rather than civic environmentalism, bottom-up ecology and climate justice frameworks. The mainstream intellectual trend talks of 'global environmental management' and thus of 'planning' and 'regulation'. It diagnoses the problem as 'market failure', or 'vested interests' such as the fuel industry, which is problematically treated as an autonomous actor within capitalist networks.[61] Among radical movements and activists, nevertheless, perspectives range: between socialist-led environmental preservation through strict state regulation, most obviously among partisan actors; eco-socialist and anarchist revolutions; deep ecological and neo-primitive views of consumption and human behaviour; and the vision of localism for a capitalism of small towns or eco-communities. Within the context of wider networks, these perspectives coexist and interact under the banner of climate justice, 'while respecting each other's ideological and tactical diversity', as one such European network of 59 distinct organisations, BY2020WeRiseUP, reminds us on its website.[62] Anti-systemic environmental and climate discourse, therefore, has on the one hand emphasised climate justice as counterposed to capitalism, while on the other hand it is itself plural in its teleology, that is, the ideal conditions for this or that form of eco-socialism or civic environmentalism.

Alex Callinicos' point, in his *Anti-Capitalist Manifesto*, about concrete measures providing remedies to problems and 'introducing a different social logic', is of essence in the current incarnations of the revolution–reform debate. Callinicos comes from a revolutionary crowd which strives for socialism but embraces reform based on a twofold argument that is historical: responding to the immediate needs of the oppressed, and changing the superstructure to make the modes of production more vulnerable to transformation.[63] The response would be that some of these positions are not realisable within the confines of capitalism and the counterargument that their responsiveness to reality and the magnitude of change they imply makes them anti-systemic and thus anti-capitalist; statist but in a substantively revolutionary sense. Overall, reform can be radical enough to require a fundamental change of political course.

In this direction the GJM broke ground as out of it an overall critique of globalised capitalism was significantly specified.[64] The GJM and its intellectual production elaborated how it is not governments that have the first say in world economic governance but international organisations, which are neither elected nor accountable. How structural adjustment programmes by the World Bank lead to the opposite of what they promise: rising poverty in underdeveloped countries. How a race to the bottom arises because developing countries are forced to compete with each other to attract multinationals pushing governments to reduce labour and environmental protections. How due to unconstrained training, hiring and firing procedures multinationals generate very little technology transfer, and that they repatriate profits, operate on brands and are linked to child labour sweatshops in Asian countries and elsewhere. How capital benefits from the increase in temporary and part-time contracts, which generate precarious labour. Given the significant weakening of union densities and collective bargaining over the years, how there are new challenges for trade unions. How increasing differences between low-skilled workers and high-skilled workers generate an explosive social climate.

At the same time, what began in the Long '68 as a shift away from historical materialism and continued with the GJM has not really shifted in the 2010s. It is succinctly described by Simon Tormey as amounting to a reshaped radical politics over the long term; what can be called anti-neoliberalism as opposition to *this*, *today's* aggressive incarnation of capitalism, but without an elaborate scheme to get there, a 'scientific socialism' foretelling history or a shared vision of socialism. Tormey outlines this as follows: 'Today's radicals are less inclined to seek out an emancipatory scheme with universal appeal and application. They are more certain of what they are against than what they are for.' Accordingly, they 'forsak[e] doctrine, certainty, and messiahs for alliances, affinities, coalitions, and dialogue'.[65] Anti-neoliberalism does not share with capitalism the latter's fixed ideology and does not necessarily include the rejection of key capitalist features such as wage labour or private property. Comparing post-1991 activism with the Long '68 and especially factoring in Cold War communism, anti-capitalism may appear to be the new minority and anti-neoliberalism the new majority.

To pose the pertinent question: has left radicalism in European societies radically changed over the long term, if only towards an increasingly anti-neoliberal view? To what extent does the anti-capitalism/anti-neoliberalism distinction hold? To state the obvious, the radicalisation of the masses during mobilisation waves does not necessarily mean the majority identify as socialists or leftists. In socio-cognitive terms, the process of radicalisation during specific mobilisations can be temporary, as demobilisation and/or co-optation can drive deradicalisation. Anti-capitalism and anti-neoliberalism are also overlapping. On one level, in certain countries, such as the UK and Greece, anti-capitalism is a more common term among radical forces.[66] It has also been constituted as a 'master frame' to provide 'unity in opposition' to neoliberalism, with the Zapatistas playing a central role in this framing.[67] Anti-capitalism is, nevertheless, a subset of the anti-neoliberal crowd that has protested since the late 1990s.

Robert Latham spoke about 'the perennial duality of reform and revolution', of which this is the most contemporary manifestation: 'the either/or of an anti-capitalism of total revolution and an agonistic, fractional post-Marxist politics working to reduce oppression and hardship within capitalism'.[68] In terms of identifying the key source of social problems as capitalism or not, a firm boundary would need to be spelled out. But that itself, to be formulated in praxis, entails a range of issues, from property rights to inheritance taxes, from profit-making firms to constrains on individual (negative) freedom to supranational governance, over which neither the anti-neoliberals nor the anti-capitalists are united in terms of position and plan. The boundary is also often made blurry due to uneven and combined development, which undermines the narrative of a 'capitalist totality', 'a singular' order.[69]

Nevertheless, together, anti-capitalism and anti-neoliberalism as the manifestations of the reformist/revolutionary divide are still minorities in society. Using data from the European Values Survey, for western European countries between the 1980s and 2017, Figure 3.1 illustrates the percentage of radical left individual identities, measured as those reporting self-placement in the first three scores (1, 2 and 3) of the left–right scale (1–10). The percentage ranges between 14.9 per cent in the 1980s to about 20 per cent in 2017. It has risen nearly linearly by about 5 per cent, showing over the long term a soft and consistent radicalisation. Across time, the percentage of radical left identities within western European societies is lower than the number of individuals approving strongly of various types of movements – which go up to 60 and 70 per cent of the population.

A gap exists between the identities of radical left movements and the mixture of identities among all those engaged in mobilisation and resistance. This is telling of the constant need for careful strategy, fronts and coalitions between radical movements themselves, and between the Radical Left and other sections of political contention. Meanwhile, the actual 'demand' for radical policies is higher than what is achieved on average by RLPs, so when we turn to parties the endeavour of electoral success is how to attract all of the ideological constituency in question.[70] As to the number of radical left identities, there is also considerable variation among countries for each period shown here, which can go up to 20 per cent (one in five). Some cases, like Spain and Greece, with a rich left tradition score close to 30 per cent. France and Italy are also higher than the average for the most part but fluctuate more. In others, such as Austria, Ireland or Malta, radical left identities score much lower but have radicalised in the

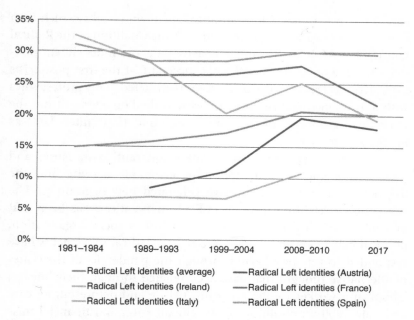

Figure 3.1   Left radicalism as self-identity in western Europe (1981–2017)

sense of roughly doubling their percentages in the 2000s. During the 2010s, no radicalisation can be recorded; in fact, on average there is a very slight decline, and in various countries (as in Italy and France) a decline of about 5 per cent.

How all this has translated into the politics of mobilisation and resistance after the 2008 crisis is seen in all of the southern European movements mentioned so far. These have included many ideological sections and produced various political organisations. The *indignados* in Spain, for example, participated in and helped build parties claiming to be part of its legacy from the left (Podemos), the politics of piracy (Partido X), as well as the centre-right (Ciudadanos). In Italy, the Italian comedian Beppe Grillo's M5S has systematically avoided a self-placement across the Left and Right, insisting that its anti-establishment stance seeks to move beyond this anachronistic schema. Its rise to prominence in the late 2000s was fuelled by post-materialist ground activity, especially among environmental movements. In Greece, parts of the Syntagma Square movements ended up in the conservative-nationalist formation Independent Greeks, which then entered into a coalition government with the Coalition of the Radical Left (SYRIZA). In Portugal, many activists chose independent politicians, some of whom were highly successful at the first post-crisis legislative elections.[71] In Spain, Podemos attracted many protest votes with anti-mainstream sentiment, distinguished on average from the established electorate of the communists and IU (United Left) as being more moderate.[72]

In the Covid-19 pandemic situation, quarantine measures and social distancing, the disruption of economic activity and the urgency for healthcare may have generated new beginnings. The perception circulating through radical interventions has been that of a major and highly threatening backshift in social organisation, political behaviour and democratic rights. Radical movements have responded to this by filtering through the pandemic all the issues of alternative thought that have accumulated through their lineage: labour and worker rights; economy, nature and deforestation; care and vulnerability; disability rights; globalisation and financial misbehaviour; feminism, social reproduction and gendered violence; prisoner rights; colonialism and indigenous populations; housing problems; and urban political economy, police states and surveillance systems. There has thus been a fusion of radical movements into the wider civil society, engaging activists in here-and-now problems and the immediate political priority of disseminating solidarity, direct action and do-it-yourself (DIY) politics so as to help society resist and autonomously defend itself.

To the extent that mutual aid and social empathy came into generalised usage, 'an ideological insurrection' has been at play, the very antithesis of the neoliberalist glorification of competition.[73] Resisting social regression, ideas of citizenship and counteracting on institutionalised authoritarianism by emergency has reopened. This is so not more than ten years since the Occupy movements, while at the same time generating performances of the state from outside of it. This is another breeding group for anarchist ideas for autonomy, an opportunity for prefiguration and expanding human possibilities, communal arrangements and collective refusal.

The pandemic also means a situation where social survival, well-being and above all human health depend on the resources states command and from which many sections of society are excluded. Hence programmatic positions of welfarism, redistribution, free healthcare for all, policies of counteracting oppression and social exclusion, and better pay and working conditions, as well as several strikes by unions in the public sector, have been set anew. E-petitions have also multiplied, and include demands for Eurobonds, suspension of rents for students or a fairer tax system to fund the Covid relief effort.[74] During the Covid-19 pandemic, social provisions and state intervention have been unprecedented in the short term, as well as desired by capitalist interests that need high levels of market-based consumption. Keynesian economic behaviour, the demand-driven capitalism which neoliberalism had displaced, arose in 2020 as the only sufficient response by many governments to managing the social situation.

For millennials especially, such high levels of state intervention and its effectiveness in many cases has been something unprecedented in their political experiences, which brings relief and is to be desired.[75] But there are already signs of renewed austerity as discourse has emerged about bloated public sectors and inefficient states. This could create an even greater focus on sustained Keynesian and demand management policies or, instead, reawaken anti-capitalism by reminding people that state intervention, as with the government economic stimuli after 2008, can only be temporary because capital will soon command states to tighten their belts so as not to stifle competitiveness. We cannot be sure at this point whether, out of the conjuncture the ideas and positions of radical social movements, the shift will be in the direction of another New Deal and regulatory governance or a more anarchist and anti-capitalist interpretation of social progress. The ideological dialectic within radical left movements may be undergoing a transition as we speak, in so far as many movements and civil society groups during the pandemic have been acting as watchdogs, organisers of material exchange and service providers, as well as anti-authoritarian resistance against state suppression of civil liberties.

SOLIDARITY AND INTERNATIONALISM

Solidarity during the pandemic reminds us that as an idea, it is not only multidimensional but also dialectical between different targets of solidarity. Solidarity can be focused the most on a particular collective subject or geographical region. This depends on the historical flow of events, such as regional integration, the dynamics of international conflict or the economy, or the pervasiveness of misery in one's own country. Internationalist solidarity means that the external supporters of a struggle provide local populations with crucial resources – legitimacy, publicity, funding and information – overall communicating resonance with their purpose. As the spaces of solidarity can change so can its overall character. It can be intensely political, as in the 1960s and 1970s, rights based as with pro-immigration movements or global as in calling for unity in diversity, as with the paradigm of the Zapatistas in the GJM.[76]

Solidarity, on one level, lies in the ambit of proletarian internationalism, which sought the unity of 'all workers' independent of country and translated into the doctrine of allegiance to the international movement of labour, led by the USSR. In the 1960s and 1970s, and as it was espoused by students, solidarity was understood mostly as a form of international alliance, central to the 'world-historical movement' as emerging in a period of global turmoil.[77] Solidarity was effectively extended beyond proletarian internationalism's stricter crowd (the workers). Revolutions in China then Cuba, and national liberation struggles in Algeria, Angola, Vietnam and elsewhere, forced Europe 'to reassess its place in the world' as its empires were receding.[78] Third Worldism combined anti-imperialism and anti-capitalism within Europe, vividly illustrated by striking Fiat workers in Turin, who, responding to Che Guevara's message, affirmed that 'Vietnam is in our factories'.[79] It also brought into focus aid to developing countries and ending apartheid. Since the late 1940s, decolonisation was gathering pace and thoroughly influenced the European Left. In both theory and practice, the Third World undermined a Eurocentric worldview, which also permeated Marxist and radical theory.[80] In the USA, France, Italy, Germany and other northern countries, the articulation of anti-colonial discourse and the production of anti-racist thinking happened 'in, through, and against Western universities'.[81]

Revolting students in western Europe had counterparts across continents in terms of perceived revolutionary potential: the Blacks in the USA, the peasants in China and Cambodia, the indigenous guerrillas in Latin America. However, the Long '68 was global, not only because it described many countries but also because it had explicitly internationalist and transnationalist policy content, shared with the GJM movements 30 years later. The post-2008 movements, on the other hand, do not strongly promote a specific, international policy agenda which resembles either the GJM's debt repayment by the 'post-colonised' Global South and terror legislation, or the anti-apartheid demands of the 1960s for no contact with countries practising it, or an end to the war in Vietnam. The contemporary period is where intra-national and European solidarity predominated over international solidarity and the indication is precisely a very thin (where existent) programmatic content linked to other regions or countries.

During the Long '68 the meanings and dynamics of migrant labour was an important issue – in France and the UK, for example, immigrants from North Africa and southern Europe or Asia were leading important social struggles, in many cases starting much earlier. In the aftermath of May '68 in France, immigrant workers set up non-union committees across the country.[82] In West Germany, the wildcat strike by Turkish workers at the Ford factory in Cologne in 1973 was a product of the 1968 groundwork for labour militancy among immigrants. It included shop-floor actions by workers, rent strikes, extended hunger strikes and mobilisations in solidarity with Palestine, as well as political organising. In the UK, the historical beginnings of ethnic and immigrant movements go back to the 1970s and 1980s. Immigrants throughout the Commonwealth and empire, needed to satisfy the industrial needs of post-war Britain and experiencing many forms of institutionalised, workplace-based and wider social racism, often became mobilised in defence of their communities.[83]

Western European trade unions varied a lot in terms of their stances towards immigrant workers. Overall, a divided working class emerged because immigrant workers posed dilemmas for established unions: on the one hand, immigrants came with specific communication deficits, work ethics, needs and cultures, while on the other, it was important to organise them to prevent divisions in the workforce. Conflicts of interest between foreign and domestic workers (as in Germany), opposition to immigration for many years (as in France and Switzerland) and the very absence of measures to combat discrimination in the workplace led to frustration.[84] Frustration with unions produced new organising sites, the 'emergence of the political subjectivity of the immigrant workers across national lines'.[85] For France, the Algerian War of Independence (1952–64) had been a crucial source of experiences that, in the circumstances of '68 and after, led to the articulation of a problematic regarding the (multi-ethnic) *condition immigré*.[86] In Germany, students from Latin America and Asia, which rapidly grew in number over the 1950s and 1960s, exposed German students to Third World ideologies.[87] For the UK, a legendary case in point is the Grunswick strike between 1976 and 1978, an instance of trade unions responding to the interests of women and members of ethnic minority communities.[88] In that country, migrants from the 'colonial states' had citizenship rights and were among the first in western Europe to engage in contentious claims beyond the workplace and the community.[89]

The popular slogan during the Long '68 in France – 'French and immigrant workers united' – became contested during that decade's historical sequence. 'It elided the specificity of the modes of subjection immigrant workers faced, and failed to capture the forms of politicisation that could address these material conditions.'[90] However, the slogan was a reaction to the conservatism and implicit racism of the corporatist trade union bureaucracies of western Europe, which in large part regarded migrant labour as temporary and thus of secondary significance. Such an opinion continues today in various union settings, depending of course on the industry. It was in the context of postcolonial dynamics that struggles waged by formerly colonised subjects would explode and gradually came to be seen as more complex and multidimensional than a labourist viewpoint could account for. Immigrant workers entered the cultural sphere too, to reflect and claim their autonomy, to channel their critique of Third Worldism within colonial states and to weave out the ways in which, contrary to communist and social democratic dogma, cultural difference in the working class was at stake politically.[91] A solidarity gap was the harsh reality of the times for immigrant populations. The established Left had to appeal to a conservative working class, which often meant negative attitudes by trade union members and communist supporters.[92]

Between the movements of the 1960s and 1970s and the GJM, solidarity with underdeveloped areas and countries was a feature of both cases, but in the latter period solidarity was not expressed so much by those who were to benefit from it. During the GJM, solidarity was more circular and thus global: 'an expression of a more extensive global consciousness that constructs the grievances of physically, socially and culturally distant people as deeply intertwined'; hence the Zapatistas serving to inspire and not merely receiving solidarity.[93] By the mid-2010s, solidarity would again shift in a unilateral direction, immigration overshadowing all other fronts of solidarity struggles. During the GJM years, a large number of pro-immigration civil society groups and radical organisations operated, but the 2010s were a watershed and witnessed the beginning of the war in Syria in 2015.

Pro-immigration positions have been, nevertheless, a feature also of the GJM's European sections. In view of the EU's Schengen Treaty in the 1990s, there emerged a novel rhetorical construction of the EU's hostile and neocolonialist attitude towards immigrants and refugees. This was expressed through 'fortress Europe' to describe a system in which freedom of movement within the EU is premised in the restriction of free movement into the EU.[94] The figure of the 'illegal immigrant' (or 'undocumented immigrant') also became politically contested and its pro and anti sides are more or less aligned with the left–right cleavage.[95] A chief struggle for radicals has thus been to challenge and deconstruct the notion of illegality as applied to mobile populations by the media or politicians – the most universal slogan to this end being 'No one is illegal'. 'Migration is not a crime' is a unifying claim through which radical activists are bound with humanitarians and appeal to immigration as an inviolable right of all human beings, at the same time as responding to the criminalisation of immigration, both by the mainstream media and government authorities. 'We are all immigrants' is perhaps the example which best echoes internationalism. It implicitly identifies the immigrant as a universal subject, between borders and within time, and in turn alludes to the internationality of the origins, destinations and sources of immigration and refugeehood.

In the 2010s, internationalist solidarity in western Europe centred primarily on millions of refugees and immigrants from Middle Eastern and African zones of conflict, famine, repression and political turmoil trying to enter the old continent. The issue has been especially politicised where the countries of 'first arrival', like Italy and Greece, are situated. Immigrant rights activists, progressive politicians and local leaders in many European cities have used citizenship claims to defend the welcoming approach of their refuge localities, where urban citizenship is defined not by refugee or immigration status but simply by place of residence.[96] Radical intellectuals have called for the left 'to predicate border politics on the potential of border struggles'.[97] As the argument goes, borders are a fundamental aspect of labour politics, which has become increasingly fragmented and sectionalised, and an important tool to use in any attempt to reimagine and construct a solid internationalism.[98]

With borders understood as crystallising and reproducing relations of domination, opening them is the way to break with domination's mechanisms and structures. Open borders has become a common position for many parts of the European Radical Left. The arguments are several: borders 'are a form of global apartheid', which preserves the power of the wealthy at the expense of the oppressed; borders and the EU's policies towards them 'produce violence but do not stop immigration'; 'blaming migrants for low wages' or 'stealing jobs' 'divides workers and creates a race to the bottom'; capital and big business already have open borders and thus, from a class or economic viewpoint, there is an unequal distribution of human rights.[99]

Free cross-border migration can operate as a counter-action to capitalist and colonial impositions.[100] But open borders takes the existence of nation states and thus borders as a fact, in a sense being more pragmatic in proposing a first step towards global equality; hence it must be differentiated from no borders. This is a more radical leap to the second step of fundamental transformation in the ways populations are territorialised without first opening borders. One such example is the No Border Network's slogan, 'No borders, no nations, stop deportations!' Effectively, the difference between 'open borders' and 'no borders' is one of framing and arises out of divergence in teleological radicalism and pragmatism – for example, is it possible to abolish borders without first opening them? Historical and contemporary ambiguities about the nation state and the fatherland echo this concern. 'Open borders' and 'no borders' don't have to be mutually exclusive. Proponents of open borders take the nation state for granted from a variety of angles (which may be market-libertarian and liberal on the Right, political-economic on the Left). No Border activists focus on contemporary border struggles and the way borders shape new subjectivities, beyond and within the nation state, eventually eroding its significance as a unit of territory. In activist practice, the distinction is blurry at best. Antifa and anarchist movements frequently protest outside immigrant detention camps. Legal activists document how conditions violate international or human rights law, and organisers expose border patrols. All these activities are transcending the border as normality.

Pro-immigration movements have spanned the whole of the radical left space, from youth and women organisations of SDPs and RLPs to Trotskyist, anarchist and other revolutionary forces. A multipurpose repertoire of contending immigration control and restriction has evolved since about the 1990s and 2000s. It includes essays, opinion articles and pamphlets that resist the branding of immigrants and seek to naturalise immigration. It includes campaigns for deportations under the EU's Dublin Regulation, and specific cases, usually including individuals from various ideological spaces. Equally, multi-ideological charity networks collect food and other primary goods. There are also festivals or camps, welcoming committees, activism in monitoring detention camps, feminist women's rights networks and initiatives of solidarity with hunger strikers, legal action and campaigns against pushbacks. In the radical literature regarding the most recent wave of pro-immigration activism, novel concepts have gained attention and attracted interventions, such as 'border regime', 'border spectacle', 'autonomy of migration' or 'border as method'.[101] These concepts and the wider interdisciplinary discussion on borders structuralise the understanding of immigration and refugeehood and thus offer a corrective discourse that deciphers these phenomena as circumstantial or chiefly economic.

Today, about 70 years after the debates opened, there is an entrenched sensitivity in radical literature centred on the immigrant's point of view as the source of true solidarity and the groundwork for any meaningful internationalism. Just as Third Worldism introduced prisms of thought to Western radicals, so too recent experiences with immigrant solidarity and struggles to decolonise the systems of the imperial core have fostered theoretical avenues that attempt to capture the immigrant subject and weave border politics into political sociology.

WAR, PEACE, INTERNATIONALISM

The other obvious axis of internationalism and solidarity concerns war, peace and their link to imperialism since Lenin. The anti-war movements of the 2010s compare little to the 1990s and early 2000s and even less to the anti-war movement of the Long '68. Over the whole of democratic western Europe, the Vietnam War was vehemently opposed by students, radical intellectuals and CPs and SDPs. But although it often characterises the period's strong sense of solidarity and the Third World's influence on Europe, Vietnam was still one war to which opposition did not mean agreement on all things related to peace. To observe a long-lasting line of conflict from the Cold War period we can look especially at the anti-nuclear movements opposed to a USSR engaged in the arms race with the USA. Since the 1950s, the new form of anti-war activism came from diverse cultural and political backgrounds, including catholic groups (e.g. this was important in Italy), as well as Protestant Christian organisations. Altogether, they challenged the post-war consensus in Europe and espoused a progressive-liberal-conservative anti-communism.[102] The USSR had its own peace movement organised and operating in accordance with the Soviet line and through nationally based sections of the World Peace Council, in addition to various other affiliated associations such as World Institute for Peace, the World Democratic Federation of Youth and the International Federation of Resistance Fighters.[103]

The CPs and the various National Peace Councils in western Europe and elsewhere sought to become a broad movement. In interaction with other mass ancillary structures of the international movement led by Moscow, they had a broad reach and a noteworthy presence across the 1960s and 1970s. At the same time, they were instrumentalised for the Soviet Union's foreign policy, supporting socialist countries and effectively mobilising under external constraints. Although the communist peace movement described itself as 'an open movement', and often fused with other local and national initiatives, a 'bloc mentality' infused it. As Wernicke summarised, 'there was a constant clash between intentions and practical realities whenever, at the international and domestic levels, concrete strategies were required to build broad peace alliances which might transcend bloc allegiance'.[104] Between the USSR and the peace and anti-war movements, solidarity was a contested notion. Both the crushing of the Prague Spring and the Soviet invasion of Afghanistan in 1983 were presented by the USSR (and contested by movements) as acts of solidarity with the people.

It is thus important to underline that historically a radical anti-war position or the broader anti-war movement does not necessarily oppose armies and all things military;[105] hence the USSR called the structures it led internationally a 'peace movement'. Let us remember that the organising principle of left internationalism since 1914 places opposition to respective imperialisms as its top priority. Thus German radical leaders Karl Liebknecht and Rosa Luxemburg mostly opposed the German, not the Russian, war effort and Lenin vice versa. Anti-militarism and anti-imperialism conflicted as the nuclear threat produced pacifist mass movements, but in the protests against Vietnam calls for peace in that country were voiced along with 'weapons for the Vietcong'. Pacifism surged by the late 1970s and early 1980s due to the rise and spread of the ecological movement. But the Radical Left of the Long '68, both students and parties, supported the notion of 'just war', the justification being anti-imperialist struggles necessary for freedom and democracy. The notion of principled pacifism was a minority position during this period and typically described as defeatist. It also interplayed with Cold War politics. For example, in the UK the European Nuclear Disarmament movement founded by key figures of the New Left like E. P. Thompson, who had split with the Communist Party after the crushing of the Hungarian Uprising in 1956, campaigned against Soviet nuclear weapons as part of its strategy of 'détente from below', while the Campaign for Nuclear Disarmament (CND, established in 1958) focused on unilateral British disarmament as the 'pro-Soviet lobby' had prevailed internally.[106]

Full opposition to war continues to divide activists and groups who, for example, refuse to sign declarations not explicitly demanding the abolition of the military. Organisations against war are distinguished into pacifist or non-violent on the one side and (in broad terms) anti-imperialist on the other side, through their names and blurbs, hence a common line of distinction is between the peace movement and the anti-war movement. Hence, CND campaigns for 'British nuclear disarmament' and 'a global ban on nuclear weapons', 'missile defense and weapons in space', 'opposition to NATO' and the 'prevention and cessation of wars in which nuclear weapons may be used'. It is also 'encouraging non-military solutions to conflict'.[107] But it includes, cooperates with and addresses both pacifists and more traditional anti-imperialists. Similar groups in Germany, such as the German section of International Physicians for the Prevention of Nuclear War or the German Peace Society – United War Resisters, neither explicitly link militarism to capitalism nor officially endorse non-violence. As in the rest of the movements in which the Radical Left participates, some groups and associations are critical of the capitalist-militarist system in its entirety and many are not. As an activist reported about the German peace and anti-war movements in 2001 at the point of declining momentum, '[i]n their peace and anti-war work, many people never reach a criticism of the dynamics intrinsic to the military, nor to a fundamental criticism of the military'.[108]

The GJM was indeed historically situated in the context of the Balkan wars and NATO's intervention in Yugoslavia's disintegration, the American invasion of Afghanistan and the US-led invasion and occupation of Iraq in the post-9/11 universe. The USA's subsequent response to the terrorist organisation Al Qaida via the War on Terror was opposed as a worldwide offensive against civil liberties. On 15 February 2003, demonstrations across many countries to oppose the

Iraq War constituted the 'largest protest event in human history'.[109] This anti-war movement generated massive demonstrations in Britain, including a very large wave of school walkouts and at times more than a million people on the streets.[110] In the rest of Europe the anti-war movement also awoke and tens of thousands protested and mobilised. In the wake of the USA-led invasion and occupation of Iraq, the multiple, local anti-bases movement became effectively internationalised; a global campaign emerged to 'map, expose, and counter the global military presence of the United States and others'. It eventually included 400 organisations.[111] At the same time, discussions of Islamophobia opened widely within European societies, especially in France and the UK with significant Muslim populations. The War on Terror cultivated, according to many anti-war movements and rights organisations, a governmentality of Islamophobia that discriminates and marginalises ethnic and cultural minorities.

After the end of the Cold War, anti-base movements were reinforced by sharing tactics and ideas against the USA's revered 'dogma of military bases abroad'.[112] Without Cold War constraints and given the considerable withdrawal of Russian military bases, the Radical Left as a whole, its movements and parties, became more cohesive in its anti-base positions. Anti-base movements were also reinforced in the context of the emerging GJM, which conveyed to anti-base activism the value of organising globally.[113] Guantanamo, the USA's Cuban outpost of extreme torture of 'suspected terrorists', became a symbol of both the anti-war movements and the GJM post-2001.[114] Shared critique identified the role of bases in enabling wars, the violation of local sovereignty as explained by the undemocratic way through which war is launched and plays out, damage and harm to local populations and their connections to global economic injustice.[115] Through deliberation at the WSF and ESFs a concrete although somewhat short-lived achievement was reached: launching the International Network for the Abolition of Foreign Military Bases (No Bases) in Quito and Manta, Ecuador, from 5 to 9 March 2007. The emphasis on bases aimed at highlighting the ways in which globalisation was premised on militarisation, itself perpetuating material and other injustice. As explained by an American activist-scholar who participated: 'without foreign military bases, wars would be so much more difficult to wage; without wars, the pursuit of geo-strategic and economic interests over democracy and self-determination would be so much harder'.[116]

The anti-war movement and its links to the Radical Left continue. Today there are many established disarmament campaigns and more than a handful of anti-war or peace organisations in each western European country. Marches outside of American embassies on key occasions have customary status, and anti-militarisation collectives and analyses through decades of interdisciplinary peace research starting in the 1950s make inroads to deconstructing peace and connecting capitalism with war. Organised support for conscientious objection is an important nucleus of activism where military service is compulsory (as in Cyprus and Greece). Large protests against visits by Donald Trump (or previously other US presidents) or NATO counter-summits are also evident. Saudi Arabia's war in Yemen, sustained by its weaponry deals with the West, although not commanding large-scale solidarity, has been opposed by dockers in France and Italy who in 2019 refused to load military equipment onto ships, their unions calling for a strike.[117]

There are sprouts of anti-war and peace activity, primarily institutional or campaign activities, demonstrations and (only then) some direct action. But the dynamic of the anti-war movement in the 2010s has been dormant in terms of mass anti-war and pro-peace mobilisations. For one thing, strategy has been recently contested. With Russia's militarism expanding and playing an important role in the conflict in Syria, the Radical Left is far from unanimous on how to end the war in terms of policy measures and even the demand for withdrawal. Indeed, the war in Syria is taking place through the multilateral intervention and support of the various local groups. It could be called 'war via representatives', rather than an explicit invasion. In opposition to any political support for a state entity, some argue that supporting Assad, or Gaddafi before him, betrays an irrationality, a 'fetishism' of state sovereignty whereby 'solidarity is ... extended to states (seen as the main actor in a struggle for liberation), rather than oppressed or underprivileged groups in any given society, no matter that state's tyranny'.[118] In the UK, the politics of the Stop the War Coalition (STWC, established 2001) have been criticised by

prominent pro-peace intellectuals, many of them Muslim, for ide-
alising the Russian-Assad side and for being more anti-West than
pro-peace.[119] Such criticisms surfaced at various points, from 2013
until 2018, and included resignations, criticism of Jeremy Corbyn for
his involvement in the STWC, open letters from Muslim activists and
intellectuals and accusations from campaign groups. In reality, the
majority of STWC is not pro-Assad, as many of the criticisms are a
result of propaganda launched by the pro-war media and lobbyists
seeking to cast doubt over the morality of STWC politics. France is
the ultimate battleground for what Tangiuef coined 'islamo-leftism'
(islamogauche) in 2002, referring to connections between radical left
and global justice activists in the early 2000s and groups like Hamas
and Hezbollah.[120] The term has since been highly politicised by the
extreme Right and its leader, Marine Le Pen, and the Right, including
the Macron government.

The Palestinian–Israeli conflict is the most central front of near
unity on the Radical Left in Europe as well as the USA. Yet, many
left-wing activists are suspicious towards the Boycott, Divestment,
Sanctions campaign, but in Britain and France the issue is more
sensitive and more easily invites accusations of anti-Semitism. A conception of Israel as an apartheid state is still widely accepted in radical
spaces across various types of movements and ideological strains,
within and outside academia, to the extent of consistent activity,
frequent pan-European initiatives and the cross-country presence of
organisations such as the Israeli Committee Against House Demo-
litions (in the UK and Finland). In Italy, the recent initiative Spazi
Liberi di Appartheid Israeliana brought together social and cultural
centres, unions, collectives and parties.

To compare the 2000s with the 2010s, it can be argued that the
Saddam regime in Iraq was no less repressive of the Left than the
Muammar Gaddafi regime in Libya against which foreign intervention was carried out; the difference was the existence in 2011
(as opposed to 2003) of massive mobilisations in the Arab world
with revolutionary ramifications. In contrast to the George W. Bush
administration (2001–9), US President Barack Obama was also
oriented towards the 'pivot to Asia' policy but tried to outsource the
Middle East to others, giving the impression to many (erroneously)

that the USA was not pursuing any regime change policies in the region anymore. Instead, the Obama administration allocated more money to war than Bush, didn't take troops out of Iraq and Afghanistan and deployed special operations in tens of countries.[121] The differences within the anti-war movement today extend the familiar divergences of the early 1900s. They concern decoding the reading of the situation (specifically, is US imperialism still dominant?) and whether to take a purely propagandistic position (i.e. against all imperialisms) or build anti-war mobilisations centred on simple demands, such as no war against Syria or withdrawal from Libya, or as during the GJM, closing the Guantanamo prison or NATO withdrawal from the former Yugoslavia.

INTERNATIONALISM AND EUROPEAN INTEGRATION

In understanding the overall internationalist outlook of the Radical Left, European integration matters in so far as it circumscribes protest and mobilisation regionally. During the bailouts in southern Europe, solidarity emerged as a feature between the activists and protestors in countries with a similar standing within the eurozone and in relation to debt. The Greek case attracted the most solidarity events from other countries. Worldwide, a campaign began called 'We are all Greeks' and 'in support of the Greek people'. Spanish activists protested the Cypriot universal haircut on bank deposits, the so-called bail-in of March 2013, which was initially rejected by parliament. In response to shared grievances, solidarities emerged between countries undergoing similar problems and pressures within the context of austerity and neoliberalism. Resonance bred solidarity in this sense, but the latter was also expressed within the hegemonic EU countries and by non-European intellectuals, politicians, groups and activists. In Germany, notably, radical groups launched multiple protests and events in solidarity with those harmed by the German government; Die Linke was an important force within the parliamentary arena, arguing that Greece was being exploited and blamed at the same time. As has been argued, '[t]his indicates that although the movement's development has been deeply influenced by the nationally uneven impact of the crisis and austerity, activists make concerted efforts to transcend the entrenched politico-economic differences between them'.[122]

As the EU was 'one of the key crisis actors for contention', radical left and other movements became increasingly concerned about the EU as a pivotal agent dictating austerity (and deciding on debt) on the continent.[123] Pan-European groups and campaigns – Democracy in Europe 2025 (DieM 2025), the hundreds of organisations calling for a 'European Spring' against austerity and anti-democratic EU policies in 2013 or the multinational strikes in 2012 – played a significant role in transnationalising the anti-austerity struggles in Europe, tying together activists and organisations both within and across European regions. An emphasis on Europe needs to be qualified in any case. Tapping into collective grievances is more effectively achieved by framing the discussion at the national, and then European, level. Put differently, the more specific the enemy (the government or the EU, or the troika, or the Eurogroup, or all of these under 'the elites') the easier it is to mobilise people and achieve impact. Radical activists of many policy domains are 'playing a double-level game' since EU institutions are increasingly targeted due to their involvement, but national government policy remains the chief locus of mobilisation and cause of protest.[124] For anti-austerity and pro-democracy movements as well as unions, the nation state or particular institutions have trumped the EU or the troika in terms of focus.[125] As a memorandum of austerity was not the case in various instances – e.g. Iceland – and in other countries – for example in southern Europe or Ireland – its peak phase had passed, the EU level as a target of protest has been progressively trumped by the national level in terms of demands and criticism. However, during severe austerity national parliaments had to approve the bailouts and the process thus became contestable in national political competition. In addition, if the initial anti-austerity movements focused on the national level, subsequent mobilisations, such as the Gilet Jaunes in France and various national or sectional strikes, were even more centred on the national level regarding both their roots and their targets.[126] The Gilet Jaunes protests ignited in response to increases to fuel prices but also echoed the destruction of the middle class and its displacement in the class map to a set of social peripheries.[127]

Meanwhile, the rhetorical framing of austerity and mobilisation against it are codified among activists as acts of resistance to problems that are global or international and thus require systemic, transcontinental transformation. The simultaneous mobilisation of Occupy movements in tens of countries legitimated these views and enhanced globalist outlooks among movement participants.[128] In the context of anti-austerity protest, 'Europe', as Della Porta and Parks report from their interviews, 'was seen as a main problem and the very identification of a European identity as problematic'.[129] There is, however, some evidence of generational divides. Where older activists appreciate Europe's legacy of twentieth-century wars and the European social model, younger activists blame neoliberal Europe and take it for granted because neoliberalism is all they have experienced.[130] Among radical movements there has not emerged a coherent or collective call for an EU exit. This is a position which neither guarantees more internationalist solidarity by itself nor clearly looks strategically superior for most activists on the Radical Left than staying in and fighting from there. Many movements and activists in the GJM were explicitly pro-European integration but disagreed with its political direction.[131]

There has been, nevertheless, a gradual Europeanisation of radical and other social movements.[132] It is defined as their capacity to mobilise with the EU as a focus and as an increasing emphasis on EU issues and European identities. It is compounded with the fragmented transnationalisation of party politics that we will discuss later. Social movements have adapted to multilevel governance by increasing their numbers of actors operating exclusively at the EU level, expanding their transnational networks and focusing on an increasing number of European targets (agencies, institutions, officials). These tendencies have been documented for deliberations over an EU constitution (*c.*2004), campaigns such as against the Bolkestin Directive's (2006) aim to create a single market for services and the Transnational Trade and Investment Partnership (TTIP, 2013–16) between the EU and the United States.[133] During the pandemic something on the left, which took both an international and transnational shape, has been the support for issuing Eurobonds as well as direct fiscal stimuli into the economies and societies of Europe, which nine countries inside the EU proposed but the hegemonic forces led by

Germany declined. In addition there is the Right to Cure campaign of the European Citizens Initiative, supported by many left-wing actors and more generally a vehement critic of the EU's organisation of vaccines and its interaction with the pharmaceutical-industrial complex.

A parallel reality is that the EU provides political opportunities to radical and other groups to mobilise in pursuit of a particular goal – against very restrictive asylum policy, for better labour rights, against the violation of civil liberties, or fighting environmental damage condoned by the national government. This is where, in some countries from time to time in others systematically, the EU serves as a progressive force to be utilised for local or national political battles. Such political opportunities can be EU law, funding from specific programmes or communiqués and interventions by EU institutions and agencies condemning or supporting developments at the national level. For all the Euroscepticism of the radical social movements, the EU's arms and branches can be a useful tool in opposing national government excesses or in support of democratising forces. This also became apparent during the pandemic, during which the European Court of Human Rights, organisations like Amnesty International and the European Commission itself became tools for reinforcing and substantiating claims against government restrictions.

In perspective, the line between Eurocentrism, Europeanisation and internationalism is thin. Eurocentrism is both a form of orientalism and imperialism to be opposed by the radical movements and a de facto reality for mobilisation and resistance given the high recognition of the role of EU institutions and policies. It wouldn't be illogical to associate this Europeanisation with the lack of solidarity during the entire 2010s towards non-EU countries and regions through formulated and collective solidarity policies or demands. In any case, post-2008 the comparatively thin internationalism of the last mobilisation wave within Europe is conjoined with a largely Europeanised protest space. This is an appropriate time for radical theory to dissect whether the concrete political situation in which movements and activists find themselves practically means overvaluing developments and agency in Europe, and depreciating the dynamic and relevance of less developed and oppressed nations, which would be Eurocentrism.

Ideological development shows lasting lines of division for which the past plays an important role – as a benchmark and spring of contestation. Ideas take up meanings that reflect their contemporary political resonance. The idea of sovereignty has evolved not in its core meaning of sovereign power but in respect of where this power is located: in the people, the nation, the locality or the food production and consumption process. Democracy has not changed in terms of the salience ascribed to democratic claims on the Radical Left but rather in what concerns its envisioned applications and protested pathologies. Solidarity shifts between the national, European and international levels and solidifies into specific policies according to each one's prominence in the public sphere, although solidarity is always found in all directions.

Differences in movement identity between the three periods of 'newness' concern how certain themes have been projected in relation to others and the way in which they are analysed, evoked and contextualised. Many of the identity traits ascribed to the post-2008 social movements – pro-democracy, neo-anarchism, anti-austerity mobilisation and the politicisation of class and its simultaneous marriage with issues that transcend material inequality and exploitation – apply to the Long '68 and in some cases much earlier, although they do not always characterise the epoch or the self-identities of activists back then. Returning to the issue of labels with which the chapter started, the radical left movements have always had multiple identities, which as we will see subsequently translate into multiple vocabularies and organisational forms. They have been pro-democracy, anti-globalisation and alternative globalisation, statist and anti-statist, anti-capitalist and anti-neoliberal, as well as anti-systemic and reformist.

We are thus prompted to return to the notion of salience ascribed to ideas and positions in the theoretical sketch of the book. This is the main issue at hand in long-term evolution. In each period, radical movement identities shift relationally when casting the mobilisation wave as a whole and radical identities within it. The NSMs envisioned a world without deprivation, hegemony, war and any form of alienation. Their vision was for equality and material abundance, against consumption-driven puritanism and authoritarian socialism. They introduced, to society and the traditional left, existential self-fulfilment, expressive freedom and sexual emancipation, civil rights for minorities and a blending of nationalism and socialism through Third World prisms and demands. A reformulated socialist longing in radical movement spaces broke with the sterile orthodoxy of the USSR, continuing a pre-emerging, wider political critique of existing socialism set off by Stalin's death.

The imaginary of the GJM was prefigurative, reformist in its policy demands, transnationally theorised and focused and speaking of social and economic justice under the rubric of anti-neoliberalism. It, too, sought to resuscitate the left, but only after a historical defeat which significantly pushed down the electoral fortune of socialist parties and CPs and oriented activism towards working outside the framework of teleological certainty and historical specificity. In post-2008 spaces, the key imaginaries coexist but also follow the sequence of emerging struggles in terms of the frames and positions driving actual mobilisation – from anti-austerity and pro-democracy, to climate justice and immigrant solidarity, to health, welfare and anti-authoritarianism.

Between the 1960s and today, it is the prominence of some ideas and positions in relation to others and in the context of mobilisation and resistance that has chiefly changed. Namely, the dynamic between revolution and reformism; claims and representations of democracy's current pathologies; evolving manifestations of solidarity; the potential and form of anti-war movements; the dialectic between anti-imperialism and pacifism; and the push and pull of Eurocentrism, Europeanisation and Euroscepticism. Thereby, change is not so concerned with the range or multiplicity of radical left claims and attitudes. These became significantly more pluralised after the 1960s, hence the discourse of NSMs offers meaning, among other things, to the ideological broadening of the European Radical Left.

4

Patterns in Social Movement Rhetoric

INTRODUCTION

The aim of this chapter is to illustrate the ways in which the post-2008 movements of the European Radical Left are distinct, or not, from those of the 1960s/1970s and the GJM in terms of rhetoric. We take a step further, based on Chapter 3, by looking more inquisitively at what rhetorical style and strategies emerge from the ideational trajectories documented so far. The chapter first considers the shift from class-based and revolutionary discourse to universalistic language and its associated features – emotions, vagueness, less doctrine, human rights and the broad category of citizen. In continuing our earlier point on the gradual passage of revolutionary positions, we elaborate on how revolution and utopia have been resignified. As a particular type of universalistic rhetoric and statist policy seeking, we then discuss 'new left populism', inquiring into the broader debate about crowds, masses and how to analyse and approach them as agents of progress. Is the alleged acceleration of left populism during the 2000s and 2010s valid?

Like populism, nationalism takes many forms according to the ideology to which it attaches. Like populism, nationalism has been an issue for the Left from its very beginnings. Like populism, nationalism works through a binary, a self-identification with the patria or nationhood as opposed to the unpatriotic or nationally treacherous. In-groupism and out-groupism can be circumscribed through local, regional or national political arenas; as with populism they evoke territoriality, but unlike populism they are horizontally defined.

UNIVERSALISM, REVOLUTION, UTOPIA, RIGHTS

The critical characteristic of both the GJM context and the post-2008 situation in Europe is dispossession; this has shaped the vocabulary of social movement politics.[1] As David Harvey explains, the mechanism affecting the relationship between neoliberalism and mobilisation against it, accumulation by dispossession – different from accumulation through the expansion of wage labour as in the 1960s – is fragmented and thus hard to oppose without appeal to universal principles evoking commonality and humanism.[2] An issue can activate emerging publics either in a universal or particularistic manner, the former meaning 'issues that have no specific reference to a well-defined social group', while the latter denotes framings in a way that issues 'are intrinsically related to specific social groups'.[3] Harvey argues that 'dispossession entails the loss of rights. Hence the turn to a universalistic rhetoric of human rights, dignity, sustainable ecological practices, environmental rights, and the like, as the basis for a unified oppositional politics.'[4] Extreme forms of exploitation under conditions of return to primitive modes of expansion produced emerging ruling classes and popular classes, which necessitated reframing opposition to exploitation. Similarly, Saskia Sassen's use of the term 'expulsions', as the human and social condition under 'brutality' and 'complexity', described the increase in disparities currently being faced by populations worldwide.[5] Like in the analysis of Harvey, Sassen's argument implies the need to recalibrate resistance, largely because it reveals atypical forms of struggles and suggests multiplicity and diversity.

In the GJM, and even more so in anti-austerity protests, traditional workers mobilised along with precarious workers, public sector workers, pensioners and the unemployed, students, farmers and indigenous people, LGBTQ (Lesbians, Gay, Bisexual, Transsexual, Queer) activists, pacifists and revolutionaries. A more encompassing language has often been the product of protests bringing together heterogeneous coalitions of citizens united as the losers and critics of neoliberal globalisation. However, they are relatively heterogeneous regarding their structural locations, their demographic features and their attitudinal traits; after all, a large part of globalisation's so-called losers, especially those with a lower educational background, unite around the extreme right. The Zapatista slogan, 'one no, many yeses', or its support for diversity of different life forms as with the phrase a 'world in which many worlds have their place', expressed this large diversity in the collective subject. Many mobilised sections of the movement were inspired to unite in an oppositional front around a shared rejection of neoliberal globalisation, but without being limited to fixed meanings. Rather, the goal was to construct a counter-hegemonic force and (in Gramscian terms) fight a war of position.[6]

In accordance with Harvey's rationale of universalistic rhetoric and what it entails – sensations, generic slogans and unspecified meanings – is above all a question of necessity and strategy under conditions of a frontal attack by neoliberal elites and unprecedented socio-political diversity among the oppressed. All-encompassing slogans are sometimes too vague to openly invoke radicalism. Consider the names of the past decade's movements: 'Get up' (Aufstehen) in Germany; 'We Can' (Podemos) in Spain or 'indignation' more broadly; 'Rising Up' (UK), 'RISE' in Scotland or 'Momentum' in the UK; or 'Common Sense' (Senso Comune) in Italy. They are connected by the call to react and demand change, and the ideological and policy net implied by their labels can be too opaque to reflect or sustain coherence. Their nominal invocations are generic, untargeted and often make mention of traits of behaviour (ability, reaction, awareness) that are more connected to motivation and emotion rather than particular ideological colours. Consider here also some of the catch-all-like statements of the Spanish 2010 movement Real Democracy Now!, such as the following, which would be unthinkable in 'a strictly left-wing' movement:

> Some of us consider ourselves progressive, others conservative. Some of us are believers, some not. Some of us have clearly defined ideologies, others are apolitical, but we are all concerned and *angry* about the political, economic, and social outlook which we see around us; corruption among politicians, businessmen, bankers, leaves us helpless, without a voice. This situation has become normal, a daily *suffering*, without *hope*. But if we join forces, we can change it. It's time to change things, time to build a better society together.[7]

In movements and protest, from strikes to demonstrations to sit-ins, emotions have a critical function. Their framing in discourse reclaims them as central to our cognitive and evaluative capacities; thus 'love', 'anger', 'indignation' and so on can be very important, legitimate and unifying elements among activist conceptions of social justice.[8] Projecting emotions is radical itself by way of bringing, in the words of Chantal Mouffe, passions into politics, which has anyway been enduringly central to political conflict, political history and political thought but dismissed as irrational by predominant perceptions of politics.[9] To the extent that it is emotional the movements' contribution is thus counter-hegemonic, given the mainstream liberal narrative of the historical and progressive victory of reason over emotions.[10] At the same time, emotional, rhetorical and other appeals are neither politically exclusive – thus they can inform a politics promoting violence, hate and discrimination – nor specific in terms of policy. They can therefore end up mixing a very heterogeneous crowd, bound only or mostly by emotions and passions rather than a collective political culture, and thus easy to demobilise or split. Indeed, counter-hegemony may be more difficult to shape without fixed meanings, that is, specific ideas about the past, the present and the future, which can be shared between the oppressed and reconcile multiple sectionalities.

To decode social movement names and appeals we have to take into consideration their organic composition and their intended audience as key indicators; both of these, in terms of movements or protests such as the above, are much broader than the space of left radicalism strictly speaking, as we saw in Chapter 3. A key part of the pragmatic formula in doing social movement politics is the perception that, as David Snow and colleagues have suggested, the successes and failures of social movements depend partly on their ability to frame grievances in ways that resonate with mainstream beliefs and values.[11] Humanism and rights are such mainstream ideas, and for coalition building with 'ideological others' pragmatism is effective. This is, in fact, an ancient realisation, reflected in the Aristotelian analysis of rhetoric. A personal account of an Occupy London Stock Exchange activist portrays succinctly the point by explaining the rationale behind replacing the banner 'Capitalism is Crisis' in the occupied space with 'All Power to the 99%': 'If we as Occupy came out full guns blazing saying we are anti-capitalists, it would have played into the mainstream frame, which would have led to fewer people listening to us.'[12]

Over time and within the broad space of radical and progressive movements, we can note a number of discursive trends: the substitution by many Anglo-American activists of terms like 'exploitation', which signifies exploiters in economic terms above all constituting the ruling class, with terms such as 'class bias', which signifies misbehaviour towards persons of low economic status, detecting a snobbish attitude rather than a problem of social and economic structure. In Anglo-Saxon settings, we can also note a shift from the language of 'oppression' to the language of 'vulnerability' or 'privilege' and 'status', which is more entrenched in identitarian concerns. Or the construction of the enemy as 'capitalism' in the 1960s and as 'neoliberalism' in the 2000s; or the notion of a 'battle', which is important in and of itself as self-serving progress, as opposed to being simply a factor in the process of 'revolution'; or the further consolidation of 'an everyday revolution', which can dampen visions of mass-scale rupture; or the near total fading of the notion of 'agitation'; importantly, also the prevalence of citizenship and the citizen as opposed to the 'workers' or the 'oppressed'.

Anarchism, for its part in revolution's shifting significations, is also a space whereby revolutionaries in both Europe and beyond 'have increasingly abandoned even talking about seizing power'. They have 'begun to formulate radically different ideas of what a revolution would even mean'.[13] Many anarchists rethought the concept in the midst of sustained incapacity for a mass overthrow. The beginning of change in the ideological thought of anarchist authors can be traced in the aftermath of World War II, when the defeat of the Spanish anarchists during the civil war (1936–9) that ended in Franco's reign made revolution look at best 'a temporally elongated phenomenon', 'without a climactic endpoint'.[14] Between the 1960s and the GJM, in the context of heated debate, the prefigurative divergence from classical anarchism was confronted with polemics and accusations of reformism. In opposition to the increasingly majoritarian position that a 'revolutionary exodus' strategy is necessary to construct an alternative infrastructure for the renewal of social relations, various thinkers and activists have persisted in the direction of overthrow. Other than this, today it is a minoritarian mode of ideological thinking.

The discontinuity in the anarchist tradition fits into a generalised shift from understanding change as a process rather than an event, thereby reconceptualising revolution and emphasising non-violence, education and opposition to 'domination' rather than 'oppression'. It is today reflected in key contemporary figures of anarchist thought – among them James Scott, Richard Day and the late David Graeber. They have sought to 'de-fetishise socio-political innovation', the very meaning of the new, by 'envisaging it as a long-term process of resistance and open, ongoing, plural experimentations rather than as an instantaneous and miraculous eruption'.[15] Occupy's anarchists, for example, like their precursors in the GJM, exhibit a strong association between utopianism and prefigurative politics. As Ruth Kinna argues, the anarchist utopian strain rejects 'scientistic', 'historicist' and 'instrumental' ways of constructing the connection between the means of struggle and its end. Rather, their utopia is evoked to assert and highlight that alternative structures, norms and behaviours are possible and to craft their way forward in a way consistent 'with their principles, precisely in order to resist unspecified abstract utopias or blueprints'.[16]

This drawn-out process, gradually changing the internal dynamics of global anarchism, is not only the 'defetishisation' of revolution, inasmuch as there has been a substantive, political repositioning gravitating towards an attitude on the state that is much more complex than the classical persuasion of smashing it. In the post-war period, the welfare system was identified as partly progressive in providing self-determination through social security and universal education. Western European countries were also becoming increasingly geared towards decentralisation and regional planning. Anarchist thought registered these developments through recasting anarchism not merely as a negative struggle of opposition to domination, but also as co-creative alongside already available infrastructures offered by the state in the service of resistance.[17] Then, the coexistence between citizenship claims and anarchist theory in the Occupy movements that was noted in Chapter 3, as well the GJM's engagement with international institutions, must thus be situated as the most recent manifestation of the gradual shift to an evolutionary understanding of revolution. This, we could argue in historical terms, makes large crowds with many anarchists inside them more plausible.

The discourse of everydayness may be driven by the response to a more general problem that has to do with modernity and therein the meaning of and right to revolt. This argument about capitalism and its consolidation through ideologies suggests that in modernity the archaic demand for self-government has been substituted by the emphasis on consent, at the same time as the average person has shifted from 'passions' to 'interests', and has no time for 'conventional' politics.[18] Since the 1970s, in a context where politics as such has been contested and redefined, revolution, and the commitment, potential, planning and other necessities for revolution, have become obsolete or nearly extinct in society. This is not to say that radical spaces lack utopian mindsets; emerging utopias have indeed commanded already significant attention.[19] One can be utopian and not expect or strive for revolution as an overthrow or a rupture – be it a 'permanent' general strike or other transformative outbreaks among the people – as understood in earlier decades.

There gradually came a phase, 1989 being a turning point and preceded by several other milestones, where vibrant utopias became completely bereft of a revolutionary plan that would realise them on a mass scale. Most other castles of revolution had been failing since the 1960s. The Soviet bloc was the biggest and more powerful one of all. For the Left, this was the end not of history but of the noble future, after which a period of existential anxiety ensued, as popular confidence in the feasibility of socialism deteriorated. Latin America's influence from the 1990s onwards also contrasted with what kind of politics was emulated or drawn upon from the other side of the Atlantic during the global 1960s. Latin American left populism has been a state-centred reformism with mass appeal, which as in Venezuela became possible due to high oil revenues and strong economic conditions.[20] In this sense, the teleological disarming of the broad Left has been a slow outcome. 'Utopias' are today back on the agenda, and in this respect all periods of 'newness' resemble each other. Over the long term and starting soon after '68, however, the very meaning of revolution on the Left has evolved, and the 'revolutionary plan' has lost its communist-inspired substance and appears weak and suspicious of criminality in the wider public sphere. Then again, an accumulation of politically motivated utopias can be a necessary, although insufficient, condition for a widely shared, relatively coherent way of transforming social relations.

In parallel, since the 1970s, the broad Left has evolved in such a way that human rights rather than anti-imperialism animate the progressive space of internationalism. Solidarity claims in support of migrants or the victims of war are today premised on arguments revolving around the legal discourse of international law and fuelled by humanitarianism.[21] This was a process that started with 1970s anti-war activists mobilising against American military intervention in northern Vietnam and subsequently siding with human rights as opposed to the sovereignty of Vietnam.[22] The 1970s was filled with 'embarrassing' instances where Third World revolutionary communism negated itself through mass slaughter, displacement and common terrorism, being accused of genocide and triggering memories of the holocaust.[23] Most relevant historical research confirms that the publication of Aleksandr's Solzhenistyn's *The Gulag Archipelago*, originally published in Russian in 1974 and focusing on the daily lives inside the Soviet system of labour camps (gulags), was a significant milestone in this direction.[24] It fed into a thorough 'ethicification' of French politics, itself generated in the aftermath of May 1968 and the subsequent discussions of its political defeat and appropriate legacy. Revolutionary zeal was also discredited in this light of revolutionary regimes being challenged on ethical terms that invoked the need for regulating systems aimed at legalising political behaviour upon the premise of respect for fundamental human principles regarding the rights of all people.[25]

This transformation sparked debate in the 1970s and 1980s, which divided radicals and progressives over, for instance, whether the Left should be 'for' or 'against' constitutionalism and the rule of law, including international law.[26] Most importantly, as the language of human rights was becoming increasingly prevalent from about the 1970s, the socialist vocabulary started to decline. This concerned France in particular as a central place for intellectual debates on political violence and rights. It was from there that Médecins Sans Frontières (Doctors without Borders) emerged to configure, or rather displace, Third Worldism and attract many leftists towards a radical humanitarianism.[27] A significant event, even before *The Gulag Archipelago*, was the Palestinian terrorist attack at the 1972 Munich Olympics, which proved important in prompting French Maoists, among others, to rethink how militant attitudes combine with politics.[28]

In both Europe and the USA, the 1960s was cast as a triumph of constitutional rights by movements. In the global context of 'universalising intellectuals' (such as Martin Luther King, Mahatma Gandhi and Nelson Mandela) and the growth in civil rights lawyers and community organising, rights guaranteed in the Constitution were forcefully defended and litigated.[29] The main advocates of 'respect for international law' were the pro-Soviet CPs, while in opposition the 'humanitarian interventionists' behind imperial powers viewed the concept of respect for sovereignty enshrined in international law as anachronistic.[30] The triumph of constitutional rights had, after all, come from below, as American and European liberalism was firmly embedded within the anti-communist Cold War consensus and only reluctantly accepted the demands of the civil rights movements.

From another angle, rights-centred politics is distrusted within a wider distrust of the law in general, their essential function perceived to serve ruling-class interests. Political polarisation arose within and across radical movement spaces because of the universality and neutrality of human rights, as if they had no political relevance, being in tension with socialist imaginaries of deep and pervasive social and political divisions. Generally, human rights discourse as a way to promote the idea of equality sat uncomfortably with radical theories of political economy, gender and race, which in recognising hierarchies of social status identify communities of the oppressed. Dissenting voices on human rights project a radical critique of liberal identitarianism, identifying it as a type of reverse puritanism and taking things such as 'political correctness' and individualism to the extreme.

The problem from the very beginning, indeed since the Universal Declaration (1948), has been that human rights are selective in identifying moral concerns, as they ignore distributive and material inequality.[31] Across time, there remain anti-capitalist sections among left-wing movements that are at best sceptical about human rights discourse and at worst totally reject their abstraction as insufficient for (or even obstructive to) emancipation. They are also uncomfortable with its class origins and its use by Western imperialists themselves.[32] The socialist critique of human rights starts from a critique of individualism as the form (and thus agency) of rights and considers them incapable of giving effect to and promoting human needs. A radical critique of rights begins therefore from a rejection of the subject of rights as the individual. From this perspective, rights discourse negates the Left's notion of solidarity as fundamental to any form of strategic opposition against the day's hegemonies. Developing out of the Marxist tradition, critical legal thinking has taken issue with the fetishism of human rights, which meant 'denying them central status as the sole criterion of questions about morality and social justice' and refusing to anchor the debate 'within the conceptual terrain of liberal legalism'.[33]

Human rights, more specifically anti-discrimination laws, have been interpreted so to prosecute activists. In prosecuting Boycott Disinvestment Sanctions activists for their involvement in peaceful boycott campaigns, French authorities utilised anti-discrimination laws in ways that conform to the standard of anti-discrimination in international human rights law.[34] Moreover, activists and movements criticise groups such as Human Rights Watch for imposing Western, orientalist standards on developing countries; standards which utilise a culturally and ideologically biased interpretation of universalism.[35] For Palestine especially, critiques of human rights point to its strategic use to undermine the political essence of the Palestinian struggle and to legitimise foreign intervention and support of Israel.[36]

Bartholomew and Breakspear wrote about 'the possibility of pursuing the development of cosmopolitan norms and institutions as part of an anti-imperialist strategy, in part by addressing the problems of the United Nations (UN), multilateralism and human rights instead of rejecting them'.[37] Many recognise, for instance, that some of the most progressive diagnoses and technical reports about health, labour or rights emerge out of the UN's specialist committees, or similarly out of the Council of Europe or organisations such as the World Health Organization. Major human rights treaties – the International Covenant on Civil and Political Rights, the International Covenant on Economic, Social and Cultural Rights, the conventions on torture, women's rights, children's rights and racial discrimination – have provided resources for social movements active in these struggles such as monitoring bodies, linking with civil society, receiving individual complaints and examining periodic reports by state members.[38]

Disagreement on the Left still remains, in so far as many activists and partisans are not convinced that the advancement of human rights is the way forward for more distributive and material justice, and more importantly for moving beyond the consolidation of rights within existing society beyond the 'mere' broadening of permissibility. The frame of human rights has, however, become a core part of most justice-related struggles across the world. The UN, multilateralism and human rights are not simply 'problems' of theory to address through reflection; they are often allies or tools, attracting supporters across multiple struggles and for issues pertaining to the West and beyond. Because defending human rights broadens the scope of solidarity expression to the largest possible extent, their advocating may be the most useful positioning for many battles on the Left. It may be too hard or too late to reformulate questions of imperialism, inequality and oppression around sharply different nodal points.

Accordingly, the strategy of engaging with, instead of deconstructing, human rights discourse through a non-liberal perspective that recognises both their imperial nature and neoliberal bias on the one side, and their cross-sectional appeal and entrenched status as a set of humanist ideas on the other side, can appear as the most logical way forward today. 'Rights talk' can be a useful toolkit of demands for a more forceful anti-capitalist politics; although their defence through litigation strategies and judicial reviews are not forms of disruption or resistance, they are tools to be used strategically and are useful under certain contingencies. As Thomas Murray points out, this is basically in line with the analysis of rights by Karl Marx in the *Grundrisse*: it treated constitutions as arenas of political conflict with many determinations, not as abstract normative or economic structures.[39] This has been internalised by anarchists and socialists, as they often, in the context of local and national mobilisations, engage in opposition to authoritarian or unjust regimes or legislation through recourse to constitutions, civil liberties and violent oppression.

One could counter-argue that, nevertheless, social rights enjoy only secondary status when human rights constitute the prevailing discourse. After all, this is why from the anarchists to the Trotskyists and democratic socialists, 'social rights' is the predominant frame of rights talk on the Radical Left, so as to restore balance away from the signification of individuality and towards the collective and material dimensions of justice. Also, other normative and economic structures, which may be independent of rights in a historical sense, impinge upon the boundaries of rights and constitutionalism as a tool for radical change in the long term. The very challenges faced by local movements confirm this in a sense. As broad ideas that infuse behaviour, rights and constitutionalism will always condemn a vague 'too much' in protests and action against 'property rights', 'law and order', '(negative) freedom', occupying private and public space and other axioms of liberalism that crop up in real-life political conflict, whereby opponents seek to demonise illiberal action.

THE FEW, THE MANY, THE PEOPLE: POPULISM AND SOCIAL MOVEMENTS

Like universalistic rhetoric and its manifestation in rights discourse and citizen claims, populism is both a rhetorical form and a discursive political strategy. Post-2008, populism has reflected progressive ends, most vividly in the case of Podemos, emerging from the Spanish *indignados* movement, SYRIZA in Greece, Momentum and Jeremy Corbyn's electoral campaigns, Jean-Luc Mélenchon's presidential campaigns and the discourse of France Insoumise (FI). A radical or progressive populism was also evident in the Occupy movements; the banner popularised in Ireland and the UK, which stands with 'the millions not the millionaires'; the Gilet Jaunes in 2018 or the Nuit Debout in France in 2016, which embraced a democratic, horizontal and thus 'counter' populism to be differentiated from the hegemonic populism of authoritarian and conservative forces;[40] and the People's Climate Marches in European and other countries, often backed by tactical arguments about inventing 'the people' of the environmental movement in the conjuncture of a climate crisis as a political opportunity.

As a sort of minimum definition, populism is the discourse which pits ordinary people against corrupt elites. It brings together people-centrism and anti-establishment discourse in a sharply different way from right-wing populism. It constructs the people as a progressive, forward-looking, inclusive and emancipatory force, in stark contrast to the people as an exclusive subject – the product of ethnic attachment, nativist, racist and xenophobic attitudes.[41] Populism in its progressive colours can prove to be a potential corrective to democracy by restoring the popular sovereignty damaged in the process of liberal democratic practice.[42] As a strategy of political mobilisation, populism can also entail organisational features that enable its discourse to survive and attract. In the final analysis, as regards the widespread claim that there is a populist surge on the European Radical Left of the 2010s, what are the differences with previous 'new lefts'? By implication, how new is today's left populism?

The 1960s/1970s movements in many ways communicated themselves as minoritarian currents within an otherwise conservative, oppressive and unjust society. They still featured populist-like rhetoric. The counter-culture movements in the USA and western Europe during the 1960s – communes, social and political satire, provocation and absurdity, alternative 'hippie' lifestyles and dress codes and other habits driven by the attempt to widen consciousness – are testament to how the enemy was perceived as the established superstructure, imposing a narrow version of possibilities in terms of social organisation and asserting dominance through morality. This collective political body was perceived as summoning forces from various parts of the ideological spectrum, pervading the educational system and social relations, and inculcating a substantial section of the working and middle classes with a robotic subservience to systemic demands. Terms such as 'alienation', 'conformity', 'authority' and 'absurdity' reverberated a negativism that was a fundamental part of the New Left's 'rhetorical structure' across both Europe and the USA. Confrontation, as embodied in the movements of the time, suggested a radical distinction between the 'haves' from the 'have nots' and a 'Manichean struggle' in which the latter, 'who confront established power do not seek to share: they demand to supplant'.[43]

Identifying an oppressive out-group as the enemy was a central feature of the 1960s and 1970s movements not only in terms of rhetoric, partly like left populism today, but also in terms of theory. This is exemplified by many social science books of the Long '68: C. Wright Mills' analysis of dominant 'vested interests' in *The Power Elite*, Louis Althusser's *Ideological State Apparatuses*, Goran Therbron's *What Does the Ruling Class Do When It Rules*, the Miliband–Poulatzas debate concerning the state and social classes in capitalism, or Stuart Hall's model of 'popular culture' as 'a battlefield where a struggle between freedom and exploitation is played'.[44] The 1960s and 1970s were the hiatus of Marxist state theory, its elaborations affecting the schemas and binaries of socialist language among militants, and around journals such as the *New Left Review* and others admired by students and intellectuals. Marxist sociology had effectively provided analytical sketches of what constitutes the establishment, the elites or the oligarchy and how these think, act and react, something which was feeding directly into mobilisation.

The very slogan '(all) power to the people' suggests the people/elites binary, as the elite is alluded to by the slogan (although not explicitly addressed). There is an implicit acknowledgement that there is an unfair distribution of power that can in turn be corrected by consigning power to the people. The history of the slogan attests to this. The Black Panthers used the slogan 'All Power to the People' to protest the domination exercised by the white, rich, ruling class. For the Vietnam War 'the people' stood against the military campaign in Vietnam and the economic and political agents driving it; that is, against the establishment.[45] American and English youth would more generally use the phrase during the 1960s as a form of rebellion against what they perceived as the oppression by the older generation, often referred to also as the establishment.[46] Indeed, 'anti-establishment' became a buzzword of the tumultuous 1960s. It was a sensibility unifying different sorts of movements (often issue specific) against 'the system' or the 'status quo'. Towards that end of fighting the establishment these movements sought to blend aesthetics, ethics and art. Songs like 'Power to the People', 'People Get Ready' and 'Everyday People'

from American soul music codified politics through cultural performance. Third World activists used the 'Power to the People' slogan
to claim self-determination and as a means of radical socio-economic change. What other call from radicals has evoked popular
sovereignty so explicitly, and so evidently connected with the oppression of the many by the few? To the extent that this slogan came to
be used by and characterised a multiplicity of radical initiatives and
groups in 1960s America and Europe across classes, situations and
organised spaces, a convergence of struggles through identification
with popular power was already achieved back then in the populist,
Laclauian sense.

It has been suggested that the post-2008 movements are distinct
from those of the 1960s/1970s and the GJM in terms of rhetoric
and more generally their framing of left radicalism through specific
notions: their communication to society at large of what they stand
for and who they are. In terms of their self-perception, while the
groups of the GJM cast themselves as struggling minorities, they
were different and clearly more radical than the average citizen in
European societies. Today's movements claim to be massive and
composed of ordinary people who detect an obvious unfairness and
an evident structural malfunctioning. These movements claimed to
be the '99%', and their orientation is majoritarianism. Some authors
contrast this with the GJM's minoritarianism, since its cultural forms
include 'common sense', 'normality' and 'respectability', where the
GJM proclaimed 'heroism' and 'antagonism'.[47] Thereby, this is both
a new strategy of communicating the struggle that emphasises unity
within diversity and a type of sloganeering reflecting a self-concep-
tion by the activists themselves that eschews the GJM's – and indeed
that of the many NSMs of the 1960s – counter-cultural orientation.[48]

Gerbaudo's point, and more generally the novelty that such arguments detect in the 2010s, have to be nuanced, as a developing appeal
to the masses is evident from earlier decades. During the GJM, an
out-group of a few elites – those who are profit seeking, self-inter-
ested, environmentally insensitive and so on – was said to exist.
The main slogan of Genoa was 'You are G8 we are 6 billion' and its
key rhetoric was the Negrian one of the 'multitude(s)' against the
'Empire', a schema veritably distinguishing between the main antag-

onists. Later ESFs insisted on being the expression of 'civil society', a political body arguably perceived as much larger than the neoliberal architects of globalisation. The messages of the GJM made use of ample people-centrism, countering the world's mass populations to the ideology and interests behind the dictatorial market, or the huge global corporations, or the international economic organisations, or a network of all three. These were perceived and communicated as deeply counter-popular, and for that matter undemocratic, economic institutions.

In terms of the populist language schemas, the picture is one of evolution rather than significant change. While the GJM criticised capitalism and multinational corporations whereas the movement of the squares identified the oligarchy as the enemy, anti-oligarchic tendencies, arguments and visions in the form of anti-authoritarian and anti-elitist thinking were evident in various manifestations of the GJM. This was also the case in the critiques of multinational corporations and the financial oligarchy that were attacking self-imposed hierarchies which effectively lacked popular democratic legitimacy. As Hardt and Negri put it in *Empire*, '[t]he transnational aristocracy seems to prefer financial speculation to entrepreneurial virtue and thus appears as a parasitical oligarchy'.[49] The terms 'oligarchy', 'elites' and 'establishment' were frequent terms in communiqués by key movements and activists of the GJM. Famously, during the 1999 protests against the WTO, the Earth Rainbow Network launched a webpage titled 'The Anti-Establishment Files'. Within the context of opposing a global neoliberal oligarchy, various new words, such as McWorld, were invented to allude to a new order of things, whereby a few conglomerate companies could decide or influence the way of life of millions of people. This rhetoric was indeed underpinned by rigorous analysis – as expressed in a bestseller from 1993, *The McDonaldization of Society* by American sociologist George Ritzer. A slogan popularised by the GJM was 'People before profit', which echoed challenges of the pursuit of maximal profit-driven GDP growth as the world's utmost objective (a discussion also taking place at the level of the UN).[50] Crowds at GJM events were heterogeneous in terms of their ideological imaginaries, social characteristics and immediate political goals, and they were large or sometimes massive. A key slogan in the Genoa protests was, 'You are G8, we are six billion'. In these ways, the populist current on the post-2008 European Radical Left can be seen as a continuation, extension and elaboration of this initially hesitant and more partial rhetoric in the GJM that was conjoined with minoritarian ingredients coming from the anarchist space.

It is not so much the language or rhetorical style of in-groupism, counter-hegemony, binaries and popular sovereignty that distinguishes the latest movement wave and the Left's participation. This is not what changes but its circumstance, specifically the theories informing left populism not merely as discourse but chiefly as strategy and politics. The relationship between socialism and populism is on the one hand historical and intricate, whereas the 'people's legacy in communist thinking (Marxism, Leninism and Maoism)' signals 'a revolutionary alliance of the oppressed (in contrast to the populist rendering of the people as an organic unity)'.[51] In the presence of pervading class divisions and distinctions, an organically unified people could only be mythical according to dialectical, materialist analysis to begin with. This is why Lenin (who was influenced by certain notions of Russian populism), as a Marxist theorist, rejected the view of 'the people' and distrusted the central role of spontaneity in populist analyses.[52]

Populism could not be reconciled with historical materialist narratives, hence it lacked an ideological formula justifying its strategic use while still remaining loyal to the pillars of classical Marxism. A portrait of the people and how they can be bounded into a collective political subject was missing in large part and had only started developing in the 1960s; there had been socialist populist rhetoric since the French Revolution, but no articulate theory of how to construe and design a counter-hegemonic near organic unity that would justify the people–elites binary. Although the translations of Gramsci's *Prison Notebooks*, beginning in 1971, had a significant effect on critiques of centralism, his approach to counter-hegemony still configured a class struggle and accorded political primacy to the working class, upon which populism could not rest with theoretical confidence. Around the time Ernesto Laclau was publishing the initial formulations of his discursive-strategic approach to populism, David Plotke, an American radical academic commenting on his country's own experience with the phenomenon, noted both positive and negative traits to populism as a left-wing strategy. He concluded that, 'while it poses the questions of broad social alliances, it has no means of understanding the dynamics of such alliances'.[53]

The shift by Laclau from Marxist to post-Marxist populism provided him with the tools necessary to formulate more specific answers to the above question, while also giving a distinct political tone to its adherents which continues today. Shifting away from historical materialism entailed eventually minimising class analysis and maximising linguistic constructs and effects. Intellectually, the move in strategic priorities from ultimate victory to challenging everyday impacts is reflected in how critical analyses of the power dynamics of everyday interpersonal interactions have become prominent and increasingly sophisticated. In parallel, there has been a relative de-emphasising of system-level causal mechanisms and teleological questions, and in turn a downgrading of the importance ascribed to political economy and critical macro-sociology. The linguistic turn within the broad humanities and social sciences, originating from the quest for methodological hybrids, bore an approach to language both as a new datum and as a perspective of analysis.[54] Discourse-oriented studies reinforced and were reinforced by the post-modern paradigm, the increasing relevance given to cultural and symbolic phenomena and the micro-logics of power. Left populism as theory and as a discursive strategy cannot be separated from the gradual abandonment of a positivist historiography.

According to some sections of the Left these trends paved the way for identity politics and have overall damaged the socialist cause – a damage understood as partly inflicted, although perhaps unintentionally, by the Left itself. Based on Louis Althusser's concept of articulation, Laclau and Chantal Mouffe abandoned the Althusserian 'last instance' of the economy, essentially class and economic analysis. They claimed that without considering a fixed-but-evolving structure the superstructure is everything. If everything is articulated through discourse, performance and communication then 'everything is constituted in that articulation'. In doing so, Laclau departed from the Marxist tradition's essentialist logic whereby everything can be reduced to a particular social foundation or a set of structures, and explored the possibility of thinking about the political beyond the dictum of base–superstructure.[55] Among many other rejections or revisions of Marxist schemas, ideas and frameworks, this was a very important one, since it subverted the analytical compass of socialists.

Earlier we noted a widely documented point: the 1970s was a period which, for a mass of left-wing intellectuals (many coming out of the revolutionary space), witnessed the realisation that an ideological and political overhaul of socialism was necessary. Both the traditional analytical tools and political demands of the Left were under scrutiny. It is by extending this rationale behind intellectual, revisionist strains to today's context that one can understand why many see class and broader counter-hegemonic struggles as determinations of discourse. While the rhetoric of movements diachronically exhibits various elements of contesting hegemony and constructing the in-group and the out-group, left populism as a discursive strategy has a distinctive, post-Marxist, theoretico-ideological content, not simply strategic implications and particular rhetorical features. Most of the things we know about left populism at the theoretical and empirical level come from academics and graduates who are sympathetic to Laclau and supportive of left populism as the way forward in constructing counter-hegemony. Discourse studies and the increasing emphasis given to political language, psychoanalysis and communication since about the 1960s are poles of attraction and output for radicals today.[56] Through processes unfolding in society and elaborated in political activism and academia there has gradually advanced a theoretical core of radical populism, consolidated in Europe by the 2010s and most celebrated in *On Populist Reason*.[57]

Because it is post-Marxist, largely refutes class analysis and revises the logic of achieving counter-hegemonic mobilisation towards discursive tactics, left populism as theory has been and still is an ideological battleground. In its articulation, according to Laclau's post-Marxism, it finds significant resistance within the intellectual and activist left. Meiksins-Wood, in *The Retreat from Class*, gave the conceptual and theoretical foundations for a still-existing line of criticism towards Laclau's post-structuralism for essentially abandoning (not only modifying) classical materialism in favour of an approach which is linguistically deterministic.[58] Laclau was criticising historical materialism, the foundations of Marxist political economy, as reductive, arriving, according to his critics, at a 'new reductionism'. This was reflected in the avoidance of 'a more complex engagement' with practices 'irreducible to linguistics', structural processes and edifices.[59] On similar grounds, Jodi Dean has challenged the more contemporary strategic implications of left populism as theory, as 'indifferent to [their] setting, as if there were no material determinations of political possibility', 'the state and the economy [...] taken as given'. 'Populist politics', she concludes, 'doesn't try to change these given parameters'.[60]

Left populist strategy is a question of conceptual and ideological analysis whereby the structural questions of radical politics are not primarily understood in terms of material conflict and politics but in the dynamics of language. This is still a broad spectrum in a sense, since degrees of linguistic emphasis and shades of anarchist, democratic socialist, communist or other backgrounds often suggest that the left 'populist crowd' is not a monolithic one. Conceptual and theoretical spin-offs in the tradition of Laclau's, Lacan's and others' cultural critiques and deconstructions of economic or even historical certainties have turned into political divisions, as in Latin America on many occasions, in Spain more recently and less so elsewhere. Chapter 7 returns to this discussion in the context of RLPs. As a preliminary point, populist theory (or more broadly discussions about populism) animates discussions about political points. For example, regarding whether populism is a successful discursive strategy for the Radical Left, whether it can save social democracy and whether the recent defeats of various parties and other parts of radical mobilisation and resistance are to be explained by populism's limitations or a more holistic examination of neoliberal politics that incorporates more (not less) economic thinking.

Whatever the case, for the time being the relationship between radical movements and populism is threefold. Populism is a frame widely used by 'movement entrepreneurs' throughout the austerity and (more recently) pandemic periods.[61] As a left-wing ideology, it characterises parts of the French and Spanish Radical Left. As a schema between oppressor and oppressed, it is much more widely disseminated across the whole of Europe and spans the environmental, communist and democratic socialist currents. In Britain, Bailey showed that four key themes reflecting real, existing problems and grievances animated the in-group versus out-group schema of the anti-austerity movements, from UK Uncut, the Anti-Tuition Fees Movement, Occupy London and Sisters Uncut: that elites are self-serving in supporting austerity; austerity is not the only alternative; austerity is damaging and counterproductive; and it is necessary to transcend politics as usual by democratising constitutional representation structures.[62] Popular identity becomes relevant when opportunities arise and enemies are specified over problems, but these openings can be of so many, various types that it is always difficult to tell if populist-like schemas have increased from a pre- to a post-crisis period, or if they merely gained more visibility through the electoral success of their agents. Anyhow, by 2020 an increasing mass of people has been (further) hit by unemployment due to the pandemic and extreme poverty is predicted to affect millions for several years, and this echoes as a new social reality the rhetoric of the 1 per cent compared to the 99 per cent, and of citizens compared to the state.

AN EVOLVING RADICAL NATIONALISM?

From its very beginnings the global Radical Left has supported oppressed ethnicities, national minorities, colonised nations, nations without a state and indigenous populations. Socialists utilised nationalism 'as a key player in the politics of modernity', 'developed in association with ideas of popular sovereignty and mass democracy bound up with ideas of the self-determination of a given people, defined by shared history and common political rights'.[63] A civic nationalist spirit has been there from the very beginning.

The European movements of the 1960s and 1970s were not preoccupied with an 'own national sovereignty problem' in many countries but were responding to Third Worldism as the instantiation of the postcolonial state through anti-colonial, national liberation struggles. National sovereignty in that context was an external idea mostly supported on behalf of the Third World's movements. The Third World's first institutional moment was the Conference of Afro-Asian Nations in Bandung, Indonesia, in 1955. That was the moment that reservations were made public about the growing Cold War between the United States and the Soviet Union, in essence signalling the establishment of the Third World as a third bloc (the Non-aligned Movement) coalescing around left-nationalist aspirations in a broader political project of decolonisation. At that conference, the territorial sovereignty of all states was asserted by the endorsement of the principle of 'non-intervention', as opposed to the Western concept of international 'anarchy' in global geopolitics.[64]

Radical nationalism was the case initially in India under Nehru, Egypt under Nasser, Indonesia under Sukarno and Ghana under Nkrumah; then Chile under Salvador Allende, Tanzania and Jamaica. In all cases, there was an 'intense valorising of anti-imperialist sovereignty around rhetorics of economic independence, popular power, social justice, and cultural dignity'.[65] Crucial in this conjuncture for the eroding hegemony of the USSR was also the Sino–Soviet conflict, the demise since the mid-1950s of the alliance between the two superpowers of national communism, which undermined not only Soviet legitimacy but that of the entire socialist camp. The revolutionary experiences of the Cuban revolution, the Algerian War of Independence, the Vietnam War or the Cultural Revolution in China, among many others, are examples of experiences in which at a practical level the approaches of nationalism were fused with socialism. 'Patria o Muerte' (Country or Death) marked the Cuban armed revolt and illustrated how revolutionary causes could be married to a nationally bounded in-group. Nationalist framings in the West also resonated well with the state ideology of 'socialist patriotism' in eastern Europe which blended imageries of socialism and nationhood. It presented CPs as heirs to national traditions and as defenders of national interests and loyalties – those of the state's own workers and peasants.[66]

A revival of movements within European states making ethnic, cultural and national claims was underway. A revived European regionalism in the 1960s and 1970s stood upon the ground of several developments. Capitalist regional planning in the post-war period was underway, and the 1950s and 1960s underwent significant socio-economic progress, including notably in the construction industry.

The impact of ideological fusions arising from May '68 and the influence of the decolonisation struggles inspired new left libertarian and revolutionary movements to adopt regionalist outlooks, distinguishing themselves from the centralist tendencies of the Old Left at both the party and state levels.[67] The centre–periphery cleavage was salient in Belgium, France, Spain, Italy, the UK and Switzerland, where both left-wing and right-wing regionalist parties formed during the 1960s, often increasing their vote shares by the 1970s. In the process of forming these parties there were contributions from or alignments with a number of NSMs, such as labourism, the peace movement and Third Worldism (as in Belgium), revolutionary and libertarian movements (as in Spain) or environmental movements (as in France and Switzerland).

Shifting sovereignty forward takes other forms. During the GJM, food sovereignty movements both in southern and northern European countries opposed corporate control of agriculture and focused on the right to healthy and culturally appropriate, locally produced and distributed food. Sovereignty was thus rearticulated in transnational terms while presenting itself as in partial contradiction to the market. GJM also contained currents fighting for indigenous sovereignty, exposing the link between the extreme deprivation of populations at the local level, corruption and authoritarianism at the national level, and the structural cruelty of modern capitalism at the global level. Popular education work, undertaken foremost through Attac, indicated the pursuit of knowledge sovereignty, away from the neoliberal ideas, formulas and doctrines of TINA and the Washington Consensus.[68] At the same time, parts of the GJM, in line with Antonio Negri, rejected sovereignty as a left-wing project in favour of the decentred 'empire', in turn leading to perceptions of the EU as potentially progressive in transforming modern life away from sovereign claims. Whereas the anti-colonial struggles against European and American imperialism in the 1960s and 1970s were firmly built on notions of national sovereignty, 'empire' denied the nation state as the main possessor of sovereignty.

Moreover, in the GJM national identities and nationalism in its cultural and political sense were far weaker forces than in the 1960s or more recently. The GJM's transnational structure and the spirit of global solidarity celebrated most by the Mexican Zapatistas' internationalism conduced to keeping nationhood away from the agenda in the global struggle against neoliberalism. As the most popular source of inspiration for the GJM, the uprising of the Zapatistas in Chiapas, Mexico in 1994 uniquely combined indigenous sovereignty with internationalist pluralism, and in this intersubjection claims to national independence could not find theoretical grounding. Certainly, debates over the trajectory and status of the nation state flourished during the height of the GJM years, but these were less guided by an interrogation of globalisation's consequences. The emerging disagreement has been one between those who argue that we live in a 'post-ethnic' or 'post-national' era and those who point out that nationalism's drive has been reinforced because of globalisation and international governance.[69]

Sovereignty has been perhaps more directly defended during the austerity period. It is often taken as the distinguishing point of the Occupy movements, challenging the sovereign rule of representatives and insisting that political power has access to collective decision-making about the commons.[70] To claim that people are de facto sovereign through the direct exercise of constituent rule is not a novel claim, yet it does constitute a counter-hegemonic conviction in democratic theory that challenges the sacrifice of popular sovereign power in the name of universal human rights.[71] Second, in the pro-democracy movements, national sovereignty was being reclaimed by countries from the markets, other hegemonic EU member states and unelected international bodies. Unsurprisingly, national flags, anthems and a sense of national pride characterised many of the anti-austerity and pro-democracy demonstrations in Europe in the aftermath of the crisis.[72]

For the first time, one of the implications of the crisis is that we can no longer speak of the sovereignty of nation states in a European context in that some of these states have the power to legislate and implement policy for their territory only formally and not substantively. The quintessence of the phenomenon of diminished sovereignty – especially in the eurozone context – that the Radical Left identifies as a problem is the lack of accountability of those implementing economic policies. This translates into inherently illegitimate governance. From this angle, national sovereignty is popular sovereignty because only national governments can be accountable to the people, who in turn can exercise sovereign power through them. Therefore, if there is not a people bounded nationally through common territory, there is no popular sovereignty. Following this, repossessing the national state and the national border as economic devices is a defence mechanism against neoliberalism as an edifice to counteract its negative consequences.[73]

But other types of popular sovereignties have been expressed on the Left as economic ideas or on scales lesser than the national one. In austerity Greece and Spain, sovereignty, or rather its loss, was cast in economic terms. In Spain, where various regionalisms limit the usefulness of exclusively defending progressive visions through underlining national boundaries to evoke the popular, 'shared sovereignties' have been called for, for example in the radical municipal campaigns of Barcelona. That is, sovereignties of different types and between national and subnational arenas of politics.[74] Sovereignty in certain contexts is not an idea exclusively utilised with the nation state in mind. If sovereignty is above all popular, then it can be claimed at a certain level of governance in so far as a territorial people can be evoked. Given that it suggests socio-economic justice it can be linked to forms of collective consumption as well as fiscal policy independence. Concerning Brexit, nationalistic arguments prevailed, while in Scotland secession was almost identified as the protection of the welfare state and as opposition to British neoliberalism. In such an environment, nevertheless, for the Radical Left the challenge is that popular sovereignty must stand firmly away from ethnocentric sovereignties if it is to avoid facilitating a generalised interpretation of anti-system politics from Left and Right with common root causes. What can count in the communicative sphere is that both Left and Right 'stage their performances of sovereigntism on, behind or inside the borders of the existing nation-states'.[75]

RETROSPECTIVE

The overarching question has been how left radicalism has (re)casted and (re)framed its struggles, and what these entail in terms of rhetorical constructs guiding theory, critique and action. The new in historical time does not always or mainly entail a break with the old. It also entails a reappropriation, adaptation and reinvigoration of historical insights into subterranean struggles, through revised tools of activist and scholarly analyses, emerging needs and the corresponding responses by movements. On some occasions, as per the contrast between the GJM's alleged minoritarianism and the populism of Occupy and subsequent movements, historical evolution can be mistaken for short-term change that boils down to the shifting conjuncture alone. In hindsight, both middle-class, subversive, counter-cultural and prefigurative minoritarianism and electoralist, populist rhetoric calling to the masses, ordinary citizens or the oppressed have been visible mobilisers in different versions of the Left's political sequence.

Likewise, nationalism has been a visible mobiliser for the Radical Left through time, but in different ways across the periods of 'newness'. The radical sovereigntist rhetoric of the students and other Third Worldist social forces in countries such as France, Germany and Italy demanded someone else's sovereignty and were entrenched in the key weapon of mobilisation in the former colonies themselves: nationalism, patriotism, independence and thus liberty and anti-imperialism. In the GJM, nationalism was trumped by globalism or an alternative globalism, a global justice, rather than a national one. After 2008, nationalist rhetoric returned but against undemocratic institutions, unaccountable EU bodies and 'internal colonialism', notably by Germany. While key rhetorical signifiers do not change, the narrative that packs them together does; the idea of national sovereignty or self-determination is always present to a greater or lesser degree, for western European countries themselves or for outside populations, and in opposition to particular enemies, be they American imperialism, German hegemony within the EU or the 'deep state' one seeks to secede from.

What transpires over time is the substance of political rhetoric – the nature and kinds of words and schemas that predominate or protrude under certain conditions: the rise of universalism and rights advocating as a response to multidimensional and rising disparities; the invention of concepts opposed to prolonged or exacerbated situations of crisis; the appeal of counter-hegemonic, post-Marxist traditions and left populism, opposed by the contemporary anti-revisionists aiming to sustain emphasis on historical materialism; and the softer tone opposing teleological praxis and the progressive undermining of revolutionary plans, then a re-ensuing search and prefiguration of utopias. Radical rhetoric and the discourses it internalises have been marked by medium-term and long-term processes of social and political change, such as the composition and alignment of popular grievances, the ups and downs of economic and political orders, the failures and overall legacies of socialism or the shifting dynamics between fragments of the radical left space.

5

Organising in
(Every Subsequent) Movement

To decipher the ways in which social movements have organised mobilisation and resistance across the three periods of 'newness' considered, this chapter examines their structural, procedural and compositional aspects. Physical space, as the 'origins' of political struggles,[1] the ever present structure of mobilisation, is addressed first, the point being how protest on the Radical Left is grounded in the spatial and operational configurations of society. Particular forms of radical activism's political geography animate both their structures and procedures. In other words, we begin with space because space is both a fundamental aspect of left radicalism's diversity and has been evoked as a signifier specifying historical novelty. Drawing on the identification of newness post-2008 as largely conditioned by the internet, we situate real and virtual spaces of resistance within radical movements across time and outline their broader implications.

In the second section, horizontal and vertical activisms are discussed and then we address debates about state legality and, opposing it, violence, disruption or civil disobedience, which denote procedurally confrontational and outspoken tactics. Empirically, how often and in what manner has violence been practised by radical left movements, and why and to what extent does it go beyond civil disobedience into physical harm and destruction? We then proceed to compositional patterns in radical left activism and theory, engaging with the social subjects and agitators of radical 'newness'. Linkage, a key part of our investigation, is not exclusively addressed here. Rather, it is discussed in the Part III, where the perspectives of movements and parties, as they concern their friends and allies, are put together. However, the movements' evolving orientations to the state as an arena of organising, the organisational counterpart of a topic we addressed in Chapter 3, are highlighted.

SPACE AS STRUCTURE OF MOBILISATION: BETWEEN THE REAL AND THE VIRTUAL

The global emergence of Occupy in 2010 and 2011 was both an occasion of protest and of experimentation with participation and deliberation. Occupy emerged in 950 cities and 82 countries.[2] The anti-austerity and pro-democracy movements of the post-2008 period 'learned democracy', it has been extensively argued, in order to reinvigorate themselves amid the decline of effect in the GJM's forum format.[3,4] To pose the historical question, does this process, described as learning in the social movement literature, tend to over-estimate 'newness' for the Radical Left?

Occupying public squares prompts us to revisit the past for the European Radical Left. As concerns the GJM, its distinctive organisational feature was that of time and conjuncture, which had an anti-establishment use for the movements rather than a particular physical space as such. Protests coincided with or followed global elite meetings. The occupation of universities, schools, factories, railway stations and housing blocks was much more frequent in the 1960s and 1970s across both Europe and the USA than it has been during the whole of the post-2008 period. In the 1960s, sit-ins, teach-ins and go-ins, which began mostly in the USA with the Students for a Democratic Society, subsequently became widely used protest methods, revolutionising political protests around the world. Occupying physical space has historically provided the powerless with rhetorical and operational openings. The unifying element of the streets among the post-2008 mobilisations (compared to the university or the factory) that connected the European Radical Left in the 1960s and 1970s denotes a previously underexplored 'space where new forms of the social and political can be made'.[5] In the more privatised world of the 2010s, squares were utilised as the last public spaces, an invocation of the commons as well as a practical response to the question of reconstituting the political.[6]

Saskia Sassen's argument that 'urban streets have become global stages for enacting political change' is a valid depiction of contemporary protest. Except for the European Radical Left, 'newness' seems to be overplayed if we follow the broad 'streets perspective'. In fact, the street, the university, the workplace and so on have all gone hand in hand when mobilisation turns to resistance; the experience of multiple struggles unfolding in parallel and feeding into each other over a decade recalls the slogan, 'Occupy everything'. The streets, after all, were claimed in the 1960s by students in France and elsewhere, an experience captured by another iconic slogan, 'Beauty is in the street'.[7] In Italy, popular slogans were 'Let us take the city', 'The city is ours' and 'Don't vote – occupy!' These social vibrations would later be codified as the strain that bore the discourse of the commons, out of which emerged the mediated tactic of occupying public squares in mass fashion.

For movements that claimed a specific territorial unit, the street and the city precisely invoked communal understandings of urban life and instrumentalised the notion of public space as a collective, social right. Protest in urban spaces was conjoined with the appearance of urban movements. In principle, public space is important for the Left because it is the negation of privatised space and a confrontation with public authorities. For the anarchists, it is the foundation of self-organisation and its story can best be told perhaps through squatters. These today do not compare to their vibrancy in the 1970s but do have a continuous presence in many western European cities. Their original goals of autonomy and decolonisation remain the same: squatting in urban or rural areas is an endeavour of community building without authority, private property and the nuclear family, adhering to values of full and unconditioned equality and a communitarian worldview.[8]

As with the idea of decentralisation and smaller scales in the struggle for democracy, social justice and the recommoning of public goods, radical municipalism has resurged during the post-2008 years. It continues and endorses the squares movements' inclination to experimentation as necessary in inventing effective modes of struggle and performing democracy. It also expresses the 'glocal' spirit voiced since the GJM when the sociological concept of 'glocalisation'

– a rescaling of governance extending both globally or upwards and downwards, towards the urban and local – came to symbolise also a mode of struggle.[9] Again, it continues the legacy of left-wing populist government in Latin America, such as Brazil at the time of the first WSF, which promoted local-level experimentation with assembly-based municipal governance. Before contemporary Spain, in other contested spaces outside of Europe, such as the Rojava territory in northern Syria, municipalism was integrated into a broader radical politics; as in Latin America also – notably the Zapatista movement in Chiapas and grassroots indigenous movements in Bolivia.[10]

In Europe the sociological study of urban movements emerged in the Long '68. In *The Urban Question*, Manuel Castells began reconfiguring the field of urban sociology, building on and also departing from previous Marxist theories.[11] French theorist and radical political activist Henri Lefebvre theorised the *Production of Space*, building on his 1968 work *The Right to the City* as a space of co-creation away from the damaging effects to life of what was seen as a raging commodification.[12] Radical theorisations of social space and urban movements came through a critique of the literature on urbanisation, highlighting the emergent, progressive social forces at the level of the city and the locality in response to the gravity of urban problems under capitalism. These problems were categorised under the heading of collective consumption: housing shortages, growing discrepancies between rents and wages, landlords' neglect of house maintenance, damage to the environment and health of local communities, and insufficient local welfare and education. Just as Castells's ideas influenced Spanish municipalism and Lefebvre French radical sociology and activism, the autonomism of Murray Bookchin regarding libertarian municipalism played into politics through his influence on the Kurdistan Workers Party (PKK) leader Abdullah Öcalan and its transmission to the Syrian branch of the PKK – the Democratic Union Party. For Bookchin, people could obtain power only through democracy, thus it was necessary to focus institutions on the local, municipal, village level where fully democratic forms, like the public assembly, can be used as decision-making bodies.[13]

As these intellectuals theorised municipalism, urban activism and the city in relation to capitalism, European governments (primarily social democratic ones) were pursuing large-scale urban renewal and modern housing projects. These were at the core of local politics and linked to housing struggles and resistance to modernisation plans and uneven urban development.[14] European cities were 'contested cities in an era of crisis'.[15] In Rome, plans over shantytowns were central during the 1970s, when the extra-parliamentary left intensified its focus on the housing issue and the city more broadly to promote agitation as the trade unions took back control of factory workers.[16] In the Ruhr, Germany, workers and social movements mixed in a series of initiatives to resist the privatisation of the workers' settlements built around 1900.[17] In response, for example, to touristification, urban movements in Italy like Centro Sociale Leoncavallo, or in Belgium like BOM, the public–private neighbourhood development agency set up in 1990, are the offspring of the 1970s movements: leftist, social cultural and political centres based on self-management and initiated by radical activists and groups.[18] The urban movements of today make visible the most recently emergent injustices and inequalities – those of gentrification and touristification – which reorient the historical debate on the right to the city towards the newly reconfigured urban conflict.

In this current of activism, horizontality translates as injecting locality into democratic and anti-austerity claims in the context of wider visions of autonomous politics and social citizenship claims. An international municipalist movement seeks to challenge the power of the nation state and the markets from the bottom up. Municipalism is effectively the organisational attempt to weave politics into the everyday spaces and lives of people. Social change should start not only from national but also with local institutions as they are close to concrete social issues. An upturn in municipalism has involved mobilisation for access to housing and welfare services at the local level; the development of mutual cooperation to counter impoverishment, gentrification driven by commercial enterprises such as Airbnb and urban degradation, or mobilisations against large speculative projects.[19]

Across Europe, urban dispossession reached a high point post-2008. Today, the European Action Coalition for the Right to Housing and to the City, which has 23 groups from western Europe, includes tenants' and housing movements, victims of eviction, those affected by debt, slum and self-built neighbourhood dwellers, squatters, campaigners and researchers.[20] Wider local participation through municipalist ideas includes notably the *foros locales* (local forums) in Madrid operating at the city-district level. Another noteworthy example has been PAH and the subsequent political trajectory of Ada Colau as a chief organiser of the citizen platform Barcelona en Comú and mayor of Barcelona. Under Colau, Barcelona implemented a number of progressive operations and policies: promoting the direct involvement of citizens in policy and budget; redistributing the excessive wages of politicians to the community; widening and promoting social and LGBTQ rights; providing refuge to immigrants in opposition to restrictive national policies; and managing municipal-controlled companies. Agendas and manifestos for these positions and policies have been based on deliberation and decisions in open neighbourhoods or discussion groups focused on particular issues. For those pursuing anti-capitalist politics, a number of questions are confronted by municipalism. These show that radical municipalism is a method for realising social and political goals, not a coherent ideological formula for constructing socialism. Without exhausting the issue, we can indicatively mention the danger of fetishising 'the local' and the debatable capacity to supersede or disobey the nation state.[21] We can additionally point out the resemblance of municipalist measures to New Public Management, a point reinforced by the very recent electoral disaster of Podemos in the 2021 Madrid elections. In retrospect, the municipalist method can be utilised by the right, which in this case won a landslide.

Perhaps the truly new relationship of radical contention to space in the contemporary period, as has been widely argued, regards expansion into a virtual, online public and political sphere. The drive towards the occupation of squares and other mass demonstrations was largely established through information and communication technologies. The internet made possible both the massiveness and the spontaneity of occupying public squares post-2008, and it also facilitated the establishment of international networks and protest events in the GJM. In a sense, the advocates of socialism via spontaneous mass uprising obtained a new weapon, as the internet fuels impulsiveness to the purposes of protest and upheaval. Real and virtual spaces are connected and coexist in mobilisation practices, hence our question is: what has the dialectic between them meant for the Radical Left?

Post-2008 is certainly a different social epoch to that in which the movements of the 1960s and 1970s operated, yet these movements in the USA and Europe did use diverse media: music and its rhetorical artefacts, concerts and radical musical events; the mimeograph machine enabling mass-produced flyers before the photocopier; and pirate radio. Their contribution to radicalism was less about content than opening up channels of expression and disturbing the social order.[22] Research on the NSMs has elaborated on the repertoires of social control and the role that science and information play in power relationships and in the growth of institutional discipline and domination mechanisms on lifestyles and human cognition. Echoing the liberating responses of thousands of middle-class activists to what were perceived as systemic tendencies towards alienation, discipline, domination and coercion, Touraine pointedly described the social environment against which the students were revolting as a *sociéte programmée*.[23]

The internet and advanced information technologies have contributed to deprogramming society. In line with resource mobilisation theory in social movement studies, resources that can be applied to obtain social and political capital, and the ways in which actors use, ignore or divide over them, is critical for collective action.[24] Online activity specifically overcomes obstacles to participation, such as time constraints, lack of skills and low income, while at the same time helping movements to stress ambitions about changing the world and downplaying controversy over their positions.[25] Information technologies offer themselves as back-end infrastructures for movements, which can be utilised both to organise and to deliberate. The spontaneity, immediacy and multimedia functions of contemporary online networks entail transmitting emotion, spreading information and forming a conduit for inspiration and hope.[26] One of the most astounding examples of how the contention of neoliberal policies can reach and attract millions within a short period of time, making a lot of oppositional noise and raising awareness that would not have otherwise existed – what media scholars call the 'amplified message'[27] – is the #ThisIsACoup hashtag on Twitter in July 2015. Born in Barcelona as a part of a collective campaign, in the passage of a few days it reached more than a billion views and prominent support.

Technological advancement has widened the audience of subversive, anti-systemic discourse and reinforced the attempts of political actors to politicise everyday life, launch spontaneous protests and initiate pressure on political elites through quick and public attention. Today's developments still resonate with the global cultural wealth of the 1960s and 1970s, when the ability to both consume and produce forms of media was transformed through various optical, acoustic and electronic innovations. Radicalism, revolt and dissent entered a phase of 'popular mediatic engagement'.[28] Resistance was elaborated in culture, through music, satire, self-destructive artistic objects and other forms of revolutionary art. In many ways, information and communication technologies in the 2000s and 2010s mainstreamed many functions that were earlier manifested through pirate radio and other radical media: the decentralisation of media; systematic feedback from the audience and a process of political learning; collective production; social and associational control; and self-organisation.[29] In these senses, across periods of 'newness', communication as a key feature of the time's socio-technical system served similar purposes for radicals.

In the 2000s and 2010s the internet aided and prefigured the emergence of a reinvigorated thirst for real democracy, while broadening the possibilities of radical action. Municipalist confluences within the context of 'Cities for Change' in Madrid, Barcelona and other Spanish cities have demonstrated innovation in participatory technologies. Under the notion of 'smart cities', metropolitan areas have rejected the neoliberal understanding of the city that is based on private entrepreneurship, and apps extract information from city data grids. Technology is instead approached through the principles of open, democratic participation and publically owned data, which can help build networks that localise how citizen needs are addressed, improve city services, encourage and support cooperative production and consumption and inject bottom-up logics to municipal decision-making.[30]

Problems do abide in the radical grounds of online activism. Social media and other electronic means such as mobile phones certainly facilitate and speed up communication among those who have access, yet given that not all people have (the same) access to these means of communication there arise inequalities between those 'within' and those 'outside' them, and by extension movements favour or disfavour certain issues.[31] This debate about digital inequalities was especially important and had implications inside many GJM groups, especially during the 1990s and early 2000s when social media and advanced mobile phone technology were just starting to provide new tools of communication. Another chief exchange has been in how social media or online activity may dampen militancy, on-the-ground work and appearance, which is important for real impact, relieving grievances and attracting mainstream media attention. The lack of real-time activity can also damage the comradeship of groups and vibrancy is difficult to maintain during 'calm' periods.[32] Digital organisation is a 'weak-tie instrument par excellence'.[33] Because it is so easy to stop and start through digital activism, it may be insufficient to create a sustainable network of activists. At the same time, the multiple expressional forms of digitality can often lead to its fetishisation as the only, necessary or most important means of generating counter-publics. Additionally, centralising tendencies and informal power arrangements lacking any form of delegated authority arise in apparently horizontal, online participation in forums and consultations.

These pathologies aside, digital tools have been fruitfully appropriated by radicals. The shift from early online resources to the later ones, from Indymedia, alternative mailing lists, autonomous servers and hacker meetings towards Facebook, Twitter, Tumblr and messaging apps, signalled change in the use of the internet as a platform of organising contention.[34] While the GJM activists used the internet to organise and coordinate 'small-group politics', the post-2008 movements turned corporate social media 'into an expansive medium of mass mobilisation', an 'emerging antiestablishment digital mass politics'.[35] Through social media, groups formed around Jeremy Corbyn, Podemos, Occupy platforms and other online spaces of political discussion, sometimes with tens of thousands of participants. These were evidence of multiple processes. For example, the facilitation of a near constant engagement with politics, the perpetuation of informal politics, the critical flow of ideas and deliberative democratic spirits. Through online activity the possibilities of engagement between different sections of the Radical Left and between the Radical Left and other political spaces are conducive to leaders becoming more aware of criticism from below, the accumulation of public argument, polemic and political knowledge, and the everydayness of publicly voicing an opinion, confronting others or scrutinising anything and everything. Compared to the exposures of the partisan and activist in the socialist tradition, the terms of social and political conduct by which radicals abide have been transformed, and the realm of sociality itself redesigned.

In spite of the internet's relevance to social movement politics (and we will return to this shortly), radical activism has been far from restricted to the virtual sphere. By the time of the GJM, radical repertoires of action had expanded in manifold ways. Indicatively, the list of actions sponsored by People's Global Action to mark the Global Day of Actions against Capitalism on 1 May 2000 included no fewer than 31 conceivable types – from strikes and demonstrations to critical mass bike rides, carnivals, street parties, handing out free food and building gardens.[36] Then occupations and forms of mobilisation evolved in response to the 'refugee crisis', involving complex networks of activists. In summing up the debate, Della Porta writes that 'while formal organisations (from left-wing to religious) have certainly been influential in supporting migrants ... research has pointed at the growing importance of self-organised groups, with informal organisational structures'.[37] Decentralisation and informality facilitated the temporal adjustment of the movement's tactics in the refugees' journey: 'If direct help was most needed at the moment of arrival, civil disobedience accompanied migrants along their route, and demonstrative protests for the integration of migrants emerged at their destination.'[38] New experiences were realised in mobilising to save lives, to make the first and most urgent arrangements, to help people at their most desperate, to keep families together, to be welcoming on their arrival and to symbolise hope for a new beginning. Groups and individuals may declare themselves apolitical and come from different social classes. Ground tactics have often been the focus of activist debate, and disagreements emerged over whether humanitarian work had to stop to shift emphasis to the protests and the policy demands of the refugees themselves.[39] Effectively, discussions or contestations of what solidarity works best in organisational terms for the subject on the receiving end are always under way.

Organising solidarity is multifold for radical activists and it includes mobilising within wider solidarity communities. The economic crisis generated a surge of poverty, exclusion and insecurity that had not been seen since after World War II. This led to an upsurge of alternative experiments in the form of cooperatives and associations focusing on the production or distribution of goods and services, as well as an increasing number of non-mainstream finance systems giving rise to an 'alternative moral economy'.[40] As neoliberalism and austerity broke down social bonds and relationships, social movements created new conditions that brought citizens closer to one another. Difficulties with the basic means of subsistence became a key mobilising factor. Solidarity initiatives and networks, as well as social mini-economies or self-organised healthcare as alternative platforms for 're-instituting socio-economic relations', have constituted survival tactics by vulnerable groups while generating loci for progressive and anti-capitalist propaganda.[41] What started in public square occupations in Greece and Spain evolved into economic solidarity movements and mutual aid networks. This happened when the occupations declined in force and attendance to a point where it was particularly evident that 'only' protesting is a politically insufficient response to the crisis.[42]

Direct social actions, as Bosi and Zamponi remind us, 'represent a significant part of the repertoire of contention ... while they tend to be less visible than protest actions, they should still not be overlooked and treated like something "new" every time they resurface'.[43] In the austerity-stricken Italy of the late 1970s, for example, extra-parliamentary left-wing activists advocated various countermeasures to the crisis, including the 'self-reduction (*autoriduzione*) of public transport fares, public utility bills and cinema and concert tickets; "proletarian shopping" (*spesa proletaria*); housing occupations; and self-management of various social services'.[44] Italian autonomist Marxism was an important intellectual and social force in this direction, although the associated forms of resistance above are much wider in appeal than Italy. Self-management, from alternative, feminist-organised kindergartens to communist collectives, or the self-reduction of public transport fares, have been relatively common practices across time and on both sides of the Atlantic.[45]

What did change between the GJM and the post-2008 conjuncture was the focus of SMOs. According to Paolo Graziano and Francesca Forno, they shifted from 'ethical' economic actions – 'political consumerism, purchasing groups, local organic food schemes, community renewable energy initiatives, community currencies'[46] – to solidarity actions developed as 'coping strategies' or 'alternative forms of resilience'.[47] This was a shift in the rational of solidarity spaces, initially to politicise (alternative) economic choices and subsequently to defend survival. Various groups, never easily defined as Radical Left but with radicals almost always participating, have employed innovative organisational and participatory tools. Organising has included both the national level – social credit systems, slow food, participatory budgeting, sustainable community management through online exchange systems, ethical banking and responsible tourism – and international organising, for example focusing on fair trade, opposition to 'sweat shop' factories, degrowth or simplicity movements.

The rise of what is more broadly understood as political consumerism was strongly connected to the GJM, which spoke of the market as an arena for political activism; to build counter-markets in a sense was understood as a necessary strategy of prefiguring alternative economic systems, so as to subsequently advocate them widely.[48] By the end of the GJM cycle and in the context of poverty, expensive housing, gentrification and exclusion, these movements reoriented their activities from the global to the local level, explaining the growth in such associations in Europe subsequently.[49] During the crisis, the prevailing pattern between northern and western Europe – where, due to cultural opportunity structures, political consumerism has been much more diffuse and close to popular imaginaries – and southern Europe has evolved. Due to the crisis and the need for cooperative and collectivist responses to counteract economic inequality and facilitate welfare outside of the mainstream markets, southern European patterns of political consumption and solidarity economy organising expanded.[50]

To what extent has this expansion grown or sustained itself? Two parameters can be raised indicating that direct action structures have confronted challenges when it comes to radical politics, and will probably remain relevant in the future too. First, the movements of self-organising producers at the end had very limited appeal and duration without leaving many traces in terms of subsequent mobilisation or institutional effect. As a setting, consumption and production mini-communities are also ideologically stratified. To ground political action in new forms of solidarity and sociability that evade free market and consumerist logic is not easy, foremost because those involved have varying attitudes towards capitalism, neoliberalism, the national Left, government and compromise. Indicatively, a divide has been uncovered in ethnographic work, between Greek 'solidarians' who are more liberal minded, softer in tone and oriented towards the state on the one hand, and 'leftists' arguing that a compromise with hegemony leads to dependency on aid and narrating political events from a more militant and radical perspective.[51] The solidarity economy and direct social action movements have not avoided the political divisions visible in the wider arena of radical left mobilisation. And once organisational experience in such spaces accumulates and the sustainability of collective projects is endangered, they often also entail shifting from the 'hardcore' to the 'soft', from the principled to the pragmatist.[52]

Second, political consumerism and new ways of organising the economy face the future in so far as its rise is strongly linked to globalisation, crisis and neoliberalism. As the Covid-19 pandemic has again challenged the current developmental system, new spaces for solidarity economies and direct social action have been opening up across the globe. Although, when compared with other types of radical mobilisation – the environmental, rights, Occupy, pro-democracy and anti-austerity movements – political consumerism and solidarity economies are a smaller structure on the whole, organising in this domain is most likely here to stay. During the pandemic, hardship funds, the global rent strikes which started in April 2020 and above all mutual aid groups have sprung up in the thousands across Europe.[53] In this situation, the lines separating activism from daily life are more blurred and horizontal procedures, and fully equal power distribution, like in the more general movement of political consumerism, is more entrenched.

Moving forward, there is another uptick in digital tools. Although this time around it is under different conditions, online facilitators of communication have been utilised profoundly. Social distancing and lockdowns during the Covid-19 pandemic generated a situation where cyberspace has been the main arena for mobilisation by social movements. Within solidarity communities and mutual aid mini-societies, activists circulate and explain toolkits and resources to increase familiarity with technology. WhatsApp, Facebook and Slack have been employed to organise solidarity initiatives or campaigns, similar to the online activity of food banks after the onset of the global financial crisis.[54] Google docs are used to disseminate useful information for DIY and sharing experiences across countries, Zoom meetings to coordinate action and threads on Signal for up-to-date community services. Individuals and groups also mobilise for education and awareness raising so as to counteract the spread of false information, fake news and conspiracy theories. It is now unthinkable to organise a local struggle without using social media platforms and tools. The split between social and economic reproduction that the pandemic has normalised through undermining social bonds and disconnecting them from labour and productive activity[55] has to an extent been undone through the digitalities of solidarity and contention.

HORIZONTALITY AND VERTICALITY
IN RADICAL LEFT ACTIVISM

Within space, distinct structures and procedures can range between the theoretical maximum point of horizontality on one pole and the theoretical maximum point of verticality on the other pole. From the spaces in which mobilisation operates on the Radical Left, we now turn to how centralised or decentralised they are. Let us begin with consensus as a distinguishing procedural feature of horizontal politics. Anti-nuclear and peace movements, squatting movements and autonomist social centres have traditionally strived for consensus and rejected any form of hierarchy. Indeed, consensus encounters the Radical Left in different ways across time. In the past, consensus has expressed the thinking behind the mobilisation of trade union militants in tripartite negotiations within the context of corporatist systems and national-level economic planning. It has also always been a practice, even an entrenched psychology, in the general secretariats or political bureaus of traditional CPs, which strived to appear united, albeit often unsuccessfully so. Crucially, consensus was interpreted very differently by democratic centralism, which suggested that consensus had to characterise the party over a decision after that decision was taken and not before.

Consensus as aversion to conflict continued into Occupy assemblies from the GJM's Social Forums, where decision-making combined limited and controlled forms of delegation with instruments encouraging the broadest possible agreement, appealing to dialogue and transparency.[56] Procedures included not upholding a proposal if there is a large minority, thus interpreting the majoritarian principle less absolutely, as in the anarchist tradition; having facilitators in the decision-making process; and allowing decisions to be brought back into discussion.[57] Consensus as a procedure for decision-making in European radical movements travelled there from the 'Zapatist consultation'. Indeed, consensus had emerged in many indigenous communities because in such societies there was 'no way to compel a minority to agree with a majority decision – either because there is no state with a monopoly of coercive force or because the state has nothing to do with local decision-making'.[58]

Mobilisation in the GJM resonated with the age of mass information and the networked society: 'networking, [a] decentered form of organisation and intervention, characteristic of the new social movements, mirroring, and counteracting, the networking logic of domination in the information society'.[59] Unlike the bureaucratic and hierarchical traditional labour unions and their concerted decision-making procedures, the GJM movements adopted a network structure, embraced solidarity and hesitated less to employ disruptive and aggressive action. The logic of networking involves building horizontal connections, autonomy of the connecting elements, freedom of information circulation and consumption, decentralisation and complex coordination, direct democracy and self-management.[60] Internal democracy was crucial, democratic participation and the democratisation of the institutions and mechanisms of globalisation were key objectives and advanced technological means were becoming available to utilise in this route.[61] We should still refrain from reducing the GJM to an anarchist revival; the cleavages within the GJM (autonomist, revolutionary left, non-governmental organisations (NGOs), Attac) have been documented in detail – this was the 'movement of movements', the 'network of networks'.[62]

Many on the Radical Left reasonably doubted that the self-selected, unelected and uncontrollable leadership of the GJM was more democratic (responsible and accountable) than the traditional leadership of parties and trade unions. Within the GJM a broad distinction between institutional action and autonomist action has been extensively documented. On the one hand, there is a permanent organisation, legitimacy accorded to the collective, voting and negotiation in decision-making procedures and a clear division of labour and authority. On the other hand, the only legitimate actor is the individual acting collectively, and repertoires of contention include self-managed projects and lifestyle activism as opposed to demonstrations and strikes, while organisation is contingent and evolves through critical reflection.[63] At the WSF of 2005, debates over the celebrated but also critiqued as self-refuting book of John Holloway, *Changing the World without Taking Power*, showed the overarching political dispute: between the horizontal-prefigurative struggle as sufficient for self-emancipation, and the more classical socialist views of the necessity to devise a political programme, distribute authority and confront the government.[64] In the absence of doing the latter, and given the GJM's funfair-like operation and atmosphere, a performative elitism by academics and NGOs contradicted the very proclamations of the WSFs.[65]

In the European public squares of the 2010s as political realms, the assembly was structured on very specific discussion and voting rules, following the logic of accommodating large crowds with divergent life stories, opinions and emotions. As Michael Hardt and Antonio Negri argued in *The Assembly*, their celebration of horizontalist movements across the globe, when the multitude assembles, radical political possibilities expand. Through 'leaderless movements', in which the assembly engenders political equality and discourages leadership personas, two organisational ideas were manifested. First, that for radical democratic change to be effective and lasting, decision-making structures need to rely on the broadest democratic base possible so that the initiative and control of strategy is undertaken by the multitude itself. Second, this is so because a leadership problem existed: 'the lack of leaders in the movements today is neither accidental nor isolated: hierarchical structures have been overturned and dismantled within the movements as a function of both the crisis of representation and a deep aspiration to democracy'.[66]

In the assembly, the foremost critics of delegation and representation – the anarchist and autonomist traditions – shaped consensus practices. The term 'democracy on steroids' came to mean 'the active (co)creation' of diverse options outside of majority voting, with the only genuinely democratic procedure being consensus decision-making, an intense but necessary form of government.[67] The chief objectives lay in satisfying the perspectives of as many people as possible, operating on modes of trust building and distributing power equally, by contrast with politics as usual. To this end, deliberative democracy theory has been central in giving certain types of answers to democratic puzzles and producing or reinforcing the activist practice of thinking beyond and around the reign of majorities in democracies.[68] Rules which were thought to facilitate movement in this direction in the Occupy assemblies and many other groups have included turn-taking, interventions limited in length, gesture codes to navigate discussion, the quick publication of proceedings, moderation and the feminisation of vocabulary to subvert patriarchy. Horizontality is more fitting for prefigurative politics, which occur in a group's own terms of political conflict. But they can be inefficient and without real impact when the terms of politics are electoral, when groups are very large and coordination is pertinent, and when quick, tactical decisions need to be taken in situations of intensified conflict.

Within the movements, horizontality has been in tension with verticality since the emergence of autonomist activism. In the seminal essay *The Tyranny of Structurelessness*, focused on the Women's Liberation Movement and its consciousness-raising groups practised across the globe, American feminist Jo Freeman suggested that the benefits of participatory and horizontal structures cannot replace the gaps left by the absence of delegation by democratic procedure, and a formal distribution of authority within the organisation.[69] Otherwise, the end result is either ineffective or subsumed under the banner of the structured organisation operating in the same political space. Informal power networks also develop, their chief difference with formal ones being that they are ad hoc and undemocratic. Freeman's remarks still resonate acutely today. The experience of what has been called a prefigurative crisis came when the GJM's dynamism was fading away while no concrete advances were achieved. Looking back over the past two decades, it became clear to many theorists and activists that anarchism's emphasis on consensus, autonomy and horizontality, spontaneous actions, informal networks and local struggles have not succeeded because campaigning organisation has not been sustained in a systematic way. The same applies to the post-2008 wave's movements: they (re)realised a need for victory in the electoral realm that would sustain some sort of effective input into the policymaking structures of neoliberalism and exercise a pull effect on capital.

What happened for the GJM and its gradual diffusion into parties and NGOs and away from the streets is a standard point for all social movements that are declining: institutionalisation. Thus, the GJM's prefigurative politics, whereby near exclusive weight was placed on 'activism' (as opposed to 'party politics as usual'), spontaneity, consensus and direct action, gave way. Without these having been abandoned, the organisational discourse throughout the 2000s and 2010s, excepting perhaps the mass pro-democracy moment, where it happened most vigorously, was more geared towards validating the absolute necessity of solid organisation building and practices that complement and go beyond planning events of spontaneous activism, direct action and prefiguration.[70] The very lesson of GJM was experienced in the 15M in Spain and facilitated its journey to the Podemos party. In this direction, a renewed interest resurfaced in Lenin, Gramsci, the party, the comradeship of socialist politics, the social movement organisation, populist politics and leadership, and communism as theoretical means to political strategy.[71]

Since the 2000s a great many parties and electoral coalitions have arisen out of partnerships and mergers between public personas, extra-parliamentary organisations and social movements: SYRIZA in Greece launched before the 2004 legislative elections, a result of Synaspismos's involvement in the Athens ESF and before that the 'Space for Dialogue for the Unity and Common Action of the Left' in 2001; the contribution of social movements to the electoral mobilisation of the Tsipras List (L'arltra Europa con Tsipras) in Italy, which won two seats in the 2014 European elections; the establishment of the Front de Gauche in France in 2009 and the expansion of its constituent groups in 2012; the establishment of the New Anti-capitalist Party (NPA) in the same country in 2009, aimed at unifying the fractured movements of the French Radical Left and mobilising primarily Trotskyists; the People before Profit Alliance and its cooperation with Solidarity (previously the Anti-austerity Alliance) in Ireland and Northern Ireland; the emergence of Respect and later Left Unity in the UK as a party of activists, whereby political organising is established from below and social movements have a strong input to the party's policymaking; and Momentum as a decentralised space, which affirmed success at the polls through the Labour Party as its prime goal.

As Wallerstein articulated, the predominant argument inside the Radical Left itself is that 'an anti-systemic movement cannot neglect short-term defensive action, including electoral action. The world's populations live in the present, and their immediate needs have to be addressed. Any movement that neglects them is bound to lose the widespread passive support that is essential for its long-term success.'[72] It is not hyperbole to argue that Europe's recent past was Latin America's earlier past. Neoliberalism aggressively hit Latin America first, resulting in growing anger from the mass citizenry when confronted with structural adjustment programmes and policies of economic austerity, and a shift to the left over the past two decades, first in society and then in the party system. The most prominent examples being the Zapatista and Appista movements in Mexico, the Piqueteros and workers' movements in Argentina, the

Chavistas in Venezuela and the Aymara coca-growers and indigenous movements in Bolivia.[73] Charismatic leaders of the left have captured state power via support from, and growth out of, these movements, left populism became a central feature of the new, leftist governments, and state management went hand in hand with non-institutional networking and activity.[74]

PROCEDURE AND STATE LEGALITY: VIOLENCE AND THE EUROPEAN RADICAL LEFT

Having seen so far that multiple ways of organising are always present among radical left movements, let us turn to one of the common accusations against them in both recent and earlier years in terms of method: that they are or can be uncivil or extremist, that is, evasive, shocking or provocative. Unlawfulness, illegality and disruption are often associated with extremism or ultra-committed doctrines, which at core pose the question about radical left movements in opposition to the state, particularly its legal system and practices of enforcing public order.

In the decades following World War II, political violence – state sanctioned, para-state and interstate – thrived as a means of engaging in social and political conflict. The international scene was one of revolutions, guerrilla warfare, coups d'état, riots and generalised upheaval in Europe, Africa, Latin America and Asia. In this context, many on the non-partisan and anarchist Left saw potential and concrete results in the 'critique of guns', which has existed since the late nineteenth and early twentieth century within the French, Spanish, Italian and Russian anarchist traditions. In the late 1960s, left-wing armed guerrilla groups grew out of the social movements of the New Left, mixing Marxism, Maoism and the ideologies of Third World liberation movements.[75]

Among the groups that emerged from the social movements were: the Brigate Rosse and Prima Linea in Italy; the Red Army Faction (RAF) and Bewegung 2. Juni in Germany; the Gauche Proletarienne and later the Action Directe in France; the Grupo de Resistencia Antifascista Primero de Octubre in Spain; and the Revolutionary Organisation 17 November in Greece. In Italy, the armed movements of the Radical Left were the largest, with around 50,000 participants, mainly in their mid-twenties.[76] Repertoires of action varied according to national context and ideological narrative and included threats, assassinations, bombings, kidnappings, small-scale attacks on industrial targets or personnel, attacks aimed at liberating imprisoned affiliates, theft of state military equipment and robberies. Unlike the looser boundaries of student groups, which were a more general phenomenon with a generational identity, revolutionary groups were characterised by a strong sense of belonging and clear boundaries between the in-group and those outside of it.[77] Activating guerrilla networks in Italy and elsewhere was a process of creating a small, secretive circle of trust, mutual claims of resistance and emotional ties.

All this occurred within a wider context in which 'defensive violence' as a sort of organisational concept was losing ground.[78] Violent tactics were often cast as counter-violence, or as a matter of active defence; revolutionary violence was understood as necessary to counteract the violence inherent in imperialist, capitalist states.[79] At the same time, violence understood as self-defence was justified as a way to provoke social upheaval and contribute to the emergence of revolutionary conditions and the opportunity for mass subversion. For all of the groups, the Maoist and Che Guevarian interpretation of violence was more or less the same, in the sense of endorsing violence as 'a necessary condition' 'for every revolutionary struggle'.[80] Many guerrillas in the 1970s sought to bring the war back into 'the belly of the beast'.[81] They were in this sense a subversion of Western normality. These notions were largely popular also outside the guerrilla groups, and counter-violence was supported in principle by many German students who protested aggressively and passionately against the handling of the RAF by the German state. As only a small, important indication, the suicide in a Stuttgart prison cell of Urliche Meinhoff, formerly herself a member of the Socialist German Student Union, unleashed country-wide protests and, followed by the death of the rest of the RAF members, a notoriety ritualised by a massive literature and popular discourse about the 'Stammheim myth'.[82]

What war meant was still at stake and the cosmos of violent, revolutionary groups had its internal debates, both moral and tactical.

Some groups embraced the 'armed struggle', such as the Red Brigades or RAF. Others rejected it as the chief strategy of action, still justifying and often practising revolutionary violence; for example, the groups Lotta Continua and Lotta di Popolo in Italy.[83] Divisions also existed over political homicide as a 'decisive event' for mass emancipation. In fact, the opposite was realised. The kidnapping and murder of former Italian Prime Minister Aldo Moro by the Red Brigades in 1978 was a decisive event demobilising violent activism and was the most representative historical case of the descent into terrorism by these groups.[84]

Debate revolved over which political objective is served by violence, and from that over how far and in what ways violence is to be exercised. Through the broader radical movements and intellectuals, a threefold distinction in responding to the question of violent action was that between 'under no conditions', 'against objects' or 'against human lives too'. These were also the main demarcation lines of feminist attitudes towards violence.[85] There was effectively a threefold response to the feminists' own intellectual production on the complex processes of systemic violence, with multiple layers – structural, representational, symbolic, gendered and racialised.[86] The chief arguments in support of and against violent action were elaborated back then by Noam Chomsky in a debate with Hannah Arendt.[87] Absolute opposition to violence may mean, 'either saying that resort to violence is illegitimate even if the consequences are to eliminate a greater evil; or saying that under no conceivable circumstances will the consequences ever be such as to eliminate a greater evil'. According to Chomsky, the first argument is irreducible moralism and highly debatable and the second is historically incorrect. Violence can be seen also in a tactical light. It can be seen as justified but is it politically effective or not? Chomsky's own defence of non-violence in the peace movement against the Vietnam War was indeed premised on the conviction that it would constitute 'suicide' because the US government had a 'monopoly of terror'. Affecting all movements is that violence 'antagonises the uncommitted' when the point is to draw them in.[88]

The wave of radical left violent groups in Europe lasted from the late 1960s to approximately the 1980s. One of the last violent, urban guerrilla organisations, the Greek 17 November, was captured in 2002. It is, though, interesting and important that until today many physiognomies of the violent left in previous decades are respected, consulted and defended by radicals, both young and old. In the case of Greece, where Nicos Koufontinas is a prisoner for life, radical activists and intellectuals from the non-communist, extra-parliamentary space, and from within SYRIZA, have routinely mobilised against the violation of his rights and the state's broader political repression through its anti-terrorism branch. The issue had also been dealt with by the Greek mainstream media as one of possible 'connections' between SYRIZA and 17 November and was utilised by its competitors to tarnish the party's image among a significant part of its milieu, which was adamantly against not fully rejecting 17 November. The Greek case, among essentially all others, shows that colourations of association with the historical or contemporary revolutionary, violent group play out, although more subtly, over a long period of time.

More recently, the focus of those connecting or debating the source of violence has been elsewhere. In western Europe, the violent Radical Left is typically identified in three types of mobilisation: radical environmental groups, the Black Bloc associated with the GJM and its more recent incarnations in the Antifa movement. Let us consider them in turn. First, small cells in the name of animal rights and the environment developed in the late 1990s, both within and outside the broader movement, and today translate into a broad movement of local and international groups of civil disobedience and environmental resistance. Second, Antifascist (Antifa) groups, often identified as a Black Bloc, engage in a number of activities confronting far-right activists, politicians and demonstrations; that is, in fighting fascism directly.

What has come to be known as 'ecoterrorism' rose from the radical sections of the environmentalist movement, which gained currency during the 1960s. The tactic of inflicting material damage on development projects that destroy the environment (and by extension a number of other things, such as threats and letter bombs), is tied to the left through the belief that capitalism and profit seeking, as well as environmentally unconscious, development inevitably lead to the despoliation of nature. Radical environmentalism thus puts forward the claim that 'if society is left unchecked', this will lead ultimately to the 'complete degradation of the environment'. In this light, the urgency of the damage done to the planet requires a more robust response than that of conventional protest.[89]

Radical ecology begins to deviate from the classical, socialist strain where it concerns the religious-like nature of certain parts of radical environmentalism, which project an indigenous-like view of 'environmental degradation as an assault on a sacred, natural world'.[90] Marginal organisations – such as Earth First, the Animal Liberation Front and (only in the USA) the Animal Recovery Mission, 'A Vanguard Defense Organisation', share a critique of society's structure and call for revolutionary change, but are not materialists and legitimise their acts as representing the weaker sentient beings in an unequal situation between humans and animals. Between the 1970s and about 2010, they carried out hundreds of 'missions' of property and infrastructure destruction or setting animals free, but remained detached from mass movements and the working class. In western Europe and North America, the liberation of animals has inspired thousands of activists, and since the 1970s it has grown into a very important social movement in its own right. Accusations by the radical left remain that animal liberation is connected to and driven by 'privileged white and middle-class concerns'. From within the movement, the concept of total liberation, adapted from Frantz Fanon and intersectionality, reflect attempts to connect with wider struggles in society through non-particularistic ideological frameworks.[91]

The post-2008 movement of radical ecology has practised 'ecoterrorist tactics' as part of a broader determination for civil disobedience, specified by activists as resistance to companies which do public harm. A 2010 Europol report outlined a number of tactics: 'blackmail, sending threatening emails or making warning phone calls to their targets, often threatening their family and committing physical assault against their property', or the 'mass release of animals', and even 'disinformation methods in order to discredit their targets and weaken their public acceptance'.[92] 'Images of sick and abused animals are embedded in video footage and made public'.[93] These are typically classified as 'ecoterrorism' by various judges across Europe, whereas activists understand and defend them as ecological sabotage (ecotage).[94] Importantly, violence is contested among ecotage groups. Far from embodying the image of 'eco-terrorists', many of 'those who carry out small-scale acts of sabotage are also often engaged in relatively conventional political activity; view sabotage as a complement to other action, not as an end in itself; and are committed to avoiding physical harm to people'.[95]

Some activists find that a non-violent ethos has prevailed, which is insufficiently useful in strategic terms and theoretically ill-informed through unfounded moralism. A known representative of this position is climate scholar and activist Andreas Malm, who has recently published *How to Blow Up a Pipeline*.[96] In it, he essentially advocates a radical upscaling in the confrontation of climate destructors, including the destruction of luxury commodities like SUVs or superyachts, and infrastructure of the fossil fuel industry such as gas stations, pipelines and refineries. Malm called out a true emergency and the necessity to behave that way in strategic terms and to bear the cost of defetishising violence if necessary. His criticism has been rebutted in differentiated ways. Leading activists in Extinction Rebellion, who do not endorse anti-capitalism, reject any form of violence. Others point out that the consequences of such acts will be devastating for those involved and the movement more broadly, since they will invite repression, which is even heavier than that of today and will be disorganising for the cause.[97]

The other commonly referenced source of violence on the Radical Left is the Black Bloc section of the GJM, especially on the occasion of the Genoa counter-summit in 2001, which was twisted into an iconic sign of destruction; a rain of Molotov bombs and stones against heavily armed and aggressive riot police. Here, the notion of 'performative violence' becomes important to distinguish between protestors' and rioters' intentions and the practice of symbolic confrontation-based rituals within a wider array of tactics, and the random and senseless violence they were portrayed as committing by the media.[98] The Black Bloc is really a tactic pursued by anarchists and other anti-authoritarians: black clothing and masks are worn and activists march in tight formation to express anonymity and solidarity as the founding stones of collective resistance whereby the group and not the individual are what matters. Other groups, like the *Tutte Bianche* in Italy, the WOMBLES in Britain and Ya Basta! in Spain typically wore white jumpsuits, put on helmets and carried shields, intended for protection as they were pushing through the barricades of police.[99] The overall GJM, which is more prominent in Europe (where the Black Bloc originated) than in the USA, is represented by civil disobedience rather than violence, as no one in these groups justifies harming people.[100] Rather, their innovations were to use blockades or lockdowns for disruption during international elite meetings, broadly understood as 'non-violent warfare', combined with carnival-like and radical art performances.[101]

Another strain is the thinking behind anti-fascist violence, suggesting the moral duty to contain neofascism with aggressive opposition when political institutions fail to do so. This also reveals the strategic assessment that there is much to achieve by confronting fascism in the streets and in social life. Within the Antifa movement, often violence is only condoned as self-defence, although common criticisms include that Antifa counter-violence often surpasses its claims. Violence, however, is not the chief mobilising force of Antifa. Well-known Antifa tactics in Europe and the USA include the disruption of far-right events and speakers, forming human chains in anti-demonstrations, monitoring reactionary groups on social media platforms, 'doxxing' or taking over the Twitter accounts of far-right groups and posting anti-fascist content. They are confrontational and provocative, except they are not at their core geared towards personal, physical violence. To connect Antifa and anarchist activist solely with violence is to overshadow all of their political, cultural, anti-authoritarian, solidarity and other actions, leaving a picture narrower than and unreflective of empirical reality. What do become central among Antifa groups are questions involving anonymity and visibility, in person and online; self-defence and organising vulnerable groups around it, as in the form of Antifa gyms; dealing with infiltrators and with infiltrating; football anti-fascism and networks across European countries with diverse social activities; state repression and anti-police tactics; festivals, social events, publications and debate; solidarity with immigrants, refugees, asylum seekers and other oppressed populations; participation in urban and municipal movements; fusing with ecological movements.[102]

Within Europe, the stark contrast between anti-fascism and its opposite became clearer than ever in October 2020, when a historic victory for the Greek anti-fascist movement was achieved. The leaders of the far-right Golden Dawn party were found guilty in court for directing a criminal organisation responsible for the murder of Antifa hip-hop musician Pavlos Fyssas, killing migrants and harming communist trade unionists, among many other acts of violence. The sentencing of Golden Dawn's fascists has been the largest indictment of Nazi crimes since Nuremberg, and the Greek Radical Left was a crucial mobilising force of activists, lawyers, politicians, opinion leaders and academics in the five-year trial.[103]

There are, of course, continuities between various anarchist, animal liberation and Antifa organisations which refuse to condemn all violence and destruction. The last two are monothematic militant groups, whereas anarchist and autonomous violence is not strictly dependent on the strategy for particular social issues, such as fascism, animals or the environment. Yet violence or illegal action often comes with less dialogical communication and thus there is more difficult linkage between Antifa communities or animal liberationists and mass movements. Examples include Antifascistisk Aktion and the Rev Front in Sweden, and the Greek Rouvikonas and anarchist student groups. As a social force within the Left, these tendencies are nevertheless a minority, but a temporal and relational point is due here if we are to argue for evolution. Although violence as terrorism is much less identified with the European Radical Left than before (e.g. during the 1970s), uncivil resistance and confrontational protest have been thoroughly documented as increasing in the past two decades on a world scale. Violence in the form of confrontations with the police, illegal action, rioting, property destruction, disruptive activities and civil disobedience have been especially common in the 2010s globally.[104]

Many instances from around Europe of illegal direct action within universities, the public sector or the local level have generated movements and led to confrontations with the police. Riots between 2008 and the mid-2010s erupted in Athens, Paris, Stockholm, London and elsewhere. Confrontational tactics by activists reflect a changing role by the police, away from what had earlier been characterised as 'the continuing institutionalisation of protest'.[105] An increasingly authoritarian response by police ended the previously alleged pacification of police conflict and the routinised forms of public order management.[106] The criminalisation of protest has grown: a rise in police brutality against protestors; anti-immigrant legislation; punishing immigrant solidarity for human trafficking, as in Italy and Greece; intrusive surveillance measures that violate individual rights and explode into scandals, like in the UK; ultraviolent police suppression, as in the Catalonian referendum in October 2017; or the anti-G20 protests in Hamburg in July 2017.[107] The shooting of Carlo Giuliani at the 2001 protests in Genoa and of Alexandros Grigoropoulos, which ignited the Athens riots of 2008, have become symbolic among radicals of a vengeful, murdering police.

Civil disobedience, a nominally extreme measure, has been a common procedure of mobilisation and resistance for radical movements, especially during heightened contention or crisis and certainly beyond Antifa. In the 1960s and 1970s, its best known manifestation was that of conscientious objection to military service in the Vietnam War in the USA. The other repertoires of civil disobedience have already been addressed: anti-fascist fighting, interruption, disruption, rioting and squatting. During the GJM gatherings, pacifists would distinctly separate themselves from the Black Bloc. During the 2010s, resistance to the implementation of austerity has included illegal utility maintenance for bankrupt households, refusal to pay toll charges and rioting at court hearings of house evictions during the crisis in Greece.[108] The Spanish 15M camp was a 'laboratory of civil disobedience'. This was expressed, for example, in the general assembly's decision to violate the Spanish 'day of reflection', during which electoral campaigning activity is suspended and a decision was taken to evict the camp.[109] When plans were announced to privatise the health sector in Madrid, employees enclosed themselves in the hospitals (*encierros*) and held massive workforce assemblies, which quickly expanded to include users of health services and gave birth to the *marea blanca*, the movement for public sanitation.[110]

In the environmental camp, civil disobedience and direct action tactics, as in the UK, helped Extinction Rebellion to grow and gain popularity, having today more than 130 groups across the country. Breaking windows or blocking public roads and bridges or commuter trains have been often referred to by Extinction Rebellion as 'escalation strategies', useful for grabbing the attention of the public and helping the organisation grow. Civil disobedience has been taken to new organisational levels, exemplified by this group's 'flopping' tactic when arrested, or their prison guides to movement participants as hundreds were arrested. More widely, with the pandemic, civil disobedience has been a contested issue between radical movements and parties and right-wing governments as in Cyprus, Greece and Italy, which implemented unconstitutional orders for banning peaceful demonstrations as part of the Covid-19 safety measures.

Between the 1960s and today, 'extremism' and 'terrorism' as understood by liberals – physical violence, paramilitary mobilisation, intentions of overthrowing the regime, unlawful behaviour – has actually diminished on the European Radical Left. At the same time, confrontational tactics and civil disobedience have again become more and more features of the disruptive 'emergent publics' within, across and beyond radical movements. Over the long term, on the Radical Left as well as more generally, terroristic violence in Europe is largely (although not entirely) gone, while disruptive action, uncivil resistance and civil disobedience have, in large part, returned.

Violence may be less identified as stemming directly from political consciousness, compared to the 1960s and 1970s. As it has been argued for the recurrent Paris riots, some violent protest repertoires denote a proto-political horizon outside of institutional politics.[111] Second, protests in the 2010s are qualitatively different from those of the GJM and the Long '68 when violent groups were explicitly on the far left or right. In the mass, spontaneous and heterogeneous movements, left-wing violence has often taken place during the same event, occasion or period as right-wing violence. A communicative problem for radicals in this context is how a 'two extremes' thesis can more easily polemicise both flanks of the political spectrum as illiberal by equalising them as inimical to democracy, irrational and senseless.

In opposing state legality and the rule of law, radical movements as a whole exhibit a large spectrum of action over time, which has narrowed towards legality but has retained large-scale civil disobedience, especially in countries with a vibrant extra-parliamentary ground.

WHICH RADICAL SUBJECTS?

The practices of the mobilised bring up the additional matter of which social categories constitute the main agitators, what in Chapter 2 was introduced as the composition of mobilisation and resistance. In Marxist and radical theory this is about the agency of revolution or progressive historical change when aligned with oppression. Revolutionary subjects as allies, substitutes or extensions of the working class had been sought by prominent Marxist intellectuals for several decades before the 1960s: the revolutionary vanguard in Leninism, the peasants in Maoist thought, the masses according to Rosa Luxemburg or the citizens in the French republican-socialist tradition. In the 1960s and 1970s, during the GJM and post-2008, original social forces and issues entered the field of protest, and each time the revolutionary subject has not been the working class, at least not the only one. Activists, intellectuals, academics and students have been important actors in agitation and more symbolically representative of the New Left; in Herbert Marcuse's line of thinking, they have been revolutionary subjects as 'arising from the struggle itself'.[112] In France and Italy especially, where 1968 has been highly contested in public memory, analyses emphasising the students' pioneering role have faced criticisms for underplaying the force and role of labour battles and not taking into account the intersections and interactions between the students and the more general mobilisations of the time.[113] Here, pursuing this problematic, we deal with today's radical protagonists and compare them to before, the idea being to connect class oppression with other socio-demographic elements of mass dissent.

The NSMs and the divisions between them and the Old Left emanated from new trajectories of political socialisation among the 1960s and 1970s youth – more open, liberal and contentious than those of the 1930s generation. In 1968, student protests occurred in 56 countries and continued in most of them throughout the 1970s. High schools students also participated in protests in the hundreds of thousands.[114] Student radicalisation arose out of the changes within capitalism, specifically the large increase in student numbers in many countries across the world and the more general transition from elite to mass education, during which universities resisted revising their traditionalist practices and maintained inadequate facilities.[115]

In the 1960s, among thinkers like Herbert Marcuse, C. Wright Mills, Howard Zinn, Andre Gorz and others, students' relationship to class interests was a flaming topic. There was a widely circulating perception of students as new possible agents of revolutionary activity. In contrast to the established left, because of their age, life stage and middle-class status many activists comprising the student movements and the 1960s New Left, were often 'despised' and treated as 'utopian', 'childish', 'destructive', 'irrational', 'hedonist' and 'reckless'.[116] In the words of Edward Short, education secretary in the 1968 Labour government: 'They are wreckers who ... are concerned only to disrupt society. Their weapons are lies, misrepresentations, defamation, character assassination, intimidation and, more recently, physical violence.'[117] In Italy, the Communist Party of Italy (PCI) denounced the new movements and activists as 'adventurist' extremists, gradually shifting to framing them as 'provocateurs' aiming specifically to damage the Left, and finally to approaching them as 'nihilistic hooligans' only interested in destruction.[118] These insights point to the widely discussed implications of a generational gap and its pervasiveness on the European Radical Left and beyond during the 1960s and 1970s. Youth and students then were a source for cultural renewal and the reformulation of radicalism and socialism, especially in the context of the university as a free space where thousands are concentrated; they embodied neither the conservatism often inscribed in traditional working-class constituencies nor the behavioural self-restraint of communist cadres and militants.

Although students in the late 1960s kicked off the events of the ensuing decade with vehement criticism of the working class, throughout the 1970s they often connected to class and workers as it became apparent how educational supply into the labour market reconfigures class relations. Sections of youth saw their social and economic expectations challenged, if not crushed, and this constituted fertile ground for their politicisation and radicalisation.[119] The working classes, albeit much more heterogeneous and disconnected in occupational terms today than before have had, in the three periods considered, a strong presence in terms of mobilisation and resistance. Economic or welfare grievances have driven demonstrations and activism. The movements of the 1960s reacted to the quandary of Fordism – the modern model of mass production, put in practice since the 1910s – while the post-2008 movements responded to the crises of neoliberalism and democracy, yet both waves demanded 'better institutions of collective consumption'.[120] Importantly, some of the largest mobilisations of the 1960s and 1970s were workplace based; for example, the French general strikes and the Italian 'hot autumn' (1969–70), the more temporally scattered strike activity in the UK or the strikes of 1969 and 1973 in West Germany. Depending on the context, strike activity included general strikes, sit-ins, walkouts, 'walk-ins', wildcat strikes and unfair labour practice strikes.

The crisis in the 1970s came with the rise in labour militancy in the context of increased industrial conflict and industrial action, especially at the factory level.[121] The *autoriduzione* movement (self-reduction of prices) spread across Italy in 1974 and worker turmoil was sustained by resistance to the austerity programme advocated in the context of the PCI's Compromeso Storico (*Historic Compromise*), the communists lending support to the Christian Democratic (DC) government between 1976 and 1979.[122] In France, the largest strikes in the twentieth century took place in 1968, along with workers' general assemblies and numerous committees of struggle and solidarity in neighbourhoods, which paralysed production and communication in the country. It would be a reductionist view to consider the social movements and broader left-wing forces of the 1960s and 1970s as merely 'counter-cultural'. This would betray 'the very content and meaning of the claims and mottos of most of the millions of Belgian, Italian or French workers whose strikes almost always had goals concerning wages or working conditions'.[123]

Two types of worker, which were previously absent from trade union struggles, played a crucial role in the 1960s and 1970s. One group was the young, unskilled workers with underpaid jobs, and the other consisted of young technicians 'skilled enough to perform delicate tasks which control the productive process, but who have no chance of joining the managerial staff'.[124] Two classic works of neo-Marxist theory, which had significant influence, were Andre Gorz's analysis of rethinking labour strategy and Serge Mallet's *Essays on the New Working Class*.[125] Both criticised the PCF's (Communist Party of France) political strategy and approach towards social stratification and towards organising the party and the unions. Theories focusing on the increasingly central role of skilled, educated, technical workers saw them potentially as the new socialist vanguard.[126]

New knowledge workers were the prime constituency of the NSMs in the 1960s and 1970s. Their preferences arose out of their social position. Theories of the 'new middle class' have documented the emergence of socio-cultural professionals and skilled service workers, which are more heterogeneous as a group, open-minded and liberal than the old middle class of white-collar office workers, managers and technical experts. At the same time, a 'new working class' including 'service and office workers with few skills' emerged alongside the 'traditional working class of craftsmen, technical workers and skilled agricultural workers'.[127] New intermediate social strata posed challenges for socialist politics as the classification of persons in relation to capitalist production (and consumption) became de facto more complex.[128]

In the contemporary social topography, a new subject envisaged as potentially revolutionary has been identified in the form of the precariat.[129] What has come to be known as the precarious generation is that group of mainly young people who find themselves in precarious employment. Processes of precarisation begin in the labour market and include temporary, fixed-term work or unemployment, as well as atypical, flexible, cognitive work. Concomitantly, these processes extend beyond the workplace to all facets of life. The precariat is a concept with a workerist (or operaist) genealogy that can be traced between Negri's (1988) 'social worker' and 'the multitude'.[130] It reflects a fervour that can be attributed to the poor, emigrants and immigrants, and other atypical figures in the world of labour, giving them the ability to resist imperial power, hence the multitude (or the precariat) is potentially a revolutionary force.

Italian workerism (or *operaismo*) of the 1960s had a significant intellectual impact on sociological analysis nationally (and to a lesser extent internationally) through its project of worker inquiries, and yielded strong theoretical journals. Due to the PCI's shift away from class by the 1960s, and the initially intra-party processes and elaborations (also within the Italian Socialist Party) that began workerism in the first half of that decade, there has since been a strong workerist bent in some Italian movements.[131] Since the 1970s, a number of activists and scholars have been engaged with the conditions of post-Fordism and how the workerist understanding of manual labour in the massive factories can be reformulated appropriately to respond to the realities of late capitalism, including the insecure settings of the gig economy. The difficulties it has faced were largely due to it being organic to Fordism and the mass factory.[132] Indeed, Standing's analysis of the precariat can be associated with endeavours to update class analysis in late capitalism and connects to the emphasis on 'precarisation' as a sign of capitalist transformation, which for some scholars is a critical juncture in historical-material development.[133]

Standing's analysis of the precariat is not exhausted by the workerist perspective; it is more connected to early 'social workers' and much less to the notion of the multitude. Yet the new social group it identifies is a product of a developing capitalist industry, exploited and alienated by its organisation of labour; financialised, to a great extent. The origins of the precariat also render it psychologically liberated from labourism (no option, no dependency) and at the same time non-commodified, that is, not entrenched in institutionalised exchange.[134] According to Standing, the precariat is a 'dangerous class', exactly because of its loose relation to the opportunities and constraints of the labour market.[135] As Andretta and Della Porta show, the precarious generation was largely present in demonstrations across southern Europe and shares multiple socio-demographic features and grievances.[136]

This is not to suggest that Standing's thesis of people in long-term precarious work gradually forming a dangerous class has not been challenged. From an empirical standpoint, Grasso and Giugni, utilising a dataset of over 10,000 protestors from 72 demonstrations (2009–13), report that 'precarity' does not form a new social base for anti-austerity protests.[137] Some scholars find it necessary to distinguish contention by those who are precarious or unemployed from that of people mobilising on behalf of them; the former can be subsumed into the movements of the latter.[138] Standing's thesis has also been negatively assessed as geographically biased, insufficiently contextualised[139] and suggesting an artificial distinction within the working class.[140]

Even if we part with the idea of a new class emerging on a global scale, precariousness in employment, precarious work and precarity as a condition of social life involve a much higher degree of social insecurity than that embodied by even the GJM middle-class activists, and certainly the 1960s and 1970s students and intellectuals. Precarity and unemployment connect youth to class antagonism. It is in this sense that the class cleavage has been partly 'redrawn into shape' by contemporary struggles.[141] An insecure occupational status can trigger political activism by precarious workers 'both at the individual and collective level', at least as a sort of temporary, political cleavage.[142] The social and economic interests of precarious youth align with those of workers and pensioners in increasingly austere public sectors and immigrant populations (which are also largely precarious), and are deeply imbued in the contradiction in capitalism between capital and labour.

If the New Left of the 1960s and 1970s introduced political issues not captured by class analysis alone, then the GJM and the post-2008 movements bestowed major significance upon class-related issues. Empirical studies based on surveys have suggested that the recession and its management have directly influenced the patterns and volume of protest. Deteriorating economic conditions, eroding labour rights and rising individual-level deprivation incentivise contention.[143] Attesting to the growing significance of class-based contention is the relevance of workers and labour issues in acts of disruption, such as factory occupations and road blockages,[144] as well as in protest participation against the neoliberalisation of the public sector.[145] Constituencies of anti-austerity protest exhibited a distinct social composition. On the whole they are younger and more precarious, more concerned with economic issues and not very embedded in political networks.[146]

During the post-2008 crisis in Europe, alternative forms of trade unionism and new modes in labour mobilisation have been observed at the local and national levels. A minority trend of 'radical political unionism' has either split from the large, mainstream trade unions or formed through autonomous establishment and organisation. Beyond its engagement in social movement activity, it emphasises class struggle and adopts politicised strategies aligned to new left-wing formations that present themselves as outsiders.[147] Anarcho-syndicalism in the European courier sector is a case in point. After the first strikes of UK Deliveroo riders in 2016 and their spillover to France, Spain, Germany, Italy, Belgium and the Netherlands, a number of anarcho-syndicalist unions got involved: in Germany, the Free Workers Union; the Independent Workers' Union of Great Britain; and the National Confederation of Workers in Spain and France. The Spanish and French unions were members of the International Workers' Association, which split in 2018, and have been since members of the Confederación Internacional del Trabajo that emerged out of it. Across countries, cleaners, food industry workers, cab drivers and others have independently organised in small, rapidly growing unions. Although the precarity and atomisation of the gig economy render this sector less prone as a whole to union struggles and power, or to shaping a radical left consciousness, unions have mobilised on issues specific to precarious workers. In doing so, precarious workers' unionism has produced several innovations, including campaigning in vocational schools, sectoral organising, community building and empowerment and consensus democracy in practice, each driven by the particular circumstances of precarious labour or their industry.[148]

Turning to age, since the late 1990s the young have been a central force both within the GJM and in the post-2008 radical movements, including, notably, Jeremy Corbyn's support base and Momentum, Podemos leaders and cadres, SYRIZA, the Occupy movements across Europe and the USA and the movements behind Bernie Sanders. The young have supported old die-hard socialists in large numbers and in diverse ways, reinjecting political force into their historical ideas. The radical youth is profoundly visible today, although things have changed: a more aggressive and austere capitalism in the West has affected the younger generation, who did not grow up enjoying safe labour markets, social security and welfare. In his account of a 'new political economy of youth', Côté explained that 'we should talk about 'youth-as-a-class', because the last two generations, Gen Y and the millennials, are victims of downward social mobility:[149] huge increases in house prices leading to a 'rent generation'; huge amounts of student debt along with a shortage of graduate-level jobs; and rising youth unemployment, sometimes fed by the extension of the retirement age under fiscal austerity programmes.[150] These sources of political grievance have driven lower age cohorts' characteristic radicalism, captured by the 'Generation Left'.[151] Born in an economic climate of crisis and generalised precariousness they understand politics differently than previous generations.

In recent years, students and youth have been tied to poverty, insecurity, lack of prospects, the austerity crisis and exploitation. As part of the New Left they were reacting against 'alienation', 'consumerism', 'bureaucratisation', 'puritanism' and the 'gerontocracy' of European politics. At first at least, youth was not experiencing a crisis of capitalism, which impoverished or adversely affected their ranks on a mass and cross-national scale. On the contrary, the post-war welfare systems that existed until roughly the 1980s allowed for substantial social mobility among working-class students, many of whom formed successive generations of technicians. There was a widespread (although not easily specified) sense that societies raised on capitalist abundance were problematic, and this pervaded intellectuals and the young during the 1960s.[152] On the other hand, as Goran Therborn pointedly observed in emphasising the lack of a generational divide, as in the 1960s, in Argentina, Portugal, Greece and Spain during the 2010s young activists protested alongside their parents.[153] Public sectors hit by austerity in bailed-out debtor countries meant a higher number of retirees hit by poverty and insecurity in light of pension reform.

We can observe a similar pattern for intellectuality and its relation to class and materiality. Intellectuals were first seen as the basis for renewing the left in the realignments and schisms that occurred in 1956 and thereafter, reflecting the concept of 'newness' through the growing, theoretical and popularised importance accorded to agency.[154] Both students and intellectuals arrived at militant positions, being decisive allies of the workers, without any meaningful pull from organised political forces.[155] By the end of the Long '68 and in the light of economic crisis, Foucault claimed that the left intellectual encountered specific, 'non-universal' problems, and in this way came 'closer to the proletariat'.[156] The encounter was realised because intellectuals, more specifically academics, began engaging in 'real, material, everyday' struggles through their work within circumscribed domains. By extension, they frequently confronted the same enemy as the working classes, 'the multinational corporations, the judicial and police apparatuses, the property speculators, etc.'[157]

Shifting forward to today, intellectuals are even closer to the proletariat due to the neoliberalisation of the university sector and the prioritisation of laissez-faire logic in education since the 1980s. Gradually, but clearly by the 2000s, the global and European university sector has exhibited certain trends: more precarious positions of employment leading to the replacement of tenured with contingent faculty; an expansion of the private college and university sector; online education and a generalised inclination to vocational, labour market-targeted training; casting students as customers through a clientele-based, private sector approach, while introducing annual evaluations and merit pay for faculty to cultivate a competitive environment and limit promotions; following new management approaches of assessing outcomes-based performance, often through narrowly quantified target-based indicators; and increased reliance on external, competitive research funding that has been decreasingly forthcoming at the university level. These developments have driven the 'proletarianisation of the professoriate' constraining the very horizons for developing scholarly capacity and social creation.[158] Between the 1960s and today, the left intellectual and student have increasingly become, in Foucault's terms, more 'specific', namely more integrated into the struggles of the lower and middle classes and multiple other oppressed groups. Newness, or rather structural change, can be registered in as much as the materialist instinct is now more than ever before entrenched in intellectuality and young age, as well as in other groups such as public servants, women and pensioners.

A distinguishing factor in the twenty-first-century movements and protests globally is that they involve the (impoverished) middle class more than before. This same middle class in the 1960s and 1970s was a beneficiary of the systemic structures it is now criticising.[159] Because of welfare and healthcare retrenchment and the downsizing of public sectors, new groups have emerged as a large organised crowd for agitation and propaganda. Since about the 2008 financial crisis, they include public sector employees, pensioners and other ex-beneficiaries of state subsidies. This is not to say that one cannot find middle-class groups in the 1960s Radical Left in Europe (students, professionals). Though as a large organised group and as a space for agitation and propaganda, these groups are for the first time engaged in contention en masse.

For movements, then, can we contend that their radical subject changes over time? No, given workers and students, various sectional groups, intellectuals and the middle-class mix across the three mobilisation waves of the Long '68, the GJM period and post-2008. Yes, because how they are aggregated into the form resistance takes, its coherence or fragmented nature, has developed into a large mass of citizens with common enemies – neoliberalism and austerity, social insecurity and post-democracy.

RETROSPECTIVE

If the multitude is important, if emergent publics are all-encompassing, then this is so at least in terms of the increased and reaccelerating multitude of struggles since the 1960s in which radicals are engaged. The Radical Left organises through multiple methodologies. Physical and organisational settings and mobilisation experiences among activists are numerous and diverse and a diachronic feature on the Radical Left, but this is not a European particularity. It is a global commonality. The spectrum of activism ranges between the collective and the individual, the institutional and the cultural; from violent, disobedient and aggressive to peaceful; from secretive to open, pluralist to particularistic, confrontational to consensual, and vertical to horizontal. Additionally, in the 1960s and 1970s, during the GJM and post-2008, new social forces and new issues entered the field of protest. Each time the mobilising subject has not been the traditional working class, or at least not the only one. The key tensions that are internal to movement demarcations and contrasts are disaggregated into the analytical dimensions of organisation in Table 5.1, summarising the narrative developed over Chapters 3–5. Altogether, they posit that distinct mobilisation waves entail particular types of tensions depending on intertwined processes in the socioeconomic context, such as generational change and the global spirit of the times. Because new structures, procedures and compositional profiles appear or old ones re-emerge in every subsequent wave, division lines are drawn and redrawn in organisational practice. Most of these tensions, in columns two and three of Table 5.1, manifest themselves concretely in a particular fashion each time.

Yet, every subsequent mobilisation wave includes both emerging sectional interests and the archetypical collective subjects of the 1960s. It includes disruptive action and solidarity-based initiatives – both the utilisation of entrenched protest repertoires and innovative or unprecedented practice. During our time frame and between periods of 'newness', what has been reconfigured the most in the case of radical organisation is the centrality or prominence of certain ways of doing politics on the left: the salience, and intellectual and political legitimacy, of organisational forms within a broad political space, whether guerrilla tactics, uncivil protest, decentralisation and horizontality, hierarchy or spontaneity. In real time, the old and the new almost always coexist in radical organisational practice during the peak of mobilisation cycles.

Table 5.1   Summary of organisational demarcations inside Radical Left movements in western Europe

Social movement organisations	Tensions within the Radical Left	Periods of 'newness'/cases
Structures	Verticality vs. horizontality	Long '68 – New Left vs. communists and social democrats GJM years – parties respond to movements post-2008 – 'movement parties' (e.g. Podemos, SYRIZA)
	Mobilisation in national vs. international arena	GJM and post-2008 – glocal shift and regionalisation of movement targets
	Social media vs. on the ground work	Post-2008 – spontaneity and mass appeal but short life of Occupy movements
	Secretive vs. transparent	Long '68 – radical environmentalism, urban guerrillas vs. others GJM and post-2008 – radical environmentalism and Antifa vs. pro-democracy and anti-austerity movements
Procedures	Centralism versus decentralisation	Long '68 – anarchism and left libertarian movements vs. orthodox communists and their ancillary structures
	Majority vs. consensus	GJM – anarchism and citizenism during Social Forums and Occupy raise practical and strategic issues
	Representation (vanguardism) vs. participation (direct democracy)	Long '68 – communist and socialist centralism vs. anarchist and libertarian left
	Confrontational vs. consensual	Long '68 – guerillas GJM – performative violence Post-2008 – precarious organising vs. mainstream trade unions
	Prefiguration vs. institutional tactics	GJM – crisis of prefigurative politics: RLPs emerge in 2000s Post-2008 – Occupy's short durability, more focus on political organisation
Composition/ radical subjects	Students vs. workers	Long '68 – generational gap, hostile exchanges but also linkage gradually
	Middle class vs. working class	Long '68 and subsequently – intermediate/technical strata increasing and diversifying (new classes), changing class analysis Post-2008 – public sector workers, impoverished middle class, pensioners, a precarious youth/student body
	Young vs. old	Long '68 – young radicals (students) criticising and reproached by established Left Long '68, GJM and post-2008 – recurring 'left generations' but generational divide mostly in Long '68 Long '68 and subsequently – intellectuality becoming more resonant with class

PART III

Past and Present of European Radical Left Parties

6
Radical Left Party Identities in Motion

INTRODUCTION

As we have seen, ideological tensions have diachronically played out between binaries such as reform and revolution, class and identity, the state and its outside, or in this book's idiom, co-optation and resistance. Here, we pursue this problematic in mapping the evolving Radical Left party family since the Long '68. In all, we return to the ideas of democracy, anti-capitalism and anti-neoliberalism, solidarity and internationalism that were previously dealt with from the perspective of movements. To interpret how RLP identities resonate in political conflict, we try to situate parties within their national party systems and the competitive dynamics of electoral democracy where this conflict occurs. A pertinent task is to ask how time and conjuncture differentiate party identity as conceived relationally, that is, with respect to other partisan identities in society. More specifically, we need to examine the processes of electoral change since the 1970s such as social cleavage realignment or dealignment and the recomposition of European party systems.[1] This perspective has been adopted across Parts I and II, looking initially at the Cold War years and then beyond them.

Part III turns to internationalism by focusing, as with the movements, on the questions of war, peace and immigration. As in Chapter 3, the issue is taken further by looking at European integration. The regional dimension of the societies, economies and political systems of European countries became increasingly important during the 1990s and 2000s, as EU legislation began to pervasively bind national economic and legal systems. In terms of public opinion this process of 'deepening' has been accompanied by a shift from a 'permissive consensus' to a 'constraining dissensus'.[2] Today this new reality is clearly evident in the shadow of Brexit.

ELECTORAL DEMOCRACY, PARTY SYSTEMS AND THE RADICAL LEFT

What has changed between the 1960s and today in the ideological universe of RLPs cannot be overestimated. Obviously, the Radical Left has had different histories across western Europe, which resist summary presentations amid country-by-country specificities. Nevertheless, trends in most parts of this region begin with the two main strands on the Radical Left that have existed since the early twentieth century: communism and social democracy. In political science one cannot find a typology of party families which does not distinguish between these two lefts, but over the long term the labels communism and social democracy have evolved both in their meaning and their place as political visions within the broader political space. These two party groups were competing against one another, particularly where the bulk of aggregate volatility took place primarily between groups of parties either on the left or the right side of the ideological spectrum, and much less in terms of electoral transfers across the two blocs of the party system.[3]

In western Europe, both communism and social democracy remained committed to the new order arising after 1945 when the market system was tempered by political power and the state was ascribed a protective role over society in opposition to the laissez-faire approach. In this way, as Claus Offe underlined, both groups disclaimed radical hopes for an end to capitalism, although both also diverged sharply and contrasted in policy spirit with the predominant paradigm of the pre-war period.[4] For both, class-centred politics was a constant of their self-definition.[5] CPs accepted the parliamentary road to socialism and aimed to present themselves as political actors who fully respect the constitutional regime. There is a rational pattern of co-optation into the post-war consensus, as summarised by Hobsbawm: 'the history of communism in the developed economies of the west has been the history of revolutionary parties in countries without insurrectionary prospects'.[6] Nevertheless, the lines of division between the two lefts historically amounted to nothing less than an (intra-Left) cleavage. This cleavage reproduced the major strands of left radicalism since the Russian Revolution (1917) – its main expressions previously being social democracy and anarchism – which remained as such until the social democratic mutation.[7]

In the first half of the twentieth century, because of the victory of the Bolsheviks and the subsequent creation of strong CPs and eventually communist regimes in many parts of the world, debates about social democracy were about whether to reform or transform capitalism. In spite of coalitions, common fronts and convergence over Keynesian policy, until well after the 1960s the debate between CPs and SDPs focused on projecting two competing economic systems, each side outlining its own ideal system's benefits and identifying flaws in the other. SDPs crucially differed on foreign policy, as most of them were hostile to the USSR or at best reserved. The decision of the SPD at its Bad Godesberg congress in 1959 'to break with Marxism' reverberated beyond the confines of Germany, and Keynesianism triumphed over Marxism as the ideological and policy toolkit of Western social democracy. Gradually, and depending on the case, SDPs would also shift towards support for the West, NATO and the EU, in most cases by the 1990s.[8]

It's more than clear how developments in capitalism and geopolitics brought about a crisis in both communism and social democracy by the 1960s. This 'double crisis' of the Left explains the beginning of an identity shift, which, as suggested by Geoff Eley, is rather ironic: 'just as Western CPs sought to shed the Soviet handicap by remaking themselves in the social democratic image, most notably via Eurocommunism, social democracy of the established kind became politically a dead end'.[9] We will cover the Eurocommunist moment in more detail later, but it is important to note it here. Both of the ideologies and identities sprouting out of the intra-Left schism of the revolution years were discredited by the 1970s. This was tantamount to the early stages of each one's historical defeats.

Focusing on party systems reminds us how drawn out this crisis can be. Among other things, RLP identity has been affected by how radicals responded to or behaved during the introduction of new ideological cleavages since the 1960s. In the 1970s, NSMs influenced western European party systems in three major ways: by producing programmatic demands and issue dimensions located outside of the realm of traditional controversies over economic issues and which various parties gradually incorporated; by spawning left libertarian parties and GPs as well as a plethora of revolutionary parties and many urban guerrilla groups; and by initiating debates on intra-party democracy.[10]

The emergence of left libertarian parties and GPs in the 1960s, 1970s and 1980s came from central and northern Europe. Today these comprise the predominant profile on the western European Radical Left. Left libertarian parties first appeared in Scandinavia (the Socialist People's Party in Denmark, 1959, and Norway, 1961), France (various forces in the 1960s and 1970s) and the Netherlands (the Political Party of Radicals, 1968) under the label of a New Left. Afterwards, GPs attracted considerable electoral support in Austria, Belgium, Switzerland and West Germany. This was not a southern European phenomenon where other cleavages initially took the place of the northern European 'new politics' conflict line: in Cyprus the national question, in Greece, Portugal and Spain the dictatorships and parliamentary democracy itself.

Left libertarian parties criticised the post-war logic of social development, were opposed to having economic growth as the centrepiece of the political agenda, advocated more and non-elitist democracy, combined libertarian commitments with egalitarian concerns and were not satisfied with the bureaucratic welfare state. The policy expression of their 'newness' came through positions that place these parties in opposition to 'established politics': the institutions of government, the unresponsive bureaucracy and the political culture of the old left-wing parties. Democracy, and the design of society as a whole, was, like in the current period of democratic crisis, a core issue for both the left libertarians and the early GPs. For the latter, the *fundis–realos* conflict during the 1980s centred on the significance of institutional opposition to non-institutional political action. This conflict within GPs concerned, among other things, how they should organise and mobilise, and more broadly how they should engage in modern politics. The conflict cross-cut any left–right distinctions that existed in some of these parties; many Greens saw themselves as part of the left although (still) not the socialist movement.

For GPs, where from the start it was claimed that the left–right divide was redundant and had to be transcended (as in the British and French Greens), the *fundis–realos* conflict issues remained unconnected to talk about visions of socio-economic transformation.[11] In the German and French GPs, until the 1990s there were strong eco-socialist tendencies that either wanted to tie the parties more closely to the socialists or social democrats and emphasise non-ecological social issues, or which detested the option of coalition building and insisted on political autonomy. Many GP activists and militants originally came from the left, although they denounced political systems and traditions, presented themselves as advocating 'new politics' and were often disappointed by the CPs or SDPs.[12]

The other manifestation of left-wing realignment in the Long '68 and its aftermath, beyond the left libertarians, went in a revolutionary direction; chiefly, Trotskyism and Maoism.[13] Trotskyism's fate was sealed largely by the historical and immoral role assigned to it by Stalin. Nevertheless, Soviet politics evolved, and with it so did the communist image of Trotskyism:

> from a 'right' deviation of communism in the late 1920s to a criminal non-ideology in the time of the purge trials to bourgeois nationalism/Zionism at the end of Stalin's life to Khrushchevian half-hearted revision to a 'left' deviation of communism in Brezhnev's time, with a growing variety of nuances among non-Soviet communists.[14]

During the 'newness' of the 1960s and 1970s, a new generation of Trotskyists was in part shaped by the changing legacy of Stalin, which had come into question, making the issue of Trotskyism a continuing problem for the CPs.[15] Otherwise, Trotskyism was grouped with other 'petty bourgeois', 'ultra-left' deviations, such as anarchism, the New Left and Maoism, and was accused of 'adventurism' or 'the substitution of revolutionary phrases for deeds'.[16] The rhetorical manifestations of such divisions are discussed in Chapter 7. Within these political circles, and in many western European trade unions, debate emerged in the late 1960s over whether workers' control over production and distribution processes was the only true socialism, which was very different from having one leader in charge of decision-making and a centralised economic system.

Maoist parties had formed in the 1960s in almost all Western countries and beyond, mostly splintering from CPs. Conflict between the Maoists and Trotskyists occurred in various places. The two currents did resemble each other in highlighting the revolutionary potential in the peasant masses in former colonial countries, denying the possibility of ceasing power peacefully and operating incrementally thereafter, and in terms of fragmentation and reactionary behaviour against potential allies.[17] Still, the Maoists all shared a physiognomy comprising elements that differentiated them from everyone else on the Radical Left. They saw the role of 'oppressed people' and 'oppressed countries' in fighting imperialism as equally important for achieving socialism as the role of the working class. They also employed a broadly populist language, often replacing 'the working class' with 'the people' in their rhetoric, and thus being accused of 'substitutionism'. To put it as simply as possible, the historical role ascribed by Marxism to the working class was widened through the lens of Third Worldism to include many more social groups. All of the main Maoist parties propagated against the CPs, which were accused of having been taken over by revisionism, either since the 1930s or at some point in the two decades thereafter: 'for many Western European radicals, China "was a stick with which to beat the undynamic Communist Party at home"'.[18]

In most of their western European and North American variants, Maoist parties were composed mostly of former students who easily engaged in competition with each other. Without substantive and long-lasting connections to the proletariat, Maoist parties typically failed to reach workers in any sustained fashion.[19] For the Trotskyist parties that had formed an International in 1938, which by the 1960s had undergone multiple quarrels and splits, sectarianism has been widely explained by the movement's social and political isolation. Callinicos specified this point with more accuracy, arguing that the movement's very small size combined with its 'historic isolation from mass working class struggles' translated into 'the inability to influence events … itself likely to encourage splits: since there is no way of settling differences in analysis or policy by practical tests, why not break away?'[20]

The revolutionary parties had a strong intellectual identity, and this explains why in some instances sectarianism arose and fragmentation was divisive enough to limit an otherwise more obvious presence in society and politics. Ideological detail matters more in the face of extensive analytical exercises, as reflected in the culture and structures of some parties. When it is combined with the falsehood of ideological purity or ideological correctness it turns into sectarianism. Hobsbawm made a relevant observation: 'There is the danger of establishing a ghetto in which intellectuals, while claiming to operate within the working class movement, really address each other, often in terms which are incomprehensible to anyone outside.'[21] On many occasions, sectarianism reflected the political manifestation of the Freudian psychological term 'narcissism of small differences', whereby competing groups would each claim the moral high ground of principles. As Chomsky argued, sectarianism was sometimes the outcome of concerns about oppression, authority and rights that became important in the 1960s taking an unhealthy form, although not commonly and not inevitably.[22] Not only did resistance become futile by blurring a coherent radical identity in society, spreading the seeds of revolutionary marginality and incapacitating Maoist alliances, collective advance and impact on political conflict, it was also damaging to the very lives of some of those involved: its record of tragic events among Maoist protagonists includes nervous breakdowns, suicides and defamations.[23]

Between the 1960s and today, Maoist and Trotskyist parties had a mild and differentiated role in shaping western European party systems. Unlike the Maoists, whose significance was notable in the social movements much more than it was for parties, Trotskyists had a double effect, although this varied from country to country. In the UK and France, Trotskyism (like the New Left as a whole) played a key role in sustaining radical politics, both extra-parliamentary action and within sections of the labour or socialist movement through entryism. After Mao's death in 1976, many small Maoist parties turned away from China and towards Albanian socialism, while by the end of the 1970s most formal Maoist parties across the West fell into decline. Some of them, as in Belgium and Norway, tried to become 'normal' CPs and disassociate themselves from the Third World's crimes, which had begun to marginalise them completely. Today Trotskyists are marginal within the broader party family, but there are numerous organisations which operate in the name of Trotskyism: John Kelly estimated that there were around 22 British Trotskyist organisations of various particularities in existence in 2017, and internationally he identified 23 Fourth Internationals.[24] In the UK, a presence inside the national parliament has only been achieved through the Labour Party. The Trotskyists are important at the municipal level and have played a critical, leading role in many struggles: the Vietnam Solidarity Campaign (1966–71); the Anti-Nazi League (1977–81); the movement of Rock against Racism and subsequently the organisation Love Music Hate Racism (1976–); the Anti-Poll Tax Federation (1989–91); and the STWC (2001–).[25]

By the GJM years, as their autonomous strength faded in most countries, Maoists and Trotskyists entered democratic socialist coalition parties – like SYRIZA, British Left Unity, the Portuguese Left Bloc, Die Linke in Germany and Podemos in Spain. In some countries, notably in Greece, they have an important role in the extra-parliamentary left (Anticapitalist Left Cooperation for the Overthrow, ANTARSYA). In the UK, 'thousands of former revolutionaries who became disillusioned by the collapse of the movements of the 1960s and 1970s' joined the Labour Party in the 1980s under the umbrella of Tony Benn's influence. Trotskyists rejoined the Labour Party under Jeremy Corbyn in 2015.[26] But it is France which remains the only country where Trotskyism commands autonomous status in left-wing presidential politics, essentially leading the organised movements of the historical anti-capitalist left. The reasons for the French exception can be loosely summarised as including Trotsky's concrete connections with French socialist militants during his exile in France between 1933 and 1934, subsequently consolidating a lasting political cultural current within the left-wing vote; the many organisational faces or nuclei of Trotskyism in the political sphere, a 'multiple Bolshevism' addressing differentiated social milieus and ideological spaces and the incredible capacity and sophistication of the Trotskyist tradition in the practice of revolutionary organisation.[27]

Revolutionary and left libertarian parties have produced new competition for the established Left since the 1970s. But new parties have been a more systematic feature for the Radical Left compared to the SDPs and GPs. Tables 6.1 and 6.2 inspect the aggregate and disaggregated levels of 'newness' for the three pillars on the Left to estimate how interparty competition therein has (or has not) become increasingly unstable and unpredictable. New parties are defined as new entrants in the electoral arena that have contested national elections for the first time and obtaining 1 per cent or more of the vote.

Table 6.1 Aggregate number of new SDPs, CPs/RLPs and GPs per western European country (1960–2019)

Country	Social democracy	Communist/socialist	Green	Total
Austria	1	0	4	**5**
Belgium	4	1	2	**7**
Cyprus	2	1	1	**4**
Denmark	2	5	3	**10**
Finland	0	2	2	**4**
France	2	7	3	**12**
Germany	0	2	2	**4**
Greece	7	6	2	**15**
Iceland	3	4	5	**12**
Ireland	2	5	1	**8**
Italy	8	6	2	**16**
Malta	2	0	1	**3**
Netherlands	0	1	2	**3**
Norway	0	3	1	**4**
Portugal	7	9	2	**18**
Spain	1	7	1	**9**
Switzerland	0	3	3	**6**
United Kingdom	2	0	1	**3**
Total	**43**	**62**	**38**	**143**

Source: Holger Döring and Philip Manow, Parliaments and Governments Database (ParlGov): Information on Parties, Elections and Cabinets in Modern Democracies, development version, 2019. Party family classifications based on ParlGov codes.

Notes: Only parties winning *more than 1.0 per cent vote share* in elections. In ParlGov, mergers and party splits count as a new party 'if the (largest) predecessor party won less than 75% of the combined vote of all preceding parties in the last election'. Otherwise such cases only count as renames not as new parties.

Table 6.2   New RLPs per decade per western European country (1960–2019)

Country	1960s	1970s	1980s	1990s	2000s	2010s	Total
Austria	0	0	0	0	0	0	0
Belgium	0	1	0	0	0	0	1
Cyprus	0	0	0	1	0	0	1
Denmark	1	0	1	1	2	0	5
Finland	0	0	1	0	1	0	2
France	1	2	0	2	1	1	7
Germany	1	0	0	1	0	0	2
Greece	0	0	1	0	1	4	6
Iceland	1	0	1	0	0	2	4
Ireland	1	0	1	2	0	1	5
Italy	1	2	0	1	1	1	6
Malta	0	0	0	0	0	0	0
Netherlands	0	0	1	0	0	0	1
Norway	1	2	0	0	0	0	3
Portugal	0	4	3	2	0	0	9
Spain	0	2	1	0	0	4	7
Switzerland	0	2	0	1	0	0	3
United Kingdom	0	0	0	0	0	0	0
Total	7	15	10	11	6	13	62

Source: ParlGov. Party family classifications based on ParlGov codes.

Notes: Only parties winning *more than 1.0 per cent vote share* in elections. In ParlGov, mergers and party splits count as a new party 'if the (largest) predecessor party won less than 75% of the combined vote of all preceding parties in the last election'. Otherwise such cases only count as renames not as new parties.

Relationally, the total number of new RLPs since the 1960s has been higher than both the Social Democrats and Greens (almost double the latter). We could understand this as a more unstable pattern of politics on the Radical Left rather than the centre-left, which is the product of many factors, including Cold War dynamics, the impact of the USSR's fall, deeper historical divisions and national institutional factors. Looking behind the numbers, we can say that almost none of the new RLPs emerging since the 1960s can be classified as a CP, although this does not mean Marxism-Leninism has been entirely out of the picture, since both Maoists and Trotskyists self-defined as Marxists-Leninists.

In certain countries no new actors emerged. In Malta, the UK and Austria (effectively also in Cyprus, the Netherlands and Belgium) new

RLPs have not appeared or were subsequently absorbed into other, established organisations. These are frozen party systems with a 'fundamental bias towards stability' that characterises western European party systems as a whole, although less so the Radical Left than the Greens and the social democrats.[28] Still, in many countries the same actors of the 1960s or 1970s or their successors dominate the political landscape. In these cases, the organisational anchor point of left radicalism in the national party system has remained the same throughout, and identities carry on through subsequent reconstitutions. Looking at trends over time, the most 'populous' decade was the 1970s, followed by the 2010s and then the 1990s and 1980s. New RLPs appear in the Long '68, the GJM years and in the post-2008 crisis period, as well as during the years of intensified Soviet crisis and dissolution. That is, across and between periods of 'newness'.

The data should be read primarily as concerning the Radical Left's identity fragmentation within the party system in a relational way. Data collection issues prevent the inclusion of all new parties. A loose view, however, which becomes clearer in subsequent chapters, allows us to underline the marked difference between the 1960s and 1970s and the 2010s. Twenty years before the end of the Cold War was the time of heavy and bitter splintering in virtually all radical spaces of European party systems. After 1990, sects, groups and micro-parties converged into a unified organisational whole. There is therefore a universalising tendency between distinct organisations analogous to the rhetorical patterns reviewed earlier. It is quite different from the bitter antagonism of the Long '68, when more historical cleavage lines ran through the Radical Left.

However, in the Long '68 'newness' did not only arrive through new parties and movements, fragmenting the identities of RLPs in party systems. It also came from within the universe of established CPs. From 1973 until the 1980s, the Italian communists under Enrico Berlinguer, the French communists under Georges Marchais and the Spanish communists under Santiago Carillo embraced what came to be known as Eurocommunism. They held various meetings across Europe, issued common statements and made collective interventions. Their ideological horizon was also largely adopted by some Scandinavian CPs, the British communists and the Greek Eurocommunists, which had split from the KKE (Communist Party of Greece) in 1968. Eurocommunism was three things overall. It was an electoral strategy aimed at appealing to the middle classes, an ideological revision that moved away from Marxism-Leninism (both as interpreted and practised in the USSR) and it was a sign of increasing disaffection with the USSR in the West.[29] This meant the espousal of an interpretation of democracy and human rights that differed greatly from the orthodox line. There came a subsequent acceptance of political pluralism, both during and after the period socialism was built. Southern European countries already had their own social democracy by the 1970s, which was labelled as communist and approached the democratic state with a positive, 'constructive' attitude, revealing a conviction that although it was controlled by the ruling classes it could still be democratised and serve popular interests if the balance of power within it was appropriate.[30]

The Eurocommunists' fate was sealed by the early 1980s. Although they emphasised the goal of electoral victory and chose strategies targeted at winning over non-communist votes, the result was far from grand electoral victories in the medium term. Between the elections of the 1970s and the early 1980s, the PCI, PCF and PCE (Communist Party of Spain) each lost about a million votes, while the KKE Interior halved its vote share.[31] By the mid-1980s, there was no such thing as Eurocommunism being practised as an alliance between parties. Yet, we must note that the paradigmatic turn away from revolution and towards reform, and the ideological spirit of the Long '68, was also present within the communist movement: 'A socialist strategy remained the ultimate and desirable goal, but the road map leading in this direction no longer contained instructions for sudden, radical breaks and associated cataclysmic events but, instead, a series of intercalated structural reforms which, in due time, would bring about the same result.'[32]

THE END OF ANTI-CAPITALISM?

During the 1990s a course of recomposition began. It had its roots in the divisions and failures emerging from the 1980s, which was nothing short of a crisis already, not least in the Soviet Communist

Party itself.[33] After the fall of the Berlin Wall, among other associated, dominant notions of historical development, it was popularly claimed that the battle of ideologies had ended and with it history itself.[34] In this 'final' ideological hegemony, it was widely claimed, liberalism emerged victorious. Communism (along with fascism) was said to have failed, liberty was the opposite of socialism, class was unimportant and eastern Europe finally became 'democratic' and could be incorporated into Western 'normality'. Policies encouraging central planning and speaking in the name of the working class raised suspicion. To be as clear as possible: the most seismic discontinuity since the 1960s was the end of the USSR and its impact on global political developments and on RLPs.

Foremost, this is evidenced within party systems rather than looking at post-1990 movements alone, such as the GJM, which had distinct dynamics involving anarchism and autonomism. A fundamental reshaping of the Radical Left took place where qualitatively new organisations or permutations of existing ones developed. There was an assortment of immediate responses to the end of 'actually existing socialism'. What they had in common was that the outcomes were produced by the internal balance of power between the Stalinist and orthodox segments and the reformist or 'renewal left'. National *perestroikas* were pursued by reformers in almost all parties and many of their advocates eventually ended up either in New Left or non-left-wing politics.

Orthodox parties in which pro-Soviet forces predominated rejected the failure of communism and continued to prioritise a socialist transformation in the means of production. These parties initially included the Portuguese Communist Party (PCP), the PCF in France, the Danish Communist Party, the Belgian Communist Party (PCB) and the KKE in Greece. The PCF and the PCB eventually shifted to change their initial interpretation. The Party of Communist Refoundation (Rifondazione) in Italy and the PCE in Spain and most of the Scandinavian parties in the 1990s argued that socialism had failed because it degenerated into Stalinism, and that the original principles of Marxism had to be redrawn and enriched with insights from the struggles of movements and local groups. Parties whose conclusion was that the collapse of communism in eastern Europe represented

165

a failure of communism itself abandoned all communist credentials and transformed into non-CPs of the Left. These were the PCI in Italy, which became an SDP, the Communist Party of Great Britain, the Communist Party of Finland and the Communist Party of the Netherlands.[35]

An identity crisis for the communist left was, moreover, coupled with its profound electoral weakening. The family's aggregate electoral strength fell from 19.1 million votes (9.4 per cent) in 1988 to 11.2 million votes (5.1 per cent) in 1993. Most RLPs lost moderately or heavily and the Radical Left as a political force across Europe was significantly relegated post-1991.[36] The end of 'actually existing socialism' has, since the 1960s, been the key moment of collective change for RLPs. In addition to electoral downsizing, this came in the form of internal conflict about left-wing memory, defeat and the past, ideological challenges and revisions, organisational weakening and fragmentation. The impact of the USSR's fall must be nuanced only in the light of continuing historical facts, of which there are two that are most important. In terms of size, the European Radical Left has been a relatively 'small party family' throughout, only in a few cases consistently getting more than 30 per cent of the vote (e.g. in Cyprus and Italy).[37] In most countries it rarely polled above about 15 per cent and in some countries, such as Austria, West Germany (until unification) and the UK, it never entered parliament as an autonomous force. Soviet dissolution thus did not transform electoral dynamics across most countries between the communists and social democrats. Indeed, the most marked electoral decline for RLPs happened during the 1980s.[38]

Initial responses to and the effects of the Soviet collapse do not of course exhaust the diversity of European RLPs today; things have changed significantly since then. Thus, for the purposes of identifying a political morphology among RLPs in Europe, the distinction between communist and non/post-communist left parties that initially emerged in the aftermath of Soviet collapse is not very useful. The last ten years or so have in many ways been unique because of the global financial crisis and its European implications, uniting RLPs around anti-austerity. This has effectively meant opposing legislation that seeks to restructure the public sector and its finances, cut back on welfare provisions, privatise public utilities and commodify the commons. Compared to the 1990s, during the crisis RLPs have been markedly different – a revitalised space, both in terms of electoral performance and movement mobilisation.

The interpretation of the post-2008 crisis by most RLPs – the communist and workers' parties excepted – is geared, as in the movements, towards a critique, not of capitalism and its underlying social processes but of the symptoms of neoliberalism: financialisation, rising inequality, precarity, welfare state retrenchment and the commodification of public goods.[39] The overall policy profile amounts to 'a new Keynesianism', combined with a plea for democratising the channels of political representation and, since the rise of the climate movements, addressing the climate emergency. One should also note that many of the battles the Radical Left has fought successfully, by proposing legislation around which majority coalitions formed (e.g. in Portugal and Greece), often concern 'new politics' issues. These issues range from domestic violence, civil rights and guarantees, the fight against racism and discrimination, gay marriage and other more localised issues, such as bullfighting in Portugal and Spain.

To add another parameter of evolving political dynamics, along the way technological development has also had implications for the Left in the context of party systems. The digital revolution played into the emergence of pirate parties and their rise since the early 2000s. This has been an uneven phenomenon limited to continental and northern Europe, where the issue was most salient. In all the cases of newly formed pirate parties they have been anti-authoritarian, aiming to enhance civic liberties, to give open access to culture through the internet and to fight or resist 'institutional corruption' and the influence of corporations. Their roots lie in internet activism and protest against digital copyright law. Although pointing to the malfunctions of capitalism, pirate parties are predominantly middle-class organisations and avoid using anti-capitalist rhetoric or putting forward ideas about extensive redistribution: 'pirate politics merely tweaks the logic of existing regimes.'[40] Statistical analysis of electoral survey data has shown that the prime driver of voting for pirate parties has been political distrust, and interviews with Pirate Party activists illustrate that they do not self-define in left–right terms.[41] In what ways then, if any, has this party family been challenging RLPs?

In those countries where pirate parties did become an important competitor in the party system, they had a twofold influence, which is very time-specific. Sections of the protest vote going to RLPs were drawn to the Pirates, most evidently in Germany. Die Linke and Rosa Luxemburg Stiftung launched a number of meetings and events to understand and respond to this party phenomenon and its implications for the Left's strategy. Die Linke also spent a period testing 'liquid democracy', out of which certain new democratic operations emerged.[42] In Sweden, in terms of both timing and extent, the Left Party, among others, has been influenced by the Pirates' presence,[43] in developing many features and online tools for organising and agenda setting, under the Pirates-initiated pretext of decentralisation and directness as the partisan manifestations of horizontalist politics.[44]

Although with a partial and faded influence, the politics of digital rights responded to emerging puzzles about communicative capitalism, bringing into focus the political economy of piracy and how this can serve as a form of resistance to the media industry and big corporations. Piracy has emerged out of the fundamental conflicts in the contemporary information society, which reshaped competition over material wealth.[45] From this perspective, pirate parties are political manifestations of a systemic phenomenon, with technological development in the free market bringing into opposition the zero-sum logic of multinational and finance capitalism, which is catalytic in diffusing digital science, and the logic of the 'commons' arising from universities and other producers of digital science.[46] This led to the politicisation of issues – access to knowledge, rights to privacy and the meaning of freedom and property in the digital public sphere.[47]

In terms that are more tangible and ongoing, the Radical Left has been confronted by a resurgent radical and extreme right, with many elements and incarnations of right-wing extremism, which has become a key competitor attracting part of the blue-collar working class. The increasing importance of working-class constituencies raises questions that are most relevant to the Left's identity. A 'proletarianisation' of radical and extreme right party constituencies was reported in the 1990s across various European countries. This process has led to the eventual predominance of working-class votes among the far-right social milieu.[48] Without a strong social policy offering, which is virtually impossible under conditions of permanent austerity, welfare chauvinism as a sort of pseudo-socialism has certainly worked electorally. According to empirical tests, support for the radical right decreases the likelihood of electoral success for RLPs significantly.[49] However, RLPs carry some of the blame over the long term. Failure in office on various occasions since the 1990s may have fed the growth of the extreme right, which could more easily claim an 'anti-establishment' identity and sell the narrative of a sold-out or 'like all the rest' left. Nevertheless, the crisis-ridden and marginalisation processes inscribed in European neoliberalism and globalisation have also generated distinct patterns of politics.

SOLIDARITY AND INTERNATIONALISM

Changing historical patterns have also translated into evolving dynamics of solidarity and expressions of internationalism. The struggles of colonialised people across the globe exposed the notion of 'national communism', since national liberation was prioritised over socialist revolution as a necessary stage preceding it. Yet, beyond mainly the PCI and the forces of the New Left, CPs clung to loyalty to an overarching centre focused on the USSR. This demarcated them from the 'internationalist revolutionaries' 'without a country', of the New Left which criticised CPs as 'social democratic' and 'revisionists' being more oriented towards the militancy and strategy infusing the writings of Frantz Fanon on peasant revolutions.[50] Still, the USSR was the self-proclaimed leader of the international peace movement and the most important financier of national liberation struggles across the world. The World Peace Council was at the centre of solidarity struggles among the communists during the entire Cold War period. For the Soviet leadership, pacifism was condemned, and 'as Third World states emerged and national liberation movements consolidated political ideologies, the concept of just war acquired new meaning within anti-imperialist discourse.'[51] That is why the USSR and all the loyal CPs in western Europe took sides in the Arab–Israeli wars and supported military intervention in Afghanistan in

1979. The Soviet invasion of Afghanistan divided the Eurocommunist parties, however – the PCI condemned it explicitly, the PCE hesitantly and the PCF realigned itself away from the 'national road' back to the 'internationalist stance' of the USSR. In doing so, the PCI joined a number of European socialist leaders – Mitterand in France, Papadreou in Greece, Soares in Portugal, Gonzales in Spain, Brandt in Germany – in the pursuit of a Third Worldism distinct from the Soviet one, as well as the backing of Eastern dissent.[52] As historian Basil Davidson pointedly observed, the Eurocommunists shared with the national liberation movements resistance to 'models imposed from outside'.[53]

What effectively differentiated the European and global context of the 1960s and 1970s from the post-1990 climate is primarily the dynamic (and organisational density) of the international peace movement. It was a time that most of the left, including SDPs, rejected European integration, either because of entrenched national traditions, as in the UK, or because of solidarity with the Third World and the EU's free market ideology. But social democracy was divided as well, into the 'right-wing "social democrats"', who supported Atlanticism, nuclear deterrence and European integration' and the ' left-wing "socialists"' who rejected them.[54] As we saw in Chapter 3, since the 1980s little remains the same in terms of how the idea of solidarity and internationalism are mobilised on the ground, as both the nature of wars changes and a unipolar geopolitics emerges. In the 2000s and 2010s, for the Radical Left there are no models to be imposed from outside in situations of war, famine or disaster. In lieu of the pre-existing Soviet, former Yugoslavian, Chinese, Vietnamese, Cuban or other models, no new ones have arisen and, ironic as this might seem, no outside models also means more negative argumentation, rather than a positive, concrete contribution to system change abroad.

On immigration, RLPs are not entirely united in their positions either. Since the 1980s, there has been a gradual but steady rise in the extreme and radical right, which reached a climax in the 2010s and is connected to, although not fully explained by, immigration. On the Radical Left, although for activists and intellectuals pro-immigration is the natural place, from the perspective of party leaders and government officials the issue is more complex. In most European countries, the Radical Left is the most pro-immigration position there is, with all parties declaring vehement opposition to xenophobia, racism and Islamophobia, and participating in struggles, demonstrations and other pro-immigration initiatives, links to anti-racist forums and immigration working groups. At the EU level, the European United Left/Nordic Green Left (GUE/NGL) has launched multiple initiatives and vigorous criticism of the EU's immigration policies and especially immigrant detention centres and conditions therein.

Immigration is fundamentally a neutral policy issue from a partisan perspective, with the exception of its evident association to the rise of the radical right. One can see this in the history of western European politics in the 1960s and 1970s, whereby both parties of the Left and the Right promoted some of the earliest policies to restrict immigration in Europe.[55] For the communists a much-cited historical case of ethnicised representations of social issues is the PCF mayor of Vitry-sur-Seine, Paul Mercieca, who just before Christmas 1980 led communist members and supporters in preventing 300 immigrants from Mali from being rehoused in a hostel in Vitry by disconnecting utilities and smashing the interior of the building. This was called a 'direct action'. A demonstration followed in support of the action in which the PCF's leadership participated.[56] In the April presidential elections of 1981, one of the PCF's campaign slogans was 'Stop immigration, official and illegal'.[57]

The PCF of today is markedly different in its immigration policy, and it was an exception even in the 1970s: for example, compared to Sweden, where both the CP and the social democrats were pro-immigration. Yet, the point remains that nationally and locally, RLPs have particular incentives to withdraw support for the multicultural ideal and restrict immigration. In essence, they face an electoral trade-off due to the different economic impacts of immigration on different segments of the electorate upon which the Left relies. Distinct policies entail costs and benefits for different income categories of the population. Native low-skilled workers lose the most from integrated markets with free movement between them, and given their reliance on publicly subsidised welfare provisions a competitive imaginary against immigrants can be created for jobs, public resources and space. The Left also seeks to 'catch' high-skilled workers and professionals, who typically have less apprehension of immigrants because they are on the 'winning side' of neoliberal globalisation. The radical right has largely cultivated and capitalised on anti-immigrant sentiments among blue-collar workers, and statistical analysis has shown that RLP opposition parties have repositioned themselves on the immigration issue by way of contagion from the anti-immigration forces on the radical and extreme right.[58] RLPs in government – the ongoing government in Spain, the SYRIZA government or German regional governments in coalitions with Die Linke – have behaved in similar ways: immigration from third countries has to be limited and regulated. Deportations by the Left have already occurred plenty of times.

Given the above-mentioned electoral dilemmas and national historical traditions, frictions arise on the issue. The most discussed case is Sahra Wagenknecht's Aufstehen (Get Up) movement, her various interventions for stricter immigration and asylum controls and laws, and the internal conflict inside the German Die Linke which led to her resignation from the party's parliamentary group leadership. Concerns were expressed that the German left-wing support for the 'open border' position, in addition to recognising the right to asylum, was pushing voters away from the party. Unchecked immigration, the narrative goes, increases pressure on Germans seeking work and domestic social systems, benefiting the (then newly emerging German) far-right Alternative for Germany (AfD). Wagenknecht's strategy was to try 'to beat the AfD in its own game', suggesting that the Left has been too consumed with political correctness and identity politics, and should instead refuse to abandon its core base support by not acknowledging their grievances as legitimate.[59]

For Wagenknecht, advocating for open borders is 'the opposite of what is left-wing because it encourages exploitation, threatens community, and undermines popular sovereignty'.[60] In German social democracy, a historical position has been that the rise of Nazism rested upon the impoverishment of the masses which migration can catalyse. This has remained entrenched as the initial and overarching interpretation of the German social democratic approach to 'uncontrolled immigration'. Oscar Lafontaine, once very distinct from Wagenknecht, is a social democratic politician involved in the

Radical Left since the 1990s, who has systematically expressed hostile positions towards the prospect of immigrants coming to Germany, including, as he had argued during the period of German unification in 1989, East German immigrants.[61] The electoralist, constituency-argued logic of politicians like Lafontaine has a historical lineage, although more recently scepticism or straight out anti-immigration by the centre-left and RLPs has been turned into an electoral weapon in opposition to a forceful extreme right and political polarisation over the issue during the post-2008 crisis.

Another important example of strict immigration positions comes from the Netherlands where, in the run-up to the 2019 European elections, the Socialist Party (SP) adopted a more 'harsh' line on asylum and immigration issues. This is partly because, since the 1980s, this party has traditionally emphasised native Dutch workers. The SP's outlook was derived from its origins as a Stalinist-Maoist party which followed the 'theory of socialism in one country' and Mao's 'mass line'. These respectively meant adopting the view that socialism could and should be built within the national state and addressing conservative constituencies with racist outlooks and grievances against immigrants.[62] In both Die Linke and the SP, the line in many ways signals old standpoints that remained present throughout. The Swedish Vänsterpartiet and Danish Socialist People's Party also witnessed internal debates or dissent over the issue. Events in the 2010s led to intensified politics over immigration-related issues, more discussions that are open and more visible disagreements. Divisions emerged over party behaviour towards immigrant communities, candidate selection in parliamentary elections or leadership statements.[63]

Historically, there has been division inside the Left between a form of socialist cosmopolitanism whereby 'workingmen have no country' and the assumption that the working class is a patriotic and authentic force of the nation.[64] The modern transliteration of this tension is between internationalist solidarity with all oppressed communities and pragmatic concern about existing pressures on the wages and social security of national constituencies – primarily, the white working class. Given marginal or non-existing overlap between the radical milieus of the two poles of the spectrum, it is the endurance of dividing lines standing out, not contagion from the radical right.[65]

The lines of division between more and less progressive, or more or less restrictive, policies towards immigration have been diachronic. Currently, we can broadly distinguish between parties with less restrictive policies towards immigration, such as the Left Bloc, SYRIZA and Vänsterpartiet, and more restrictive policies, such as the Dutch SP, or Jan Luc Mélenchon's France Insoumise and (for some time) Jeremy Corbyn, who do not endorse in principle free movement within the EU.[66] We can observe disagreement among RLPs as manifested in roll call votes among members of their group inside the European Parliament (EP).[67] On solidarity, the partisan trajectory is positionally variegated and on average different from the movements of the Long '68 to today. It is through activism primarily, and not institutional politics, that open borders are being promoted on the Radical Left in terms of political work. A significant part of this activism is through the youth, syndicalist, women's and other organisations that operate through parties, like in the KKE and the extra-parliamentary Left in Greece, Podemos and IU in Spain, the Labour Party in the UK or the Scandinavian radical and labour parties. Nevertheless, a dissonance remains between the internationalism of pure and uncompromised solidarity and the pragmatics of leadership, governance and electoral opportunism.

INTERNATIONALISM AND EUROPEAN INTEGRATION

European integration is a key part of the Radical Left's story post-1991, affecting its internationalist prisms. How so becomes clear only when compared with the Cold World period, because the acceleration of integration in a neoliberal direction roughly coincides with the events of 1989–91. In the 1970s, the Eurocommunists aside, all other parties stood against European integration per se by rejecting the Common Market and in most cases any form of association agreement between their own country and the EEC.[68] CPs were concerned that the EEC institutions would consolidate the USA's control over western Europe and play a reactionary role in the Cold War context. The idea of European integration came to the forefront of European politics as a means to reaccelerate economic growth in Europe, as well as a response to the strategy of the USSR that contested the interests of the USA.[69] Since, in many cases, an anti-EEC platform also accrued electoral benefits, a policy of what would today be called full-blown Euroscepticism went easily uncontested in various countries.[70] The EU was equalised with NATO, in both analysis and slogan. It was conceived as the regional, political arm of Western imperialism, behind its pro-peace and cooperation discourse; an economic project of capitalist accumulation with internal contradictions among competing hegemonic states, trumping labour rights and creating obstacles to socialism expanding westwards. Divisions on European integration had already emerged among CPs in the 1950s and 1960s, and in the 1970s they were particularly important because of Eurocommunism.

The PCI, PCE and the Greek KKE Interior in particular approached the question of European integration differently from the orthodox view. It is in this political strain, starting in the aftermath of the first New Left, that a 'soft' Euroscepticism emerged, which did not oppose an altogether different process of integration, and was willing to engage with liberal, intergovernmental and transnational institutions. Its purpose was not to overturn European integration, but rather to democratise its politics and institutions, in the same way as it sought to democratise national institutions. If in the Long '68 something important happened on the communist left in relation to the EU, it was a convergence on the necessity to be represented within EU institutions. With democracy as a key signifier, CPs could not easily refuse representation in the institution that commands parliamentary control over the executive at the EEC level. The first concrete steps to establish relations with the EEC were taken in 1963 by the PCI-controlled Confederazione Generale Italiano dei Lavoratori. By 1971, leading Central Committee members of the PCF issued a positive view of participation in the EP, stating that the communist-socialist coalition programme would include 'participation' in 'European institutions' more broadly.[71]

The Communists and Allies Group in the EP was established in 1973 and initially had two members – the CPs of Italy and France. The group was subsequently joined by the KKE, PCP and PCE in the 1980s. It lacked a coherent group policy and there was no agreed outline towards institutional change in the community, including the questions of direct elections and the EP budgetary powers; the control of multinational corporations and any checks and balances to constrain them; or matters directly emerging from détente and its instrumentalisation between the USA and the USSR.[72] The European policies of communists diverged over support or rejection of the internationalisation of the productive (capitalist) forces, and their broader relations with the USSR were at odds to an extent.[73]

The transformation of the PCI into an SDP after its 1990 congress and its official departure from the European United Left group inside the EP was catalytic in this sense because it led to the group's collapse and redrew lines of division. In this conjuncture, a key moment was the Treaty of Maastricht, ratified in 1992 and introducing, among other things, the criteria necessary for the European Monetary Union (EMU) to be realised. The anti-Maastricht platform which characterised the vast majority of European RLPs contributed to the creation of GUE/NGL and thus fed into launching the most sustained transnational political group of the Radical Left so far. From Maastricht a four-part criticism of the EU's socio-economic terrain emerged:

1. Against the restrictions on national budgetary autonomy as foreseen in the EMU's convergence criteria and the Stability and Growth Pact, and in turn associated with cuts in public and welfare spending.
2. Support for a 'social Europe', where articulate and generous welfare is institutionalised and employment is prioritised.
3. The lack of democratic accountability in relation to the European Central Bank.
4. Popular sovereignty through the EP.

Maastricht signalled a 'new' type of critique by the European Radical Left, expressed extensively and more cohesively across parties of the democratic socialist type, as well as movements in the European sections of the GJM. Maastricht was a key moment in a quadruple sense. It was a watershed in terms of what seeking radical change within the EU meant; it consolidated reformism towards the EU via soft Euroscepticism; it helped produce some unity and consolidate the networking capable of formulating a collective criticism of the EU (as an evolved entity); and it subsequently mounted opposition against the Treaties of Amsterdam and Nice. Launching opposition to Maastricht also meant the re-emergence of national sovereignty as a key theme; this was raised first as a red flag by the French communists more than 30 years before.[74]

At the same time, the evolving relationship between the national and European arenas in radical left politics, which we examined in Chapter 3 in relation to social movements, plays out even more clearly in parties. A sign of historical change has, since the 1990s, been the transnationalisation of radical left politics at the European level. A number of organisations have been formed alongside GUE/NGL. The establishment of the European Left Party (ELP, 2004), the European Anti-Capitalist Left (EACL, 2004), the Northern Green Left Alliance (2004), the Initiative of Communist and Workers' Parties (INITIA-TIVE, 2013) and Democracy in Europe 2025 (DiEM25) all came in the context of realising that regional politics mattered.

The foundation of the EACL may have responded to the ELP's foundation, yet its activity is not as important compared to the Fourth International meetings.[75] Like the orthodox communist and workers' parties, these are more purely internationalist.[76] The ELP, on the other hand, is the Europeanist left, funded largely by the EU. This shows that Europe as a centre of gravity for the international affiliations of RLPs is itself contested, at least between anti-capitalist and democratic socialists. Aiming to reform the EU from within, most forces within the ELP have become increasingly open to broader progressive alliances. These include, although are not limited to, the social democrats. This has been the line of parties such as Rifondazione and the IU in the late 1990s and early 2000s, which, for example, engaged with the campaign initiatives of Ken Coates, a New Left veteran and Labour Party MEP from 1989 to 1998 until his expulsion, and then an independent member of GUE/NGL from 1998 to 1999.[77]

SYRIZA's U-turn in 2015 concerning the Greek bailout was a critical moment. After the 'No' result in the July referendum on whether to accept the offer of Greece's creditors for a bailout, the party sidestepped the result and complied. Some parties left the ELP and founded Now the People, associated with Plan B, for structurally reforming the EU treaties, while warning that if EU elites refuse concessions then disobedience (that is, exit) would be the only option. The Northern Green Left Alliance is an association within the Nordic Council. Some of its parties are also part of NGL inside the EP, which was created during Europe's 'Scandinavian engagement'.[78] Others have joined the Greens. INITIATIVE is largely carried by the KKE in Greece, which organises meetings among some 28 parties, mostly without parliamentary representation, and views the EU as 'an imperialist core'.

At a peak of fragmented transnationalisation today, there are at least five different organisations with European-level coordination outside the EP. Within these five groups there are parties and MEPs who have left the GUE/NGL (such as the KKE); and all of them exclude left-wing forces belonging to the Greens or to the social democrats. At the same time, parties such as Podemos, SYRIZA and DiEM25 are connected with some SDPs or GPs, their delegates participating in initiatives under the framework of organisations such as Friedrich Ebert Stiftung, the think tank of the SPD, or other social liberal entities. Left-wing Euroscepticism is deeply divided in its political expressions and institutionalised at the European level in multiple bodies, hindering the potential of establishing an EU-wide, counter-hegemonic, historical bloc (in Gramscian terms).

The regionalisation of a radical left politics has been a gradual process facilitated by transnational linkages between parties and accelerated by the crisis, and it coincides with an ideologico-political paradigm shift. In the terms of Fritz Scharpf, the Radical Left has shifted from predominantly a critique of 'negative integration', for example, the elimination of custom and trade barriers, towards 'positive integration', which is concerned with the EU's regulatory powers and its potential to intervene in the capitalist economy.[79] At present, the predominant position on the European Radical Left echoes the argument articulated within critical political economy that neoliberal dominance within the EU is relative, contested and explained by the political weakness of European social democracy from Maastricht onwards.[80] It is thus potentially temporary and worth fighting for under a social democratic programme. The Keynesian paradigm updated to fit the current stage of European integration appears to be necessary and sufficient. As a result of this and a number of other political convictions, among the most electorally successful RLPs a soft Euroscepticism has taken centre stage. Although it does suggest far-reaching reforms in all aspects of EU policymaking, it no longer contradicts the spirit of further European integration based on the free market and pooled sovereignty. This broader shift to a softer Euroscepticism materialised for RLPs in the 1990s and 2000s.[81]

By the 2010s, a policy repertoire developed that had been shaped within distinct parties during the 1990s – the French, Italian, Spanish, Portuguese and some of the Scandinavian Radical Left. It arose partly in the context of the European sections of the GJM, and the relevant campaigns of the time had attracted the majority of electorally relevant parties at the transnational level. The predominant democratic socialist proposals among RLPs on the EU are reflected in the policy positions of the ELP and DiEM25, which have an overall orientation of moderating the excesses of the market via intervention from the state, while at the same time rebuilding a 'Social Europe'.[82] This general policy orientation in what concerns the economy comes with a democratic redesign of the EU's architecture, constraints on the financial sector, state-centred environmentalism and more generally a progressive (equally if not more than the social democrats and the Greens) attitude towards 'new politics issues'. Most of the key programmatic positions are addressed in Table 6.3. All of these policies in essence reflect a general conviction that the EU must be a regulatory state, in line with positive views of European integration.

During the immediate aftermath of the eurozone crisis, many argued that to beat austerity Greece or any other country must break free from the euro. This was the broad policy content symbolised in the term 'rupture', which echoed across southern Europe. SYRIZA and many others, however, have insisted on fighting austerity from within the eurozone, thus rejecting the option of exit. Some of its initially prominent party-associated intellectuals, such as Costas Lapavitsas, forcefully defended exit during the bailout negotiations of 2015. In this way, ceding sovereignty, abolishing national currencies or accepting EU law and regulations as supreme prevent a real break with austerity and neoliberalism. In fact, authors like Lapavitsas – an MP only for six months in 2015 – argue that eurozone and

EU membership eliminates the possibility of initiating socially trans-formative policy measures.[83] Others go one step further, arguing that exiting the EU 'also represents a form of internationalism: if the EU is the common enemy of the subaltern classes in Europe, the only way to actually fight is by means of a series of exits'.[84]

Serious threats of an exit have not really been launched by European RLPs, and although sovereignist factions have been strengthened across the board, the crisis has not really increased Euroscepticism

Table 6.3   Main policy positions of the ELP and DiEM25 by domain (2019)

Policy domain	Policy position	
	ELP	DiEM 25
Economy and finance	No to Lisbon Treaty (no constitu-tionalisation of neoliberal order) New pact on growth, full employ-ment and social and environmental protection to replace Stability and Growth Pact Debt redemption for poorest coun-tries and reformulation of World Bank/IMF Structural Adjustment Programmes Opposition to the Transatlantic Trade and Investment Partnership and the USA–EU free market Tax on financial transactions	No to Lisbon Treaty (no constitutionali-sation of neoliberal order) An investment-left recovery and con-vergence programme Break up 'too-big-to-fail' banks European Clearing Union for exchange rates (Keynesian inspired) Universal dividend Pan-European Coordination, to max-imise outcomes across euro and non-euro countries. Tax on financial transactions Opposition to the Transatlantic Trade and Investment Partnership and the USA–EU free market
Social and Environ-mental Policy	EU minimum wage/pension Free universal, public healthcare More investment on alternative energy sources Decrease emissions by 30– 40 per cent until 2020 In support/developing Charter of Fundamental Rights	An Emergency Social Solidarity Pro-gram (housing, anti-poverty, jobs guarantee) EU minimum wage/pension Free, universal, public healthcare More investment in alternative energy sources (and Green agency) Progressive CO_2 tax based on the level of a country's development and emissions.
Foreign Policy	Ending EU military engagement abroad Dissolution of NATO and replace-ment with a new International Coop-erative Security System Opposition to the EU's anti-terror-ism policy Replacement of defence agency with disarmament agency Reform of UN	A foreign policy where non-Europeans are 'ends in themselves' Opposition to the EU's anti-terrorism policy Independence from NATO/anti-NATO

Policy domain	Policy position	
	ELP	*DiEM 25*
Agricultural Policy	Reform Common Agricultural Policy in an anti-neoliberal direction; transform European industrial, agricultural and land-use policy to be environmentally friendly	Reform Common Agricultural Policy in an anti-neoliberal direction; transform European industrial, agricultural and land-use policy from to be environmentally friendly
EU Institutions	Referenda on landmark EU decisions Popular control over EU institutions EP to gain legislative initiative PR electoral system in Euroelections	Popular control over all sovereign authority Democratise macroeconomic management Full transparency (including EU Council, Economic and Financial Affairs Council, European Central Bank and Eurogroup meetings to be live streamed) Constitutional Assembly (within two years) Against EU–Turkey migration deal – raising the issue at the European Court of Justice

Source: Adapted from Richard Dunhpy and Luke March, *The European Left Party* (Manchester: Manchester University Press, 2020), pp. 216–20; European Left Party, Political Document – Reset Europe, Go Left, 2019, www.european-left.org/wp-content/uploads/2019/12/Political-Document-Final-version-EL-Congress-2019.pdf; DiEM, European New Deal, 2019, https://diem25.org/wp-content/uploads/2017/03/European-New-Deal-Complete-Policy-Paper.pdf; DiEM25, The European Union Will Be Democratised, Or It Will Disintegrate, 2019, https://diem25.org/wp-content/uploads/2016/02/diem25_english_long.pdf; DiEM25, The Green New Deal for Europe, 2019, https://diem25.org/wp-content/uploads/2016/02/diem25_english_long.pdf.

beyond mostly confirming the already Eurorejectionist views of orthodox CPs.[85] The year 2015 saw a break among Eurocritical forces, with some actors reasonably feeling the need to differentiate themselves from SYRIZA's 'capitulation' to the austerity demands of Greece's bailout creditors. Yet the majority position is far from advocating an exit. If eurozone exit was discursively on the table in the early 2010s, and various RLP bureaus across Europe were looking into it as an option and weighing the costs and benefits, it was left deep inside the drawers of the rest of that decade. For SYRIZA itself, eurozone exit was never officially a defended political option to begin with.

During the Brexit years, leaving the EU was a minority position in the UK within the space from Labour to its left. The predominant position argued that none of the problems faced, including economic recession, climate change and military conflict, can be resolved on a national basis. Rather, only by creating concrete links across European and international borders can they be addressed.[86] The minority position posited that Britain's future depended much more on the domestic economic policies of future governments and much less on the result of the battle between Brexit and Remain. The minority position was that many aspects of the Labour manifesto under Jeremy Corbyn – such as the renationalisation of public utilities, state support for companies or the adoption of capital controls – would be constrained under EU law. Almost certainly they would have been challenged by the European Commission and European Court of Justice, according to the defenders of nationally based socialist politics.[87] The Left Party in Sweden shifted its long-standing pledge for Swedish exit from the EU and did not campaign for 'Swexit' in the double election of May 2019. In the same European elections in Denmark, one seat went from the hard Eurosceptic Danish People's Party to the Red–Green alliance, a softer critic of the EU. These results are not to be perceived as surprising; as concerns the euro, there are also precedents in the opposite direction of criticising it: in the 1990s, RLPs in Italy, France and Finland contributed to the introduction of the European single currency as junior partners in centre-left governments.[88] In 1992, the Coalition of the Left and Progress, the predecessor of and main party inside SYRIZA, had voted in favour of Maastricht in the Greek parliament.

Reclaiming sovereignty by advocating exit from the eurozone and the EU is projected by those in favour as necessary for meaningful statist regulation of the economy. On the other hand, left sovereignism creates fear that extreme forces will benefit from a resolute Euroscepticism in public opinion. Especially in the event of a series of exits, and more broadly a disintegration process set in motion by Brexit or otherwise, the majority of parties within the Radical Left may worry about an extremist backlash with consequences not worth risking.

RETROSPECTIVE

How have the ideas and programmatic positions of European RLPs developed since the Long '68? Discontinuity has manifested itself above all in the dialectics internal to the radical left space. The prevailing identity on the European Radical Left evolves because the relative position of this political family's historical currents, tendencies or traditions changes. Over the long term, change is significant. Between the 1960s and today, social democracy exited the radical party space and in the 2010s showed some signs of repositioning, most notably in the Labour Party under Jeremy Corbyn, the Scottish National Party's centre-left turn under the leadership of Nicola Sturgeon and the Portuguese Socialist-Radical left coalition. Trotskyism remains fragmented and important in France and (less so) in the UK and Ireland. Stalinism almost died out, and only survives in minuscule forces in Europe outside of parliament, beyond only the KKE's explicit defence of Stalin. Maoism has no distinguishing contemporary theory, and communism is no more than a unifying claim to a past identity. Red–Green alliances, still the stronger in Scandinavia and northern Europe, have effectively expanded southwards, in an analogous way to the environmental, feminist and anti-nuclear movements.

Democratic socialism now claims the vanguard role of this party family, and it becomes what social democracy more or less was, rallying behind it both reformists and anti-capitalists. Whether social democracy is called radical today or not – which depends on the country concerned – does not change its underlying paradigm of state intervention in the economy, guided by demand-driven macro-economics and the political initiative and pragmatism required to do this. Taking everything together, a Eurocommunist heritage, and a reradicalised social democracy, runs through the veins of most contemporary RLPs. It is the counterpart or rather reflection of social movements' anti-neoliberalism, while also incarnated in the softer versions of Euroscepticism predominant today.

RLP adaptation and change in the ideational and programmatic realms appear in historical retrospect as both necessarily familiar and novel or particular. Here we must once again emphasise that the events of 1989–91 created shockwaves, leading to massive change on the Left. Those events changed the global balance of power and shook up the Left in all of its manifestations, putting it on the defensive. Nonetheless, for multiple processes of morphological change in tune with the very compositional patterns of this family, the starting point was the Long '68 (its cultural, social and political manifestations) and the precedent dynamic generated in the 1950s. What prevailed in the 1950s and 1960s was radical dissent from Stalinism and communist orthodoxy. It morphed into Eurocommunism (where the social democratic space was available) or left libertarianism, where the post-materialist/identity cleavages were mature enough to be turned into politics. A long, historical process is at play that incorporates the effects of the USSR's end as the most critical moment, although it cannot be reduced to it. It was then that democratic socialism started climbing up the ideological ladder. Dissent from the Soviet model circulated widely, reformism and Keynesian democratic politics became increasingly consolidated and environmentalism turned into a mass although decentralised movement, which subsequently entered institutional politics.

Finally, changing party systems brings into focus issues that were not treated as significant by the Left or were not previously incorporated into Marxist and critical analysis, at least by parties. The electoral incentive to do so arises in the context of 'new' competitors or neighbours in the form of both movements and parties – whether the left libertarians and the Greens of the 1980s, the pirate parties in the 2000s or the extreme right, particularly in the 2010s. In embodying new social divides, new competitors make it necessary to craft new strategies that previously were not urgently articulated. Each time, this means the RLP is judged anew based on more (and intersecting) issue dimensions than the labour–capital dichotomy.

7

Continuities and Changes
in Radical Left Party Rhetoric

INTRODUCTION

To articulate resistance and fuel mobilisation a political vocabulary is employed within a broader public sphere of diverse, more or less predominant discourses. This chapter inspects how RLPs have been framing their electoral and political mobilisation since the 1960s and during each episode of the New Left examined in the book. The chapter starts by considering the names and labels of CPs and RLPs, their ways of addressing allies or competitors and the key rhetorical signifiers of their identity. Ideological aspects of their operation such as their (de)legitimising impact on the wider political system can be fruitfully addressed in terms of party verbal behaviour.[1]

Bearing in mind that the Radical Left has been increasingly understood as populist, and that this is a relatively new strategy or novel perspective, our subsequent goal is to revisit the question of populist schemata as political language, continuing from the twofold premise of the analysis in Chapter 4: left populism as a diachronic and contested discursive strategy. In the third section we turn to the nexus between socialism and nationalism. In the movements, this becomes clear through the prism of Third Worldism and regional sentiment, blended with anti-capitalist or progressive ideologies. In displaying how the European Radical Left interplays within nationalist and patriotic framings in different historical eras and political settings, we approach nationhood as a schema of framing various types of grievances. The aim is to resist dichotomous and thus very rough understandings of the relationship in question – a nationalist versus a non- or anti-nationalist Radical Left.

ELECTIONEERING, RADICALISM AND PRAGMATISM

Above all, in framing their identity the majority and the most successful parties to the left of social democracy today define and label themselves as 'Radical Left' or simply 'Left'. How has such an all-encompassing definition of 'left radicalism' come about and what preceded it?

Since Lenin and during the whole Cold War period, three doctrines defined the official communist ideology: the 'dictatorship of the proletariat', which marked how socialist society is organised, identifying the transitory political system to communism; proletarian internationalism, briefly discussed in Chapter 3; and 'democratic centralism', examined in Chapter 8, which defines how CPs would organise and mobilise. There were also many other circulating signifiers of western European communist language – 'advanced democracy', 'bourgeois democracy', 'socialism' and 'socialist democracy', 'new type of state', 'undivided popular sovereignty', 'revolution', 'proletariat', 'struggle', 'masses', 'the guiding party' and 'against the rule of the bourgeoisie'. Many of these were slightly modified versions of Slavic expressions found in the communist lexicon in Russia and eastern Europe. Communist discourse centred around the party, the working class and the masses (or 'the people'), against 'imperialists' and 'warmongers', 'tyranny' and 'fascism', 'revisionism' and 'reactionary social democracy'.[2] Words like 'the people' and 'popular' signified both labour and the nation as a whole. In language more than in actual experience, the communists' enemies were both of the other lefts – the social democrats and ultra-left – and the capitalists. This said, the Marxist vocabulary of self-labels, schemas and teleological convictions was shared by the SDPs well after World War II. While, in many cases, the social democrats were clearly anti-communist, some of the main social democratic agents in western Europe – the British Labour Party, the German SDP and the French Section of the Workers' International – still appealed to socialist notions and persuasions, despite internal pulls and pushes.

'Revisionism' was always meant to signal a break with the 'truth' of Marxist 'scientific socialism' and Bolshevik orthodoxy. The original debate on revisionism took place in the 1890s, largely in response to Eduard Bernstein's social democratic formulations as opposed to the revolutionary current in the European labour movement. By the 1940s and 1950s, revisionism was used to defend a Soviet and Stalinist orthodoxy from critics who advocated a more independent and even, at times, revolutionary path. Tito's Yugoslavia was condemned as revisionist after 1948 when it broke its Soviet ties, and during the Sino–Soviet split from the late 1950s each side condemned the other as revisionist. Eastern European militants who voiced the need for a more humanistic socialism, as in Hungary in the 1950s or Czechoslovakia in the 1960s, were also 'revisionists'. During the 1970s, Eurocommunists had been condemned as revisionist by orthodox parties. At the same time, student movements and dissidents from communist and socialist parties attacked the revisionism and 'bureaucratic centralism' of the Old Left – notably, the PCI and Socialist Party in Italy, the KKE in Greece and the PCF in France. Trotskyist critiques of 'deformed workers' states', or 'state capitalism', a concept by the historic British Trotskyist leader Tony Cliff, signified the worse kind of revisionism: that at state level. Accordingly, the relationship between the state and workers was the equivalent to that between private employer interests and workers in the West.

Revisionism has been a key signifier of the Left's doctrinal history, and its absence today indicates the gradual fading away of doctrine itself in this space. But the 1950s revisionism was different from that of the late nineteenth century. In the debates of the 1890s revisionism was a right-wing deviation from communism, with different views on issues like the prospects of capitalism, the debate on gradualism versus revolution and the merits of bourgeois democracy. In contrast, revisionism was intrinsically connected to dissent from Stalinism from the 1950s and those labelled as revisionists were often more radical (or to the left) than the defenders of orthodox communism.[3] Accordingly, radical revolutionaries with strong credentials, utopians and libertarian Marxists and anti-fascist violent groups, were all 'revisionists' and at the same time 'ultra-left' and even 'extreme'. By way of a historical twist, the 'two extremes' thesis that has been used fervently against the left during the post-2008 crisis period, and has also developed into a strain of academic arguments, was utilised by the communist leaders in the late 1970s. It identified the student radicals as equally dangerous to the fascists in order to maintain a distance between their own ranks and the radicalised left youth, who were often organised in violent groups.

Another fashionable concept in the 1960s, illustrating the need to navigate between protest and legitimacy, between revolutionary credentials and war of position, was that of 'structural reforms', a term often used to distinguish between the 'true' Left and the revisionists. These were not merely reforms but 'structural reforms', meaning that they were meant to be deeper and implemented with a horizon for socialist transformation, unlike the attempts of social democratic rivals at reforming capitalism. They were nonetheless 'reforms' and thus non-insurrectionist or agitative in direction. The concept was used by CPs in western Europe in opposition to social democracy, and seen as aiming to sustain capitalist structures rather than eventually overthrow them. Eurocommunists referred to structural reforms to signify economic policy change combined with political democratisation. Within the revolutionary Left, the term was used mostly with the addition of the prefix 'anti-capitalist', but was also contested as it came up against more difficult criteria and could persuade only if it directly challenged the capitalist base: the means of production. In an important article defending the position of 'workers control' during a time when it was 'on the order of the day' among the European anti-capitalist left, Belgian Trotskyist leader Ernest Mandel argued that 'workers' control is ... an anti-capitalist structural reform *par excellance'*. He went on to illustrate the ease with which accusations of reformism were launched: 'At this point, we can dismiss an objection raised by sectarian "purists": "Calling for anti-capitalist structural reforms makes you a reformist," they tell us. "Doesn't your demand contain the word 'reform'?".[4]

Communist rhetorical identity was underpinned by a revolutionary spirit, carrying forward as a discursive culture expressed in the parties' journals and newspapers, the writings and letters of party leaders, and the symbolisms of party culture. Political reality was ritualised through youth festivals, local-level commemorations, tributes to past party leaders, the glorifying of past heroes and institutionalised cultural creation via the party and its ancillary structures. Communist discourse and cultural performance suggested anti-capitalism and offered a background ideology which sustained coherence in the face of tactical compromise, political defeat or alliance-driven communication by the leadership. In reality, most communist and workers parties in western Europe talked in revolutionary terms, used Leninist language and communicated an insurrectionary vision but played fully by the rules of parliamentarism and capitalism. In Italy, this was often referred to as a policy of *dopienza* (duplicity), as expressed in the PCI's slogan of the 1970s, *di lotta e di governo* ('a party of government and a party of struggle'). Duplicity of identity played into the evolution of party rhetoric. In most places, leadership rhetoric strived to navigate the tensions between two functions: being anti-system parties and voicing intense, dramatic, overplayed, confrontational and revolutionary language; while also being an opposition loyal to the regime, 'responsible' towards the nation state, and thereby opposed to any kind of revolutionary and spontaneous agitation.

To understand the balancing acts of communists in terms of doing and saying things, one has to factor in the socio-political environment in the West during the Cold War. It was intensely anti-communist, with anti-communism conceived as 'the rejection, exposure or suppression' of communist manifestations.[5] Anti-communist hysteria – the 'red scares' facilitated by the media, capital and the state, and opposition to communism as a foreign intervention, as a challenge to the catholic faith and as an agent of modernity and thus an enemy of tradition, culture and custom – used confrontational language and could often put the Left on the defensive. From the 1950s, a literature was also developing that would soon morph into the 'totalitarian' approach of Soviet politics, which has been gradually mainstreamed in the social sciences and especially political science.[6] According to the totalitarian approach, communist ideology is habitually understood as bearing certain qualities – impersonal address, repetition, limited informational value, tautology – so as to better enforce authoritarianism through rhetorically manipulating the audience.[7]

As Soviet statehood became cast as totalitarian, the social transformations that CPs aspired to were delegitimised, and terms such as the 'dictatorship of the proletariat' came to be challenged, rethought or abandoned. The concept had been rendered less relevant in 1961, when the Soviet communists declared that the phase of the 'dictatorship of the proletariat' had ended. This was soon followed by the dropping of the concept by western European communists: the Finnish Communist Party dropped it first in 1961, then Italy and France; Eurocommunism was espoused, among other things, by dropping the dictatorship of the proletariat.[8] Today, very few parties sustain the term, again, with the exception of the Greek communists. What remains today is the struggle of hegemony. It goes back to Gramsci's refashioning of the Leninist 'dictatorship of the proletariat' into the 'hegemony of the working class', but it no longer identifies a transitory state (dictatorship of the proletariat) or the forces of government therein (proletariat or working class). Having 'proletarian dictatorship' as a concept of teleology reflected a Leninist heritage, which subsequently came to be revised, contested or dismissed. How could it not, given the shifting class composition of Western societies, Third World 'dictatorships of the proletariat' turned violent, global protest diversified beyond labour conflicts and human rights discourse?

In the 1960s all the forces associated with the New Left in Europe, including Trotskyists, Maoists, violent groups, Guevarists and anarchists, as mentioned in Chapter 6, were cast as an 'ultra-left' and other nationally based variations. The term was used pejoratively by Marxists for groups and parties advocating revolutionary or violent strategies that were considered to overestimate political consciousness within society or underestimate the long-term consequences of what they were proposing.[9] 'Left-wing radicalism' also described these same groups as left-wing deviations from the Marxist-Leninist 'general line'. On the right, deviations were expressed by 'revisionism', 'opportunism', 'social democratism' or 'reconciliationism', terms that were frenetically deployed.[10]

In *Left-Wing Radicalism: An Infantile Disorder*, Lenin had argued that 'extreme revolutionarism' had a class character, and lacked in endurance, organisability and discipline. By the 1970s this discourse would be slightly differentiated depending on the country. In Italy, instead of 'left-wing radicalism' one often spoke of the 'ultra-left' and of 'left-wing extremism', while in France 'left-wing radicalism', 'left-wing extremism' and 'gauchism' were seen as 'synonyms'.[11] In all countries, a petit bourgeois consciousness was identified in these non-communist spaces and blamed for the deviations. Communist critiques of left-wing radicals often dismissed their stratagem as overplaying the tempo and dynamic of development, proposing initiatives that downplayed the limits to militancy and overestimated its intensity and the appeal of violence, and not appreciating the risk of overturning the milestones of historical democratic struggles. Unlike Leninist orthodoxy, the 'ultra-left' believed in the proletariat's spontaneous revolt. The ultra-left was thus an issue that reached beyond the Stalinist USSR and the Eastern Bloc, where they were understood most vehemently as 'opportunists' or 'revisionists'. Yet, during Lenin's time, the Radical Left was not an anti-Stalinist left (Stalinism did not exist), while in the 1960s and 1970s it was that above all. Lenin was in many respects reclaimed rather than deconstructed by ultra-leftists, through Trotsky, Mao, Che Guevara and Castro, Ho Chi Min and other Third World theoreticians and political leaders.

The discourse inherited from Lenin's time would continue until the 1990s, where in academia many scholars would not initially go beyond the communist–post-communist distinction. The term Radical Left as a self-label of a new space arrived in parallel with the rightward shift of traditional social democracy to a mainstream one. For those to the left of social democracy it was crucial to emphasise that the latter was no longer 'radical' or 'left'. Between the 1990s and the 2000s various parties appeared in Europe which made reference to themselves as a 'radical left' or simply 'the left': the Left Bloc in Portugal, Die Linke in Germany, Rifondazione in Italy calling itself 'la sinistra radicale', the Swedish Left Party, the IU in Spain, the Parti de Gauche in France, the Finnish Left Alliance and SYRIZA in Greece. The problematic of labelling oneself in the midst of historical defeat is vividly portrayed by the case of Ari Setälä, a Sweden-based Finn, who noted in one motion to the Swedish Left Party-Communists' twenty-ninth congress in May 1990: 'Communists we are no longer, Social Democrats we can never be, so let us be Left Socialists.'[12, 13] That congress eventually voted for another name, simply calling itself the Left Party.

By the 1990s social democracy was damaged as a framework by important parties in its own tradition. The 'third way', as it was labelled in the UK, or the New Centre (*Neue Mitte*), as it was launched in Germany, signalled the rejection by SDPs of a socialist, even left-wing identity. By the early 2000s, the discourse of social democracy had changed, becoming effectively neoliberal and focused on 'efficiency', 'prudent state finances', responding to 'new challenges', transcending the socialist–capitalist dichotomy and prioritising 'growth' and 'the markets' while treating taxpayers as 'customers'.[14] For many parts of third way philosophy, the left–right distinction was old and meaningless because politics was no longer adversarial and therefore it was all about valence politics: who does what better.[15] By calling themselves left, left wing or radical left, RLPs in the 1990s were in part responding to the space made available by the social democratic drift towards the centre and under the hegemony of neoliberalism. Simple, explicit referents to the left can be a defence of its politics' continuing relevance, a reminder of the inherently conflictual nature of capitalist affairs.

The left and left radicalism becomes an important term in the post-socialist universe where new realities in the battle of ideas and language were consolidated. While many parties continue to embrace 'socialism' in their official names, few new parliamentary parties emerging in the 1960s and especially the 1990s and beyond use orthodox terms such as 'communist', 'socialist' (only), 'Marxist-Leninist' or 'workers' party'.[16] This was an era in which communist discourse and Leninist framings had become empty rhetoric, as the regimes of 'actually, existing socialism' lacked and lost legitimacy. As the discourse of those challenging the USSR and international socialism prevailed, rhetorical constraints came into play for those marked by its defeat.[17]

Rhetorical evolution among RLPs must be nuanced on two grounds: ideological and electoral. Initially, given that rhetoric is connected to different ideological traditions on the Radical Left, it should reflect distinct rhetorical styles in terms of self-descriptions, schemas, concepts and teleology. And it does. Luke March's typology of contemporary RLPs, although based according to the author on distinct ideological traditions, reveals a lot about differences in the rhetorical styles of certain types of parties compared to others.[18] Anti-capitalists (e.g. the KKE, the PCP and Trotskyist parties) denounce all compromise with 'bourgeois' political forces, including social democracy, and define capitalism and profit, and not merely neoliberalism, as the enemy.[19] They are, after all, self-labelled as communist, Marxist-Leninist or workers' parties, which are party names that imply a certain ideological heritage. They also speak more about economic and labour issues in their manifestos.[20] Red-Green and democratic socialist parties (e.g. SYRIZA, Podemos, the Swedish Vänsterpartiet, the Norwegian Socialist Left Party (SV) or the Finnish Left Alliance) 'define themselves in opposition to' both 'totalitarian communism and neo-liberal social democracy', while giving more attention to feminism, environmentalism, self-management, direct democracy and the rights of minorities. Their emphasis on socio-cultural issues is greater than for the CPs.[21]

These patterns are also evident across the distinct transnational radical left groupings that we reviewed in Chapter 6. The rhetoric of GUE/NGL, ELP and DiEM25 stands apart from that of the communist INITIATIVE or the EACL. In the last two groups, declarations centre around 'peace and socialism', a critique of imperialism, capital and monopolies, and more emphasis on economic interests, demands and categories. For the organisations of parties that are not strictly anti-capitalist, a softer repertoire of signifiers is utilised: a 'people's Europe', a 'social Europe', a 'democratic Europe', 'more and better jobs', 'the enforcement of human rights', 'against elites', 'anti-fascism' and 'anti-racism' and 'sustainable economic development'.

Moreover, rhetorical evolution due to changing geopolitical dynamics aside, there are electoral pulls for all RLPs. Competing in the liberal capitalist public sphere bears constraints. This becomes particularly evident in electoral slogans, the epitome of pragmatist contingency. To set our discussion again a concrete empirical base, Appendix 2 presents the campaign slogans of various parliamentary CPs and RLPs in eight countries between the 1960s and today – France, Greece, Italy, the Netherlands, Norway, Portugal, Sweden and Spain. Some elements of RLP rhetoric are diachronic, ideological change and electoral necessity notwithstanding.

There are four discernible patterns. First, there are universalistic framings: catchy but vague language is always present and very different from revolutionary, technical and ideological discourse. Within electoral slogans, one cannot find words like 'revolution', 'proletariat', 'working class', 'insurrection', 'capital', 'bourgeois' or even 'socialism' for the most part, and not one reference against capitalism. Understood in terms of party politics, western European CPs are electoral entities and their slogans, like all slogans, are relatively short, catchy and broad, evoking emotion and ambivalence. Electoral sloganeering entails pragmatism as an endogenous condition. To attract the youth, slogans need to be in the range of direct experience. Yet even judging them within these boundaries, radical left electoral slogans are not provocative, explicitly subversive or specific in terms of their targets, visions or tools of struggle. Subsequently, radical left electoral rhetoric does not really reproduce the lexicon of communist and socialist discourse because that's the discourse of the party and partisans, not the electorate or broad alliances. Through the consistency of avoiding such rhetoric in key electoral slogans, we can see one of electoralism's constraints, which is shared by other party families: teleology and official ideological discourse, as enshrined in party statutes, is systematically, avoided.

By comparison, Trotskyist and Maoist appeals, names and schemas remain more fixed, like the wider beyond-slogans discourse of parties such as the KKE and the PCP. For the Socialist Workers' Party in the UK and Lutte Ouvrière in France, the workers figure centrally in their festivals, and there is still debate over when communist states 'degenerated' after the revolution. The French NPA reminds us by name that it is anti-capitalist; previously it was the Ligue Comuniste Revolutionaire. ANTARSYA in Greece translates as Anticapitalist Left Cooperation for the Overthrow.

Second, we can assume that the European Radical Left, like social democracy, does what was identified in Jeremy Corbyn's campaigns. That is, it has a preoccupation with 'the Old, the New, "new times"', 'renewal, finding the true original path, making the journey to a better place, being true to an original purpose and all of these in relation or contrast to the practical, rhetorical exigency of gaining power'.[22] This 'newness' has always been there, was problematised by Marxist theory and is a logical corollary of emphasising one's capacity to imagine alternative futures and differentiate from the incumbent status quo. 'Newness' was also ingrained in Cold War dynamics; changing the world would accord one side more legitimacy as it was the only way to 'prove' the universal applicability of their ideology, including through a 'war of the mind'.[23] In crude terms, having an anti-system profile and being excluded from power combine to produce an oppositional tone geared towards improvement rather than sustenance. The ongoing expression of the need for a journey, a transition which makes things better and fairer, is 'the alternative' used across different types of actors and responding to the 1980s Thatcherite maxim TINA. Yet, terms such as 'new', 'renewal', 'change', 'departure', 'social reconstruction', 'turn' and 'structural or new democratic reform' are always there.

Third, we can observe a consistent appeal to democracy in the movements – 'democratic change', 'democratic majority', 'democratic state', 'democratic government', 'democratisation', 'popular democracy' and 'socialist democracy'. The language of democracy for radical left movements is diachronically present in RLP rhetoric as well. In a sense it is 'democracy' which becomes the *telos* of RLPs in terms of policy during office. This is a softer, more generic *telos* to promote electorally in preference to the dictatorship of the proletariat. But although generic, one can identify distinct spaces in the Cold War left according to how they framed democracy and associated concepts: for example, 'democratic centralism' (communist), 'proletarian democracy', 'state capitalism', 'economism' (Trotskyist), 'socialist democracy' (social democrats), 'advanced democracy' (communist), 'degenerated workers' state' and 'bureaucratic centralism' (Trotskyists), 'direct democracy' and 'democratic socialism' (libertarian) and 'microbureaucracies' (anti-Trotskyist).

The fourth pattern we can flesh out of Appendix 2 concerns the social subject to which electoral slogans make reference. It is almost always much broader than the working class. Although it has been reasonably suggested that since 1990 all RLPs have defined the 'working class' more widely than the traditional blue-collar strata, and nationalistically in terms of presenting themselves as 'defending national workers and not Moscow's foreign policy',[24] in Appendix 2 the pattern is more consistent and starts earlier than commonly suggested. Only in a few cases do we see mention of 'workers' (and there is no such reference anywhere in Appendix 2 after the 1980s), while on most occasions the social subject is 'the people' or the country, and this is evident since the 1960s. Again, the pattern can be accounted for by the nature of sloganeering, but we are looking here into electoral rhetoric as a product of opportunities and constraints within capitalist liberal democracies. To say the least, therefore, in terms of their electoral communication, parliamentary RLPs are in certain respects like all other parties: making use of signifiers with a wider scope than their official ideology's concepts. But people-centrism in particular was a central signifier of both the SDP and CP strategies to enable the conditions of the workers to constitute themselves as a class. Both lefts talked of the 'simple people', the 'have nots', 'the subaltern classes', 'the people' or the 'uneducated', which have sovereign power opposite capital, itself realised through organising the working class.[25] Patriotism and nationhood had discursive utility in this vein, as frames of a national people, in its majority from the working and lower middle classes. To investigate the rhetorical social subject of the Left between popular and national sovereignty, we now continue with these notions of 'people', 'country' and 'nation', as conjunctions of elections and the theory of counter-hegemonic strategy.

POPULISM AND EUROPEAN RLPS

It is evident from the political rhetoric of social movements that 'new left populism' has special relevance for parties. Much of what has been written has to do with electoral strategies and the discourse of party leaders and politicians.[26] This is not surprising since the contestation of political power has directly engendered a lot of populist and deceptive electoral mobilisations across the whole of the political spectrum. This strain of research is rich and insightful, and above all effective in differentiating progressive populism from conservative and authoritarian facets of the phenomenon. However, it needs to be nuanced in so far it suggests 'newness' for the left. To do this, the story cannot be reduced to a dichotomous question – is today's left or that of the 1970s communist and other RLPs populist or not? This would miss the complexity entailed in how people–elite binaries can serve or inhibit, divide or unify, socialist struggle.

Although Marxism-Leninism had defeated populist ideology for CPs, upholding dialectical materialism as the only 'scientific socialism', in political language people-centrism won the day early on. This was largely due to the experience of the Popular Fronts, especially where anti-fascist resistance became a national movement, as in Italy. People's Republics, people's museums and people's daily newspapers have all been the subject of historical struggle communicated in communist discourse systematically, widely and in diverse forms. Its political history develops out of the Cold War, when 'people's democracy' became a standard term to euphemistically describe socialism in eastern Europe.[27] This rhetorical practice of socialist states casting themselves in popular terms initially represented a new communist nomenclature that retheorised the development of 'actually existing socialism'. It went beyond distinguishing between non-socialist, 'bourgeois' regimes and socialist states as the dictatorship of the proletariat. The Soviet leadership argued anew that the present was the stage of gradual mixing between state and society, as per the predictions of Marxist theory, whereby the bureaucratic state based on the dictatorship of the proletariat gradually withers away into socialism.[28]

Beyond the social democratic and communist construction of a popular imaginary, in the 1950s and 1960s populism appeared in debates about decolonisation, the conceptualisation and future of 'peasantism' and the origins and developments of Maoism. Consider the following passage written by Mao Zedong and appearing in *The People's Daily* in June 1957:

The concept of 'the people' varies in content in different countries and in different periods of history in a given country. Take our own country for example. During the War of Resistance Against Japan, all those classes, strata and social groups opposing Japanese aggression came within the category of the people, while the Japanese imperialists, their Chinese collaborators and the pro-Japanese elements were all enemies of the people. During the War of Liberation, the U.S. imperialists and their running dogs – the bureaucrat-capitalists, the landlords and the Kuomintang reactionaries who represented these two classes – were the enemies of the people, while the other classes, strata and social groups, which opposed them, all came within the category of the people. At the present stage, the period of building socialism, the classes, strata and social groups which favour, support and work for the cause of socialist construction all come within the category of the people, while the social forces and groups which resist the socialist revolution and are hostile to or sabotage socialist construction are all enemies of the people.[29]

French and European Maoism, like the passage above, cast socialist struggles in terms of binaries, addressed the popular masses and evoked people-centrism constantly, called for people's power, posited that true socialism is one 'from the masses to the masses' and acknowledged contradictions within the oppressed, borrowing from a language already consolidated in Mao's writings and political initiatives by the 1950s. In Maoist experiments of 'going to the people', militants and intellectuals joined workers on factory assembly lines before and after May 1968 in France – the process known as *itablissement*. 'May was about losing one's self to the masses in a quasi-religious abjection, and losing one's individual voice to the cadences of "militant-speak," the *langue de bois*.'[30]

Multiple other historical instances stand out as representative of left-wing populist-like movements or intellects in Europe: Eurocommunist people-centrism inherited from the Popular Front-era CPs, striving for alliances across class strata; late nineteenth-century French socialist thought reflected in the Blanquists' attunement with mass politics and populism, as inherited from the Jacobin tradition during the years of the French Revolution and as a form of anti-parliamentarism;[31] the writings of the Russian populists and also the early Marx, which often referred to the people without specifying whom it included.[32] Considering this diachronicity in the problematic of left populism, it is right to claim that populism can sound 'thin or perfunctory' in contrast to deep and carefully articulated socialist commitments.[33] Pauline Johnson specified populism's 'demagogic reformatting of democratic justification' as colluding with neoliberal power.[34] Demagoguery replaces the intent to build a 'rational consensus about matters of social justice', as it involves flattering of the audience, projecting the blame away, avoiding any sort of reflectivity and self-criticism, repeating apparently obvious policy positions and making extremely generous promising.[35]

Because of left populism's slippery slope unto demagoguery, uncritical reflection and schematic language without explanation, there lies a partial incompatibility with socialism as a series of analytical doctrines. Tension is evident above all historically: neither in the 1960s, nor earlier or more recently, has the Radical Left, even its 'new' component alone, reached a consensus on populism. This point was already raised earlier for populism and radical movements in terms of theory, so here let us look at strategy in terms of party competition. Theoretical divisions over left populism in the case of parties concern above all electoral technique and the performative qualities of particular political personas. Neither in terms of language use nor in relation to theorising imminent struggles is there, or perhaps can there be, unanimity on such complex issues as framing the in-group, the out-group and the relationship between them in an attempt to conduce effective counter-hegemony. In the 1970s, Trotskyists were criticising Maoist populism for being too vague and indeed counter-revolutionary in replacing the opposition between Right and Left by the one between us and them, the people and the elites, or the underdogs and the privileged. Others considered that Leninism and Maoism are connected; the former can help organise the party (the leadership element), while the latter can help organise the masses (popular element).[36]

In *Populism Left and Right*, Marxist academic and member of Attac France, Eric Fassin, considered explicitly populism's strategic use. He cautioned against the alleged potential of populist politics on the left for transforming right-wing resentment of migrants and minorities into contention against economic elites.[37] This has been a chief aspiration among the adherents of left populism, which often responds to the capacity of the radical right over the last four or so decades to mobilise the white middle classes through cultural populism by formulating its own civic and counter-hegemonic populist genus.[38] The presupposition here is that the fury and rage of the far-right support base can be reoriented away from racist populist movements and towards socialist ones. Fassin dismisses this left-wing populist idea as he considers the orientation of far-right supporters to be more structural and immovable towards the Radical Left than assumed by the left populist analysis. It is argued that the left cannot benefit from entering into cultural and identity 'warfare', which was in the first place initiated by the radical right and has so far served neoliberalism.[39]

The political positions that these criticisms (like the earlier ones we considered) inform, can be described as at least a reserved and partial endorsement of populism in certain contexts, and at worse as left-wing 'anti-populism'. In the spirit of internally contested mobilisation waves, not all of the radical left aligns behind populism in the period after the 2008 financial crisis or more generally in the 2000s. While some Trotskyist and other extra-parliamentary currents, for example, denounce post-Marxism and populism as its derivative strategy for undermining the prominent role of class and the labour–capital dichotomy in the development of society and the design of socialist strategy, others have participated in broad parties such as the Die Linke in Germany, the Left Front in France and Podemos in Spain. Certain radical feminist critiques of populism suggest that it is an obstacle to feminising politics and is actually reinforcing patriarchal systems;[40] this is not an unfair criticism given that a woman has rarely led radical left populism in either Latin America or Europe. The orthodox communists, the KKE and PCP, do not deviate from a strict and absolute class-based understanding of contemporary struggles so their people-centrism and anti-establishment discourse is intentionally left short of a left populist strategy and theory. This applies to any communist or workers' party in Europe, no matter how small or large they are. Communist orthodoxy dislikes populist theory and strategy.

Clearly, left populism is a majoritarian phenomenon today on the European Radical Left. Its main representative cases are quite strong and successful in comparative terms. Its key frames are also predominant – people-centrism, variations of 'the many, not the few', crisis and urgency, popular sovereignty, ordinariness and massiveness.[41] Yet, when we turn to culture rather than ideology the picture becomes even more complex. Pointedly, some of the parties identified as representative examples of party populism, such as SYRIZA in Greece and Die Linke in Germany, approach populism mostly as an ideological *dispositif* and not a positive self-description like Podemos or FI. Populist strategy and the Radical Left are connected according to the country and history in question, and are partly related to native understandings and uses of the very term itself. Few Scandinavian militants or partisans would identify as left-wing populist, especially given a particular socio-economic development and an overall context where it is mostly nationalist and nativist identifications that engage in populist politics.[42] Spain, on the other hand, has Latin American influences and a more turbulent domestic environment and historical trajectory. Until about 2018, it also had no electorally relevant competition from the extreme right. Parties like SYRIZA and Die Linke may to all intents and purposes voice populist rhetoric but certainly do not defend a populist strategy, which in their national-cultural contexts is synonymous with cheap and superficial politics – the politics of many promises and no actions.[43]

In the most emblematic case of patriotic populism as a party strategy, Podemos experienced a deep ideological rift between its two main groups that crystalised after the 2015 general election. On one side were those in favour of consolidating support among leftist voters through emphasising the radical identity of the party (a position represented by party leader Pablo Iglesias and former IU members). On the other were those advocating a broader appeal, primarily relying on 'populist reason' and less so on anti-capitalism that would more effectively attract moderate and centre-left voters. This latter position was represented by the party's former secretary for policy, strategy and campaigning, Iñigo Errejón, and his supporters who left the party to found another platform in 2019.[44]

On the one hand, populism is embraced by anti-capitalists, communists and social democrats, partisans and activists, cutting across older divides. On the other hand, it is also either rejected en masse as a theory-informed discursive practice or as a label, or still debated and scrutinised as a broader political strategy, depending on the organisation in question and its internal balance of power. In particular, the usefulness for and association of populism with electoralism is contested. The 'populist' style of mobilisation has often been accused of reformism or opportunism because it propagates all-inclusive formulas for counter-hegemony. As James Petras explained about the

1970s socialist left, 'the indistinctness of the slogans, in terms of specifying which class interests would benefit or be adversely affected, was considered by many in the Left as a clever electoral tactic to secure lower-class support without alienating the middle class'.[45] The problem, he continues, is that '[i]n the aftermath of the elections, the vagueness of the promises allowed several of the Socialist leaders to state that they had not in fact promised any radical social reforms and therefore were following the same political-economic trajectory traced out before the elections'. In short, populism may work against accountability and pledge fulfilment.[46] According to Seraphim Seferiades's definition, populism is itself a deceptive politics.[47]

Be that as it may, left populism is also specifically ideological. Left populist forces are 'not anti-statist but directed towards the state and its "return to the people", through a transformed, collective posture towards the vehicle of electoral representation'. Effectively, the state can create and defend the politico-economic sovereignty of the subordinated.[48] Post-Marxism channelled into party systems the embrace of combining populism and realpolitik; a point made by Boris Frankel in the late 1990s after almost two decades into neoliberalism and one decade after Soviet dissolution.[49] We are now four decades ahead of these phenomena and populism is still combined with realpolitik, and more specifically office seeking. Populism's rhetorical package, as it has been pointedly remarked, can read 'like a wish list for a socialist and radical-democratic agenda'.[50] Left populism as theory has always predominantly come in reformist colours, as the rhetorical strategy of piecemeal reforms in a progressive direction. Populist strategy and theory do not primarily arise from as strict a dichotomy as that of capital–labour. Rather, they generalise the contradiction and in the process end up with a redistributive, Keynesian, inclusive, welfare-oriented and democratised capitalism.

NATIONALISM, PATRIOTISM AND FRAMING RESISTANCE

Since the mid-nineteenth century, left-leaning sovereignist discourse has always existed. For our purposes we can begin with the 1960s. In Belgium, state-wide parties collapsed after the regionalist mobilisations experience at that time, while in the UK devolution politics ensued and in Northern Ireland the Irish Republican Army (IRA) was established (1969–72) and the civil rights movement was under way. In France, it was the first time that the Jacobin conception of an indivisible and centralised France was challenged by the Left. In all cases, this left regionalism had cultural and democratic justifications, consolidating and respecting: the pluralism of popular cultures; territorial self-management; alternative models of policymaking that break with capitalism and the oppression of peripheries by its policies aiming at a uniform society; and revisiting revolutionary rupture through the fusion of regional and national arenas as loci of struggle. This leftist regionalism is premised on cultural and democratic justifications: respect for and development of popular cultures, and self-management of territorial issues by those concerned. It also has a cognitive and strategic dimension.[51]

Radical regionalism was different from the CPs' love of country. Nationhood tapped into the student–CPs dividing line. For instance, radical student leaders would typically snub the French flag while the CP raised it. For the CPs, revolution was not on the agenda, and patriotism, as David Broder argued, dressed up their reformism, which was to nationalise industry and fight imperialism.[52] This patriotism served as 'social lever', as in the case of the PCF. Combined with anti-fascism, it served to strengthen the party's working-class constituencies and attach it both to France and to the many immigrants seeking integration and joining its activities.[53] In Italy, national framings also appeared in the context of critique towards the USSR and its satellites and the attempt to establish 'polycentrism'. In the 1950s, historic PCI leader Palmiro Togliatti had theorised the need for Italian independence and a different geopolitical system than that institutionalised through the Cold War.

This framing of nationhood – the national road to socialism and the patriotism that was intended to appeal much beyond the pro-Soviet sections of society – was different from the PCF's historical attachment to the Soviet leadership for most of its Cold War existence. Rather, the ideological explanation of the PCF's nationalism and sovereignist rhetoric lay exclusively in their anti-imperialism and specifically their analysis of the French ruling class as organically connected to the exterior of the USA, betraying the French nation in this way.[54] Yet in both cases during the 1960s and 1970s, seeking popular votes through here-and-there invocations of national grandeur continued the post-1945 strategy of using republican referents. The passionate love for country was often associated with the claim that 75,000 PCF members had been killed during the resistance.[55] Precisely in the same manner, Greek Cypriot patriotism was animated with anti-fascism, to which AKEL (Progressive Party of Working People), the CP of a small island, was proud to say that it contributed by sending volunteers to the war.

Between the Cold War and the RLPs during the GJM years, there has been a key discontinuity, the same one as for movements and protest. The centre–periphery cleavage has been reactivated in the context of the delegitimation of the nation state as caused by economic globalisation and European integration. The growing geographical polarisation of European populations into major urban areas and declining rural areas and towns have restructured European party competition since the 'new regionalism' of the 1980s, whose initial vibrations derived from the Long '68. Many regionalisms and localisms surfaced at the time, as altogether the above processes translate into geographical inequalities. Perceptions of local or regional decline can drive populist voting and work through electoral in-groupism based on the locally shared community.[56] By the middle of the last decade, subnational claims to self-determination came to the fore in western Europe through the cases of Catalonia and Scotland and then the electoral success of Sinn Féin in Ireland towards the end of Brexit. The shared sovereignties discourse we saw in Chapter 4 finds electoral resonance.

Left nationalism has also come through austerity and has had 'patriotism' and civic nationhood as its anchor points. Although SYRIZA, Podemos or its splinter platform More Country (Mais Pais) are the most discussed cases, many more parties from various ideological traditions employ patriotism.[57] Left patriotism and an ethnocentric outlook that advocates people-to-people solidarity is shared among all periods of 'newness' and among all traditions. Through time, therefore, one unchanging rhetorical trait of left radicalism in contesting elections and building political capital is an identification with the country in question, which can of course range from high to low and inform multiple policy positions but is always there. The patria is the institutional platform upon which a number of progressive political tasks can be taken – consolidating a plethora of social, political and economic rights so as to: include minorities and the oppressed, which comprise altogether a large majority; provide free and generous welfare for everyone; and undo the democratic deficits generated by capitalism, imperialism and neoliberal globalisation.

The eurozone crisis also fuelled analyses about the European centre and the periphery. Southern European countries were, according to many activists, taken advantage of by the hegemonic states of the EU, such as Germany and France, which were to benefit the most from the EU's economy. This way of framing the crisis was popular among the office-seeking Left in Greece, for example, but was also premised on an ethnocentric economic narrative different from movements, which saw a 'plan C' in constructing the commons from below.[58] The diagnosis in this narrative was essentially that the main structural problem of Greek capitalism is the transfer of fiscal and monetary control to EU institutions, which do not operate for the good of the country but are synchronised with the needs of the hegemonic EU states and their export-based economies.

In the opposite camp, the defenders of austerity and neoliberalism referred to the PIIGS (Portugal, Ireland and/or Italy, Greece and Spain), where they argued there lies a cultural and historically pervasive predisposition to laziness, corruption, patronage and clientelism, blame shifting and wasteful spending. A key term for legitimising neoliberal discourse in the Greek case, for example, was 'anomy', used to construct the crisis as the outcome of Greek political culture, irrational and lawless.[59] These claims pointed to a conclusion: it was the peripheral countries that were to blame in explaining the eurozone crisis, and more specifically their public sectors and economic models. It was them that had to change as a result. Moreover, the efficient, productive and hard-working German (and other European) taxpayers were unfairly paying for the anarchic Greeks. A form of intra-European orientalism abounded in these media-driven polemics. A historical analogy is pertinent in revealing the evolving impact of neoliberalism on European politics – the southern European periphery presents itself as the new 'Third World', it bears the debts once born by Latin American, African and Asian countries by former colonial powers or international institutions. Debt capitalism has essentially expanded geographically, further sharpening the divide between countries regarding economic hegemony and subordination.

Within this broader agenda, crises of the public sector became contested domestically, as national capital in countries such as the UK, Cyprus, Ireland, Italy and Spain overemphasised the bad condition of the state and the responsibility of overblown and unproductive civil services, in an attempt to legitimise cuts and welfare retrenchment. Trade unions, along with left-wing parties and movements, contested this narrative, and held that the need for austerity-driven bailout programmes was the responsibility of the banks. Movements such as UK Uncut presented themselves as exposing malpractice and lies, deconstructing mainstream soundbites, such as 'We are all in this together', and in turn defending the position that there *is* an alternative.[60] We can see here contestation over the locus of crisis: on one side, blame shifting to the 'inefficient, south European state' or the public sector in line with neoliberal convictions; and on the other side, exposing the lack of state oversight over financial fraud and the banking system's self-imposed problems, in line with the anti-austerity forces.

Hegemonic framings of the peripheral member states of the EU depoliticised and racialised economic and distributional questions, as well as signalled the return of colonial dynamics back into Europe through the culturalisation of politics, complementing the post-political neoliberal hegemony.[61] The very thesis of southern European exceptionalism was an axis of political conflict in the years of the crisis. Its delegitimisation was a task undertaken by radical scholars and activists as part of their opposition to the EU's economic policy, the bailouts and their defenders domestically. In this setting, centre-periphery schemas have been employed widely to describe and explain responses to the crisis. Accordingly, the eurozone crisis can be understood as the outcome of a structural imbalance between core and periphery countries.[62] It is against this theoretical backdrop that much of the anti-Germanism mentioned earlier took a substantively neo-anti-imperialist form, as crafted by RLP strategy.[63]

The examples are so numerous and consistently present in the Left's history that we should consider patriotism and nationhood at the regional or country level as useful, tactical propaganda tools for socio-economic struggles. We saw how the great proletarian internationalists had a national flavour to declare: a defence of country and a people that guards its sovereignty against imperialism. Wallerstein's analysis is illuminating in this respect: the rise of nationalist movements can be attributed to their locally rooted realisation that as a 'weak majority' in a 'weak state' their best option is that of a 'state structure'.[64] When it comes to nationalism, as Connor Walker discussed, it is thus one thing to be a believer in ethnic particularism and another to be a manipulator, shrouding socialism in a national rhetoric to attain political goals, as communists sought to do.[65] Nationalism and patriotism can be strong performative weapons motivating and energising civic engagement.[66] Patriotic appeals allow the electorate to feel proud of their country or region in supporting specific socio-economic goals and political actors.

Accordingly, there is sometimes a strategic calculus by socialists who seek to encourage and channel nationalist claims or transmit a patriotic aura. One could theoretically argue, however, that the strategic value of casting an economic and social struggle as patriotic and national may increase or decrease, on average, over time. The strategic use of nationalism may backfire, and it often has. This is implied in evaluations of left nationalism as a constrained manifestation of the progressive vision since at least the 1990s. Arresting this tendency is an article titled, 'The Movement that Dare Not Speak Its Name'.[67] In the contemporary period, amid the global rise of the authoritarian ethno-populist Right, anti-terrorism and liberals speaking of ties between 'the extremes', the Left cannot legitimately frame its struggles as national and patriotic because this is the distinctive feature of its far-right opposition and other key opponents: locally, nationally, regionally and globally. With such framings, easy accusations would be prompted and labels such as the 'populist left' or the 'extremist left' would more easily resonate.

Political opportunities for nationalism's emancipatory content open and close. In Scotland, the referendum of 2015 triggered a mass progressive social movement and an explosion of working-class activity that was far greater than previous campaigns related to the GJM or the anti-war movement.[68] Yet the 'left turn' of the centrist Scottish National Party, under the leadership of Nicola Sturgeon, absorbed energy and votes from radicals, and the same time many Scottish nationalists adopted an elastic attitude towards neoliberal politics.[69] For Sinn Féin's historic electoral success in Ireland in 2020, the reawakening of anti-British nationalism as a result of Brexit may have helped. This resembles the era before the Good Friday Agreement that ended the Troubles, as during the 1960s civil resistance movement many political actors tried to combine the republican tradition with left-wing politics. Ireland's nationalist past, as an observer remarked, 'broke through' to again become a vote winner when tied to the left. This has been so in spite of Sinn Féin's connections to the IRA military council, which echo the dark (militaristic and violent) side to its nationalism in the public sphere.[70] In a country where housing was a flaming topic, Ireland's neoliberal model was under scrutiny, and as there are no nativist or strictly anti-immigration parties, left nationalism and national unity thrives mostly in egalitarian colours.

Yet the strategic value of framing party mobilisation according to the stipulations of nationhood also varies according to domestic circumstances. On one side, radical left claims to secession in Scotland, Spain and Ireland are expressive of radical contention's deep roots in the traditional cultures of mobilisation (such as nationalism) which have pervaded the class structure. When understood as cultural resources, these pre-existing legacies and traditions may account for current manifestations of left patriotism and nationalism; for example, in order to explain why Podemos could innovate by reclaiming patriotism from the Francoist tradition, which during the Spanish dictatorship of about 40 years killed tens of thousands in the name of the fatherland.[71] Podemos did have a challenge to overcome: patriotism's links to fascism in the collective memory. Yet the mere existence of this past allowed it to call for patriotism in the first place, so as to erase the Francoist shadow and return patriotism to its pre-Francoist heritage of democratic, libertarian, republican, socialist and communist credentials. Common decency as opposed to the fatherland itself, where the people are located and which the people constitutes, was a relevant post-ideological signifier in its mobilisation.[72] In Northern Ireland, the IRA achieved mass recruitment for the purposes of armed activism in the late 1960s through an invocation of dignity, honour and pride in oneself and one's community, as well as a struggle for recognition from the opposite side – the Northern Irish establishment, loyalists and the British army.[73] These elements of recruitment were subsequently institutionalised within the IRA's political wing, Sinn Féin, which has never had a nativist or nationalist competitor to trigger these emotions for racist and xenophobic reasons. In Greece, the rhetoric of national independence during austerity worked in favour of SYRIZA because it reminded people of the discourse of the once glorious Panhellenic Socialist Party (PASOK) and worked to mobilise many progressives.

Claims to the fatherland and national sovereignty by Basque, Catalan, Scottish and Northern Irish radicals, in addition to the Greeks perhaps, do not negate internationalist sympathies but coexist with them. Yet such coexistence seems less viable in the socialist imaginary in other parts of Europe where left nationalism has traditionally been a regressive force. In Cyprus, for example, nationalism in both the north and the south has been the chief obstacle to bicommunal peace. Since about 1968 (and more concretely, since 1974, after the junta-instigated coup in Cyprus and the subsequent Turkish invasion), AKEL has not spoken about nationhood. The Cypriot (not the Greek) flag, as opposed to the nationalist Right, define its performances. Its policy on the country's de facto division is markedly different from the other parties, and it is historically tied to the peace and reunification movement. Similarly, nationalism is incompatible with the Workers' Party of Belgium, which owns the 'franchise' of the only bilingual and bicommunal party system actor in Belgium, operating in both Wallonia and Flanders. How progressive nationalism can be is determined by domestic historical legacies, political opportunities and constraints.

Notwithstanding this, peripheral nationalisms and the ways they shape the political agenda are topics towards which the Radical Left in Europe again remains divided. Many on the Spanish and European Left have voiced suspicion at the rise of Catalan separatism, seeing it as a nationalist phenomenon, which can be and is used by the ruling classes to divide the economically oppressed.[74] Even though the Radical Left since Lenin is sympathetic to the right of self-determination, many activists distrust both the leadership of separatist forces and the potential effects of secessionism on the national left and society more broadly. Others frame the Catalan question, and along with it the Kurdish, Corsican, Scottish and Palestinian movements, not as national questions (ones which concern above all the sacredness of the nation state) but as questions of democracy, regarding above all the democratic right to self-defence of the minority and its right to separation or secession. What remains of political essence across all cases is the civic component of nationalism, which can blend with socialism.

RETROSPECTIVE

How has Radical Left rhetoric evolved since the 1960s and between three distinct waves of intensified contention? How are the distinct processes of rhetoric and ideology associated, in terms of ideological changes leading to shifting rhetorical representations of political reality? Many patterns are common to both parties and movements – the language of democratic socialism, a break with doctrinaire teleology, democracy translated according to ideological tradition, anti-capitalist versus critical social language and its predominance as a fact of historical defeat. As with ideas, the process of change began when the Soviet legacy came increasingly into question – a period marked by the Long '68. The critical moment which removes the burden of frames that derive from outside the parties themselves was the end of the Cold War and its associated trends, such as social democracy's rightward shift under the predominance of neoliberalism. These processes together challenged and then ended the ideas driving international communism's political language. Having said this, with RLPs there appears to be more change in their ideological culture and more consistency and continuity in the pragmatism of their communicative expressions in the context of elections. The sloganeering and generic and emotional appeals observed in the movements are nationally inclusive, diffuse more easily and gain attention, but with an ideological cost. This cost may not be triggered if a background ideology, a cultural radicalism, is sustained in an organised fashion – this was certainly the case for the mass western European CPs that allowed for a double identity, a purist and catch-all rhetoric at one and the same time.

As a schema of in-group versus out-group binaries, left populism is utilised for a strategic puzzle that at root is as old as the left itself: how to construct popular hegemony out of the majority's partly distinct and partly overlapping grievances, many of which may not align closely with the party's ideas. As we see later, the mass party line underpins the complexities of this strategic puzzle. Party populism on the Radical Left is thus not 'new' in the exclusive, definitional sense of new as a 'break with the old', or from the perspective of a highly successful, cross-country political trajectory for the European Radical Left compared to the past. The contemporary manifestations of populism signal something 'other than the old', which evolves between continuity and change, innovation and tradition, enthusiasm and rejection. At the same time, it is the object of a wider, long-lasting conflict between materialism and discursive critical theory, class and identity, confrontation and collaboration, anti-capitalism and anti-neoliberalism, socialist strategy and national culture. Not least, as in the movements, this left populism is never revolutionary as theory, like Maoist populism was, but always combines oppositional identification and a structural root-and-branch vision with a social democratic solution and a statist spirit.

Much 'newness' can be granted to the left populism of the twentieth century, in the sense of evolution, or fluctuation towards conditions of severe crises which favour it as a rhetorical strategy and performance. There has been no rupture with the past, in the sense of: a very recent historical discontinuity in the ideational realm; politically novel claims that escape the identity of post-Marxist reformism and declassing critical analysis; universally exceptional success; resonance across cultures, or easy agreement over issues of theory, strategy and the state. Left populism is a conflictual type of politics because it is highly variable in both normative and empirical terms. Nationalism, across time and like populism, is also a partiality and variable across context, a 'double-edged sword' that has a dark side and brings upon the Radical Left ideological and strategic contestability.[75] Its utility in alliance building and inspiring mobilisation risks a difficult coexistence with internationalism and can easily slip into romanticism, or worse a veiled mainstreaming. Yet the 'newness' in nationalism itself changes with each period considered. For the 1960s and 1970s, new was regionalism; for the GJM, new was its anti-nationalism and connection between levels of governance; while for post-2008, it has been economic sovereignty from the hegemonic forces of the EU.

8

Party Organisation on the European Radical Left

INTRODUCTION

Like movements, parties are political communities with particular structures, procedures and linkages to other organisations. As with movements, these interplay with ideology; in other words, traditions on the Left are associated with particular organisational forms. Moreover, as society changes parties have to respond in order to legitimise the performance of their key functions: representation, recruitment, policy formulation, participation and mediation between the state and the public. While, in the industrial age, parties were formed to mobilise the demands of a society empowered by democracy, the information age changed a number of things, including more spontaneous engagement with political parties and a lack of permanent commitment. Taking party and party system evolution as a given, in order to delimit trends and variability in the organisational anatomy of the Radical Left, this chapter first consults the broad framework of party models. As was noted in Chapter 2, the shifting party models across time are organisational responses to social and political developments and are connected to distinct procedures, structures and linkages. In broad terms, we are interested in how the RLP organisation refracts democracy and the tension between verticality and horizontality through conducing in this or that direction of power distribution within the wider party body and between institutions and their environs. The spatial analogy to movements is, at the most basic level, whether RLPs face towards the streets or the parliament, and how they utilise and absorb digital spaces.

To this end, a subsequent focus is placed on parties' intermediating function as a linkage between the state and society, from a twofold perspective of the party itself and the movements. Specifying the structure that divides and also connects RLPs and movements, the capitalist state and seeking office in government, we further evaluate the general conviction that this party family tried to travel 'from the margins to the mainstream', although with uneven, unimpressive and, even when it was impressive, with unsustained electoral success.[1] How do state structures affect party policy and the party organisation? Finally, this chapter turns to the voters and supporters of RLPs to elaborate further the radical subject in time. This is done by looking into the composition of electoral constituencies – their social, material and political features.

STRUCTURES AND PROCEDURES:
SPACES AND PARTY MODELS

RLP organisational practice since the 1960s is presented schematically in Figure 8.1, where the proceeding analysis is summarised. Our axes of discussion are party models, the continuum between vertical and horizontal structures, and their corresponding top-down to bottom-up linkage strategies based on the broad distinction between being ancillary to the party and independent civil society actors.

In the Long '68, the strongest pillars of party organisation were found in the communist and social democratic traditions. Between them, there were significant differences, which were the product of their origins and versions of socialism, at the same time as they also shared distinctions from the 'other left'. SDPs became mass parties first, and communists developed into mass parties primarily because of the broader 'Popular Movements' which they directed.[2] A propagandist strategy aimed at establishing a solid, social and cultural counter-hegemony. They always had a youth organisation, trade unions linked to the party, other front organisations such as for peasants and women or war veterans, the pro-peace and anti-imperialist movement (which operated as a pole for democratic citizens), a party press which typically included a newspaper and a theoretical journal among other local or regional publications. These were ancillary structures, that is, they were associated with the party by statute or constitution and primarily served the objectives of the party

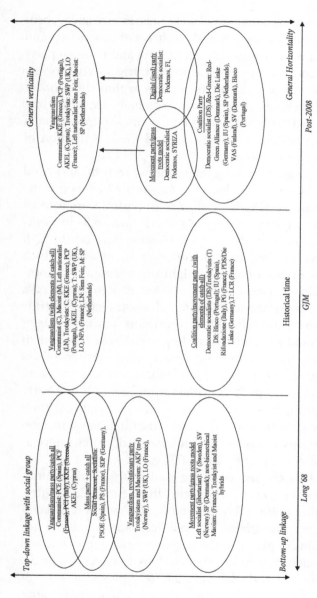

Figure 8.1 Party organisations on the European Radical Left (ideal-type organisational model, ideological denomination, indicative examples)

Abbreviations: AKEL – Progressive Party of the Working People; AKP (m-l) – Workers' Communist Party (Marxist-Leninist); FI – Unbowed France; IU – Left Unity; KKE – Communist Party of Greece; LCR – Communist, Revolutionary League; LO – Workers' Struggle; NPA – New Anti-Capitalist Party; PCE – Communist Party of Spain; PCI – Communist Party of Italy; PCF – Communist Party of France; PCP – Portuguese Socialist Party; PG – Left Party; PS – Socialist Party; PSOE – Spanish Socialist Workers' Party; SPD – Social Democratic Party of Germany; SF – Socialist People's Party; SP – Socialist Party; SV – Socialist Left; SWP – Socialist Workers' Party; SYRIZA – Coalition of the Radical Left; VAS – Left Alliance leadership. The CP was also connected, as in Italy, France and Cyprus most notably, to private businesses in the spheres of production and consumption, culture and sports. Its youth, local and national party festivals, affiliated cooperatives and the broader organic civil society that encircled it operated as a counter-society within the broader capitalist social life. In being vibrant, organisationally diversified and multisectoral, CPs and SDPs of the mass type politically appropriated space through their widespread branches and the mobilisation of party activists in neighbourhoods.

A long chain of decision-making bodies began with the local and workplace cell for the CPs or the local cell for the SDPs. Whereas the local cells of the traditional cadre and socialist parties were formed in geographical areas, communist groups also formed cells in workplaces. This original element of their organisation gave rise to high levels of solidarity resulting from a common occupation, which was more effective in contributing to tight organisation and community and mobilising capacity than residence. Workplace cells were more focused on practical questions of labour, with less time for open-ended debate and substantive constraints on the agenda of that debate. This could also differ according to the industrial area in question, specifically the density of workplace cells.[3] Party members had demanding duties: to recruit new members, endorse the party programme, defend unity, protect matters relating to internal party affairs, regularly account for their activity and 'self criticise' their personal stance or activity. The cell system inscribed the principles in organisational terms and offered useful means of contact, propaganda and recruitment during periods of illegality.

After the cell came the sectional, regional and federal committees, then the party congress which elected the Central Committee, after that the smaller political bureau and finally the general secretariat which ran everyday affairs. The political bureau was the key agenda-setting and veto player in the decision-making process, and traditionally, although not always, its decisions were carried at the Central Committee. The broader principle of democratic centralism was one of vertical unity in action, meaning that dissent after a decision was made was punishable by the leadership. Discussion would be organised from the bottom up and application of decisions from the top down. In applying the axes of democratic centralism, the communists would typically develop behaviour with certain key elements. Chiefly, factions were (and are still today in orthodox CPs) banned, although intra-party tendencies have existed almost invariably across time. This meant that their potential functions were entirely concentrated in the central leadership, such as mobilising participation in the party's affairs, articulating issue-oriented interests and representing certain groups or ideological traditions.[4] To prevent the formation of factions, horizontal discussion in the archetypical CP was banned, while vertical structures also facilitated a quicker transfer of information between the top to the bottom and vice versa.

The institution of apparatchiks (paid party personal) meant that militant activism was intermediated by cadres co-opted by the party. When extending to the cadres of associated organisations, often part of the party's leadership, it becomes clear how the mass and centralist party was organisationally designed to reinforce the leadership line. Nevertheless, in spite of their discipline, which has been higher compared to their opponents, the internal critics of CPs have been many. Across countries, they were systematically put through the party's disciplinary mechanisms, with expulsions as the ultimate punishment. Critics called into question the Leninist structures and demanded, among other things, horizontal communication, secret voting with the opportunity to promote particular candidates and a decrease in the role of paid officials.[5]

Democratic centralism was nevertheless variable across time and place, its trajectory determined by the relation between its constituent parts: centralism and democracy. Each in relation to the other was applied and verbalised by historical communist leaders in a fashion that reflected the conflict at stake within the party and their side and position in that conflict.[6] During the 1960s and 1970s, democratic centralism was interpreted in relation to debates over the centralisation of state socialism in the USSR, eastern Europe and China.[7] Casting the issue in wider terms, party bureaucracy has been the CPs' (and SDPs') chief strength. Part of this bureaucracy was ideological education. It was organised through specific party bureaus, regional and local seminars on theory, theoretical periodicals and the funding of working-class history projects, museums and memorials. At the same time, agenda setting, veto functions and the crafting of the ideological and political line rested in the highest organs. While the party organisation was so deeply and thoroughly rooted in wider society that the party bodies could easily absorb, receive and consider vibrations from all corners of social life among their constituencies.

Democratic centralism was disputed by the students of the 1960s within a larger discussion about bureaucracy, hence a typical critique of the New Left ran along the lines of 'centralised organisation equals bureaucracy equals degeneration'. Critiques of 'substitutionalism', typically attributed as a term to Trotsky, claimed that Leninist party organisation operates by replacing the working class with the party and inevitably leads to personalisation and power abuse by the leadership. From a Leninist viewpoint, the critique was somewhat different: that in Lenin's own conception of party democracy, vanguardism and the centralism necessary for careful direction from the top were historically limited.[8] 'Under conditions of political freedom our party will be built entirely on the elective principle. Under the autocracy this is impracticable for the collective thousands of workers that make up the party.'[9]

Trotskyist and Maoist parties did not significantly diverge from the communist model of organisation. Their structure was that of the 'new type of party', premised in democratic centralism and having the same decision-making chain as the communists. The Trotskyists, however, invoked 1921 as the moment which determined the CPs' organisational rigidity and blamed Lenin for misinterpreting his own principles and arriving at a centralist position. Ernest Mandel wrote that 'nothing in Lenin's writings suggests that the period of the dictatorship of the proletariat allows for only one party', something which attests to why the Trotskyists appealed to 1921 in order to legitimise the formation of tendencies.[10] To be more specific, for both the Trotskyists and the Maoists there was a certain variability in the distinctions between currents and organisational spirits.[11] Some parties, like the Socialist Workers' Party in the UK and the Communist Revoutionary League in France allowed tendencies, while others – such as Workers' Struggle in France and the Workers' Party of Norway – did not. Maoism came in hierarchical as well as non-hierarchical forms (e.g., GP and one of its predecessor organisations, the Union of Young Communists (Marxist-Leninist) in France). The latter was more oriented towards a movement-party form, and used a method known as *enquête* – going out to the people and learning from them – as a preparatory stage for a 'true centralist party' whereby the individual and the collective were in absolute harmony.[12]

In particular, what came to be known as the left libertarian tradition – which cut into Trotskyist and Maoist spaces and had connections to feminism and the environmental movements – can be credited with democratising radical spaces away from vanguardism, centralism and uniformity. Since the time of the Hungarian reform movement, and its crushing in 1956, democratic centralism had come under increasing scrutiny. Especially after the crushing of the Prague Spring and with bottom-up groups and mobilisations appearing in the thousands in western Europe, the communist organisation was also criticised from within, although not in all CPs. The Long '68 still marked a critical moment in the verticality/horizontality tension that was at play from the twofold emergence of left radicalism in the nineteenth century, through anarchism and social democracy; the main historical transmutation being that the original intra–extra-institutional division became an intra-institutional one, as if anarchism was given ideological space in the socialist tradition. Across subspaces on the historical Radical Left – the communist, Trotskyist and Maoist – it was argued that the institutionalised suppression of tendencies affected the party on multiple levels, inhibiting autonomous theoretical work, sufficient levels of pluralist expression, collective agency, flexibility and the appreciation of its own living and inevitable contradictions.[13]

A more pluralist organisation would have been more reflective and representative of the diverse opinions of citizens with socialist allegiances, rather than allowing for the easy imposition of a common framework without meaningful participation in decision-making procedures. Given diversity and pluralism the party should also be, by nature, sufficiently competitive. 'Thinking for oneself' was the intellectual fuel for many activists, which emanated from radical literature and culture.[14] Where they were more influential depending on the ideological background of parties, these ideas, meant a number of organisational changes. In Scandinavia, the New Left parties of the 1960s and 1970s espoused a non-Leninist organisational grid which abandoned democratic centralism. The Norwegian SV, established in 1972, offered an innovative organisational model to the extent that it was less hierarchical than its predecessor party organisation, developed a participatory organisational structure and sustained interaction with external social movements and citizens' initiatives. From the beginning, SV also had a 40 per cent quota for both sexes at all levels in party bodies. The Swedish Left Party-Communists in 1978 introduced a quota for as many women as female party members, in a wider process of explicitly committing to parliamentary politics, rejecting democratic centralism and taking a more cautious and distant stance towards the USSR.

The Eurocommunists also underwent change on organisational issues, which began to be debated and posed by the leadership two to three decades earlier. The year 1969 was when the Spanish and Italian CPs criticised democratic centralism as a communist organising principle. Six years after that, the Rome Declaration by the PCF and PCI in November 1975, as well as other meetings in Berlin and Paris, committed to a plural party, the independence of trade unions, workplace democracy and opening state institutions to the working class.[15] In accordance with the PCI's heritage views, the party always blended class struggle with the democratic ideal. And these horizons were connected in the quest for more autonomy from the USSR and the latter's loss of a sacrosanct appeal. Without officially abandoning democratic centralism and the theory of the revolutionary vanguard, the Eurocommunists made openings on a number of fronts, not least in order to appeal more to the middle classes and catholic sections of society:

- The party's links with society at large and social groups in particular: becoming more oriented to emerging currents and allowing participation in the party as well as in independent SMOs.
- In the PCF, during the Eurocommunist phase, between 1977 and 1979, the PCF's position on workers' control (*autogestion*) was changed to an enthusiastic one, to the extent it was now enshrined in party statute.

- The traction between the mass membership and militant cadres: leading to revisions of earlier criteria and procedures for recruiting members and approaching sympathisers, or commitment to full transparency for members.
- Modifying democratic centralism and engaging with more pluralist arrangements: more tolerance for criticism and dissent, including the quasi-unofficial existence of currents and imposing no measures on dissidents.
- Debates and in some cases policies to enhance democracy in the electoral process, which are today standard, such as more candidates than places to be filled on the ballot, reflecting the increased significance of competition.
- Democratising the ideological process through more vibrant discussions at party congresses, where dissenting opinions are not institutionally undermined.[16]

In 1976, in East Berlin, the Conference of European Communist Parties promoted diversity by institutionsalising it in its statutes and argued for respect for different roads to socialism.[17] Further democratisation on the Radical Left came gradually. The Eurocommunists did not break from democratic centralism until later, and therefore a tension arose here as well as between their attempts to democratise and their homogeneous, closed structures, with stringent procedures governing entry, participation and exit, and a centrally disseminated framework for interpreting the world and militancy through party obligation. That said, the period of the Long '68, from the New Left to the Eurocommunists, signalled the initial and polymorphous critique of communist organisational orthodoxy through ideological revision within the party systems and movement spaces of western Europe. All this was happening in the broader context of rising individualism, after the 1960s, in which the new, central significance placed upon the individual does not fit into the discipline of democratic centralism.

Today, RLPs mostly abide by the democratic principles of liberal democracy as constitutional practices at the level of the nation state. In their majority, they are participatory, representational, internally competitive, responsive and transparent.[18] By the 1990s, parties like

Rifondazione, IU and Left Bloc practised policy consultations with movements and civil society in their manifesto-drafting processes. The SV in Norway and Vänsterpartiet in Sweden also employed this practice. DiEM25 used party member surveys for its policy formulation process in the 2019 European elections. Today more than ever, any uniformity of ideas has come to be taken as fictitious. Demarcations have been carried forward, indeed, mainly as concerns about centralisation as opposed to decentralised structures – hence most Marxist-Leninist parties – AKEL, the PCP and the KKE – have maintained agenda-setting and veto power for the higher echelons, most often the Central Committee. CPs are also different in their perception of competitive elections for party office and especially for the party leader – hence the long tenures in AKEL, the KKE, the PCP and the Dutch SP effectively translate into the absence of competitive elections when the time comes, as a consensus pre-emerges in the central committees and ensures the supremacy of one selected nomination.

In these parties, democratisation processes that effectively reduced the top leadership's power have not only been avoided for the most part but in certain cases the change has been towards centralisation. In the fluid environment of the Greek crisis, for example, the KKE, which still operates on the basis of democratic centralism, tightened the conditions for the readmission of members who were expelled or had left the party, having found that 'few actually managed to reintegrate'. The KKE's leadership also reintroduced powers allowing it to periodically review the party's membership to ensure that members are suitable.[19] Nevertheless, centralist features are not exclusive to the CPs. SYRIZA's government experience led to centralisation and the concentration of power in the leadership, and the leader himself – Alexis Tsipras. Podemos functions 'like a typical centralised party', in terms of decision-making and candidate selection procedures;[20] Sinn Féin has concentrated power over its leadership under Gerry Adams due to its military and clandestine past. Parti de Gauche, the party of Jean-Luc Mélenchon, has had no proper process of leadership elections, as it was established as a political vehicle for the promotion of its leader. Formal procedures can also be circumvented through tactical manoeuvring to outbid opponents.[21]

Wider social processes of party organisational change have interposed power distribution within RLPs. We can register during the Long '68 a reorientation towards attracting votes from all social cleavages and classes, thus expanding outside of traditional communist constituencies. This was also a more generalised shift of many parties, diluting their ideological base in order to expand their electoral base in the light of increasing problems faced by the mass model. Chiefly: a decline in membership and party identification, with consequent decreases in newspaper readership and subscriptions, the erosion of voluntary partisanship, a transformation towards a more balanced social profile in terms of groups and classes, and declining membership fees in total and in relation to overall party revenue. In this reality, a catch-all perspective could accrue most benefits in the age of declining political loyalties.[22] In subsequent decades, Otto Kircheimer's original diagnosis was in many respects reinforced in empirical terms, and indeed Eurocommunism in the 1970s showed a strong element of the catch-all mentality. It specified the middle classes as the target of an expansive electoral strategy.[23]

A key aspect of such transformations – membership – has declined dramatically in European party systems. This includes RLPs, although not all of them. The main outliers are still the PCF, PCP, AKEL and SP, which have about 51,000, 64,000, 15,000 and 44,000 members respectively, which translates into a membership density of about 15 per cent in each case.[24] Membership density is the number of members compared to the total number of members of all political parties in the country, and it has gone down dramatically since the 1970s when the stronger CPs of France, Italy, Cyprus and Finland ranged between a third and half of all the members of the countries' political parties.[25] If we widen the scope to the 'societal strength' of parties, as measured by the number of RLP members compared to the electorate, the decline is even higher. It is estimated by Chiocchetti, based on a sample of eight western European countries, that it fell from about 1.5 per cent in most of the 1960s and 1970s to about 0.02 per cent in the 2010s.[26] Many aspects of party organisation have been affected: a decline in militant activists, problems of internal coordination and cohesion, gaps in communication with constituencies, difficulty in developing ties of identification without social roots, poorer capacity to initiate protest and lower utility of extra-parliamentary mobilisation as a driver of political success.[27]

To a certain extent, these factors explain the next organisational reconfiguration of the Radical Left party family in terms of structures. It came in the 1990s and 2000s, when this space stood out in five main cases of coalition party building (and various minor ones), whereby pre-existing parties or groups came together into a unified organisation: Left Bloc, SYRIZA, Die Linke, the NPA and the Front de Gauche, and less importantly the Scottish Socialist Party (SSP). Their chief predecessors were the IU from 1986 and the Danish Red–Green Alliance since 1989. Within the IU, Red–Green Alliance, SSP and Front de Gauche the parties have been preserved as organisational units within the whole, while in Left Bloc they dissolved after six years and have been operating since then as factions. The same has happened to Die Linke, where the German Party of Democratic Socialism and Labour and Social Justice – The Electoral Alternative officially merged in 2007 a few years after they engaged in negotiations. Unlike the RLPs of the 1960s and 1970s, the starting point builds on an acknowledgement of fragmentation and pursues the objective of a plural party trying to unify as much as possible. For the CPs, the point of departure was full and undisturbed unity, which in due course witnessed divisions and splinters. The road to unity is hard nevertheless, especially the beginning: in Die Linke and the Left Bloc it took six years after the mergers to arrive at a common programme or platform, and in the Red–Green Alliance this took nine years.[28] The Left Bloc rests on structures of routinised factionalisation. More broadly, factionalism has been naturalised on the Radical Left. The overarching perception progressively taking shape is that all groups and opinions have the right to exist and this is challenging. It is, however, healthier as a transition stage towards the establishment of counter-hegemony than dogmatic discipline.

At the same time, more inclusive though looser linkages opened up through the participation and responsiveness potential of digital politics. Many political parties have taken the idea of the public square assembly to the internet, creating participatory online platforms for their members, and aspiring to provide members and supporters with more influence in the party decision-making process. Emulating and departing from the pirate parties, Momentum inside the Labour Party acted as a campaign group for recruiting party members, and Podemos and FI have largely operated through open, accessible and user-friendly forums of deliberation and online primary elections and referendums. On these platforms the organisational machinery of the party is substituted by software: for example, Rousseau, Plaza Podemos and My Momentum. In the age of the social media, parties extract data from their supporters' online behaviour, which can be used for the purpose of adaptating to their opinions or any shifts therein.[29] The outcome of platform-based party organisation can be more vertical than expected or believed by participants. The frequency of supermajority results supporting the party line in online and highly inclusive elections, referendums and policy decisions betray the tendency of concentrated and vertical power distribution, which remains unresolved by digital forms of organisation.[30] The very use of social media individual-level data for navigating public opinion is nothing short of a definitive operational feature of the ideal-type cartel party: wide inclusivity combined with agenda-setting and veto power by the leadership. Processes of mediatisation, professionalised political communication and digitalisation are assumed to centralise parties by enforcing the party in central office and its professionals, which control communication strategy and central access to digital means of collective mobilisation.

Through digital access to politics, the membership boundary has been blurred. Most notably in Podemos and FI, all affiliates have voting rights (and most people vote online). Podemos' Asamblea Ciudadana is a permanent body making decisions between conferences through online decision-making processes. One can acquire membership by registering on the website. SYRIZA has been getting closer to this approach. During its membership recruitment campaign, the leadership utilised the slogan 'Take SYRIZA in your hands', and promoted a digital platform – currently utilised for member registration – that they hope will become a website through which members can participate actively, express opinions and vote. Suspicious reactions from party officials warned that 'if our members are people who vote on the criterion of popularity, the social media, and the physical appearance of officials, then our future will be foreboding'.[31]

The shift in boundaries is formally one towards open plebiscitary intra-party democracy, with democracy defined by its level of inclusiveness and a 'fully democratic' party as one that includes all citizens.[32] Moving in this organisational direction reflects the discourse of citizenism in so far its mobilisation practice suggests that members and non-members should be equally involved in all organisations by and for citizens. This variant of internal party democracy departs from the dominant approaches to party democracy driven by conceptualising the party as an organisation with clearly defined boundaries, as in the Leninist tradition. Yet, given that entry requirements are so low, members have almost no obligations, which is in stark contrast to the archetypical communist, Trotskyist and Maoist parties of the past. It may thus appear more democratic to grant members many rights and no obligations; nevertheless, this severely undermines political belonging by eliminating commitment.

Mobilising through virtual space works in some respects but not in others. Based on her experience of the Occupy movements, Dean made the case for imagining and adapting the CP as an organisation that can reinvigorate socialist strategy and radical political force. This, she argues, is necessary for weaving the bonds of a 'weness' between radical subjects, something which classical socialist politics did very successfully.[33] But to the extent that doing the above requires the physical presence – rituals, festivities, education groups, press, etc. – to be rolled back into a central organisation, the ideological tension not only remains but is much stronger than the 1960s and 1970s, a period when CPs still reigned with communist legitimacy as highly centralised entities. A multitude of innovations has been recorded, for example, Labour-backing bots on Tinder, the daily use of memes for political propaganda, broadcasting anti-fascist confrontations or live streaming movements and party leader interventions, or using Google docs to organise meetings. Across the world, parties have responded to the decline of their memberships by introducing ways to get people involved. But are they sufficient to produce the principle of 'one for all and all for one'? In the terms of Jodi Dean, this would be a realm that channels belonging into the political Left through combining rights and commitments, and in turn projecting a collective spirit into radical action.[34]

The overall mobilising capacity of these tools compared with a socially rooted organisation entailing political participation through all walks of life is at the least insufficient. Digital tools can thus support spontaneous, transparent, inclusive and tactical mobilisation, solidarity and protest. But alone they cannot substitute for the day-to-day mass-scale 'societies within societies' of the mass CP and its respective organisational reach. And they do not always translate into more party democracy.[35] Virtual space may not be sufficient for comradeship, which is the result of concrete bonds, networks, relations, commitments, connections and norms, and the subsequent sense of belonging it brings about. Meanwhile, virtual space is not free of democratic deficiencies. Transcending physical space through virtuality can be helpful but insufficient for a strong socialist force that is not networked into the everyday lives of people and does not inscribe a collective political culture into its militants.

HORIZONTALITY AND VERTICALITY THROUGH THE LENS OF LINKAGE

Our dominant motif of the central role of linkage in mobilisation and resistance returns to centre stage because party models and spaces are relevant for linkage. They reflect the nature of top-down or bottom-up strategy and which organisation commands more social and political capital. The horizontality–verticality continuum takes shape through parties' internal decision-making procedures as well as in connection to society. Here, we develop a linkage between organised entities on the Radical Left, combining the strategic viewpoint of each key actor involved: movements and parties. Enthusiastic statements that highlight 'newness', such as 'a close interaction or even organic relationship with such movements seems to be one of the key characteristics that singles out newer parties of the populist left', can be highly misleading.[36] Today's linkage on the European Radical Left has a strong sense of historicity.

In spite of the divisions and conflict between communist leaderships and students movements, there was substantive interaction on the Radical Left in the aftermath of 1968. Approximately 27 per cent of delegates to the 1979 provisional party congresses of the PCI followed a 'new' or 'mixed' pathway to party membership, involving activism in a social movement organisation.[37] A shared similarity of activist inflow into communist organisations is further documented by Michael Waller, who surveyed western European CP congress delegates' characteristics in the 1970s, showing a 'new member' factor. A militancy 'different in kind from that characteristic of traditional Stalinist democratic centralism' was brought into the CPs. Over the long term, it both helped the CPs to reinvigorate in the electoral market and contributed to internal fragmentation and splintering, often igniting pre-existing divisions.[38] The 'new member factor' for all parties was the product of a changing European society and economy, at the apex of economic growth, with social mobility mostly the product of education. Parties as receptors of educational, occupational, demographic and other changes translated social developments into political ones.

For the PCI, the inflow of young people and women 'contributed to slowing down the decline that the PCI had been experiencing over the 15 years previous to 1968'.[39] As an ex-PCI militant, and critical figure of the extra-parliamentary Italian left, Rossana Rossanda described it: 'the overlapping of the political shift of the historic compromise and the mass movement, from which the PCI extracted its political capital between 1968 and 1975'.[40] In various struggles, communist militants linked resources and conviction to local movements, from the feminists to the ecologist and anti-fascist fronts. Although nothing (as shown later on) is to be taken for granted (as was the case in Italy), the PCI (and especially its left wing under Pierro Ingrao) was constantly oriented towards the party machine and the outside realm of radicals working in the same direction of social change as the communist militants. Following an initially hesitant approach, which saw these movements become largely disassociated from the working class and its problems, by the 1970s it was participating in working groups with the peace and environmental movements, although not incorporating some of their central demands about nuclear power and ecological sustainability.[41] During the Eurocommunist turn, the party's approach to social movements was changing nevertheless. As a feminist PCI militant, Laura Lilli, argued, the party consented to communist women being active in both the PCI and the movements, thus introducing 'a further, original Italian attempt at a "third way"'.[42]

In Norway, Sweden and Finland, the CPs had made the peace movement a top priority from the 1950s and into the 1960s, and in their endeavour to fuse with society they often connected parliamentary work to local and national assemblies, which also served as consultations of its parliamentarians and the party leadership.[43] Across the board, the Trotskyists and Maoists, without a parliamentary presence, were constantly engaged in organising neighbourhood assemblies, issue campaigns, protests, strikes and cultural events within networks of other organised groups. At the same time, a vertical design operated, as in the CPs. Detailed bulletins of contact work were circulated by the party for militants and members, refined into principles, tasks, hierarchies, distinctions, categories and specific intents, and reached into leisure time.[44] Trotskyist parties' resilience – their existence over time in multiple countries without any sort of electoral power – directs us to their hybrid nature, comprising party, social movement and sect features.[45] Which one prevailed was highly dependent on case and context.

Linkages with movements also formed in the so-called Eurosocialist parties emerging in the 1970s in southern Europe and distinguishing themselves from the classic SDPs of central and northern Europe. Notably, the Socialist Workers' Party of Spain was radicalised in the late 1970s due to widespread anti-Franco sentiment and the economic crisis that country was undergoing. It fathered momentum among disenfranchised and pro-democratic sections of the organised grassroots movements. In France, post-'68, the Socialist Party (PS) grew from 10,000 members in 1968 to about 200,000 in 1981 under the leadership of Mitterand, outpolling the PCF by 1978.[46] The small Parti Socialiste Unifié attracted both revolutionaries and reformists in their common rejection of anti-Stalinist views and the 'old' SDPs. In Greece, local citizens' movements and a variety of new left organisations formed PASOK's backbone. The proliferation of social movements in France, Spain and Greece would produce the upsurge of electoral socialism, which in turn came to talk about women's issues, cultural renewal and ecology.[47] In the UK, Tony Benn advocated workers' control, more transparency, critical reflection on bureaucracy and power abuse, emphasis on extra-parliamentary work, feminist values and alternative economic policies with emphasis on economic democracy. As with the CPs and newly emerging parties, the inflow of *movimentismo* into the rising social- ists in Greece, Scandinavia and the Iberian peninsula translated into a diversified composition, and thus a social basis that was broader and more multiclass than that of traditional social democracy.[48]

During the GJM years, the prefigurative crisis that we outlined in Chapter 5 facilitated the 'return of politics' by movements. From the point of view of parties, since the GJM linkages with movements have maintained the status of a noble and strategic commitment in the fight against neoliberalism. Emulating Latin American mobi- lisation on the Left, parties such as Rifondazione, IU, Left Unity, Left Bloc and Synaspismos established departments focusing exclu- sively on social movements and often included hearings from civil society in their manifesto-drafting processes. In the Genoa Social Forum, alternative globalist and pacifist organisations came together on a permanent basis with Rifondazione in 2000–1 to discuss and organise demonstrations and common activities. Rifondazione con- ceptualised the appropriate place for the party in relation to the movements as 'contagion', receiving cultures of activism, positions, ideas, concepts, methods and repertoires of action, and incorporat- ing them into the party's deliberations and political narrative.[49] The first European transnational structure of left-wing parties and RLPs allowed for individual and movement membership beyond party- based participation.[50]

In France, the Collectifs du 29 Mai/Collectifs Unitaires Antilib- eraux were organised by cadres of political parties and SMOs, coming together in 2005–7 to continue the coordination of the 'left of the no' to the European Constitutional Treaty, and to propose a common candidate for the subsequent presidential election. In Spain, Espacio Alternativo was created for the explicit purpose of bringing social movements closer to the IU. In Sweden, leading figures of Vänster- partiet helped to organise Attac.[51] Similar phenomena continued into the 2010s. In Germany, Die Linke supported and contributed to the protests against the G20 in Hamburg in July 2017. Its think tank, Rosa Luxemburg Stiftung, is a network connecting academ- ics and activists of the democratic socialist tradition. In the UK, Left Unity has actively collaborated with the STWC, UK Uncut, the

Women's Assembly and Black Activists Rising against the Cuts.[52] In Spain, Podemos and IU have supported PAH. In France, the *marée populaire* demonstration on 26 May 2018 was jointly organised by parties (most importantly the FI and PCF), trade unions (most importantly the General Confederation of Labour) and civil society organisations. Under Marie-George Buffet, the PCF's leader after the disastrous participation in the Lionel Jospin government, the party emphasised extra-parliamentary mobilisation and wide participation in social and political struggles. In Sweden, links and common local campaigns against spending cuts were undertaken between Vänster-partiet and Megafonen, especially after the dramatic youth riots in Stockholm in 2013.[53] In Greece, the youth organisations of the KKE, SYRIZA and ANTARSYA, through the network structure of their presence in labour and other groups and associations, contributed to the organisation of several protests.[54]

There are many more examples. However, it is highly questionable whether this has led to a widespread redefinition of the political space on the Radical Left in western Europe,[55] since party–movement linkages and transversal and sectional interconnections between mobilising agents of left radicalism have rarely led to successful new RLPs. With Podemos, SYRIZA, the Labour Party and the Belgian Workers' Party entering parliament in 2016 as the exceptions, in the rest of western Europe a realignment in left political competition has not been triggered: either a break into parliament, the emergence of a new successful RLP or radically altering the balance of power towards the left of the political spectrum. This is so, in spite of many dramatic declines in the vote for SDPs and ensuing internal upheaval.

Beyond temporal variation there is spatial variation as well. A macro-historical pattern is that perceptions of how top-down or bottom-up societal linkage needs to be is associated with ideological traditions. For the communists, the party as vanguard was irreplaceable, whereas Gramsci identified the workers' councils as the most significant collective organ of the proletariat. The Trotskyists have also been traditionally understood (and often (self-)satirised) for their revolutionary party militancy. In the ESFs, they were the most insistent on 'more action, less movement'. A symptom of partisan, militant behaviour is the accusation (common in several campaigns in the UK) that the Trotskyist vanguardists try to take over the movement or campaign.

The democratic socialist tradition, including some of the early Greens, has veered between *movimentismo* and partisanship. The traditional communists criticised movement and individual membership inside the ELP and produced a fierce critique of the ESFs. The KKE called them opportunist, questioned their financing practices and did not participate in the Athens ESF once it realised it could not take over, while the PCP was softer in its approach, although still markedly different from parties like Rifondazione.[56] Since early on, CPs and many Trotskyist parties, for example Workers' Struggle in France, made a clear distinction between workers and the petit bourgeois when it came to entry into the party. Probationary periods were a characteristic mark of this space, and this remains the case today in all the examples we have examined. AKEL in Cyprus barely engaged in a dialogue about movements, and disagreed about membership by individuals and movements inside the ELP.[57] All of these parties are more selective because they can be: they have ancillary structures which organise important and well-known events that attract attention. Their annual youth festivals, for instance, are telling, and their branched structures enable proximity to events and information across the country. Communist linkage necessitates that we understand dense, diversified and interactive party structures as conducive to strong linkages. This is top down on the one hand, but on the other it sustains social roots in the long term and ingrains political belonging.

The extremity of crisis conditions did not alter preformed strategies towards civil society at large: orthodox parties continued to rely heavily on selected labour-related groups and ancillary structures, following exclusive, top-down strategies, while dismissing riots, students and youth movements. In contrast, the democratic socialists created channels of communication and interaction with them, accepting a mutual direction of influence to begin with.[58] The patterns of the GJM years inside the Radical Left party family continued into the 2010s. It seems, therefore, that the ideas of socialism in their particular colours continue to contribute towards shaping particular targets, conditions and perceptions about radical civil society.

This is how ideology feeds into organisational practice. Still, the common factor across all RLPs – the ideological legacy of socialism and opposition to capitalism (or the establishment) – is what dictates a constant concern with linkage, whether bottom up or top down.[59]

How, then, should we assess the widespread talk of movement parties as a popular model of party organisation in the 2010s? En Marche! in France, Podemos in Spain and comedian Beppe Grillo's M5S in Italy are parties of the crisis which tried to sustain many characteristics of the movements out of which they emerged. SYRIZA in Greece and the Green Alternativet in Denmark invested immense energy in transposing movement demands into electoral politics. Podemos grew out of the *indignados* and 15M movements. Momentum in the UK has tried to influence the Labour Party from within. Movement parties span a large space on the political spectrum and are favoured by an anti-party tendency within the electorate and a political environment of widespread protest and grassroots politics. Bottom-up processes, network-like structures, blurry member boundaries and mobilisation through activism and protest can overcome obstacles to popularity.

Movement parties are not new phenomena strictly speaking, at least not for the Radical Left. It is important to note their continual existence, which validates rather than disposes of the tension between horizontality and verticality, and more broadly between the realm of civil society and the state. In the 1970s and 1980s, the New Left libertarian parties arose out of networks and coalitions between NSMs, espousing egalitarian politics and promoting inclusiveness and direct participation. The GPs' *fundis–realo* debate revolved largely around the distinction between movement and party and its navigation. Out of the 1980s, a participatory organisation did not translate into the realisation of a rich membership and a fully democratic party. It was recurrently limited or resisted by parliamentarisation and thus the prioritisation of the party in public office.[60] For the historical Left, although not for early ecological thought, this was the debate about the people, the masses, the revolutionary subjects, the 'multitude' and whether they should be hegemonised or could rise to the challenge themselves.[61]

Podemos is the modern exposition of the dilemmas between institutional and non-institutional politics, both at the individual and collective level. It is ritualised between factional competition within the party through recourse to or dismissal of the expression 'party-movement'.[62] Momentum's 2017 Constitution centralised the organisation compared to its previous branch-like structure, concentrating democratic activity online in a mass open space, and by implication sidelining the Trotskyists. It required all new members to be Labour Party members. In Greece, since 2015, movements demobilised in their support for a left government and the party was centralised in its new course of moderation that approximates more the ideological profile of PASOK than a Radical Left identity aiming at root-and-branch change. In fact, in Greece, Portugal, Cyprus and Spain anti-austerity protests demobilised while the Radical Left has been in government within a wider framework of austerity-driven governance.

THE GOVERNMENT, THE STATE, THE RADICAL LEFT

Linkage can be fully addressed when parliamentary office, government and the capitalist state are taken into account, as the difference between opposition and power also informs party and movement strategies. We will return to this, after registering the relation of RLPs to the structures of governance, which radicals seek to enter and use as structures of resistance. These mediate any dynamics between electoral and non-electoral forces. If programmatic statements show what the party says (or promises), time in office reveals what the party does, and if this is consonant with its pre-office declarations, statutory rules of operation and the support it has been asking for from the movements and trade unions.

In dealing with the strategy of the vanguard CP in pre-revolutionary and revolutionary situations, Lenin addressed the question of coalitions and, more specifically, the kinds of coalition that should be formed by CPs in advanced capitalist democracies and the reasons for their formation.[63] Parliamentary opposition and coalition formation in pre-revolutionary situations had to be tactical, according to Lenin, that is, to 'exploit conflicts of interest among the bourgeois parties'.[64] The problem has always been what 'tactical' actually means in particular circumstances. As an indication, it's relatively easy to suggest that for revolutionary parties, tactical compromises mean manoeuvres which do not alter the commitment to the regime's overthrow, although it may be much more problematic to apply the term to a movement which does not challenge the regime itself and works *in principium* to change it from within. All parties agree on a twofold strategy on the basis of two axes – parliamentary and extra-parliamentary pressures (e.g. strikes, demonstrations and ideological battles). This is also the root of the problems that parties oriented exclusively towards office, the so-called empty vessels, do not entertain.

Until the 1980s, governmental involvement of CPs was limited by geopolitical considerations, most importantly the ups and downs of the foreign policy crafted in Moscow. The events of 1989–91 worked in the direction of more governmental strength: their average governmental strength as measured by 'relevant seats', within the cabinet or parliamentary support, during 1994–2015 is reported by Chiocchetti as double that between 1945 and 1988.[65] Table 8.1 lays out further insights into cross-national patterns and comparison with SDPs and GPs. It enumerates CP/RLP, SDP and GP participation in distinct government cabinets per decade since the 1940s. When it comes to the actual decision to participate in a cabinet, independent of seats and the actual result of the coalition, there is equal frequency since the 1960s. Between 1945 and 2019, SDPs have participated in government a total of 224 times. SDPs have been closest to the state and their advantage begins on average in the 1940s or earlier. GPs, since the 1980s when they became established across many countries in Europe, enter government with more or less the same frequency as RLPs on average. At the same time, there has always been considerable variation across countries, which is higher for the RLPs compared to GPs. In certain cases, the Radical Left has never participated in or supported government – Portugal until 2016, the Netherlands, Austria except in the immediate post-war period, West Germany, the UK except through the Labour Party, Switzerland and Malta.

Whether we are concerned with the contemporary or historical Left, government participation leads to policy compromise and to working towards defusing popular unrest and preventing a radicalisa-

Table 8.1 Communist/Radical Left, Social Democratic, Green parties and government participation in western Europe (1960–2019)

	1945–9	1950–9	1960–9	1970–9	1980–9	1990–9	2000–9	2010–19	Average (1945–2019)	Total (1945–2019)
CPs/RLPs	4	5	4	5	6	4	7	5	5	40
SPs/SDPs	22	25	25	30	33	32	29	28	28	224
GPs	–	–	0	1	0	5	4	6	2	16

Source: ParlGov.
Notes: Countries included as in Table 6.1. Numbers show the number of party participation in distinct government cabinets.

tion of the political process. This in turn creates problems of identity, feeding into electoral losses whereby radical constituencies withdraw support from the Radical Left because they do not feel that their interests or ideas are any longer represented, or to punish the party for going against their preferred direction. In the 1960s and 1970s, the experience of the PCI during its 'historic compromise' is most revealing. The PCF's participation in the early 1980s under Francois Mitterand led to a large drop in the polls, from 16.1 per cent in 1981 to 9.8 per cent in 1986. More recently, such was also the experience of Rifondazione's time in office during the first and second Romano Prodi governments in the late 1990s and 2006–8, respectively, which pushed the party out of parliament. Again, the PCF almost halved its vote after participating in the Lionel Jospin government between 1997 and 2002 as part of the Plural Left coalition (Gauche Plurielle). During the 2000s, in Sweden, Finland and Norway, participation in government by the respective RLPs halved or significantly reduced their vote share. In Cyprus, AKEL lost about 4 per cent (30,000 votes) by 2016 and another 2 per cent (10,000 votes) by 2021.

On many occasions of government participation, radical left programmes actually turned into moderate neoliberal reform. In addition, policy achievements on various fronts are often easily undone or reversed by the right-wing government that follows. For these parties, the result of participation in national governments has been negative in both ideological and electoral terms.[66] Electoral losses, it was observed, were the highest in countries with 'discriminatory electoral systems and a high number of small or newly emerging outsider parties' acting as radical competitors.[67] Post-crisis accounts confirm this pattern; in most cases of government participation, support was lost in the next election.[68] Because government participation leads to problems with their image as radical or protest actors, RLPs also tend to shift emphasis back to their ideology once they leave government.[69] This would be the essence of what in communist, revolutionary discourse is called opportunism.

Policy changes due to incumbency are the result of co-optation, with very few exceptions. Co-optation as an outcome, and as form, is the institutional endorsement of neoliberal, free market-inspired or otherwise mainstream economic and social policies, combined with a very soft reformism in areas unconstrained by neoliberal doctrine and capital accumulation. Commentators have pointed to the similar radicalism, its aspirations and its eventual fate, between Alexis Tsipras and SYRIZA, and Francois Mitterand who swept into office in 1981 as the first president from the Left in the history of the Fifth Republic, who formed a government with communist ministers for the first time after more than 30 years.[70] Mitterrand's 'road to Social Democracy' utilised radical rhetoric concerning revolution, 'rupture' with capitalism, the exploitation of man and the need to build a class front. The Common Program subscribed to by the PS, the PCF and the Left Radicals in June 1972 contained a lot of this kind of rhetoric, as did SYRIZA's campaigning towards the elections of 2015, which took it to power.

On both occasions, two historical moments for electoral socialism turned into co-optation and in essence ideological defeat. Compromise and retreat came in different ways across the two governments. In 1980s France it came through a combination of factors that were both external (largely international currency speculation) and internal (declining and unsustainable industry and pressure from within the state). Mitterand's policies started off as markedly different from the UK's Thatcher government. Mid-way the two converged through the French government's 'tournant de la rigueur' (return to austerity).[71] In 2015, Greece co-optation came via the perceived lack of an alternative to the EU's bailout programme, under immense pressure to repay the country's accumulated debt and a refusal by EU elites to annul even part of it. The tangible outcome was the same for both Mitterand and Tsipras: the government reversing its own policies of redistributive planning in line with the demands of capital. In both cases, the policies which cohered with the government's initial pledges were readjusted in the light of elections or holding office. Indeed, these very pledges already signalled various steps back from earlier declarations; the government programme embodied only a part of the radicalism that brought these forces to power. The sequence of this politics was similar: radicalism – anticipation – step back; victory and euphoria – initial radicalism – several steps back; disagreements and splits; still electorally successful (to sustain government). This last fact may have, in both cases, changed the acceptable parameters of left-wing governance by way of legitimating political compromise or inculcating it as inevitable and necessary modernisation. If Mitterand's 14 years in office is any indication, it proved to be a disaster for the PCF, as noted above, and contributed to liberalising French socialism.

For both the older CPs and the contemporary RLPs, a vital part of the story concerns the social democrats, always intermediating the causes and effects of co-optation by the parties to their left. From the 40 governments that the CPs and RLPs have participated in since the 1940s, and the tens of other cases where they lent parliamentary support, the vast majority have been centre-left governments in which the main party was the social democrats. In one of the three ongoing coalitions in western Europe where the Radical Left has been participating recently – namely Portugal – the dilemma played out in four ways: the coalition's rejection of legislative proposals by the PCP and Left Bloc, which interfere with economic commitments to the EU; the simultaneous 'relaxed framing' of the two radical lefts, so as to disassociate themselves from policies which contradict their political positions while still making sure the socialist government continues; the renewal of the government in 2019, on the basis of negotiating majority support in parliament bill by bill;[72] the drop of the PCP's vote at the 2019 elections, which also lost voters to the emerging Portuguese right-wing extremists.

RLPs have been typical coalition partners for centre-left governments, as they also benefit from the social democratic protest vote: the 'dissatisfied social democrats', estimated at above 25 per cent of the votes gained by RLPs.[73] While this refers to the contemporary period, overlapping electorates between communist/RLPs and the social democrats are a historical fact, since these electorates were mostly derived from the working class.[74] Still, the argument that 'the Right needs to go' always occupies strong ground within radical left constituencies and leaderships, and thus the memory of recent mistakes and compromises can fade relatively quickly. The boundaries between resistance and co-optation while in office become blurred in light of this argument of emergency that characterises periods of long tenure by right-wing and neoliberal governments.

Paolo Chiocchetti argues that the radical left electorate's bipolar mentality would struggle to understand the refusal to enter a centre-left government to oust the Right.[75] Reading this formula, the mediating factor appears to be the party system. Multi-party systems generate different incentives to two-party systems; fragmented party systems also translate into multi-party governments, in which parties face more negotiators or 'veto players'.[76] Further, social democrats cooperate with the forces to their left when both sides perceive a mutual benefit, which, during the crisis for example, has only been the case in Spain and Portugal, not Greece or Italy.[77] But SDPs often do need a certificate of progressive authenticity, which RLPs can provide. This by itself may suggest that radical constituencies or the need for symbolic credentials for 'the necessary radicalism' within SDPs can pull some of them into coalitions with the Radical Left.

However, given a number of recurrent patterns, the ever present, systemic challenge for RLPs does not concern exclusively the national level. Neither is it entirely dependent on the historical context, nor chiefly on leadership. It has been on average possible to enter executive office across western European countries, yet, as Miliband argued in outlining his theory of a 'state system', 'the left has acceded to governmental power at various points in the twentieth century but not been able to conquer state power in its diverse forms and places'.[78] This goes back to historic French socialist leader Leo Blum's dictum of 'administrating power' and 'conquering power'.[79] If it was an issue in need of theoretical reflection and strategic conception in the 1930s, this conquest appears even less plausible and meaningful today than before. This is the time of more fragmented electoral bodies, the hollowing out of neoliberal political systems and the corresponding forms of public administration in fashion, the penetration of public institutions by corporate and private interests, the entrenchment of 'deep states' globally, structural pressure for budget deficits and the powerful EU dimension of national politics. All this may not be tantamount to saying that the Radical Left in western Europe cannot capture state power through government participation and sustained linkage with movements. At the very least, however, this has been an incrementally difficult undertaking. It recurrently causes both movement demobilisation and leads to the weak position of being compromised and tarnished by 'politics as usual'; at least in so far as more radical choices are avoided, such as quick and in-depth restructurings of the public sector, the democratisation of the armed forces and central planning, which would translate into both executive and structural power.

The Radical Left has inspired widespread hope for redistribution and political reform. It has also always succumbed to pressure and relinquished, even if temporarily, the weight of its identity. In a sense the reason(s) for which it campaigned for votes in the first place have been contradicted. In Marxist terms, capitalist power can turn left-wing governments into 'instruments of its own interests'.[80] Some authors who acknowledge these historical problems are hopeful: 'while it is true that such [radical left] formations would recreate many of the same contradictions in pre-war social democracy, this does not necessarily doom them to the same result'.[81] But the question remains whether government reform by radicals must be the end result or one necessary step in a revolutionary direction. In response, it might be argued, 'it is only through the collective experience of winning tangible victories and testing the limits of reformism that a majority will be won to revolutionary politics'.[82] Though winning tangible victories collectively is an arduous task, if it is not also subjective how concrete previous victories have been. What constitutes 'tangible' will of course be politicised and potentially can serve as a way to suppress alternative views to a given struggle or to undermine the government.

For socialism as a globalist vision, government participation on a national scale is less important if it does not lead to contagion across other countries. If this doesn't happen, socio-economic change can be easily backlashed into place by the forces of globally organised capital and in the absence of effective global organisation by the oppressed and labour. Although neither of these points makes it futile for the Radical Left to fight for and within government, the prospects do not look good. For governments that rely on national planning, it is crucial to keep unprofitable industries solvent, or to retain a strong welfare state and avoid austerity. The financial burden will affect the fiscal position of the state and limit its ability to finance other kinds of reforms, as well as stifle competitiveness. This happened with Mitterand and even more with Tsipras and Greece. Such governments are also likely to witness chronically low investment rates and constant capital flight, which in the grand scheme of things becomes amplified through the mainstream media.[83] From Mitterrand to Tsipras things have become much more challenging of course, the first of them initially followed the alternative of seizing control over investment by nationalising the banks. Must the Left incorporate into its strategy a plan of appropriating private investment? Within the EU, this is legally and politically impossible, and a task requiring the restructuring of the EU's financial system regulations from the ground up.

Perhaps the problem is not so much that seeking government is justified, but that it is not sufficiently grounded in theory and vision. As Carl Boggs deplored for the New Left tradition, a 'debilitating feature is the lack of a systematic theory of the state, of the relationship between class or social forces and politics upon which the actual forms of democratic socialism could be articulated'.[84] Certainly, 'systematic' theory necessarily means advanced arguments about how class politics can translate into socialist political goals. Yet, from the vantage point of 2020, more specific challenges to putting capital on the defensive through institutions may be evident. In particular, the elaboration of strategies for state capture is nearly absent except for certain texts premised on populism research, and Marxist theories of the state are far from blossoming. Within academia, Marxist theories of the state, society and utopia have little or no relevance in public administration and public policy, organisational studies, economics, international peace and development or qualitative and quantitative political science.

All the acceptable versions of alternative systems of governance are founded upon SDP alliances to enter into government and provide high levels of employment, welfare services, taxation and redistribution. Simultaneously, all such governments will have to finance their state investments through economic growth and by extension the capitalist profitability driving it. The question then becomes how to find effective replacements for economic growth that do not harm the planet, while at the same time sustaining profitability. Even further, how is this possible through alliances with the centre-left and upon a two-dimensional axis of competition – on economic and non-economic issues? Otherwise, what happened to the SDPs in the late 1970s (the UK's Labour Party), 1980s (French, Greek and Spanish Socialist Parties) and 1990s (Swedish Labour Party) will happen again: the Left in government liberalising the economy in order to increase profitability as the only way to boost investment and restore growth, which was affecting all constituencies.[85]

There is an organisational story to co-optation as well, as it can only compound problems of policy drift away from one's original goals. During government participation the flow of power within parties changes – they become more centralised, personalised and demobilised in terms of their base. During incumbency, local branches may end up serving mostly as mediators to the party in executive office. The victory or success of parties that are movement allies has also witnessed reactive mobilisations on the part of the movement after the electoral contest. Podemos was initially engaged in a long-term, ongoing debate about its political profile that included frictions between radical activists and the party's institutional actors; the Trotskyist Anticapitalista tendency left the party not even a year into the Spanish Socialist-led government that Podemos is currently a part of. In the case of Momentum and the Labour Party, a thin line has been trodden between prioritising Labour's electoral success and operating in a bottom-up mode, especially when it came to drafting and redrafting the organisational outline and Constitution.[86] Within Momentum the main tension has been between older labour activists and Trotskyists committed to the mass party, delegation and representative democracy, and young militants socialised in horizontal spaces, such as the Occupy London and student movements, who are suspicious of delegated authority.[87]

Given the party in central office is on average a weaker organisation than in the age of the mass party, participation in government entails a shift of personnel from party to government positions: for SYRIZA during 2015 and 2019, 104 out of 151 members of its Central Committee had been assigned a government post.[88] This effectively means two things. One, the party cannot easily differentiate its activity from that of the government; it appears as 'the governing party', which may not always be wise in tactical terms. This is particularly the case when there is co-optation towards the centre by the government, and the distance may at least signal the potential for the party to revisit and scrutinise its incumbency period. Two, the central office and the office on the ground are weakened as party cadres shift their attention to the state, meaning demobilised social penetration and working from the bottom up. For the Left Bloc, its 'dual strategy' – of using institutional politics to gain credibility among 'former centre-left voters', combined with pursuing a differentiation from systemic parties – is inhibited by its lack of mobilisation capacity due to a relatively small core militant constituency. The strategy is also contradicted by heavy reliance on the mainstream media, and investing most of their resources in parliamentary work.[89] In the case of Finland and Norway, participation in government meant the later challenge of mending relations with social movements and trade unions.[90]

During office, the autonomy of the core party leadership to undertake key government decisions can happen in such a way that carries no legitimacy by the party body through the appropriate participation of party organs and members in deciding key issues. In line with theories of party government, the policy of the state should be drawn from within the party or parties running the government.[91] If it is not, then the core leadership and their inner coterie, often including politicians that are not party members, remains unaccountable to the party, the very organisational vehicle which allows partisans to become state officials. By limiting the internal accountability of party leaders, their external accountability as public office holders can be affected.[92] Tsipras's profound impact on the positive result of the first electoral test of SYRIZA in government in September 2015 confirmed what had happened back in July before the referendum, when the Central Committee of the party was not properly consulted or convened during the high-level negotiations with the troika. Between 2012, when SYRIZA shot up to more than 30 per cent from merely 4 per cent, and the present day the Greek Radical Left has been personalised.

This democratic deficit reflected the reality of EU politics during the eurozone crisis: the overrunning or bypassing of parliaments through speedy processes and agreements behind closed doors negotiated in the most elitist way between a few individuals in the Council of the

EU. Thus, as the Radical Left in capitalism is posited to manage the state's affairs, it has been incapable of not internalising the democratic deficits of liberal governance, and manifests organisational characteristics that are not very different from the establishment parties which systematically staff the executive. We are therefore prompted to return to the 'movement party'. This may exist as an ideal-type organisation, but on most occasions, with the Radical Left recently as with the Greens since the 1980s, this turns into a typical political machine.

De facto then the movement party, on the broad left or otherwise, is a transitional party model.[93] Having entered party competition, this model confronts political professionals and incorporates mainstream organisational party features. It also moderates the initial planning for a loose, activism-based and grassroots physiognomy. The Radical Left's challenge is then to sustain *movimentismo* while fighting elections and interacting within the state apparatus. To do this, it needs to transcend no less than the very distinction between the extra-institutional realm and the entrenched hierarchies and self-reproducing ways of doing things inside liberal institutions.

THE RADICAL SUBJECT AS VOTERS OF RLPS

Government incumbency, office seeking and any attempt to conquer the state become even more intricate when considering the social agents that condition participation in government affairs. Broadly, the social and material bases of mobilisation and resistance, within as well as beyond parties, are important. Let us, therefore, turn our attention to the evolution of RLP support within society and across demographics and class, having previously addressed the theories to the revolutionary agency that distinct eras ushered in. CPs in the 1960s and 1970s, as we have seen, did not give youth (or any other category except the working class) the status of being destined to carry the future. Youth could thus only be organised as an appendage to the blueprint of the vanguard party. Maoist, libertarian and Trotskyist parties recognised the significance of youth more vocally. Some parties, such as the French Maoist Union of Marxist-Leninist Communist Youth, explicitly recognised youth as the subject that commanded priority as potentially radical and important.[94] This was also the case with the British International Marxists Group, which engaged extensively with youth culture.[95] The overall approach, not unique to France and the UK, was that students, petty bourgeois intellectuals and nationalist leaders are the vanguard force, which can bring about a revolutionary consciousness in the subaltern classes.

The CPs were also confronted with debates on youth and student movement positions. In Sweden, the CP responded with relative success to the tension between the 'Old Reds and Young Greens'. In Finland, the students were drawn to the Bolshevik wing of the CP. The PCI profited electorally by incorporating the new member factor, whereas the PCF's support eroded as it lost parts of the working class without compensating with inflows from NSMs. In other countries, such as Cyprus and Belgium, the CPs lost out.[96] For the CPs competition from the ultra-left (Maoists, Trotskyists, anarchists) was most pronounced in those sections of society for which the communist environment was rather hostile – the sub-proletariat of low-paid immigrant workers, disregarded by the unions and with no voting rights, and intellectuals who demanded a place in designing socialism but could see the constraints on free criticism or recognised the brutalities of Stalinism.[97] Communist electorates were, in the past, mostly composed of blue-collar workers,[98] although they were not always the most supported by workers among the available party options. The leading electoral force of the working-class vote in the 1960s and 1970s and before were the SDPs.[99] Even in Italy, where the PCI's vote had one of the highest working-class shares among CPs in Europe, its percentage of wage earners was a minority.[100] Therefore, before moving on to explicate contemporary class politics, it should be cautioned that the class relations of the CPs were much more nuanced than their own vision of the working-class party suggested.

Because of modernisation processes, changes in economic structure, the mass entry of women into the labour force, rising global economic interconnections and immigration, Europe's workforce has become highly heterogeneous in terms of both salaried or non-salaried wage workers and occupational experiences.[101] The traditional industrial working class and new lower-skilled service workers are on average less in number as an electoral base for RLPs compared to professionals, which include skilled and semi-skilled service workers and white-collar employees.[102] Skilled workers in the service sector and social professions are equally or more likely than the archetypical working class to vote for the Left.[103] This creates electoral quandaries because these sections of the population typically have more culturally liberal attitudes. It was part of the problem for the students in the 1960s that came from the middle classes and were differently oriented from the working class on socio-cultural issues such as religion, patriotism and sexuality, and the question of democracy and intellectual autonomy.

To say the least, many CPs hesitated to adjust their worldviews in the face of these profound shifts. To mention the two most visible examples, the PCF and the PCI in the late 1960s expelled Roger Garaudy and the Il Manifesto Group, respectively, upon their similar suggestions to grant more theoretical and practical status to intellectual workers and technicians. Effectively, they placed them on an equal footing with the working class and retheorised the relation between these two social sections. In France especially, a rigid *ouvrierisme* (labourism) refused to identify the new forces as classes. It rather spoke of them as strata. The PCF's refusal to recognise non-manual workers as part of the proletariat cost it dearly: in the 1970s, because of these votes flowing into the PS, the latter overtook the communists in electoral strength.[104]

During the Long '68, it was clear that youth and women became targets of communist electioneering. CPs were getting old and turned to the votes of those comprising many of the NSMs, mainly out of electoral necessity. One position which emerged in Sweden, illustrating the communist attempt to steer gender issues, was the offer of baby-sitting services to women by the Communist Party of Sweden so they could attend more party activities.[105] Moreover, the class composition of CPs had already changed between the immediate post-war period and the 1960s and 1970s. For the PCI, for example, 30 years after the war its electoral share was more skewed towards pensioners and housewives than factory workers. The schema between a proletarian and bourgeois constituency, which CPs traditionally tried to seal by reporting the social categories of their congress delegates or members, was already a crude one by the 1960s. It was not easy to ascribe a class or the potential for a class consciousness to 'permanent

officials of a party who were briefly workers but have been professional politicians for decades; or students; or housewives; or retired
people; or intellectuals; or land-owning peasants; or the executives of
communist business enterprises; or brain workers ... .'[106]

Predictive statistical modelling of contemporary RLP voting has
recurrently identified a higher likelihood to choose an RLP in elections for voters who identify with the working class and who are
union members, atheist, on the left of the political spectrum, young,
dissatisfied with democracy and more educated.[107] Class politics has
not ended, rather its map was 'redrawn into shape'.[108] Traditional
parties of the Left gradually became parties of the new working and
middle classes, specifically the expanding white-collar employees in
the state's civil service and elsewhere; during the post-2008 crisis,
the size of the public sector energised distributive conflicts.[109] Most
importantly, however, the two-dimensional axis of competition in
most of Europe, whereby class and identity politics cross-cut, has
meant RLPs drawing in middle-class voters to the Left because of
their libertarian politics. New Left or new politics voters are indeed
located to the right of those from traditional communist or other
socialist parties.[110] In the meantime, working-class voters who are
less educated and more conservative on average may turn to radical
right parties. Elderly citizens who rely on welfare state services and
government subsidies tend to desire their continuation or expansion, while they also have less tolerance for cultural openness.[111] In
the globalisation age, a progressive economic programme has been
disassociated from socio-cultural dynamism. Cosmopolitanism is
highly associated with open economic exchange, while traditionalist
and culturally introvert views go hand in hand with protectionism.[112]
This feeds into a sort of conflict line between the New Left and right-
wing extremist forces.[113]

It has been extensively argued that RLPs have lost their working-class profile and accommodate mostly the middle classes. It is,
however, faulty to suggest an effect on the RLP vote of a declining
working class.[114] The working classes have certainly changed location,
but voters at the low end of the service industry, or the non-active
population, are still found in many statistical analyses as being highly
likely to support the Radical Left. While, over the period between

the 1960s and the 1990s, one could more easily make the case, à la Inglehart, that material and collectivist issues faded towards irrelevance in the West, at least in the face of intergenerational change and individualistic cultures, the past 20 years have evidently suspended this scenario amid extreme inequalities and a series of economic and social crises. Even using the archetypical occupation-based categorisations of social class, in the majority of European countries the middle class has declined over the crisis years and wealth polarisation has increased.[115]

More generally, if we follow class classifications adopted by liberal scholars – Giddens, Goldthorpe and others – then the working class decreased during the 1970s, 1980s and 1990s. Goran Therborn, aptly summarises the global pattern:

Discourse about the new middle classes has grown into an avalanche over the past decade. In and about Africa, Asia and Latin America it is predominantly triumphalist – about Eastern Europe, often more cautious – proclaiming the arrival of mass markets of solvent consumers. Whether right or wrong, class discourses are always socially significant, so the global surge of middle-class discourse is a noteworthy symptom of the 2010s … The working class is vanishing from Chinese and Vietnamese Communist Party documents, while in German-led Europe the ideal of an 'entrepreneurial society' has replaced the mid-twentieth century self-image of the 'wage-earner society'. Political commentators generally see the middle classes as a promising foundation for 'sound' economics and liberal democracy … In the US, by contrast, the prevailing tone is of worry about the middle class's decline in economic status and social weight.[116]

To understand 'potential RLP voters', it is thus crucial to combine substance with perspective and ask what each combination produces. If class is defined in income-related and occupational terms in the relevant scales, it misses the key Marxist proposition that relations to means of production, and thus forms of capital or the absence thereof, is what determines class. Pursuing this line of inquiry, Erik Olin Wright devised a social class classification schema capturing the middle class as one of three things: workers with a managerial function and thus control in the productive process; cognitive capital in the form of a unique skill or specialised knowledge that is marketable within the labour market as a form of capital; and petty capital as in owners of small and medium-sized enterprises.[117] These categories did not change much until the crisis, when the impoverishment of the middle strata started to grow. From a Marxist perspective, 'a rising middle class represented the vanguard of capitalist development in nineteenth century Euro-America; no longer. Finance capital and the multinational corporations have long since usurped that role. Instead, the middle classes have to take sides in sharply polarised societies.'[118] This reading of the social basis of resistance is pertinent, as it subverts the understanding of labels like left populism as twisting political rationalism and reality. It documents a different reality to begin with, which is more resonant with the populist schema than liberal analyses of the class cleavage in European societies.

From class to age there remain patterns across the three periods of 'newness'. 'Younger people are often more likely to vote for left-wing parties than older people', and some studies suggest the trend is 'particularly pronounced among women'.[119] At the same time, RLPs with libertarian orientations (like the GPs) are caught in a dilemma: between (1) advocating welfare retrenchment and market liberalisation to curb spending in pension benefits and health care, which target the elderly, and thus investing more in the young through better education and childcare so to sustain or enhance their status among younger private business people, students and public sector employees; and (2) not alienating their traditional, economically leftist voters who, in the light of RLP liberalisation, may shift to abstention or the SDP, or get tricked into the 'cast a valid vote' strategy of their opponents.[120]

In trying to see how the tendencies of distinct periods translate into long-term trends, we must be careful to balance short-term strategic moves and difficulties by parties and their outcomes across countries. To observe ideological or demographic changes over time, Figures 8.2 and 8.3 show time-series data for RLP and SDP voters based on the Eurobarometer survey and European Social Survey. The time series presents the evolution for both types of parties in the percentage of radical voters (1–3 on the 1–10 self-placement scale and 0–2 on the 0–9 scale), the young (18–24 and 18–35) and women.[121] Both party families share certain trends: a decline in youth support and support from radical left identities, and a relatively stable trend for women and those aged 18–24. For both cases, the deradicalisation of their electoral constituencies began after the end of the Cold War, which supports the claim that the 'end of history' had an ideological impact for the Left within society as well as in party systems. For RLPs the electoral share of radical identities drops from about 80 per cent to about 40: it is essentially halved. For SDPs it drops from about 30 to about 20: the drop is higher for RLPs. It is also noteworthy that about one in five voters of essentially neoliberalised parties (SDPs) identify with the far left of the political spectrum.

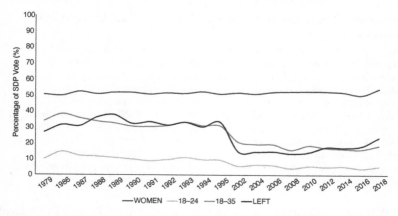

Figure 8.2 Social democratic vote by gender, age and left–right self-placement (1979–2018)

Sources: Schmitt, Hermann, and Evi Scholz. Manheim Eurobarometer Trench File, 1970–1999, 2nd ICPSR version (Mannheim, Germany: Mannheimer Zentrum fur Europaische Sozialforschung and Zentrum fur Umfragen, Methoden und Analysen [producers], 2001) (Cologne, Germany: Zentralarchiv fur Empirische Sozialforschung/Ann Arbor, MI: Inter-university Consortium for Political and Social Research [distributors], 2002), http://doi.org/10.3886/ICPSR03384.v2; European Social Survey Cumulative File, ESS 1-8 (2018). Data file edition 1.0. NSD – Norwegian Centre for Research Data, Norway – Data Archive and distributor of ESS data for ESS ERIC, http://dx.doi.org/10.21338/NSD-ESS-CUMULATIVE.

Notes: Years that had very few data were excluded from the analysis. Weights were applied to ensure that each country is represented in proportion to its population size given the group of all countries is the object of one study.

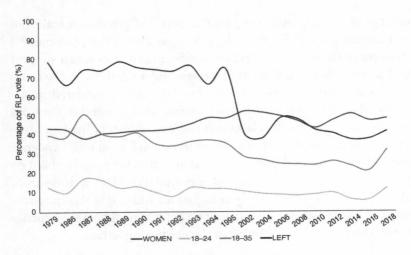

Figure 8.3 Communist/Radical Left vote by gender, age and left–right self-placement (1979–2018)

Notes: Years that had very Sources: Schmitt, Hermann, and Evi Scholz. Manheim Eurobarometer Trench File, 1970–1999, 2nd ICPSR version (Mannheim, Germany: Mannheimer Zentrum fur Europaische Sozialforschung and Zentrum fur Umfragen, Methoden und Analysen [producers], 2001) (Cologne, Germany: Zentralarchiv fur Empirische Sozialforschung/Ann Arbor, MI: Inter-university Consortium for Political and Social Research [distributors], 2002), http://doi.org/10.3886/ICPSR03384.v2; European Social Survey Cumulative File, ESS 1-8 (2018). Data file edition 1.0. NSD – Norwegian Centre for Research Data, Norway – Data Archive and distributor of ESS data for ESS ERIC, http://dx.doi.org/10.21338/NSD-ESS-CUMULATIVE. Few data were excluded from the analysis. Weights were applied to ensure that each country is represented in proportion to its population size given the group of all countries is the object of one study.

We can additionally argue that contemporary CPs and RLPs have faced increasing difficulty in reaching the young due to the emergence of new parties which could be seen as competing to the Radical Left, and which in various cases, especially the Greens, attracted high numbers of young voters. That those between 18 and 24 only drop very slightly for both SDPs and CPs/RLPs may imply that structural changes in the economy, combined with cultural evolution, have not significantly altered their voting choices. The decline appears to begin in the 1970s or 1980s. This is not as pronounced for those between 18 and 34, who show a decline in both party families, meaning this age group underwent a differentiated experiential transition from its younger subset between the pre- and post-Cold War period when the decline was recorded. It is also possible that this age group correlates the most with left radicalism as an individual identity, potentially explaining the parallel declines in these variables. Because of proprietary features that facilitate non-institutional politics, young people are typically protest subjects, but among them macro-political narratives of triumph and revolt 'no longer provide [them with] a readable map of systems of belonging'.[122]

This may explain the dissonance with the picture of social movements. Academics, students and civil society have lost economic ground, as we saw in Chapter 5, and radical movements (and some RLP candidates) are very strongly associated with young age. Yet this is not so for most RLPs, with the exceptions of Corbyn in the UK and France.[123] More widely, a part of the radical identities we saw in Chapter 3 opts either for abstention or another party rather than RLPs.

The stability for women RLP and SDP voters suggests that, as has been argued elsewhere, gender issues have been invariably present in the appeals of left-wing parties.[124] Female voters tend to support left parties in general, not favouring any specific strain of left-wing thought or practice, rather choosing a party depending on which value or policy (economy, environment, peace, social care or other) they prioritise.[125] An increased likelihood for young women choosing the Left has not in any case radically shifted the percentage of this group in RLP vote shares.

Further on, an empirical study, which mapped congruence between the positions of RLPs and those of their voters, comparing it to agreement between voters and parties on the extreme right, found that this depends on the issue dimension, and is on average higher for the latter group than RLPs.[126] In addition, the demand side of RLPs is not really distinguished from the social democratic or Green voter or supporter in terms of socio-demographic characteristics but rather mostly on attitudinal variables, such as satisfaction with democracy, political trust and attitudes towards redistribution.[127] Most RLPs also accommodate both traditional, mostly working-class, Eurosceptic supporters and those who are anti-austerity while holding pro-EU positions. RLP electorates are not and have never been wholly defined by a Marxist consciousness and typical radical left identities. Again, there is a historical parallel here with the attitudes of PCF and PCI voters in the 1970s. As registered in various polls of the time, the majority did not desire revolution, they were split on issues of income inequality and nationalisation, many of them supported inheritance and property and their overall positive attitude towards socialism eroded between the 1970s and 1980s. In Italy, the majority of PCI voters, who were more influenced than the party leadership by the 'bad governance' attributed to the DC, supported Europe.[128] Any strict particularism about 'revolutionary subjects' in the Radical Left's mobilised agency during elections finds at best partial corroboration. What echoes through history is Marcuse's diagnosis that '[t]he *immediate* expression of the opinion and will of the workers, farmers, neighbors – in brief, the people – is not, per se, progressive and a force of social change: it may be the opposite.'[129] How the last mobilisation wave we have been discussing has ended, as regards the Radical Left's electoral relevance, renders Marcuse's diagnosis very real.

RETROSPECTIVE

Many of the tensions inside social movements and between social movements and parties, as identified in Table 5.1, are also present inside most parties and within the party family: the horizontal–vertical dynamic; the choice between confrontation and moderation; the potential of youth and alliances with the movements; the working-class vote in capitalism; institutional politics as opposed to the prefiguration that partisan mobilisation inherently entails; and the turn from *movimentismo* and revolt to party membership and support which took place during all periods of 'newness'. Organisational variations between parties correspond partly to ideological differences – RLPs, GPs, SDPs, left libertarians, Trotskyists and Maoists. They also undercut them, as distinct types sometimes employ similar organisational logics. Since the 1960s no distinctive model of party organisation characterises or has represented the Radical Left as a whole. Neither is there a fixed relation with government, linkage and the opportunities of movements feeding into parties. There has been, nonetheless, a realignment to the organisational practices of democratic socialism taking the ideological lead.

Today's RLPs are more inclusive, diversified and encroached on by the state, and are weaker in organisation and membership than the traditional CPs. They are in many respects simply following generalised trends for most political parties. Hence, to a certain extent they become co-opted into trends of organisation that tamper with their original and militant intents. Yet time and again, movement–party interaction is so vigorous and active citizenship so vibrant that by the standards of democratic theory, which sees democracy beyond elections as a key criterion for democratic quality, the Radical Left's contribution is systematic, even if unstable in linkage patterns.

Each period of 'newness' has increased the extra-institutional arm of activity within the political family and challenged party conventionalisms, and this has heightened both the interpenetrative momentum and the tension and conflict between the movements on the one hand and parties on the other. A chief strategic continuity today, above all reflected in the years of Eurocommunism, concerns 'the centrality of the electoral objective, perceived as the sole key for acquiring popular legitimacy and embarking on social transformation'. This 'tended to lead to the party's programmatic moderation, bureaucratisation, and the absorption of its desires for change within the limits of the capitalist state'.[130] Processes like this have been present for essentially all parties that view the electoral objective as participating in power. Manifestly, how the ideas and positions of RLPs relate to office seeking and incumbency appears more as a historical matter and less associated with moments of 'newness' or 'crisis'. Resistance always turns into (more or less) co-optation or defeat, or both, under the rubric of running the state without having captured it.

To capture the state would mean (under any circumstances) pursuing policies satisfying at least one's supporters: both voters and organised groups. Turning, therefore, to RLP vote composition, this is the conundrum of pursuing state power. Clearly, youth, students, feminists, ecologists and the lower classes have always played a central role in each period of 'newness', and are structurally more likely to opt for the Left in elections. Under neoliberalism a vast population experiences dispossession. However, there is no historical subject standing out across time in terms of an electoral alignment between the RLPs and the majority of that group. Long-term RLPs increasingly become parties of white-collar workers, which doesn't necessarily mean that the voters they attract are mostly the middle classes. Rather, both the working and middle classes are important as an electoral milieu, but their form, composition and ideological orientation evolves. There is, still, always a certain sectional and ideological distance between archetypical RLP identity and its electorate. Post-1989, it was reinforced by a decline in the share of radical left identities among RLP voters.

9

Conclusions: A Unified Retrospective

How are we to rethink the new in the political sociology of western Europe's Radical Left recently or during previous waves of contention? What signs of continuity and change in radical agency and the context delimiting it? What does the evolution of the European Radical Left tell us about left radicalism as situated in capitalism and neoliberalism? And what are the prospects for the Radical Left if one is to briefly estimate the future of political families by looking at their past? 'Newness', our guiding scheme, has entailed a multidimensional perspective as a framework – movements and parties in terms of ideology, rhetoric and organisation. To conclude, we aggregate these into an overall assessment of evolution and its cross-national bearing, so as to consider the ways in which cross-actor and cross-dimension generalisations can or cannot be made about the presence, degree and meaning of 'newness'.

The arguments about continuity and change made in the preceding chapters are summarised in Table 9.1. The table provides a synopsis of identified, near universal patterns (or trends), their temporality between the three episodes of 'newness' and during their interim periods, and the broad mechanism triggering and facilitating change or interpreting continuity. Although the future remains unpredictable by common reason, so far most 'newness' was produced in the 1960s and foregrounded in the collective break with the socialist orthodoxies that had emerged prior to the 1960s. The Long '68 stands out as a major critical juncture in the development of left radicalism, and the first New Left was markedly different than what emerged out of World War II in western Europe, which was the product of wider generational and societal change. Indeed, not only the New Left but the whole political space had changed by the end of the 1970s. The NSMs and the broader emergence of a Left to the left of communism

257

Table 9.1 Summary of patterns inside the western European Radical Left (Long '68–2020)

Evolutionary process within the Left (change/continuity)	Proximate temporality (Long'68, GJM, Post-2008)	Broad mechanism
Radical Left identities (Chapters 3 and 6)		
Democracy	Diachronically present as a preoccupation	Critique of democracy adapting to how it is negatively affected by capitalism
Democratic socialism emerging and rising, decline and end of communist identity	Since Long '68	Criticism and drawn-out defeat of USSR and Third Worldism (esp. 1989–91)
Continuing reformism, defence of the Keynesian state as majority; with revolutionary interruption in the Long '68	Since post-war (for anarchist turn) and since Long '68: in the ensuing TINA period, reform and regulation become the chief opposition to neoliberalism	The Fire Last Time: global revolution subsides, the neoliberal onslaught
Alternative critiques of mainstream, socialist and social democratic welfarism	Since Long '68: post-materialism, rights activism, second-wave femininism and violent groups	Changing social values due to generation gap, new actors atypical of the blue-collar working class
Crisis of Marxism leads to rethinking socialist strategy, revolutionary subjects, class and utopia	Since Long '68	New cleavages in society bring new thinking which challenges class analysis; in post-industrialism higher salience of identity, freedom and community
Red-Green parties, environmental radicalism	Since Long '68	Changing intergenerational values (and anti-nuclear, disarmament and environmental movements as precedent)
Increasing recognition of the immigrant subject	Since Long '68 and recurrent debates	Students and refugees from the Third World and workers from within Europe engage in struggle, forcing recognition and focus beyond labour
Internationalist solidarity challenged by anti-immigration attitudes	Diachronic	Party politics: mass party imposes constraints on Radical Left in immigration-receiving countries; ideological appeal to national working class
Radical Left rhetoric (Chapters 4 and 7)		
From doctrinal/revolutionary language to universalistic	Long '68, catalysed by neoliberal advance	Extreme exploitation enlarges the pool and diversity of the oppressed
Electoral sloganeering	Diachronic but also intra-family demarcation between reformists and revolutionaries, anti-capitalists and anti-neoliberals	A combination of party system effects, ideological tradition, broader normative trends in democratic capitalism and communication effects
Left populism (as rhetoric)	Diachronic	The signifiers of populism are politics itself and broad enough to manipulate audiences
Left populism (as discursive strategy)	Long '68, GJM, post-2008	Post-Marxism/increasing role of agency and cultural turn/Latin American influences
Left nationalism (self-determination and ethnocentric discourse)	Since the debates of the early twentieth century	A world of nation states in which national rhetoric is variably ethnocentric and national demands emerge out of the centre–periphery cleavage

Radical Left organisation (Chapters 5 and 8)

	GJM	
Space: transnationalisation as an evolved international communist movement		Globalisation and network societies, regionalisation of European politics
An evolving place for violence	Radical Left terrorism largely dies out after 1980s, post-2008 more generalised violent protest	Global patterns of oppression/evolving political culture
Democratisation of party organisation: challenge, fall and replacement of democratic centralism, emergence of successful coalition parties	Since Long '68, more apparent in 1990s	Fragmentation and dissent in a broader mounting critique of Stalinism challenges democratic centralism; leadership initiative still commonly powerful across types of RLPs
Decline of mass party	1980s onwards	Cartelisation, personalisation and professionalisation, declining memberships and increasing reliance of parties on the state
Digital politics	GJM and especially post-2008, the social media age	The internet as a resource for assembly democracy and virtual space as a resource to approach voters in innovative ways; technological advance offers both opportunities and constraints to radical organisation
Reinvigoration of party–movement linkage	Long '68, GJM and post-2008: recurring 'movement parties'	Parties and unions turn to movements in opposition and when the latter are vigorous, but this is intermediated by government experience and the level of dissent to centralisation and hierarchy
Office-seeking	Long '68, GJM and post-2008: majority inside Radical Left geared towards statism as only or crucial means for change	A continuation of the anarchist–social democratic split of the twentieth century as organisational tension across movements, within parties and between the two
Government impact: demobilisation and co-optation	A diachronic phenomenon	Inability to capture the state, made near impossible by neoliberal globalisation
Changing 'radical subjects' and changing RLP electorate	1968 (new classes, students, 'technicians', NSMs); post-2008 (public sector, precarious workers, pensioners, immigrants)	A developing capitalism creates a large and heterogeneous crowd of oppressed much more fragmented than the working class, while European party systems have reconfigured since the 1960s into two-dimensional political systems whereby identity cross-cuts class; capitalist crises and neoliberalism brought changes in the location of grievances (universities, state employees, part-time workers)

and social democracy was paralleled in party systems by Eurocommunism, Maoism, Trotskyism and left libertarianism.

In the realms of ideas, many processes unfolded from within the Long '68: the defeat of revolution, rights advocacy, second-wave feminism and other movements oriented towards alternative readings of post-war welfare capitalism; demands that reached beyond labourism; revisions of working-class orthodoxy and discussions of new revolutionary subjects. Simultaneously, nothing short of a cultural revolution occurred. If the French Revolution signalled the emergence of the Left around the idea of political equality and developments in the second half of the nineteenth century, and up to the Russian Revolution made economic equality the next mark of the historical movement, the Long '68 extended the Left's horizon to culture and civil rights. Meanwhile, the rise of post-materialism, post-structuralism and post-modernism brought a crisis upon Marxism, as historical materialism was gradually relegated in terms of attention and perceived explanatory power.

The Long '68 additionally spurned many organisational elements that were foreign and dissented against or diversified from the traditional CPs and SDPs, including unprecedented performances of cultural critique, squatting and centring resistance upon and through the university; uncivil or 'unethical' agitation alienating the conservative working classes; the opening of the CP organisation; and reconfigurations of working class form. The first seeds of a more democratic, pluralist, descriptively representative and decentralised (as well as declassed) party form were planted in the 1960s and 1970s across the whole of Europe. Processes of wide aggregation unravelled, but without a referent point which was sacrosanct and universal across the mobilised. Party systems began changing because social cleavages realigned, the New Left (and subsequently the Greens and the liberal predominance therein) being the first signs.

The GJM period was an era for the Radical Left in so far as it brought unprecedented developments: a transnationalised Left succeeding the international communist movement as the force against American and Western neo-imperialism, through a growing front of EU-wide groups of movements, unions and parties. It began its unfolding through opposition to the Maastricht Treaty. Post-2008 radical left movements, from the internet to the squares, from labour to radical ecology, political consumerism and urban movements are the same actors which mixed in the GJM. These are versions of the past in a different organisational format and in their experiential dimension – be it Occupy or precarious workers' unions, solidarity mini-economies, organising on roundabouts, or pro-immigration mobilisation. They reflected emerging generational developments, and the processes they led to, such as radicalised youths, striking public sector employees, precarious organising or striking school children are the product of multiple capitalist pathologies.

Beginning with the Long '68, and highlighting certain aspects of change during each following wave, must not diminish the world-scale transformation of politics that came about with the events of 1989–91, throwing the communist movements into disarray and dislodging their fixed meanings and their already diminishing apparatuses. Yet multiple processes of evolution had begun earlier, and were thus catalysed or sealed, not caused, by the fall of the USSR and subsequent developments. Out of the 1970s emerged a Left in crisis, social democracy shifting towards the centre and neoliberalism, and communism losing ground and in part becoming social-democratised. In other words, the fall of the USSR did not really disrupt the linearity of deradicalisation and retreat, the Radical Left taking a defensive position and eventually wavering between strong and soft reformism, a rebuilt social democracy of the 1960s and 1970s, which had been abandoned by its original original claimants, the SDPs. For the western European Radical Left at least, 1989–91 was also a part of a linearity in generalised trends towards co-optation, the broader context of the modernity shift from passions to interests, and the Keynesian bust and ensuing social, political and economic doctrines inspired by the free market and the globalised movement of capital. What the end of the Cold War did do, which is something that explains both the nature and the initial attitude towards parties of the GJM, was to seal the end of the communist identity. It ensured that subsequent forces of left radicalism had no pre-planned future scenario to fight for and necessitated a process of adaptation and rebuilding, a re-networking on incredibly fragmented foundations.

Above we described the Long '68 as a milestone for the Radical Left, expanding its penetration into social structures through engagement with cultural and post-materialist critique, performance and subversion. The GJM was a similar milestone in confronting the legal system – the overall institutional aspect of globalised capitalism – at its transnational nucleus. It reconfirmed an underlying imperialism that is more complex and plural, with features of a transnational capitalist class that interlocks political power but nevertheless is articulated on imperialistic strategy. What, then, can be dissected as new in the 2010s? To begin, a number of elements that have been heralded as new are not entirely novel or particular. If the above processes signal an evolving Radical Left in western Europe, which changed again and again, sometimes to something very different than what it was, sometimes switching back to a previous self, many aspects of RLP functions recur. In other words, they resemble diachronic processes that need to be connected not (only) to historical events but primarily to the realities that do not change as these events unfold. We have seen municipalism and local-level action, citizenship as a way of claiming rights, nationalism and populism as frames of sovereignty, the relevance of regionalism and self-determination for the Left in the light of the centre–periphery cleavage, being triggered again and again in certain places and at a European level. Moreover, during all three periods of 'newness' there are recorded tensions as well as aggregations, with initial protesting as the contention wave begins being suspicious of parties and unions, but as time passes there begin to develop intersections, networks, the impacts of office or office seeking and a subsequent reorientation by parties towards movements and by movements towards parties.

Linkage is intermediated by another continuity: the Radical Left's statism and electoralism, its office seeking and general striving to enter government, and its tendencies before, inside and after it. Democratic participation was won through radical struggles and arose out of much worse circumstances. Yet liberal democracy creates dilemmas and a very complex electoral game, which at root is the gradualist nature of change through political conflict in capitalism. On the other hand, if state power is necessary for root-and-branch change, as Carl Boggs argued, 'the opposite is equally true: an egalitarian, self-managed society cannot be built strictly upon the terrain of state power'.[1] Repeatedly, radical movements and the tensions of linkage between parties and movements raise this issue, and a growing rejection of capitalist liberal democracy reflects it by definition, save for the fact that we have not reached a coherent and uniting theory on how to remake the national state. The bigger question – why should Keynesianism and statism not come to an end this time? – cannot be answered with confidence. Utopias, utopian thinking and utopian theory have never been incorporated into left-wing electoral politics. Like for all parties, RLPs show that electoralism, necessary as it is, can erode social roots, cause reactive dissent and induce demobilisation. And in the conflict between horizontal and vertical forms of politics, the institutional and extra-institutional or anti-constitutional recurs again and again, each time as the next manifestation of the original anarchist–social democratic dichotomy of the early socialist movement; and it unfolds within movement milieus, within party milieus and between them.

All these are diachronic encounters, all contested from within the political family, all rooted in the systemic setting and not merely in political circumstances. Capitalism, neoliberalism and processes that unfold therein propel grievances to come forward, but also bring about co-optation as if by design. In certain respects, then, and in spite of economic crisis, there has been more continuity than change in the sense of previous trends being carried forward. RLPs enter government and find themselves in a hostile environment, in coalition relations with more moderate actors, facing electoral dynamics between co-optation and policy seeking, and drifting between the movement and the government, although in a particularised form. They succeed in elections then recede or drop or change organisationally after incumbency towards a cartel-like or less socially rooted form. They never monopolise the working and popular classes. Their potential for success is highly dependent on the format and mechanics of the party system. Relations between movements and parties have been reinvigorated during all periods of 'newness', though they are still strained by the same contradictions as before. And there has not been a spike across the board in the absorption of the working and popular classes or realignment within the left spaces of party systems back towards anti-capitalism and revolutionary spirits.

Various fragmented critics of the Soviet Union since the 1950s – Maoists, Trotskyists, anarchists, social democrats, radical libertarians, pacifists and ecologists – evolved into a more unified space of democratic socialist radicals at the intersection of movement–party mindsets and organisations. Today's most powerful RLPs cannot be significantly differentiated from the Eurocommunist political mould, British democratic socialism of the 1970s or Swedish social democracy in its glory days. In the long term, Eurocommunism continues as a policy package, a discourse oriented towards preaching and practising democracy, a third way that was a second way to begin with and an internationalism that defies existing geopolitical powers. Moreover, the crisis has changed little on average in terms of left-wing electoral fortunes. Within and across the three analytical dimensions of collective action, we can evince significant evolution as well as recurrent patterning on the Radical Left in western Europe across different historical phases. But at the time of writing, the Radical Left is in a situation of marginality. Across most European countries, it is not in government (except in Spain, where it is losing electoral ground, Sweden and Finland), while its narrative on the pandemic has neither influenced policy nor seems to be gathering mass momentum for a comeback. If the immediate post-2008 period witnessed a refuelled radicalism by 2020, this wave of left-wing militancy and political hope has conceded much of the ground it initially occupied, both at the ballot box and in the streets.

Mechanisms of cross-country continuity and change are of a double geographical nature. Some events and processes are particular to Europe, but most are global. Events on other continents (North and South America, Asia and Africa) inspire, fuel or catalyse action within western Europe in solidarity, but also by way of emulation and adaptation to the national and European context. The Radical Left is embedded within a broader anti-systemic globality and it cannot be comprehended if separated from this. Its particular forms in time – violent guerrillas in the 1960s, movement-driven left-wing governments in the 2010s, Third Worldism, nationalism and regionalism, municipalism and so many other things – are grounded in transcontinental mobilisation and resistance.

Particularly because left radicalism's evolution between the 1960s and today has been a multi-factorial progression, intra-regional patterning and sequencing is still explained by the local manifestations of, or exceptions to, general trends. So we need to spell out the general points of variability, because this is something to look for in assessing the prospects of a cohesive western European counter-hegemony led by the organised Radical Left. While the broad processes outlined in Table 8.1 have been more or less pervasive across all western European countries, national specificities refract rather than import European and global tendencies. There is always a plural presence on the Radical Left, but in some places some of its aspects are more popular and disseminated within the space as a whole. Consequently, what each national Radical Left in western Europe looks like is a matter of which ideological lineage, rhetorical performance and organisational practice has consolidated itself over others. To enumerate the chief points of differentiation within the political family:

- The main receptors of the vibrations from the Long '68, the GJM years and post-2008, have been the central and northern countries in western Europe, with the biggest – France, Germany, Italy and Spain – experiencing the most pronounced cases of mobilisation and resistance during each period of 'newness'.
- Austria, Belgium, the Netherlands, the Scandinavian countries (including Iceland) and Switzerland have also hosted labourist and 'new politics' movements and parties, both over time and during the three periods in question.
- Cyprus and Malta have had a very different historical trajectory. In Malta, the two-party system, and consensus and clientelistic politics, have sustained very limited protest potential. In Cyprus the cleavage around the conflict between the Greek Cypriot-dominated Republic of Cyprus and the Turkish Cypriot northern parts of the island have consumed most of the oxygen; and radical NSMs appeared only in the 2010s, about 50 years later than the rest of western Europe.

- The environmental movements originated from central and northern Europe and so did the Red-Green and pirate parties. There is, therefore, a need to consider how the distinct political culture of the North has both meant different temporalities in such things as more horizontality and democracy, and constituted the starting geographical space for ideological and organisational phenomena, today forcefully espoused across the continent.
- Across all countries, the theme of radical mobilisation and resistance reflects the domestic arena. Nuclear movements have flourished in countries with nuclear programmes; environmental activism was sidelined where there was ethnic or religious conflict, where conditions instead invited a fierce anti-imperialism (as in Cyprus or Ireland); the politicisation of austerity (and anti-austerity) is the strongest where neoliberal policies are most intensified.
- Certain parties' internationalist solidarity is diluted or challenged by an ethnocentric stance on immigration, reflecting electoral pressures from the mass party model and historical legacies about the national working class.
- Left nationalism is an organic manifestation of the Radical Left in certain regions within states, but in other countries national identity is connected to dark forces and is perceived to refute internationalism.
- Left populism is always associated with RLPs and social movements and is typically present on the Radical Left today, but in certain countries RLPs utilise it as theory and strategy, while in others the party system is frozen or stable. Even as a strategy of capitalising on crisis, this is unlikely to produce results.
- Certain movements (e.g. violent groups and protest) do not appear in some places, such as Austria, Norway or Cyprus, while they diachronically flourish in others, such as Greece. They are conditioned by political cultural traditions such as consensus or majoritarian politics, bipolarity and the resulting institutionalisation or ostracisation of violence and civil disobedience.
- In Greece, anti-systemic discourse on the Left and 'institutionalised' civil disobedience and violence, such as university

occupations, is much more widespread than elsewhere due to the presence of a large extra-parliamentary space and the legacy of student repression by the junta state of the 1970s.

- Communism in the party system has not remained strong anywhere except for Greece and Portugal; labourism has been the only platform on the Left in the British party system; Trotskyism has a comparatively strong presence in France; left populism as theory is adopted by some but not other democratic socialist parties.

- The parties with a long-standing organisational legacy and with relatively large membership organisations, such as the former clandestine CPs in Greece and Portugal, or the SP in the Netherlands, are also the only cases of electorally relevant Marxist-Leninism.

- Electoral endurance is thus associated with organisational density, but electoral success is chiefly a party system phenomenon and needs to be evaluated mostly in a relational sense, against the histories, organisational capacities and relations to the state of the Radical Left's competitors.

- In spite of systematic patterns, the organisational conjoining of the Left – the linkages between movements, unions and parties – are also partly determined by an organic history or its absence, ideological views and the incentives and constraints groups have to coalesce or divide, including being in opposition or government.

- Because of country legacies, the institutionalisation of the Radical Left across party systems also varies with regard to the line of separation between an anti-capitalist (revolutionary) and a reformist, democratic socialist-like left.

WHAT GOES FORWARD?

For both movements and parties, different radical left currents develop at different stages, and while they ebb and flow and sometimes seem to have disappeared, they nevertheless reappear later as reverberations of their earlier selves, combining with each other to produce subsequent radical left movements, unions and parties:

a melange of currents and organisations. Responding to specific puzzles, opportunities and constraints may not be sufficient for a fundamental reconfiguration in the morphology of a political family's ideational core, but it necessarily shapes the lexicon, mobilisation and impact of social and political actors. The differences evident from this macro-historical view signal the presence of innovation and evolution on the Radical Left, although this is less so in terms of core practices, ideas and axioms, and more because of the way in which the struggle unfolds in space and historical time: through projecting certain ideas over and in relation to others; by framing collective identities differently (recognising or not social forces); and via utilising and embodying pre-existing or emerging material and symbolic resources.

The three waves of mobilisation and resistance on the European Radical Left constitute syncopated expansions of this political family's cycle, gradually enlarging its ideational, organisational and discursive scope beyond the main pillars of traditional communism and social democracy. This is the case even without changing its position and range on the political spectrum or its fundamental functions in the societal arena. Simultaneously, however, the European Radical Left is reconstructing its experienced meanings in a process of reflexive self-evaluation, inheriting and processing ideas, practices and discourses from its own historical trajectory rather than innovating out of thin air or borrowing from competing political camps. Still, it is antagonistic to liberalism but also prone to acknowledging, incorporating or succumbing to some of its analytical tools and policies, subsequently modifying radical left strategy and igniting debates about when socialism stops being 'new' and ends up being replaced by an entirely different thought system. What changes importantly regards and reflects the status of the European Radical Left's constituent traditions and their corresponding ideas, rhetoric and organisation.

In all periods of 'newness', the bequest of previous struggles is both a legacy to be drawn upon or emulated and a political toolkit that is insufficient for the new era, and thus a limit to be overcome – a form of mobilisation and resistance to be reinvigorated and appropriately designed based on ongoing exigencies. Hence, any 'newness' on the European Radical Left has not happened as a crushing break with the past. This is more a situation of macro-historical cross-fertilisation between different traditions within left radicalism – a reshuffle of principles, values and actions across time so that some features of the political family become more accentuated than others as currents within the historical movement. These currents, or strains, of radical thought cross-cut parties and movements and are (at least somewhat) variable across countries.

Because demobilisation and co-optation, and thus the annulment of resistance, have happened so vividly, suddenly and pervasively during the three occasions of 'newness' considered, the limits of party and institutional politics clearly stand out, especially in the realities of cartelised, state-encroached parties and generalised electoral abstention. This is not to question the argument of perceiving them as structurally necessary to incite radicalism and propagate change. This popular normative approach notwithstanding, within the context of multiple, self-reproducing and intersecting constraints, what stands out in hindsight for all three periods of 'newness' is, above all, a historical update in political argumentation – a shift from intellectual retreat to intellectual advance and back again; a further solidification of small-scale resistance and autonomous self-organisation; and an expansive renewal of the radical democratic imaginary through acute intellectual ferment and activism – rather than an exceptionally successful regional contestation of political power, or the lasting and effective control of the state.

This, in turn, prompts us to highlight that for future purposes, the concern of those supporting or studying the Radical Left should not be merely RLPs and their relation to liberalism and capitalism. Rather, having linkage politics in mind, at stake is how RLPs, radical movements and other actors mobilise in parallel, both within and outside the state, in a way that is capable (or not) of tilting the political power balance. Paraphrasing Marx, our interest must lie in whether and how the Radical Left can turn from a political family *in itself* to one *for itself*.

Appendix 1
Historical Context and the
Three 'New Lefts'

	Late 1960s/1970s	Late 1990s/2000s	Late 2000s–2020
Major processes/ events	Cold War (USSR's leading role vs. USA's leading role) Crisis and critique of USSR continuing from the 1950s after Stalin's death/Soviet invasion of Czechoslovakia Post-colonialism/Third Worldism: Vietnam War (and many other revolutions, wars and conflicts) Chinese radicalism: global socialism split (Sino–Soviet split) Gradual delegitimisation of Third World liberation movements Profitability crisis (oil crises; end of post-war consensus) Post-materialism, cultural and value change	Unipolar global landscape Yugoslavian wars and NATO's offensive/NATO's expansion into eastern Europe Invasion of Iraq and beginning of 'War on Terror' Latin American and Asian economic crises (IMF and World Bank as creditors and structural reform programmes) A series of global crises starting in the USA: dot.com bubble, Enron scandal 9/11 – terrorist attacks on WTC's Twin Towers in 2001 and subsequent War on Terror Neoliberalisation of the EU starting with Maastricht (1992) Rising Euroscepticism (from 'permissive consensus' to 'constraining dissensus') Pink tide in Latin America (resurgence of the Left)	A renewed rift between Russia and the West Civil wars in Syria and Libya Immigration crisis and 'cultural backlash' Populism and anti-populism (Donald Trump in the White House) Economic crisis, extreme inequalities (bailout agreements in the European periphery) Terrorist attacks in Europe Far-right surge and increasing neoliberal authoritarianism Brexit and rise of regionalism – referendums for secession in Scotland and Catalonia Climate change takes centre stage Climbing disruption, violence and protest Covid-19 pandemic: social distancing, lockdowns (2020)
Major processes/ events between periods	End of Cold War/'End of history' Neoliberal globalisation Intensification and enlargement of the EU Transformation of social democracy (beginning) Significant party system change (new party families, voter realignments, catch-all and cartel parties)		Rapid expansion of information and mobile technologies (beginning of social media age) and later 'fake news' Significant party system change (new party families, voter realignments, digital parties) Transformation of social democracy Dealignment, absention, anti-politics Global financial crisis (2007–8) spreading from the USA

Appendix 2
Electoral Slogans of RLPs in Seven Countries (1960s–2010s)

*PCF (French Communist Party)**

1962 **To the future**
[Vers l'avenir]

1968 **From the first round – Vote Communist – To guarantee the benefits gained by the united struggle of workers**
[Des le premier tour – Votez Communiste – Pour garantir les avantages acquis par la lutte unie des travailleurs]

1973 **Changing Course – Program for a Democratic Government of Popular Union**
[Changer de Cap – Programme pour un Gouvernement Démocratique d'Union Populaire]

1978 **Updated Common Government Program**
[Programme Commun de Gouvernement Actualisé]

1981 PCF slogan in legislative elections:
French Produce
[Produisons français!]
Mitterand's slogans in presidential elections:
Change Life
[Changer la vie]
All of France's forces
[Des toutes les forces de la France]
Unified France
[La France unie]

1986 **Sen sortir, c'est possible. Avec le vote communiste**
[Getting out is possible. With the communist vote]

1993 **Six proposals for France**
[Six propositions pour la France]

1995 Presidential elections:
Avec Jospin Jospin c'est clair
[With Jospin, it's clear]
The President of true change
[Le président du vrai changement]

2002	**Program of the French Communist Party for the 2002 legislative elections. 10 Priority Objectives of the Communists for the next five years**

2002   **Program of the French Communist Party for the 2002 legislative elections. 10 Priority Objectives of the Communists for the next five years**
[Programme du Parti Communist Français pour les elections législatives de 2002. 10 objectifs prioritaires des communistes pour les cinq ans à venir]

2007   **Another Politics on the left**
[Une autre politique a gauche]

2012   Left Front Coalition:
The programme of the Left Front and its joint candidate Jean-Luc Mélenchon – Human First
[Le programme du Front de gauche et de son candidat commun Jean-Luc Mélenchon – L'humain d'abord]
Place au people
[The place of people]
Prenez le pouvoir
[Take the power]

2017   Left Front Coalition:
Legislative elections – 11 & 18 June – The people in the National Assembly – The left standing for the human first!
[Élections législatives – 11 & 18 juin- Le peuple à l'Assemblée nationale – La gauche debout pour l'humain d'abord!]
Presidential elections:
The future in common
[L'avenir en commun]
I vote, they clear out
[Je vote, ils dégagent]
The force of the people
[La force du people]

PCI (Italian Communist Party)/Rifondazione Comunista

1963   **Beat the DC. Strengthen the PCI. The electoral programme of the PCI**
[Batterre la DC. Rafforzare il PCI. Il Programma elettorale del PCI]

1968   **Time to change, you can change: PCI's programatic appeal**
[E ora di cambiare, si può cambiare: appello programma del PCI]

1972   **The communists' programme: for a government of democratic change**
[Il programma dei comunisti: per un governo di svolta democratica]

1979   **The communist programme for the eighth legislature – defence and reform of the democratic state**
[Il programma dei comunisti per l'VIII legislatura – difesa e riforma dello stato democratico]

1983	**The alternative proposal for the Change** *[La proposta alternativa per il Cambiamento]*
1987	**The PCI for the tenth legislature. The fundamental programmatic commitments** *[Il PCI per la decima legislatura. Gli impegni programmatici fondamentali]*
1992	**Electoral programme. From the opposition to the alternative** *[Programma elettorale. Dall'opposizione per l'alternativa]*
1996	**Start again from the left for the alternative** *[Ricominciare da sinistra per l'alternativa]*
2001	Joint programme of Ulivo (Olive Tree): **Let's renew Italy together** *[Rinnoviamo l'Italia, insieme]*
2008	Sinistra L'Arcobaleno: **Election programme for the 13 and 14 April 2008 elections of the Left the Rainbow: Make a Choice of Departure** *[Programma elettorale elezioni 13 e 14 Aprile 2008 de la Sinistra l'Arcobaleno: Fai Una Scelta Di Parte]*
2013	Rivoluzione Civile: **Coalition 'Rivoluzione Civile': I'm In** *[Io Ci Sto]*
2018	**It's time to make a stand** *[official translation]* *[Abbiamo aspettato troppo… Ora ci candidiamo noi!]*

PCP (Portuguese Communist Party)

1975	**The PCP and the political moment** *[O PCP e o momento politico]*
1979	**Joint programme of Alianca do Povo Unido (United People's Alliance): 'A programme for Portugal in April'** *[Joint programme of APU Alianca do Povo Unido (United People's Alliance): 'Um programa para Portugal de Abril']*
1980	**Joint programme of APU Alianca do Povo Unido (United People's Alliance): With the PCP with the APU – Democratic majority, defeat of AD** *[Joint programme of APU Alianca do Povo Unido (United People's Alliance): Com o PCP com a APU – Maioria democrática, derrota da AD]*
1987	**Joint programme of United Democratic Coalition: For a Democratic Majority and a Democratic Government** *[Para uma maioria democrática e um governo democrático]*

1991   **PCP electoral programme: Project for the future for a better Portugal: Elections for the Assembly of the Republic**
[Programa eleitoral do PCP: Projecto de futuro para um Portugal melhor: Eleições para a Assembleia da República]

1999   **PCP electoral programme – A Left-Wing Politics for Portugal**
[Programa eleitoral do PCP – uma politica de esquerda para Portugal]

2002   **For a left-wing policy – Change for the Better – PCP's electoral programme**
[Por uma politica de esquerda – mudar para melhor – programa eleitoral do PCP]

2009   **A breaking, patriotic and left programme – A commitment to workers, people and the country – Yes, a better life is possible.**
[Programa de Ruptura, Patriotico e de Esquerda – Um Compromisso Com os Trabalhadores, o Povo e o Pais – é possível, uma vida melhor]

2011   **PCP's Electoral Commitment: For a patriotic and left-wing policy**
[Compromisso Eleitoral do PCP: Por uma política patriótica e de esquerda]

2019   **PCP Electoral Programme – Patriotic and left politics – Solutions for a Portugal with a future**
[Programma Electoral do PCP – Política Patriótica e de Esquerda – Soluções para um Portugal com futuro]

SP (Socialist Party – Netherlands)

1994   **Vote Against Vote SP**
[Stem Tegen Ṣtem SP]

1998   **Resistance! Election Program of the SP 1998–2002**
[TEGENGAS! Verkiezingsprogramma van de Socialistische Partij 1998–2002]

2002   **First Road to the Left: Vote for social reconstruction**
[Eerste Weg Links: StemVoor Sociale Wederopbouw]

2006   **A Better Netherlands for the Same Money**
[Een beter Nederland, voor hetzelfde geld]

2010   **A Better Netherlands for Less Money**
[Een Beter Nederland Voor Minder Geld]
Choose a major clean up
[Kies voor de grote schoonmaak]

2017   **Take the Power**
[Pak de Macht]

V-C/V/VKP (Left Party-Communists/Left Party/Communist Party of Sweden)

1960   **For workers' victory on the election!**
[Fram för arbetarseger i valet!]

Electoral Slogans of RLPs in Seven Countries (1960s–2010s)

1968	**Main lines for left-wing politics** *[Huvudlinjer för vänsterpolitik]* **With VKP for left victory** *[Med VKP for vänsterseger!]*
1976	**Labour Policy and socialism for a better future** *[Arbertarpolitik och socialism för en bättre framtid]*
1979	**Programme for the 1980s: Radical workers' policy – The road to socialism** *[ProgramFor 80-Talet: Radikal arbetarpolitik Vägen till socialism]*
1982	**Your Vote for VKP is a vote for a socialist policy** *[Din röst för VKP är en röst för en socialistisk politik]*
1985	**Politik för socialism på svenska**
1988	**For Sweden 1988** *[Till sverige 1988]*
1991	**Valet 1991: Arbete – Rättvisa – Demokrati – Grön Miljo** *[Elections 1991: Justice-Democracy- Green Environment]*
1998	**Time for justice!** *[Dags för rättvisa!]*
2002	**Mission Justice** *[Uppdragg rättvisa]*
2006	**Work – Democracy – Justice** *[Arbete Demokrati Rättvisa]*
2010	**Shared Security – Individual freedom – A sustainable world** *[Gemensam trygghet – individens frihet – en hållbar värld]*
2018	**A Sweden for everyone – Not just for the richest** *[Ett Sverige för alla – inte bara för de rikaste]*

PCE/IU/Unidos Podemos (Spanish Communist Party/United Left/United We Can)

1977	PCE: **A communist vote is a vote for democracy.** *[El voto comunista es un voto por la democracia]*
1979	**The useful vote is the communist vote. Electoral programme general elections 1979** *[El voto útil es el voto comunista. Programa electoral elecciones generales 1979]*
1982	**Electoral programme of the Communist Party of Spain: approved by the Central Committee of the PCE at its meeting on 15 and 16 September 1982** *[Programa electoral del Partido Comunista de España: aprobado por el Comité Central del PCE en su reunión de los días 15 y 16 de septiembre de 1982]*

1989   IU:
Elecciones Generales 1989 – We are the alternative
[Elecciones Generales 1989 – Somos la alternativa]

1993   **Yes, Izquierda Unida is the necessary alternative**
Si, Izquierda Unida La Alternativa Necessaria

1996   **Decide**
[Decide]

2000   **We are necessary – 2000 General Elections programme**
[Somos Necesarias – Elecciones Generales programa 2000]

2008   **More Left – Electoral Program – General Elections**
[más izquierda – Programa Electoral – Elecciones Generales]

2011   As United Left-The Greens: Plural Left:
Rebel!
[Rebelate!]

2016   As Unidas Podemos:
The smile of a country
[La sonrisa de un país]

2019   As Unidas Podemos:
(November) Main slogan – **A government with you** *[Un Gobierno contigo]*
Manifesto title – **Program for a New Country** *[Programa para un nuevo país]*
IU manifesto:
Program for a country that fights – Programme for a country with a future
[Programma para un pais que lucha – Programma para un pais con futuro]

KKE (Communist Party of Greece)

1981   **For the Right to go away – For the change**
[Για να φύγει η δεξιά – Για την αλλαγή]
Democratic cooperation, no more '63
[Δημοκρατική συνεργασία, όχι άλλο '63]

1989   Synaspismos – Coalition:
Nothing, nothing stops us, now ahead with the Left
[Τίποτα, τίποτα δεν μας σταματά, τώρα μπροστά με την Αριστερά]

1993   **A Left Answer**
[Αριστερή Απάντηση]

1996   **People, counter-attack, with a strong KKE**
[Αντεπίθεση Λαέ, Ισχυρό ΚΚΕ]

2000   **KKE Strong Popular Front. The people has the power** – *[the people]* can change the course
[ΚΚΕ Ισχυρό Μέτωπο Λαϊκό: Ο λαός έχει τη δύναμη – μπορεί να αλλάξει την πορεία]

2009   **Powerful people with a strong KKE to undo their anti-popular plans**
[Δυνατός λαός με ισχυρό ΚΚΕ για να τους χαλάσουμε τα αντιλαϊκά σχέδια 2009]

2012 (May) **Vote KKE – A new storm is coming – Strong KKE for the victory of the people – Don't scatter your vote right and left**
[Ψήφισε ΚΚΕ – Έρχεται νέα θύελλα – Ισχυρό ΚΚΕ για να νικήσει ο λαός – Μη σκορπίζεις την ψήφο σου δεξιά και αριστερά]

2019   **Your power on the next day**
[Η δύναμή σου την επόμενη μέρα]

* For France, which has a semi-presidential system, presidential nominations supported by the PCF are included.

Sources: Manifesto Project.wzb.eu, Archive.org, scribd.com, archivoelectoral.org, polidoc.net (author translations, except where official).

Note: Coalition platforms or parties, and evolving party names, are noted in the table. Missing years could not be retrieved. Some parties ran for election for the first time in the 1970s (KKE, PCE, PCP).

Notes

PREFACE

1. Giorgos Charalambous, Reclaiming Radicalism: Discursive Wars and the Left, *tripleC: Communication, Capitalism and Critique*, 2021, 19 (1), pp. 212–30.

CHAPTER 1

1. Magid Shihade, Christina Flesher Fominaya and Laurence Cox, The Season of Revolution: The Arab Spring and European Mobilisations, *Interface: A Journal For and About Social Movements*, 2012, 4 (1): pp. 1–16; Cristina Flesher-Fominaya, European Anti-austerity and Pro-democracy Protests in the Wake of the Global Financial Crisis, *Social Movement Studies*, 2017, 16 (1), pp. 1–20; David Bailey, *Protest Movements and Parties of the Left: Affirming Disruption* (London: Rowman and Littlefield International, 2017). Mary Kaldor and Sabine Selchow, Introduction – In Search of Europe's Future: *Subterranean Politics and the Other Crisis in Europe*, in Mary Kaldor, Sabine Selchow and Tamsin Murray-Leach (eds), Subterranean Politics in Europe (London: Palgrave Macmillan, 2015), pp. 1–30.
2. Richard Day, *Gramsci Is Dead: Anarchist Currents in the Newest Social Movements* (London: Pluto Press, 2005).
3. Saul Newman, *The Politics of Postanarchism* (Cambridge: Polity, 2016).
4. Paolo Gerbaudo, *The Mask and the Flag: Populism, Citizenism and Global Protest* (London: Hurst, 2017).
5. Ibid.; Manuel Castells, *Networks of Outrage and Hope: Social Movements in the Internet Age* (Cambridge: Polity Press, 2012); Paul Mason, *Why It's Kicking Off Everywhere: The New Global Revolutions* (London: Verso, 2012).
6. Benjamin Tejerina, Ignacia Perugorría, Tova Benski and Lauren Langman, From Indignation to Occupation: A New Wave of Global Mobilisation, *Current Sociology*, 2013, 61 (4), pp. 1–16.
7. Paris Aslanidis, Populist Social Movements of the Great Recession, *Mobilization: An International Quarterly*, 2016, 21 (3), pp. 301–21.
8. Cristina Flesher Fominaya and Laurence Cox (eds), *Understanding European Movements: New Social Movements, Global Justice Struggles, Anti-austerity Protest* (London: Routledge, 2013).
9. Lauern Langman, Occupy: A New New Social Movement, *Current Sociology*, 2013, 61 (4): 510–24.

10. Paolo Gerbaudo, *The Digital Party: Political Organisation and Online Democracy* (London: Pluto Press, 2019).

11. Giorgos Katsambekis and Alexandros Kioupkiolis (eds), *The Populist Radical Left in Europe* (London and New York: Routledge, 2019).

12. Barry Buzan and Richard Little, *International Systems in World History* (Oxford: Oxford University Press, 2002); Martin Shaw, *Theory of the Global State* (Cambridge: Cambridge University Press, 2000).

13. George Katsiaficas, *The Subversion of Politics: European Autonomous Social Movements and the Decolonization of Everyday Life* (Atlantic Highlands, NJ: Humanities Press, 1997). Donatella della Porta and Dieter Rucht, Left-Libertarian Movements in Context: A Comparison of Italy and West Germany, 1965–1990, in J. C. Jenkins and B. Klandermans (eds), *The Politics of Social Protest. Comparative Perspectives on States and Social Movements* (Minneapolis: University of Minnesota Press, 1995), pp. 113–33; Bert Klandermans and Sidney Tarrow, Mobilization into Social Movements: Synthesizing European and American Approaches, in B. Klandermans, H. Kriesi and S. Tarrow (eds), *From Structure to Action* (Greenwich, CT: JAI Press, 1988), pp. 1–40; Alberto Melucci, The Symbolic Challenge of Contemporary Movements, *Social Research*, 1985, 52, pp. 789–816; Allain Touraine, *The Voice and the Eye: An Analysis of Social Movements* (New York: Cambridge University Press, 1981); Giovanni Arrighi, Terence Hopkins and Immanuel Wallerstein (eds), *Antisystemic Movements* (London: Verso, 1989).

14. Abby Peterson, Mattias Wahlström and Magnus Wennerhag, European Anti-austerity Protests: Beyond 'Old' and 'New' Social Movements? *Acta Sociologica*, 2015, 58 (4), pp. 293–310; Laurence Cox and Alf Gunvald Nilsen, *We Make Our Own History: Marxism and Social Movements in the Twilight of Neoliberalism* (London: Pluto, 2014); Donatella della Porta, *Social Movements in Times of Austerity: Bringing Capitalism Back into Protest Analysis* (Cambridge: Polity Press, 2015).

15. For the 1930s, see Donald Sassoon's analysis of the PCI as a new mass party, diverging from the Leninist vanguardist model. Donald Sassoon, *The Strategy of the Italian Communist Party: From the Resistance to the Historic Compromise* (New York: St Martin's Press, 1981). For the 1950s, see Stuart Hall, Life and Times of the First New Left, *New Left Review*, January–February 2010, 61, pp. 177–96; Geoff Andrews, The Three New Lefts and Their Legacies, in G. Andrews, R. Cockett, A. Hooper and M. Williams (eds), *New Left, New Right and Beyond: Taking the Sixties Seriously* (London: Palgrave Macmillan, 1999), pp. 66–84. For the 1960s and 1970s, see Andrews, The Three New Lefts; George Katsiaficas, *The Imagination of the New Left* (Boston: South End Press, 1987); Maurice Isserman, *If I Had a Hammer: The Death of the Old Left and the Birth of the New Left* (New York: Basic Books, 1987); and hundreds of other examples. For the 1990s and 2000s, see Jeffrey Juris, A New Way of Doing Politics? Global Justice Movements and the Cultural Logic of Networking,

Recherches Sociologiques et Anthropologiques, 2007, 28 (1), pp. 127–42; David Graeber, The New Anarchists, *New Left Review*, January–February 2002, 13, https://newleftreview.org/II/13/david-graeber-the-new-anarchists; Emmanuel Wallerstein, New Revolts against the System, New Left Review, November–December 2002, 18, pp. 29–39; Kate Hudson, *European Communism since 1989: Towards a New European Left?* (Basingstoke: Palgrave Macmillan, 2012).

16. Bailey, *Protest Movements*; Marcos Ancelovici, Pascale Dufour and Héloise Nez (eds), *Street Politics in the Age of Austerity: From the Indignados to Occupy* (Amsterdam: Amsterdam University Press, 2014); Donatella della Porta and Alice Mattoni, *Spreading Protest: Social Movements in Times of Crisis* (Colchester: ECPR Press, 2014); Tejerina et al., From Indignation to Occupation.

17. Gerd-Rainer Horn, 1968: A Social Movement *Sui Generis*, in Stefan Berger and Holger Nehrin (eds), *The History of Social Movements in Global Perspective: A Survey* (London: Palgrave Macmillan, 2017), p. 537.

18. Gerd-Rainer Horn and Padraic Kenney, *Transnational Moments of Change: Europe 1945, 1968, 1989* (Lahnam, MD: Rowman and Littlefield, 2004).

19. The term New Left is written with capitalised first letters when referring to the 1960s and 1970s.

20. Key moments in the early 2010s were the demonstrations and revolts in the Arab world, especially Egypt's Tahrir Square, known as the Arab Spring.

21. Bill Wanlund, Global Protest Movements: Can They Lead to Lasting Change? http://library.cqpress.com/cqresearcher/document.php?id=cqresrre2020050100.

22. For similar, article-length interrogations about 'newness' in the 1960s as compared to more recent mobilisations, see Michel Wieviorka, After New Social Movements, *Social Movement Studies*, 2015, 4 (1), pp. 1–19; David Plotke, What's so New about New Social Movements?, *Socialist Review*, 1990, 20, pp. 81-102.

23. E.g. Hans Haferkamp and Neil J. Smesler, *Social Change and Modernity* (Berkeley: University of California Press, 1992); Mark M. Blyth and Robin Varghese, The State of the Discipline in American Political Science: Be Careful What You Wish For? *The British Journal of Politics and International Relations*, 1999, 1–3, pp. 345–65.

24. Alexandros Kioupkiolis Acts, Events and the Creation of the New, *Constellations*, 2017, 23 (1), p. 31.

25. Ian H. Angus, Emergent Publics: An Essay on Social Movements and Democracy (Winnipeg: Arbeiter Ring Pubications, 2001).

26. Shlomit Barnea and Gideon Rahat, Out with the Old, in with the 'New': What Constitutes a New Party? *Party Politics*, 2010, 17 (3), p. 308.

27. Giovanni Arrighi, Globalization and Historical Sociology, in J. Abu-Lughod (ed.), *Sociology for the Twenty-First Century: Continuities and Cutting Edges* (Chicago: Chicago University Press, 2000), p. 120.

28. Jeffrey Haydu, Making Use of the Past: Time Periods as Cases to Compare and as Sequences of Problem Solving, *American Journal of Sociology*, 1998, 104 (2), pp. 341–3.

29. James Mahoney, Strategies of Causal Assessment in Comparative Historical Analysis, in J. Mahoney and D. Rueschemeyer (eds), *Comparative Historical Analysis in the Social Sciences* (Cambridge: Cambridge University Press, 2012), p. 365.

30. Haydu, *Making Use of the Past*.

31. Paul Pierson, Big, Slow-Moving and … Invisible, in J. Mahoney and D. Rueschemeyer (eds), *Comparative Historical Analysis in the Social Sciences* (Cambridge: Cambridge University Press, 2003), p. 203.

CHAPTER 2

1.   Peter Mair and Cas Mudde, The Party Family and Its Study, *Annual Review of Political Science*, 1998, 1, pp. 211–29. See also Klaus von Beyme, *Political Parties in Western Democracies* (Aldershot: Gower, 1985), pp. 29–158.

2.   Seymour Martin Lipset and Stein Rokkan, Cleavage Structures, Party Systems, and Voter Alignments: An Introduction, in S. M. Lipset and S. Rokkan (eds), *Party Systems and Voter Alignments: Cross-national Perspectives* (Toronto: The Free Press, 1967), pp. 1–64.

3.   Valeria Camia and Danielle Caramani, Family Meetings: Ideological Convergence within Party Families across Europe, 1948–2005, *Comparative European Politics*, 2012, 10, pp. 48–85.

4.   Nikolaos Papadogiannis and Leonidas Karakatsanis, Introduction: Performing the Left in Greece, Turkey and Cyprus, in N. Papadogiannis and L. Karakatsanis (eds), *The Politics of Culture in Turkey, Greece and Cyprus: Performing the Left since the Sixties* (London and New York: Routledge, 2017), pp. 1–30.

5.   Because the distinction between the radical and extreme right is not always clear, the terms radical, far and extreme right are used interchangeably in the text.

6.   Karl-Dieter Opp, *Theories of Political Protest and Social Movements: A Multidisciplinary Introduction, Critique, and Synthesis* (London and New York: Routledge, 2009), p. 40.

7.   Donatella della Porta and Mario Diani, *Social Movements: An Introduction*, 2nd edition (Oxford: Blackwell, 2006), p. 20ff.; Sidney Tarrow, *Power in Movement: Collective Action, Social Movements and Politics* (Cambridge: Cambridge University Press, 1998), p. 2.

8.   Mario Diani, The Concept of Social Movement, *Sociological Review*, 1992, 40 (1), pp. 1–25.

9.   Tarrow, *Power in Movement*, p. 2.

10. David A. Snow and Pamela E. Oliver, Social Movements and Collective Behavior: Social Psychological Dimensions and Considerations, in K. S. Cook,

G. A. Fine and J. S. House (eds), *Sociological Perspectives on Social Psychology* (Boston: Allyn and Bacon, 1995), p. 571.

11. According to the classic definition of MacCarthy and Zald, '[a] social movement organisation is a complex, or formal organisation which identifies its goals with the preferences of a social movement or a countermovement and attempts to implement those goals'. John D. McCarthy and Mayer N. Zald, Resource Mobilisation and Social Movements, *American Journal of Sociology*, 1977, 82 (5), p. 1218.

12. Raphael Schlembach and Eugene Nulman, Advances in Social Movement Theory since the Global Financial Crisis, *European Journal of Social Theory*, 2018, 21 (3), pp. 376–90.

13. Gideon Rahat, Reven Y. Hazan and Richard S. Katz, Democracy and Political Parties: On the Uneasy Relationships between Participation, Competition and Representation, *Party Politics*, 2008, 14 (6), pp. 663–83.

14. Kay Lawson and Peter H. Merkl (eds), *When Parties Fail: Emerging Alternative Organizations* (Princeton: Princeton University Press, 1988).

15. This point has been well documented in the literature. For instance, see Ingrid van Biezen and Petr Kopecký, The Cartel Party and the State: Party–State Linkages in European Democracies, *Party Politics*, 2014, 20 (2), pp. 170–82. The mass party is described in detail in Chapter 8, generally referring to the socially rooted, centralised and ideological parties of the period between the 1940s and 1970s, with only some remnants of this model having remained intact in some cases.

16. Adam Roberts, Introduction, in A. Roberts and T. G. Ash (eds), *Civil Resistance and Power Politics: The Experience of Non-violent Action from Gandhi to the Present* (Oxford University Press, 2009), p. 2.

17. Stellan Vinthagen and Mon Lilja, Resistance, in G. L. Andersson and K. G. Herr (eds), *Encyclopedia of Activism and Social Justice* (London: Sage, 2007).

18. Ibid.

19. Paul Routledge, The Imagineering of Resistance: Pollock Free State and the Practices of Postmodern Politics, *Transactions of the Institute of British Geographers*, 1997, 22, p. 361.

20. Simon Thorpe, In Defence of Foucault: The Incessancy of Resistance, *Critical Legal Thinking*, 7 February 2012, http://criticallegalthinking.com/2012/02/07/in-defence-of-foucaultthe-incessancy-of-resistance/.

21. Vinthange and Lija, Resistance; Michael Walzer, The Politics of Resistance, *Dissent*, 1 March 2017, www.dissentmagazine.org/online_articles/the-politics-of-resistance-michael-walzer.

22. David Couzens Hoy, *Critical Resistance: From Poststructuralism to Post-Critique* (Cambridge, MA: MIT Press, 2014).

23. This is alluded to by the concept of 'tempered radicals', introduced by Debra Meyerson in leadership and workplace studies. Tempered radicals, on the one hand, espouse the dominant culture through their experiences, while, on the

other hand, they seek to change the system from within, and thus first accept it. See Debra E. Meyerson, *Tempered Radicals: How People Use Difference to Inspire Change at Work* (Cambridge, MA: Harvard Business School, 2001).

24. Giorgos Charalambous, *European Integration and the Communist Dilemma: Communist Party Responses to Europe in Greece, Cyprus and Italy* (Farnham: Ashgate, 2013).

25. Jonathan Olsen, Michael Koß and Dan Hough (eds), *Left Parties in National Government* (London: Palgrave, 2010).

26. Adam Przeworski and Jonathan Sprague, *Paper Stones: A History of Electoral Socialism* (Chicago: University of Chicago Press, 1986).

27. Michael Freeden, *Ideologies and Political Theory: A Conceptual Approach* (Oxford: Oxford University Press, 1996).

28. Michael Freeden, The Morphological Analysis of Ideology, in M. Freeden, L. T. Sargeant and M. Stears (eds), *The Oxford Handbook of Political Ideologies* (Oxford: Oxford University Press, 2013), pp. 114–37.

29. Mark Bevir, New Labour: A Study in Ideology, *British Journal of Politics and International Relations*, 2 (3), pp. 277–301.

30. Goran Therborn, *The Ideology of Power and the Power of Ideology* (London: Verso, 1999), p. 2.

31. Teun A. Van Dijk, Ideology and Discourse Analysis, *Journal of Political Ideologies*, 2006, 11 (2), pp. 115–40; Charles Henry Whiteley, *Mind in Action: An Essay in Philosophical Psychology* (Oxford: Oxford University Press, 1973).

32. Robert E. Lane, *Political Ideology: Why the American Common Man Believes What He Does* (New York: Free Press of Glencoe, 1962).

33. Bevir, New Labour, p. 277.

34. Ibid.

35. John Gerring, Ideology: A Definitional Analysis. *Political Research Quarterly*, 1997, 50 (4), pp. 666–7.

36. John Schwarzmantel, *Ideology and Politics* (London: Sage, 2008), pp. 26–7.

37. Andrew Heywood, *Political Ideologies: An Introduction* (London, Palgrave, 2007), chapter 1; John T. Jost, Christopher M. Federico and J. M. Napier, Political ideology: Its Structure, Functions and Elective Affinities, *Annual Review of Psychology*, 2009, 60, pp. 307–37.

38. Alain Touraine, *The Self-Production of Society* (Chicago: University of Chicago Press, 1977), p. 388. See also Hank Johnston, Enrique Laraña and Joseph R. Gusfield (eds), *New Social Movements: From Ideology to Identity* (Philadelphia: Temple University Press, 1994).

39. Cas Mudde, *The Ideology of the Extreme Right* (Manchester: Manchester University Press, 2000), p. 7.

40. Mair and Mudde, *The Party Family*, p. 220.

41. James Martin, *Politics and Rhetoric: A Critical Introduction* (London: Routledge, 2013), p. 72.

42. Doug McAdam, *Political Process and the Development of Black Insurgency* (Chicago: Chicago University Press, 1982), xxi.

43. David Snow and Robert D. Benford, Master Frames and Cycles of Protest, in Aldon D. Morris and Carol McClurg Mueller (eds), *Frontiers in Social Movement Theory* (New Haven: Yale University Press, 1992), p. 137.

44. John Gaffney, Rhetoric and the Left: Theoretical Considerations, in J. Gaffney and J. Atkins (eds), *Voices of the UK Left: Rhetoric, Ideology and the Performance of Politics* (London: Springer, 2017), p. 5. See also James G. March and Johan p. Olsen, The New Institutionalism: Organizational Factors in Political Life, *American Political Science Review*, 1984, 78 (3), pp. 734–49.

45. Jonathan White, Left and Right as Political Resources, *Journal of Political Ideologies*, 2011, 16 (2), p. 138.

46. Alan Finlayson, Rhetoric and the Political Theory of Ideologies, *Political Studies*, 2012, 60 (4), pp. 751–67.

47. Benjamin Moffit and Simon Tormey, Rethinking Populism: Politics, Mediatisation and Political Style, *Political Studies*, 2014, 62 (2), pp. 381–97; Rogers Brubaker, Nationalism and Populism, *Nations and Nationalism*, 2020, 26 (1), pp. 44–66.

48. Andre Krouwel, Party Models, in R. S. Katz and W. Crotty (eds), *Handbook of Party Politics* (London: Sage, 2006), pp. 249–69.

49. For the seminal study of party organisation's different organisational faces, see Richard S. Katz and Peter Mair, The Evolution of Party Organisations in Europe: The Three Faces of Party Organization, *The American Review of Politics*, 1993, 14, pp. 593–617.

50. For linkages from a party-centred perspective, see Kay Lawson, Linkage and Democracy, in A. Römmele, D. M. Farrell and P. Ignazi (eds), *Political Parties and Political Systems: The Concept of Linkage Revisited* (London: Praeger, 2005), pp. 161–70. For a perspective more equally centred across social and political actors, see Jack Goldstone, Introduction: Bridging Institutionalised and Non-institutionalised Politics, in J. Goldstone (ed.), *States, Parties, and Social Movements* (Cambridge: Cambridge University Press, 2013), pp. 1–26.

51. Hilary Wainwright, Once More Moving on: Social Movements Political Representation and the Left, *Socialist Register*, 1995, 31, p. 90.

52. Peter Lange, Cynthia Irvin and Sidney Tarrow, Mobilization, Social Movements and Party Recruitment: The Italian Communist Party since the 1960s, *British Journal of Political Science*, 1990, 20 (1), pp. 15–42.

53. Sven Hutter, Hanspeter Kriesi and Jasmine Lorenzini, Social Movements in Interaction with Political Parties, in D. A. Snow, S. A. Soule, H. Kriesi and H. McCammon (eds), *The Wiley Blackwell Companion to Social Movements* (Oxford: Blackwell, 2018), pp. 322–37.

54. Daniela R. Picchio, *Party Responses to Social Movements: Challenges and Opportunities* (Oxford: Berghahn Books, 2019), p. 172.

55. Jack Goldstone, Introduction: Bridging Institutionalised and Non-institutionalised Politics, in J. Goldstone (ed.) *States, Parties, and Social Movements* (Cambridge: Cambridge University Press, 2003), p. 2.
56. Ibid.
57. See, e.g., Mildred A. Schwartz, Linkage Processes in Party Networks, in A. Römmele, D. M. Farrel and P. Ignazi (eds), *Political Parties and Political Systems: The Concept of Linkage Revisited* (Westport, CT: Praeger, 2005), pp. 37–60.
58. See Elin H. Allern, *Political Parties and Interest Groups in Norway* (Colchester: ECPR Press, 2009); Elin H. Allern and Tim Bale (eds), *Left-of-Centre Parties and Trade Unions in the Twenty-First Century* (Oxford: Oxford University Press, 2017). See also, Angelo Panebianco, *Political Parties: Organisation and Power* (Cambridge: Cambridge University Press, 1988).
59. Maurice Duverger *Political Parties: Their Organization and Activity in the Modern State* (London: Wiley, 1954).
60. Kay Lawson and Mildred A. Schwartz, Parties, Interest Groups and Movements: Shall Change Be Midwife to Truth?, in S. Mitra, C. Spies and M. Pehl (eds), *Political Sociology: State of the Art* (Leverkusen: Barbara Budrich Publishers), pp. 51–64.
61. Panebianco, *Political Parties*, p. 191.
62. Doug McAdam and Sidney Tarrow, Social Movements and Elections: Toward a Broader Understanding of the Political Context of Contention, in J. Van Stekelenburg, C. Roggeband and B. Klandermans (eds), *The Future of Social Movement Research: Dynamics, Mechanisms, and Processes* (Minneapolis: University of Minnesota Press, 2013), p. 328.
63. Hutter et al., *Social Movements in Interaction*.
64. Picchio, Party *Responses to Social Movements*, p. 24.
65. Ibid.
66. Andre Krowel, Party Models, in R. Katz and W. Crotty (eds), *Handbook of Party Politics* (London: Sage, 2016), pp. 249–69.
67. Ibid. See also Richard Ganther and Larry Diamond, Species of Political Parties, *Party Politics*, 2003, 9 (2), pp. 167–99.
68. Richard S. Katz and Peter Mair, Changing Models of Party Organization and Party Democracy, *Party Politics*, 1995, 1, pp. 5–28.
69. Ingrid van Biezen, Peter Mair and Thomas Poguntke, Going, Going, ... Gone? The Decline of Party Membership in Contemporary Europe, *European Journal of Political Research*, 2012, 51 (1), pp. 24–56.
70. Ingrid Van Biezen and Thoma Poguntke, The Decline of Membership-Based Politics, *Party Politics*, 2014, 20 (2), pp. 205–16.
71. Luke March and Cas Mudde, What's Left of the Radical Left? The European Radical Left After 1989: Decline and Mutation, *Comparative European Politics*, 2005, 3 (1), p. 25.
72. Ibid.
73. Magnus Wennerhag, Radical Left Movements in Europe: An Introduction, in M. Wennerhag, C. Frohlich and G. Piotrowski (eds), *Radical Left Movements in Europe* (Abingdon: Routledge, 2018).

74. Chiocchetti, *The Radical Left Party Family*, p. 10.

75. Standard dictionary definitions of radicalism define it as pertaining to the origins or roots, or most fundamental aspects of something, be it an opinion, a system or a truth.

76. Allan Cameron, Introduction, in Norberto Bobbio, *Left and Right: The Significance of a Political Distinction* (Cambridge: Polity Press, 1996), p. ix.

77. For a review, see Ruth Kinna and Uri Gordon, Introduction, in Ruth Kinna and Uri Gordon (eds), *The Routledge Handbook of Radical Politics* (London: Routledge, 2019), pp. 4–6.

78. Kai Arzheimer, Radical Attitudes, in B. Badie, D. Berg-Schlosser and L. Morlino (eds), *International Encyclopedia of Political Science* (London: Sage, 2011), p. 2199.

79. White, *Left and Right*, p. 126.

80. For an analysis of social democracy as the 'new mainstream' and early signs of centrist repositioning, see Sherry Berman, *The Primacy of Politics: Social Democracy and the Making of Europe's Twentieth Century* (New York: Cambridge University Press, 2006), esp. p. 7.

81. See Gerassimos Moschonas, *In the Name of Social Democracy: The Great Transformation, 1945 to the Present* (London: Verso, 2002), pp. 320–1; Ashley Lavelle, *The Death of Social Democracy: Political Consequences in the 21st Century* (Farnham: Ashgate, 2010).

82. See especially, Lavelle, *The Death of Social Democracy*.

83. Moschonas, *In the Name of Social Democracy*; Stephanie Mudge, What's Left of Leftism? Neoliberal politics in Western Party Systems, 1945-2004, *Social Science History*, 2001, 35 (3), pp. 337–80.

84. March and Keith, *Europe's Radical Left*, p. 6.

85. Carl Boggs, *The Impasse of European Communism* (Colorado: Westview, 1982). See also Neil McInnes, *The Communist Parties of Western Europe* (Oxford: Oxford University Press, 1975), pp. 167–70; and Chapters 6 and 7 .

86. Ralph Miliband, *Parliamentary Socialism: A Study in the Politics of Labour* (London: The Merlin Press, 1964).

87. Olof Palme was indeed a representative example of early democratic socialism: class oriented but libertarian at the same time, arising within the ground of social democracy and its years of socialisation with the New Left during the 1960s.

88. March and Mudde, *What's Left of the Radical Left?*

CHAPTER 3

1. Cristina Flesher-Fominaya, European Anti-austerity and Pro-democracy Protests in the Wake of the Global Financial Crisis, *Social Movement Studies*, 2017, 16 (1), pp. 1–20; Rafal Soborski, *Ideology and the Future of Progressive Social Movements* (Rowman and Littlefield, 2018); Bailey, *Protest Movements*.

2. E.g. Cathrine Eschle, *Global Democracy, Social Movements, and Feminism* (London: Taylor and Francis, 2001); Immanuel Wallerstein, Antisystemic Movements, Yesterday and Today, *Journal of World-Systems Research*, 2014, 20 (2), pp. 158–72; Donatella della Porta (ed.), *The Global Justice Movement: Cross-national and Transnational Perspectives* (Boulder: Paradigm Publishers, 2007).

3. Marianne Maeckelbergh, The Road to Democracy: The Political Legacy of '1968', *International Review of Social History*, 2011, 56 (2), p. 301. Author's emphasis.

4. Horn, 1968.

5. Maeckelbergh, *The Road to Democracy*.

6. Bailey, *Protest Movements*, chapter 5.

7. Stefan Berger and Christoph Cornelissen, Marxism and Social Movements: A Forgotten History? In S. Berger and C. Cornelissen (eds), *Marxist Historical Cultures and Social Movements during the Cold War* (Basingstoke: Palgrave Macmillan, 2019), p. 4.

8. See Oliver Marchart, *Post-foundational Political Thought: Political Difference in Nancy, Lefort, Badiou and Laclau* (Edinburgh: Edinburgh University Press), chapters 4 and 7; Ernesto Laclau and Chantal Mouffe, *Hegemony and Socialist Strategy: Towards and Radical Democratic Politics* (London: Verso, 2013).

9. Lasse Thomassen, Radical Democracy, in M. Bevir (ed.), *The Sage Encyclopedia of Political Theory* (London: Sage), pp. 1141–3.

10. For the relevance of mobilisations in the Global South in leading up to the GJM in Europe and North America, see Susan Eckstein, *Power and Popular Protest: Latin American Social Movements* (Berkeley: University of California Press, 2001).

11. David Graeber, The New Anarchists, *New Left Review*, January–February 2002, 13, https://newleftreview.org/II/13/david-graeber-the-new-anarchists. For the anarchist core of the GJM, see also Mark Rupert, Anti-capitalist Convergence? Anarchism, Socialism and the Global Justice Movement, in M. Steger (ed.), *Rethinking Globalism* (Lanham, MD: Rowman and Littlefield, 2003), pp. 121–35.

12. Saul Neumann. *The Politics of Postanarchism* (Cambridge: Polity, 2016), p. 51.

13. Katsiaficas, *The Subversion of Politics*.

14. Susan Epstein, Anarchism and the Anti-globalization Movement, *Monthly Review*, 2001, 53 (4), p. 1; David Graeber, The New Anarchism, in T. Mertes and Walden F. Bello (eds), *A Movement of Movements: Is Another World Really Possible?* (London: Verso), p. 212.

15. Žiga Vodovnik, A 'New' Anarchism: On Bifurcation and Transformation of Anarchist Thought and Practice, *World Political Science*, 2012, 8 (1), pp. 58–65.

16. Alan Finlayson, Rhetoric and Radical Democratic Political Theory, in Adrian Little and Moya Lloyd (eds), *The Politics of Radical Democracy* (Edinburgh: University of Edinburgh Press, 2008), pp. 13–32.

17. Marianne E. Maeckelberg, *The Will of the Many: How the Alterglobalisation Movement Is Changing the Face of Democracy* (London: Pluto, 2009), p. 36.

18. The central question of the Icesave dispute that lasted between 2008 and 2013 was whether Iceland should be held liable for the collapsed, high-interest rate accounts offered by subsidiaries of Landsbanki in the United Kingdom and the Netherlands and guarantee savings up to 20,887 euros per depositor.

19. Eiríkur Bergmann, *Iceland and the International Financial Crisis: Boom, Bust and Recovery* (Basingstoke and New York: Palgrave Macmillian, 2014).

20. Leonidas Oikonomakis and Jerome Roos, A Global Wave for Real Democracy?, in M. Ancelovici, P. Dufour and H. Nez (eds), *Street Politics in the Age of Austerity: From the Indignados to Occupy* (Amsterdam: Amsterdam University Press, 2016), pp. 277–49.

21. Maria Citrin and Dario Azzellini, *They Can't Represent Us! Reinventing Democracy from Greece to Occupy* (London: Verso, 2014).

22. Marco Giugni and Maria Grasso, *Austerity and Protest: Popular Contention in Times of Economic Crisis* (London and New York: Routledge, 2016).

23. Colin Crouch, *Coping with Post-democracy* (London: Fabian Society, 2000).

24. Magnus Wennerhag, The Politics of the Global Movement, *Eurozine*, 2 May 2008, www.eurozine.com/the-politics-of-the-global-movement/.

25. Ian Bruff, The Rise of Authoritarian Neoliberalism, *Rethinking Marxism: A Journal of Economics, Culture and Society*, 2014, 26 (1), pp. 113–29.

26. See Matthew Wood and Matt Flinders, Rethinking Depoliticisation: Beyond the Governmental, *Policy and Politics*, 2014, 42 (4), pp. 151–70.

27. Stephen Thomson and Eric C. Ip, COVID-19 Emergency Measures and the Impending Authoritarian Pandemic, *Journal of Law and the Biosciences*, 7 (1), 2020, https://doi.org/10.1093/jlb/lsaa064.

28. See particularly, Claus Offe, The Capitalist State, *Political Studies*, 1983, 31–4, pp. 668–81.

29. Colin Barker, Some Reflections on Student Movements of the 1960s and early 1970s, *Revista Crvtica de Cikncias Sociais*, 2008, 81, pp. 43–91.

30. Daniel Bensaid, *Strategies of Resistance and 'Who Are the Trotskyists?'* (London: Resistance Books, 2013), p. 79.

31. Nanni Balestrini, *Vogliamo Tutto* (Milano: Feltrinelli, 1971).

32. Chris Harman, *The Fire Last Time* (London: Bookmarks, 1988), p. vii.

33. One of the most comprehensive descriptions is by Robert J. C. Young, *Postcolonialism: An Historical Introduction* (London: Wiley Blackwell, 2001).

34. Kostis Kornetis, 'Cuban Europe'? Greek and Iberian *tiersmondisme* in the 'Long 1960s', *Journal of Contemporary History*, 2015, 50 (3), pp. 486–515.

35. Robert Gildea, The Global 1968 and International Communism, in Juliane Fürst and Silvio Pons (eds) *The Cambridge History of Communism*, Volume 3, *Endgames? Late Communism in Global Perspective, 1968 to the Present* (Cambridge: Cambridge University Press, 2017), pp. 23–49.

36. Ronald Inglehart, *The Silent Revolution: Changing Values and Political Styles among Western Publics* (Princeton, New Jersey: Princeton University Press, 1977), p. 231.

37. Ibid.

38. Barker, *Some Reflections*.

39. Barbara Foley, Marxism in the Poststructuralist Moment: Some Notes on the Problem of Revising Marx, *Cultural Critique*, 1990, 15, p. 37.

40. See Bryan D. Palmer, The Eclipse of Materialism: Marxist and the Writing of Social History in the 1980s, *Socialist Register*, 26, pp. 111–46. Louis Althusser's legacy, in the corpus of his analyses of the state, ideology and theory, came to be an important foundation for post-structuralist thinking in the 1970s among students and Maoists. By 1977, Althusser would talk of 'Marxism's (historical materialism's) pretension to being a science'. Stathis Kouvelakis, Beyond Marxism: The 'Crisis of Marxism' and the Post-Marxist Moment, in A. Callinicos, S. Kouvelakis and L. Pradella (eds), *The Routledge Handbook of Marxism and Post-Marxism* (London and New York: Routledge, 2020), p. 340.

41. Tony Judt, *Marxism and the French Left: Studies in Labour and Politics in France, 1830–1981* (New York and London: New York University Press, 2011), p. 171.

42. Perry Anderson, as cited in Kouvelakis, *Beyond Marxism*, p. 340.

43. Immanuel Wallerstein, New Revolts against the System, *New Left Review*, November–December 2002, 18, p. 30.

44. Ibid.

45. Nancy Fraser, A Triple Movement? Parsing the Politics of Crisis after Polanyi, *New Left Review*, May–June 2013, 81, pp. 119–32.

46. Barker, *Some Reflections*, p. 80.

47. Workerists in 1970s Italy, for example, largely conceived of themselves as 'intellectuals of the crisis'. See Mario Tronti, Our Operaismo, *New Left Review*, January–February 2012, 73, pp. 119–39.

48. Jürgen Habermas, *Legitimation Crisis* (Boston: Beacon Press, 1975).

49. Immanuel Wallerstein and Paul Starr (eds), *The University Crisis Reader: The Liberal University under Attack* (New York: Random House, 1971).

50. E.g. David Held, At the Crossroads: The End of the Washington Consensus and the Rise of Global Social Democracy, *Globalizations*, 2015, 2 (1), pp. 95–113; Alain Touraine, *A New Paradigm to Understand Today's World* (Cambridge: Polity Press, 2007 [2005]).

51. See also Bailey, *Protest Movements*.

52. Bart Cammaerts, *The Circulation of Anti-austerity Protest* (Cham, Switzerland: Palgrave Macmillan, 2018), p. 39.

53. Ibid., p. 166.

54. Giacomo D'Alisa, Federico Demaria and Giorgos Kallis, *Degrowth, a Vocabulary for a New Era* (New York: Routledge, 2014).

55. Corinna Burkhart, Matthias Schmelzer and Nina Treu (eds), *Degrowth in Movement(s): Exploring Pathways for Transformation* (Alresford: Zero Books, 2020).

56. One exception is the French Parti pour la Decroisance, founded in 2006, which is, however, very marginal.

57. Mattias Wahlström, Magnus Wennerhag and Christopher Rootes, Framing 'The Climate Issue': Patterns of Participation and Prognostic Frames among Climate Summit Protesters, *Global Environmental Politics*, 2013, 13 (4), pp. 101–22.

58. Donatella della Porta and Louisa Parks, Framing Processes in the Climate Movement: From Climate Change to Climate Justice, in M. Dietz and H. Garrelts (eds), *The Routledge Handbook of the Climate Change Movement* (London and New York: Routledge), p. 25.

59. Ibid.

60. Herbert Docena, *Capitalism versus Climate Justice, Global Dialogue: Magazine of the International Sociological Association*, https://globaldialogue.isa-sociology. org/capitalism-vs-climate-justice/.

61. Ibid.

62. See the network's website, https://by2020weriseup.net/.

63. Alex Callinicos, *An Anti-capitalist Manifesto* (London: Wiley, 2003).

64. Some of the key books inspiring and reflecting the GJM, widely discussed with their authors at the ESFs and WSFs, include Naomi Klein's *No Logo*, Urlich Beck's *What Is Globalisation?*, David Harvey's *A Short History of Neoliberalism*, Pierre Bourdieu's *Acts of Resistance* and *Firing Back* and Joseph E. Stiglitz's *Globalisation and Its Discontents*.

65. Simon Tormey, Anti-capitalism, in G. Ritzer (ed.), *The Wiley-Blackwell Encyclopedia of Globalization* (Oxford: Wiley-Blackwell, 2012), p. 70.

66. Ibid.; Callinicos, *An Anti-capitalist Manifesto*.

67. Josep Ibrahim, *Bourdieu and Social Movements: Ideological Struggles in the British Anti-capitalist Movement* (Basingstoke: Palgrave Macmillan, 2015), pp. 21–2.

68. Robert Latham, Contemporary Capitalism, Uneven Development, and the Arc of Anti-capitalism, *Global Discourse*, 2018, 8 (2), 169–86.

69. Ibid.

70. Luke March, Radical Left 'Success' before and after the Great Recession: Still Waiting for the Great Leap Forward?, in March and Keith, *Europe's Radical Left*, p. 31.

71. See Andre Freire and Marco Lisi, Political Parties, Citizens and the Economic Crisis: The Evolution of Southern European Democracies, *Portuguese Journal of Social Science*, 2016, 15 (2), pp. 153–71.

72. Luis Ramiro and Raul Gomez, Radical-Left Populism during the Great Recession: Podemos and Its Competition with the Established Radical Left, *Political Studies*, 2017, 65, pp. 108–26.

73. Rebecca Solnit, The Way We Get through This Is Together: The Rise of Mutual Aid under Coronavirus, *The Guardian*, 18 May 2020, www.theguardian.com/ world/2020/may/14/mutual-aid-coronavirus-pandemic-rebecca-solnit.

74. E.g. Geoffrey Pleyers, The Pandemic Is a Battlefield: Social Movements in the COVID-19 Lockdown, *Journal of Civil Society*, 2020, https://doi.org/10.1080 /17448689.2020.1794398; Donatella della Porta, Social Movements in Times of Pandemic: Another World Is Needed, *Open Democracy*, 23 March 2020, www.opendemocracy.net/en/can-europe-make-it/social-movements-times-pandemic-another-world-needed/.

75. See Steve Matthewman, Disaster Communism, *Thesis Eleven, Critical Theory and Historical Sociology*, 2020, https://thesiseleven.com/2020/07/15/disaster-communism/.

76. Thomas Olesen, Globalizing the Zapatistas: From Third World Solidarity to Global Solidarity, *Third World Quarterly*, 2004, 25 (1), pp. 256–9.

77. Katsiaficas, *The Imagination of the New Left*, p. 3.

78. Ian Bircall, Third World and after, *New Left Review*, March–April 2013, 80, p. 152.

79. Kristin Ross, *May '68 and Its Afterlives* (Chicago: Chicago University Press, 2002), p. 81. For Italy, see Antonino Scalia, The Manifold Partisan: Anti-fascism, Anti-imperialism, and Leftist Internationalism in Italy, 1964–76, *Radical History Review*, 138, pp. 11–38.

80. For an intellectual history of how the French Left was effectively reshaped by events in the Third World, as France's empire receded during the 1950s–1980s, see Christoph Kalter, *The Discovery of the Third World: Decolonization and the Rise of the New Left in France, c. 1950–1976* (New York: Cambridge University Press, 2016).

81. Gurminder K. Bhambra, Dalia Gebrial and Kerem Nişancıoğlu, Introduction: Decolonising the University?, in K. Guriminder et al. (eds), *Decolonising the University* (London: Pluto, 2018), p. 3.

82. Maud Bracke, May 1968 and Algerian Immigrants in France: Trajectories of Mobilisation and Encounter, in G. G. K. Bhambra and I. Demir (eds), *1968 in Retrospect: History, Theory, Alterity* (Basingstoke: Palgrave Macmillan, 2009), pp. 115–30.

83. Anandi Ramamurthy, *Black Star: Britain's Asian Youth Movements* (London: Pluto Press, 2013).

84. Ramdin, *The Making of the Black Working Class* (London: Verso, 2017); Stephen Castles and Godula Kosack, *Immigrant Workers and Class Structure in Western Europe* (London: Oxford University Press, 1985); Annie Phizacklea, Robert Miles and Paul Keagan, *Labour and Racism* (London: Routledge, 1980).

85. Patrick King, Introduction to Lenin, Communists, and Immigration, *Viewpoint Magazine*, 15 January 2019, https://viewpointmag.com/2019/01/14/introduction-to-lenin-communists-and-immigration/.

86. Bracke, *May 1968*, p. 116.

87. See Quinn Slobodian, *Foreign Front: Third World Politics in Sixties West Germany* (Durham, NC and London: Duke University Press).

88. See Sundari Anitha, Ruth Pearson and Linda McDowell, From Grunwick to Gate Gourmet: South Asian Women's Industrial Activism and the Role of Trade Unions, *Revue Française de Civilisation Britannique*, 2018, 23 (1), pp. 1–23.

89. Davide Però and John Solomos, Introduction: Migrant Politics and Mobilization: Exclusion, Engagements, Incorporation, *Ethnic and Racial Studies*, 2010, 33 (1), pp. 1–18.

90. Patrick King, *Introduction to 'Lenin, Communism and Immigration'*.

91. Angeline Escafré-Dublet, Demander l'autonomie culturelle: Le tournant de l'année 1973 dans le mouvement de défense des travailleurs immigrés, *Hommes and Migrations*, 2020, 1330, pp. 111–18.

92. Castles and Kosack, *Immigrant Workers*; Però and Solomos, Introduction.

93. Olesen, *Globalizing the Zapatistas*.

94. Note the common slogans, 'Solidarity against your Fortress Europe' and 'Your wars, our dead'.

95. Jane Freedman, The French 'Sans-Papiers' Movement: An Unfinished Struggle, in W. Pochman (ed.), *Migration and Activism in Europe Since 1945* (New York: Palgrave Macmillan, 2008), pp. 81–96.

96. Harald Bauder, Migrant Solidarities and the Politics of Space, *Progress in Human Geography*, 2020, 44 (6), pp. 1066–80. Relevant grassroots campaigns in Europe included 'Solidarity City Berlin' and 'The Whole World in Zurich'.

97. Sandro Mezzadra and Brett Neilson, *Border as Method: Or, the Multiplication of Labor* (Durham, NC: Duke University Press, 2013).

98. E.g. Harald Bauder, Perspectives of Open Borders and No Border, *Geography Compass*, 2015, 9 (7), pp. 395–405.

99. Cihan Aksan and Jon Bailes, One Question: Open Borders? *State of Nature*, 31 January 2019, http://stateofnatureblog.com/one-question-open-borders/.

100. Ibid.

101. Maribel Casas Cortes, Sebastian Cobarrubias, Nicholas De Genova, Glenda Garelli, Giorgos Grappi, Charles Heller, Sabine Hess, Brendt Kasparek, Sandro Mezzadra, Burt Neilson, Irene Peano, Lorenzo Pezzani, John Pickles, Federico Rahola, Lisa Riedner, Stephan Scheel and Martina Tazzioli, New Keywords: Migration and Borders, *Cultural Studies*, 2015, 29 (1), pp. 55–87.

102. Benjamin Zeimann, A Quantum of Solace? European Peace Movements during the Cold War and Their Elective Affinities, *Archiv für Sozialgeschichte*, 2009, 49, pp. 341–89.

103. The World Peace Council was established between 1948 and 1950 to promote the USSR's foreign policy and to campaign against nuclear weapons, which at the time only the USA had.

104. Günter Wernicke, The Communist-Led World Peace Council and the Western Peace Movements: The Fetters of Bipolarity and Some Attempts to Break Them in the Fifties and Early Sixties, *Peace and Change*, 1998, 23 (3), 297.

105. David Vine, No Bases? How Social Movements against U.S. Military Bases Abroad Are Challenging Militarization and Militarism, *Current Anthropology*, 2019, 60 (19), pp. 158–72.
106. Ziemann, *A Quantum of Solace?*, p. 366.
107. See https://cnduk.org/.
108. Tobias Pflueger, Antimilitarism in the (New) German Peace and Anti-war Movement after 11 September, *Peace News*, 1 June 2002, www.imi-online. de/2002/06/01/antimilitarism-in-th/.
109. Stefan Walgrave and Dieter Rucht, *The World Says No to War: Demonstrations against the War on Iraq* (Minneapolis: Minnesota University Press, 2010), p. xiii.
110. Chris Nineham, *The People v. Tony Blair: Politics, the Media and the Anti-war Movement* (London: Zero Books, 2013), chapter 4.
111. Wilbert van der Zeijden, Building the Global No-Bases Movement, *Peace Review*, 2010, 22 (2), p. 107.
112. Vine, No Bases?
113. Andrew Yeo, Not in Anyone's Backyard: The Emergence and Identity of a Transnational Anti-base Network, *International Studies Quarterly*, 2009, 53 (3), p. 581.
114. For a culturalised critique of imperialism and warmongering, see the collaborative song by Greek low-bab band, Active Member, 'Let's Go (to Guantanamo)', which includes lyrics in Italian, French, English and Spanish.
115. Vine, No Bases?
116. Herbert Docena, An Anti-bases Network Finds Its Base, *The Transnational Institute*, 14 March 2007, www.tni.org/en/article/an-anti-bases-network-finds-its-base.
117. David Broder and Giacomo Marchetti, We Won't Load Your Ships of Death: Italian Dockers against Saudi War Machine, *Jacobin*, 25 June 2019, www. jacobinmag.com/2019/06/italian-dockers-boycott-saudi-weapons-strike.
118. Leila Al Shami, The Anti-imperialism of Idiots, Leila's Blog, 2015, https:// leilashami.wordpress.com/2018/04/14/the-anti-imperialism-of-idiots/.
119. Alex Callinicos, Fighting the Last War, *International Socialism: A Quarterly Review of Socialist Theory*, 2015, 147, https://isj.org.uk/fighting-the-last-war/; Al Shami, The Anti-Imperialism of Idiots.
120. Pierre-André Taguieff, *Les Contre-réactionnaires: Le progressisme entre Illusion et Imposture* (Paris: Denoël, 2007).
121. Ashley Smith, US Imperialism's Pivot to Asia, *International Socialist Review*, 2019, 88, https://isreview.org/issue/88/us-imperialisms-pivot-asia. Obama's Covert drone war in numbers: Ten Times more Strikes than Bush, *The Bureau of Investigative Journalism*, 17 January 2017, www.thebureauinvestigates.com/ stories/2017-01-17/obamas-covert-drone-war-in-numbers-ten-times-more-strikes-than-bush.

122. Bernd Bonfert, Allied against Austerity: Transnational Cooperation in the European Anti-austerity Movements, doctoral thesis, Radboud Universiteit, Nijmegen, 2020, p. 229.

123. Angela Bourne and Sevastie Chatzopoulou, Social Movements and the Construction of Crisis Actors: Collective Responsibility, Identity and Governance, *International Journal of Public Administration*, 2015, 38 (12), pp. 874–83.

124. Robert Putnam, Diplomacy and Domestic Politics: The Logic of Two-Level Games, *International Organisation*, 1988, 42 (3), pp. 427–60.

125. Mario Pianta and Paolo Gerbaudo, In Search of European Alternatives: Anti-austerity Protests in Europe, in M. Kaldor and S. Selchow (eds), *Subterranean Politics in Europe* (Basingstoke: Palgrave Macmillan, 2014), pp. 31–59. See also, Cristina Flesher Fominaya, European Anti-austerity and Pro-democracy Protests in the Wake of the Global Financial Crisis, *Social Movement Studies*, 2017, 16 (1), pp. 1-20.

126. In France, the target was the Emmanuel Macron government, in office since 2017.

127. Christophe Guilluy, *No Society: To Telos tis Mesaias Taxis tis Disis* (Athens: Ekdoseis Politia).

128. Donatella della Porta and Lousia Parks, Social Movements, the European crisis, and EU: Political Opportunities, *Comparative European Politics*, 2018, 16, pp. 85–102.

129. Ibid.

130. See, e.g., the ethnographic illustration of these in Geoffrey Pleyers, Alter-Europe: Progressive Activists in Europe, in M. Kaldor, S. Selchow and T. Murray-Leach (eds), *Subterranean Politics in Europe* (London: Palgrave Macmillan, 2014), pp. 200–30.

131. Donatella della Porta, Social Movements and the European Union: Eurosceptics or Critical Europeanists? Working Paper, Notre Europe Etudes and Recherche, 2006, Policy Paper no. 22, p. 9.

132. E.g. Carlo Ruzza, Civil Society Actors and EU Fundamental Rights Policy: Opportunities and Challenges, *Human Right Review*, 2014, 15, pp. 65–81.

133. Donatella della Porta and Louisa Parks, Europeanisation and Social Movements: Before and after the Great Recession, in S. Börner and M. Eigmüller (eds), *European Integration, Processes of Change and the National Experience* (Basingstoke: Palgrave Macmillan, 2015) pp. 255–78; Manuela Caiani and Paolo Graziano, Europeanisation and Social Movements: The Case of the Stop TTIP Campaign, *European Journal of Political Research*, 2018, 57 (4), pp. 1031–55.

CHAPTER 4

1. Donatella della Porta, Political Economy and Social Movement Studies: The Class Basis of Anti-Austerity Protests, *Anthropological Theory*, 2017, 17 (4), p. 465.

2. David Harvey, *A Brief History of Neoliberalism* (Oxford: Oxford University Press, 2005), pp. 172–9.

3. Joris Velhust, Mobilizing Issues and the Unity and Diversity of Protest Events, unpublished doctoral dissertation, University of Antwerp, Belgium, 2011, p. 55.

4. Harvey, *A Brief History*, p. 179.

5. Saskia Sassen, *Expulsions: Brutality and Complexity in the Global Economy* (Cambridge, MA: Harvard University Press, 2014).

6. William K. Caroll, Crisis, Movements, Counter-hegemony: In Search of the 'New'. *Interface: A Journal for and about Social Movements*, 2010, 2 (2), pp. 175–6.

7. As cited in Marco Briziarelli and Susana Martinez Guillem, *Reviving Gramsci: Crisis, Communication, and Change* (London: Routledge, 2019), p. 100. Author's emphasis.

8. James M. Jasper, Constructing Indignation: Anger Dynamics in Protest Movements, *Emotion Review*, 2014, 6 (3), pp. 208–13.

9. Paolo Cossarini, Protests, Emotions and Democracy: Theoretical Insights from the *Indignados* Movement, *Global Discourse*, 2014, 4 (2–3), pp. 291–304.

10. Lasse Thomassen, The *Indignados*, Populism and Emotions in Political Theory: A Response to Paolo Cossarini, *Global Discourse*, 2014, 4 (2–3), pp. 305–7.

11. David A. Snow, E. Burke Rochford, Jr, Steven K. Worden and Robert D. Benford, Frame Alignment Processes, Micromobilization, and Movement Participation, *American Sociological Review*, 1986, 51 (4), pp. 464–8.

12. As cited in Cammaerts, *The Circulation of Anti-austerity Protest*, p. 167.

13. David Graeber, *Fragments of an Anarchist Anthropology* (Chicago: Prickly Paradigm Press), p. 3.

14. Benjamin J. Pauli, The New Anarchism in Britain and the US: Towards a Richer Understanding of Post-war Anarchist Thought, *Journal of Political Ideologies*, 2015, 20 (2), p. 137.

15. Kioupkiolis, *Acts, Events*, p. 27.

16. Ruth Kinna, Utopianism and Prefiguration, in S. D. Chrostowska and James D. Ingram (eds), *Political Uses of Utopia: New Marxist, Anarchist, and Radical Democratic Perspectives* (New York: Columbia University Press, 2016), p. 208.

17. Pauli, The New Anarchism.

18. Albert O. Hirschman, *The Passions and the Interests* (Princeton: Princeton University Press, 2013 [1977]).

19. See Erik Olin Wright, *Envisioning Real Utopias* (London: Verso, 2010).

20. See, e.g., Lavelle, *The Death of Social Democracy*, pp. 16–17.

21. For the argument that human rights organisations 'scarcely seem very anti-systemic', and an analysis of their trajectory and public profile as more the 'adjuncts of states than their opponents', see Wallerstein, *New Revolts*, p. 269.

22. Salar Mohandesi, From Anti-imperialism to Human Rights: The Vietnam War and Radical Internationalism in the 1960s and 1970s, PhD thesis, University of Pennsylvania, 2017.

23. Eleanor Davey, *Idealism beyond Borders: The French Revolutionary Left and the Rise of Humanitarianism, 1954–1988* (Cambridge: Cambridge University Press), pp. 114–26.

24. The first signs of these realities appeared in 1963 when Solzhenitsyn's *One Day in the Life of Ivan Denisovich* had been translated in English.

25. Davey, *Idealism beyond Borders*, p. 9.

26. Amy Bartholomew and Jennifer Breakspear, Human Rights as Swords of Empire, in L. Panitch and C. Leys (eds), *Socialist Register 2004: The New Imperial Challenge* (London: Merlin Press), p. 139.

27. Davey, *Idealism beyond Borders*.

28. Ibid., p. 3.

29. Duncan Kennedy, The Critique of Right in Critical Legal Studies, in Wendy Brown and Janet Halley (eds.) *Left Legalism/Left Critique* (Durham and London: Duke University Press, 2002), p. 182.

30. See Richard Seymour, *The Liberal Defense of Murder* (London: Verso, 2008).

31. Samuel Moyn, *Not Enough: Human Rights in an Unequal World* (Cambridge, MA: Harvard University Press, 2018).

32. See Bécquer Seguín, Imperialists for 'Human Rights', *Jacobin*, 19 December 2014, https://jacobinmag.com/2014/12/imperialists-for-human-rights.

33. Amy Bartholomew and Alan Hunt, *What's Wrong with Rights?*, *Law & Inequality*, 1991, 9 (1), pp. 8–10.

34. The Boycott, Divestment and Sanctions Movement, organised and coordinated by the Palestinian Boycott, Divestment and Sanctions National Committee, is a global campaign established in 2005, promoting various forms of boycott against Israel, demanding that the country adheres to international law. Charles Tripp, *The Power and the People: Paths of Resistance in the Middle East* (Cambridge: Cambridge University Press, 2013), pp. 125–6. See also Marco Perolini, Whose Human Rights? The Marginalisation of Dissent in France and Spreading, *Open Democracy*, 20 April 2018, www.opendemocracy.net/en/whose-human-rights-marginalisation-of-dissent-in-france-and-spreading/.

35. Seguín, *Imperialists for 'Human Rights'*.

36. David Landy, Talking Human Rights: How Social Movement Activists Are Constructed and Constrained by Human Rights Discourse, *International Sociology*, 2013, 28(4), pp. 409–28.

37. Bartholomew and Breakspear, *Human Rights as Swords*, p. 139.

38. See Kiyoteru Tsutsui, Claire Whitlinger and Alwyn Lim Annu, International Human Rights Law and Social Movements: States' Resistance and Civil Society's Insistence, *Review of Law and the Social Sciences*, 2012, 8, pp. 367–96.

39. Thomas Murray, *Contesting Economic and Social Rights in Ireland: Constitution, State and Society, 1848–2016* (Cambridge: Cambridge University Press, 2016), p. 349.

40. A note of caution is that there are significant differences between these two French protest movements, their common progressive populism notwithstanding. Enzo Traverso, Understanding the Gilet Jaunes, *Verso Blog*, 15 February 2019, www.versobooks.com/blogs/4242-understanding-the-gilets-jaunes.

41. Yannis Stavrakakis and Giorgos Katsambekis, Left-Wing Populism in the European Periphery: The Case of SYRIZA, *Journal of Political Ideologies*, 2014, 19 (2), pp. 119–42.

42. Cristóbal Rovira Kaltwasser, The Ambivalence of Populism: Threat and Corrective for Democracy, *Democratization*, 2012, 19 (2), pp. 184–208.

43. Robert L. Scott and Donald K. Smith, The Rhetoric of Confrontation, *Quarterly Journal of Speech*, 1969, 55, p. 3.

44. See, respectively, C. Wright Mills, *The Power Elite* (Oxford: Oxford University Press, 1956); Louis Althusser, *Lenin and Philosophy and Other Essays* (London: Monthly Review Press); Goran Therbron, *What Does the Ruling Class Do when It Rules?* (London: Verso, 2007); Caspar Melville, The Politics of Everyday Life, *Eurozine*, 3 September, 2014, http//:Eurozine.com/the-politics-of-everyday-life/.

45. One can point to the newspaper *PEACE* (People Emerging Outside of Corrupt Establishments), a British newspaper 'by and for GIs to foster a more humane military', which denounced both communism and capitalism along with anarchism, calling for the right to refuse 'illegal' orders to fight 'in the illegal, imperialist war in South Asia'. See *PEACE*, 1970, 1 (2) in the archives of the University of Warwick, The Library: Modern Records Centre, https://warwick.ac.uk/services/library/mrc/archives_online/exhibitions/peace/.

46. Richard Havers, Power to the People: John Lennon's Revolutionary Statement, *Undiscover Music*, 12 March 2021, undiscovermusic.com/stories/power-to-the-people/.

47. Gerbaudo, *The Mask and the Flag*, pp. 103–4.

48. Ibid.

49. Michael Hardt and Antonio Negri, *Empire* (Cambridge, MA: Harvard University Press, 2000), p. 316.

50. The slogan reversed and posed as a demand, Chomsky's diagnosis of 'profit over people' under neoliberalism. See Noam Chomsky, *Profit before People: Neoliberalism and Global Order* (New York: Seven Stories Press, 1998).

51. Jodie Dean, *Crowds and Party* (London: Verso), p. 22.

52. See, e.g., Richard Mullin, The Russian Narodniks and their Relation to Russian Marxism, in G. Charalambous and G. Ioannou (eds), *Left Radicalism and Populism in Europe* (London and New York: Routledge, 2019), pp. 33–51.

53. David Plotke, Eurocommunism and the American Left, in C. Boggs and D. Plotke (eds), *The Politics of Eurocommunism: Socialism in Transition* (London: Macmillan, 1980), p. 418.

54. Richard M. Rorty (ed.), *The Linguistic Turn: Essays in Philosophical Method* (Chicago: Chicago University Press, 1992 [1969]).

55. Omar Acha, From Marxist to Post-Marxist Populism: Ernesto Laclau's Trajectory within the National Left and Beyond, *Historical Materialism*, 2019, 28 (1), p. 15.

56. One recent study of this tradition argued that social movements create new institutions that bring about social change through alternative discourses. See Oscar Garcia Augustin, *Sociology of Discourse: From Institutions to Social Change* (London: John Benjamin Publishing Company, 2015).

57. Ernesto Laclau, *On Populist Reason* (London: Verso, 2005).

58. Helen Meiksins-Wood, *The Retreat from Class: A New 'True' Socialism* (London: Verso, 1986).

59. Acha, *From Marxist to Post-Marxist*, p. 16.

60. Dean, *Crowds and Party*.

61. Aslanidis, *Populist Social Movements*.

62. David J. Bailey, Mapping Anti-austerity Discourse: Populism, Sloganeering and/or Realism?, in G. Charalambous and G. Ioannou (eds), *Left Radicalism and Populism in Europe* (London: Routledge, 2019), pp. 92–3.

63. John Schwarzmantel, Rethinking Marxism and Nationalism in an Age of Globalization, *Rethinking Marxism*, 2012, 24 (1), p. 148.

64. Geoff Eley, Historicizing the Global, Politicizing Capital: Giving the Present a Name, History *Workshop Journal*, 2007, 63, pp. 154–88.

65. Ibid., p. 169.

66. See, e.g., Martin Mevius, Reappraising Communism and Nationalism, *Nationalities Papers*, 2009, 37 (4), pp. 377–400.

67. See Tuddi Kernallegenn, Les Gauches Alternatives à la Découverte des Régions dans les Années 1968, *La Revue Historique*, 2018, 685, pp. 147–66.

68. Vincenzo Ruggiero, 'Attac': A Global Social Movement? *Social Justice*, 2002, 87–8 (1/2), pp. 48–60.

69. See Danielle Conversi, The Left and Nationalism: Introducing the Debate, *H-Net: Humanities and Social Sciences Online*, 2017, https://networks.h-net.org/node/3911/discussions/588345/left-and-nationalism-monthly-series-left-and-nationalism.

70. Alexandros Kioupkiolis, Common Democracy: Political Representation beyond Representative Democracy, *Democratic Theory*, 2017, 4 (1), p. 52.

71. Andreas Kalyvas, Popular Sovereignty, Democracy, and the Constituent Power, *Constellations*, 2005, 12 (2), p. 223.

72. Della Porta and Mattoni, *Spreading Protest*, p. 7.

73. Aristotle Kallis, Populism, Sovereigntism, and the Unlikely Re-emergence of the Territorial Nation-State, *Fudan Journal of the Humanities and Social Sciences*, 2018, 11, p. 301.

74. Oscar Garcia Augustin, *Left-Wing Populism: The Politics of the People* (Bingley: Emerald, 2020), p. 70.

75. Kallis, *Populism*, p. 185.

CHAPTER 5

1. David Harvey, *Spaces of Hope* (Edinburgh: Edinburgh University Press, 2000), p. 241.

2. Manuel Castells, *Networks of Outrage and Hope: Social Movements in the Internet Age* (London: John Wiley and Sons, 2012).

3. Della Porta and Mattoni, *Spreading Protest*, chapter 3. See also, Jenny Pickerill and John Krinsky, Why does Occupy Matter?, *Social Movement Studies*, 2012, 11 (3–4), pp. 279–87.

4. Ibid.

5. Saskia Sassen, The Global Street: Making the Political, *Globalizations*, 2011, 8 (5), pp. 573–4.

6. Ibid.

7. It was used as the title of a book of posters in support of the May 1968 events, produced by the Atelier Populaire (Popular Workshop), established in May 1968 by students and faculty at L'ecole des Beaux-Arts taking over their college's lithography studio.

8. See Katsiaficas, *The Imagination of the New Left*, pp. 16–19.

9. The connections between the global and the local have been of unprecedented interest among scholars of mobilisation, political economy and social theory. As praxis, many left-wing activists have engaged with the digitisation of music and other forms of cultural heritage precisely as an activity which globalises and celebrates the local roots of diverse populations and by extension diverse forms of mobilisation and resistance, sharing global identities. The Working Class History group, or the Working Class Movement operating from the library in Salford with the same name, are such examples.

10. Indicatively, see the Rojava Charter of the Social Contract: https://peaceinkurd-istancampaign.com/charter-of-the-social-contract/.

11. Manuel Castells, *The Urban Question: A Marxist Approach* (Boston: MIT Press, 1972).

12. Mark Purcell, Excavating Lefebvre: The Right to the City and Its Urban Politics of the Inhabitant, *GeoJournal*, 2003, 58, pp. 99–108.

13. Debbie Bookchin, How My Father's Ideas Helped the Kurds Create a New Democracy, *New York Review*, 15 June 2018, www.nybooks.com/daily/2018/06/15/how-my-fathers-ideas-helped-the-kurds-create-a-new-democracy/.

14. Margit Mayer, The 'Right to the City' in Urban Social Movements, in N. Brenner, P. Markuse and M. Mayer (eds), *Cities for People, Not for Profit: Critical Urban Theory and the Right to the City* (London: Routledge, 2012), pp. 132–3.

15. Martin Baumeister, Bruno Bonomo and Dieter Schoft (eds), *Cities Contested: Urban Politics, Heritage, and Social Movements in Italy and West Germany in the 1970s* (Frankfurt am Main: Campus Verlag, 2017).

16. Luciano Villani, The Struggle for Housing in Rome: Contexts, Protagonists and Practices of a Social Urban Conflict, in Baumeister et al., *Cities Contested*, pp. 322–7.

17. Christian Wicke, Urban Movement à la Ruhr? The Initiatives for the Preservation of Workers' Settlements in the 1970s, in Baumeister et al., *Cities Contested*, pp. 247–71.

18. Jorge Sequera and Jordi Jorge, Urban Activism and Touristification in Southern Europe: Barcelona, Madrid and Lisbon, in J. Ibrahim and John M. Roberts, *Contemporary Left-Wing Activism*, Volume 2, *Democracy, Participation and Dissent in a Global Context* (London: Routledge, 2019), pp. 88–105.

19. Such as the Turin–Lyon high-speed railway and No-TAV (No to the High-Speed Train) movement in the Susa Valley in Piedmont, Italy, which arose in opposition to it, broadly based on the notion of locally unwanted land use.

20. Their website is https://housingnotprofit.org/.

21. Plan C and Bertie Russell, Radical Municipalism: Demanding the Future, *Open Democracy*, 26 June 2017, www.opendemocracy.net/en/radical-municipalism-demanding-future/.

22. Michael Goddard, *Guerrilla Networks: An Anarchaeology of 1970s Radical Media Ecologies* (Amsterdam: Amsterdam University Press, 2018), p. 189.

23. Alain Touraine, *The Self-production of Society* (Chicago: University of Chicago Press, 1977).

24. J. Craig Jenkins, Resource Mobilization Theory and the Study of Social Movements, *Annual Review of Sociology*, 1983, 9, pp. 527–53.

25. Deanna, A. Rohlinger, Leslie A. Bunnage and Jesse Klein, Virtual Power Plays: Social Movements, Internet Communication Technology, and Party Politics, in B. Goffman, A. Treschel and M. Franklin (eds), *The Internet and Democracy: Voters, Candidates, Parties and Social Movements* (London: Springer, 2014), pp. 83–109.

26. Castells, *Networks of Outrage and Hope*.

27. Ahmed Wasim, *Amplified Messages: How Hashtag Activism and Twitter Diplomacy Converged at #ThisIsACoup – and Won. Impact of Social Sciences Blog*, 7 January 2016, https://wasimahmed.org/2016/01/08/amplified-messages-how-hashtag-activism-and-twitter-diplomacy-converged-at-thisisacoup-and-won-2/.

28. Andrew Lison and Timothy Scott Brown, Introduction, in A. Lison and T. S. Brown, *The Global Sixties in Sound and Vision: Media, Counterculture, Revolt* (Basingstoke: Palgrave Macmillan, 2014), p. 10.

29. Goddard, *Guerilla Networks*.

30. Vicente Rubio-Pueyo, *Municipalism in Spain: From Barcelona to Madrid, and beyond* (Berlin: Friedrich Ebert Stiftung, 2017), p. 17.

31. For an empirical study on the class–digital divide, see Jen Schradie, The Digital Activism Gap: How Class and Costs Shape Online Collective Action, *Social Problems*, 2018, 65 (1), 51–74.

32. It is within the context of such disputes that in leftist circles one can find satire or criticism of what is pejoratively called 'the Twitter left', 'couch activism' or 'slacktivism'.

33. Andrea Kavanaugh, Debbie Denise Reese, John M. Carroll and Mary Beth Rosson, Weak Ties in Networked Communities, *Information and Society*, 2005, 21 (2), pp. 119–31.

34. Paolo Gerbaudo, Populism 2.0: Social Media Activism, the Generic Internet User and Interactive Direct Democracy, in D. Trottier and Christian Fuchs, *Social Media, Politics and the State: Protests, Revolutions, Riots, Crime and Policing in the Age of Facebook, Twitter and YouTube* (London: Routledge, 2014), p. 69.

35. Ibid.

36. People's Global Action Manifesto, 2000, www.urban75.com/Action/manifesto.html.

37. Donatella della Porta, Conclusions, in Donatella della Porta (ed.), *Solidarity Mobilizations in the 'Refugee Crisis', Contentious Moves* (Basingstoke: Palgrave Macmillan, 2018), p. 335.

38. Ibid., p. 333.

39. Lorenzo Zamponi, From Border to Border: Refugee Solidarity Activism in Italy across Space, Time, and Practices, in della Porta, *Solidarity Mobilizations*, pp. 114–15; Leonidas Oikonomakis, Solidarity in Transition: The Case of Greece, in della Porta, *Solidarity Mobilizations*, p. 94.

40. Angela Wigger, From Dissent to Resistance: Locating Patterns of Horizontalist Self-management Crisis Responses in Europe, *Comparative European Politics*, 2018, 16, pp. 32–49. An example from bottom-up gardening is the Incredible Edible international network, which has experienced significant growth between 2008 and today and shares the values of ethics, equality and community. See www.incredibleedible.org.uk/.

41. Athena Arampatzi, Constructing Solidarity as Resistive and Creative Agency in Austerity Greece, *Comparative European Politics*, 2018, 16, pp. 50–66.

42. Bailey, *Protest Movements*, p. 183.

43. Lorenzo Zamponi and Lorenzo Bossi, Direct Social Action and Economic Crises: The Relationship between Forms of Action and Socio-Economic Context in Italy, *PArtecipazione e COnflitto*, 2015, 8 (2), p. 367.

44. Ibid.

45. Proletarian shopping was first theorised by the Tupamaros movement in Uruguay and was utilised by the RAF in the late 1960s to finance their activity. In Italy, it was also organised by the Autonomous Workers' Committees. See Steve Wright, *Storming Heaven: Class Composition and Struggle in Italian Autonomist Marxism* (London: Pluto Press, 2003), pp. 158–62.

46. Zamponi and Bossi, Direct Social Action; see also Francesca Forno and Paolo R. Graziano, Consumer Culture: Sustainable Community Movement Organisations, *Consumer Culture*, 2014, 14 (2), pp. 139–57.

47. Maria Kousis and Maria Paschou, Alternative Forms of Resilience: A Typology of Approaches for the Study of Citizen Collective Responses in Hard Economic Times, *PArtecipazione e COnflitto* , 2017, 10, pp. 136–68.

48. Michele Micheletti, *Political Virtue and Shopping: Individuals, Consumerism and Collective Action* (New York: Palgrave Macmillan, 2003).

49. Forno and Graziano, Consumer Culture, pp. 156–7.

50. Eleftheria J. Lelakis and Francesca Forno, Political Consumerism in Southern Europe, in Magnus Boström, Michele Micheletti, and Peter Oosterveer (eds), *The Oxford Handbook of Political Consumerism* (Oxford: Oxford University Press, 2019), pp. 457–78.

51. Dimitrios Theodossopoulos, Philanthropy or Solidarity? Ethical Dilemmas about Humanitarianism in Crisis-Afflicted Greece, *Social Anthropology*, 2016, 24 (2), pp. 167–84.

52. Ibid.

53. Geoffrey Pleyers, *The Pandemic Is a Battlefield*.

54. Cristina Flesher Fominaya, How Do You Protest When You Can't Take to the Streets?, *Open Democracy*, 12 May 2020, www.opendemocracy.net/en/can-europe-make-it/how-do-you-protest-when-you-cant-take-to-the-streets/.

55. Ale Mezzandri, A Crisis Like No Other: Social Reproduction and the Regeneration of Capitalist Life during the COVID19 Pandemic, *Development Economics*, 20 April 2020, https://developingeconomics.org/2020/04/20/a-crisis-like-no-other-social-reproduction-and-the-regeneration-of-capitalist-life-during-the-covid-19-pandemic/.

56. Maeckelberg, *The Will of the Many*, p. 17.

57. Such practice was employed in networks and groups such as British Rising Tide, the Italian Rete Lilliput, the Spanish Espacio Alternativo, Dissent! and A Network of Resistance against G8. Autonomist groups such as the Disobedienti acted only upon unanimity. See Donatella della Porta, Making the Polis: Social Forums and Democracy in the Global Justice Movement, *Mobilization: An International Quarterly*, 2005, 10 (1), pp. 73–94.

58. David Graeber, *There Never Was a West: Or, Democracy Emerges from the Spaces in between*, 2007, p. 11, http://genealogiesofknowledge.net/wp-content/uploads/2016/04/david-graeber-there-never-was-a-west.pdf.

59. Manuel Castells, *The Information Age: Economy, Society and Culture, Volume 2, The Power of Identity* (Cambridge, MA and Oxford: Blackwell, 1997), p. 362.

60. Manuel Castells, *The Internet Galaxy: Reflections on the Internet, Business and Society* (Oxford: Oxford University Press, 2001), p. 55.

61. For the organisational and procedural elements of radical democratic ideas, see Chapter 5.

62. Donatella della Porta and Lorenzo Mosca, Global-Net for Global Movements? A Network of Networks for a Movement of Movements, *Journal of Public Policy*, 2005, 25 (1), pp. 165–90.

63. Christina Flesher Fominaya, *Social Movements and Globalization: How Protests, Occupations and Uprising Are Changing the World* (Basingstoke: Palgrave Macmillan, 2014), p. 68.

64. See John Holloway and Alex Callinicos, Can We Change the World without Taking Power? A Debate at the World Social Forum, 27 January 2005, www.marxists.org/history/etol/writers/callinicos/2005/xx/holloway.html.

65. Owen Worth and Karen Buckley, The World Social Forum: Postmodern Prince or Court Jester?, *Third World Quarterly*, 2009, 30 (4), pp. 649–61.

66. Michael Hardt and Antonio Negri, *Assembly* (Oxford: Oxford University Press, 2017), p. 8.

67. Vodovnik, *A 'New' Anarchism?*, p. 64.

68. See Claus Offe, Microaspects of Democratic Theory: What Makes for the Deliberative Competence of Citizens?, in A. Hadenius (ed.), *Democracy's Victory and Crisis* (Cambridge: Cambridge University Press, 1997), pp. 81–104.

69. Joe Freeman, *The Tyranny of Structuralness*, 1972, www.jofreeman.com/joreen/tyranny.htm.

70. Peter D. Thomas, The Communist Hypothesis and the Question of Organization, *Theory and Event*, 2013, 16 (4), https://muse.jhu.edu/article/530491.

71. E.g. Jodi Dean, *The Communist Horizon* (London: Verso, 2019); Paolo Gerbaudo, The Return of the Party, *Jacobin*, 22 October 2018, https://jacobinmag.com/2018/10/mass-party-labour-podemos-neoliberalism.

72. Wallerstein, *New Revolts*, p. 40; See also Geoff Eley, *Forging Democracy: The History of the Left in Europe, 1850–2000* (Oxford: Oxford University Press, 2002), p. 7.

73. Jennier Leigh Disney and Virginia S. Williams, Latin America Social Movements and a New Left Consensus: State and Civil Society Challenges to Neoliberal Globalisation, *New Political Science*, 36 (1), pp. 1–33.

74. Patrick Barrett, Daniel Chavez and César Rodríguez-Garavito, *The New Latin American Left: Utopia Reborn* (London and Chicago: Pluto Press, 2008).

75. For an overview, see Klaus Weinhauer, Terorrism between Social Movements, the State and Media Societies, in Berger and Nehrin, *The History of Social Movements*, pp. 543–77.

76. Donatella della Porta, *Social Movements, Political Violence, and the State: A Comparative Analysis of Italy and Germany* (Cambridge: Cambridge University Press, 2006), p. 17.

77. Lorenzo Zamponi, *Social Movements, Memory and Media Narrative in Action in the Italian and Spanish Student Movements* (Basingstoke: Palgrave Macmillan, 2018), p. 65.

78. Donatella della Porta and Sidney Tarrow, Unwanted Children: Political Violence and the Cycle of Protest in Italy, 1966–1973, *European Journal of Political Research*, 1986, 14, p. 614.

79. Consider indicatively the notion of 'counter-terror' in Lotta Continua, see Aldo Cazullo, *I Ragazzi che Volevano Fare la Rivoluzione, 1968–1978: Storia di Lotta Continua* (Milano: Arnoldo Mondadori Editore, 1998).

80. Armed struggle supporters or reckless radicalised teenagers referenced Mao's Red Book, as captured in the reading scene of Bernardo Bertolucci's *The Dreamers* (2004), where Theo reads aloud the following passage: 'A revolution is not a dinner party, or writing an essay, or painting a picture, or doing embroidery; it cannot be so refined, so leisurely and gentle, so temperate, kind, courteous, restrained and magnanimous. A revolution is an insurrection, an act of violence by which one class overthrows another.'

81. This was a typified phrase for imperialist states waging wars in former colonies.

82. This was the name of the Stuttgart prison.

83. Cazzulo, *I Ragazzi*.

84. Donald Sassoon, *A Hundred Years of Socialism: The West European Left in the Twentieth Century* (London: I.B Tauris, 1998), p. 402.

85. Ingrid Gilcher-Holtey, On the Legitimacy of Violence as a Political Act: Hannah Arendt, Susan Sontag, Ulrike Meinhof, and Bernadine Dohrn, in Sarah Colvin and Katharina Karcher (eds), *Women, Global Protest Movements and Political Agency: Rethinking the Legacy of 1968* (London: Routledge, 2018), https://research-information.bris.ac.uk/ws/portalfiles/portal/154621826/Introduction_Vol_1_SCKK_final_3_.pdf.

86. See Colvin and Karcher, *Women, Global Protest Movements*.

87. The Legitimacy of Violence as a Political Act? Noam Chomsky debates with Hannah Arendt, Susan Sontag, et al., https://chomsky.info/19671215/.

88. Ibid.

89. Gerry Nagtzaam, *From Environmental Action to Ecoterrorism? Towards a Process Theory of Environmental and Animal Rights Oriented Political Violence* (Cirencester: Edward Elgar, 2016), pp. 1–12.

90. See Bron Taylor, Religion, Violence, and Radical Environmentalism: From Earth First! to the Unabomber to the Earth Liberation Front, *Terrorism and Political Violence*, 1998, 10 (4) p. 10.

91. Will Boisseau, Animal Liberation, in Ruth Kinna and Uri Gordon (eds), *The Routledge Handbook of Radical Politics* (Abingdon: Routledge, 2019), pp. 41–52.

92. As cited in Manuel Mirenau, The Criminalisation of Environmental Activism in Europe, *LeftEast*, 24 September 2014, www.criticatac.ro/lefteast/author/manuel-m/.

93. Ibid.

94. For a review of criminal cases against activists across the world, and the broader utilisation of 'terrorism' as discourse against environmental protest, see ibid.

95. Alexandra Plows, Derej Wall and Brian Doherty, Covert Repertoires: Ecotage in the UK, *Social Movement Studies*, 2004, 3, p. 199.

96. Andreas Malm, *How to Blow up a Pipeline: Learning to Fight in a World on Fire* (London: Verso Books).

97. See James Wilt, How to Blow up a Movement: Andreas Malm's New Book Dreams of Sabotage but Ignores Consequences, *Canadian Dimension*, 3 March 2021, https://canadiandimension.com/articles/view/how-to-blow-up-a-movement-malms-new-book-dreams-of-sabotage-but-ignores-consequences.

98. Jeffrey Juris, Violence Performed and Imagined: Militant Action, the Black Bloc and the Mass Media in Genoa, *Critique of Anthropology*, 2005, 25 (4), pp. 413–32.

99. Liz Highleyman, The Global Justice Movement, in I. Ness (ed.), *Encyclopedia of American Social Movements* (London: Verso), pp. 1009–13, www.black-rose.com/articles-liz/globjustice.html.

100. Ibid.

101. Graeber, *The New Anarchists*.

102. Frequently, rainbow or immigrant solidarity banners are raised in stadiums by the 'ultras' of such teams as St Paoli in Germany, Livorno in Italy, Omonoia in Cyprus and Celtic in Scotland.

103. See Thanasis Kampagiannis, *Me tis Melisses I me tous Lykous?* (Athens: Politeia, 2020).

104. Hank Johnston and Seraphim Sepheriades, The Dynamics of Violent Protest: Emotions, Interaction, and Disruptive Deficit, in H. Johnston and S. Sepheriades (eds), *Collective Violence in Violent Protest, Contentious Politics, and the Neoliberal State* (Aldershot: Ashgate, 2012), p. 3.

105. Hélène Combes and Olivier Fillieule, Repression and Protest Structural Models and Strategic Interactions, *Revue française de science politique*, 2011, 61, pp. 1047–72.

106. Ibid.

107. For an overview, see Donatella della Porta, Interview with Donatella della Porta: The Growing Criminalisation of Protest, *Open Democracy*, 4 December 2017, www.opendemocracy.net/en/protest-donatella-della-porta-interview/.

108. The I Don't Pay Movement (Kinima den plirono) in Greece reached its peak in 2010–11 and among demonstrations and marches that carried out consecutive acts of civil disobedience against toll taxes. Copwatch in France was a hacking-driven virtual space which documented and condemned police misconduct and brutality. The wider movement network is active across the Atlantic but it

originated and remains stronger in the USA. In France it was blocked in 2011 after a court order.

109. Flesher Fominaya, European Anti-austerity and Pro-democracy Protests, p. 10.

110. Bailey, *Protest Movements*, p. 135.

111. Anne Muxel, Political Radicalism among the Younger Generations, *Youth and Globalization*, 2020, 2 (2), pp. 123–36.

112. David Kellner (ed.), *The New Left and the 1960s: Collected Papers of Herbert Marcuse*, Volume 3 (London: Routledge, 2005), p. 146.

113. Zamponi, Social Movements, Memory, p. 60; Irene Pereira, Mai 68 et ses héritages contestataires, Sens public, 2008, www.sens-public.org/articles/634/.

114. Detlef Siegfried, Understanding 1968: Youth Rebellion, Generational Change and Postindustrial Society, in A. Schildt and A. Schildt (eds), *Between Marx and Coca-Cola: Youth Cultures in Changing European Societies, 1960–1980* (New York: Berghahn Books), p. 59.

115. Barker, *Some Reflections*.

116. Eley, *Forging Democracy*, p. 354; Carl Boggs, Rethinking the Sixties Legacy: From New Left to New Social Movements, in S. M Leyman (ed.), *Social Movements: Critiques, Concepts, Case Studies* (London: Palgrave Macmillan), p. 332.

117. As cited in Eley, *Forging Democracy*, 354–5.

118. See Edwards, *Struggling to Protest: The Italian Communist Party and the Protest Cycle, 1972–77*, PhD thesis (Salford: University of Salford, 2005).

119. Both upper-class (the inheritors as Bourdieu called them) and petit-bourgeois youth or ones from agricultural families. See Thanasis Alexiou, Apo tis Koinnikes Taxis stis Stratigikes Taftotitas,: Anadiarthrosi tis Paragogis kai Nea Koinonika Kinimata, *Theses*, 2002, 79, pp. 75–77.

120. Mayer, *The 'Right to the City'*, p. 66.

121. See especially, Colin Crouch and Alessandro Pizzorno, (eds) *The Resurgence of Class Conflict in Western Europe since 1968* (London: Palgrave Macmillan, 1978).

122. Michael J. Sordaro, The Italian Communists and the Politics of Austerity, *Studies in Comparative Communism*, 1980, 13 (2–3), pp. 220–49.

123. Erik Neveu, The European Movements of '68: Ambivalent Theories, Ideological Memories and Exciting Puzzles, in O. Fillieule and G. Accornero (eds), *Social Movement Studies in Europe: The State of the Art* (New York: Berghahn Books), p. 32.

124. Lucio Magri, The May Events and Revolution in the West, *Socialist Register*, March 1969, 6, p. 37.

125. George Ross, Marxism and the Middle Classes: French Critiques, *Theory and Society*, 5(2), 163–190.

126. See also Chapter 8.

127. Daniel Oesch, *Redrawing the Class Map: Stratification and Institutions in Britain, Germany, Sweden and Switzerland* (Basingstoke: Palgrave Macmillan, 2006).

128. Val Burris, The Discovery of the New Middle Classes, *Theory and Society*, 1981, 15, pp. 317–49.

129. Guy Standing, *The Precariat* (London: Bloomsbury Academic, 2011).

130. Antonio Negri, Archaeology and Project: The Mass Worker and the Social Worker, in *Revolution Retrieved: Selected Writings on Marx, Keynes, Capitalist Crisis and New Social Subjects 1967-83* (London: Red Note, 1988).

131. Tronti, Our Operaismo.

132. For the initial attempt to rethink autonomia in post-Fordism, see Sergio Bologna and Andrea Fumagalli, *Il Lavoro Autonomo di Seconda Generazione: Scenari del Postfordismo in Italia* (Milan: Feltrinelli, 1997).

133. Andrea Fumagalli and Sandro Mezzadra (eds), *Crisis in the Global Economy: Financial Markets, Social Struggles and New Political Scenarios* (Los Angeles: Semiotext(e), 2010).

134. Guy Standing, *A Precariat Charter: From Denizens to Citizens* (London and New York: Bloomsbury Academic, 2014), p. 14.

135. Ibid.

136. Massimiliano Andretta and Donatella della Porta, Contentious Precarious Generation in Anti-austerity Movements in Spain and Italy, *OBETS: Revista de ciencias sociales*, 2015, 10 (1), pp. 37–66.

137. Maria Grasso and Marco Giugni, Do Issues Matter? Anti-austerity Protests' Composition, Values, and Action Repertoires Compared, in T. Davies, H. Ryan and A. Peña (eds), *Protest, Social Movements and Global Democracy Since 2011: New Perspectives. Research in Social Movements, Conflicts and Change* (Bingley: Emerald, 2016), p. 39.

138. Marco Giugni and Jasmine Lorenzini, Quiescent or Invisible? Precarious and Unemployed Movements in Europe, in. O. Fillieule and G. Accornero (eds), *Social Movement Studies in Europe: The State of the Art* (New York and Oxford: Berghahn Books, 2016), pp. 111–12.

139. Ronaldo Munck, The Precariat: A View from the South, *Third World Quarterly*, 2013, 34 (13), pp. 747–62.

140. Jan Breman, A Bogus Concept? *New Left Review*, November–December 2013, 84, pp. 130–8; Richard Seymour, We Are All Precarious: On the Concept of the 'Precariat' and Its Misuses, *New Left Blog*, 2012, www.newleftproject.org/index.php/site/article_comments/we_are_all_precarious_on_the_concept_of_the_precariat_and_its_misuses.

141. Della Porta, *Political Economy and Social Movement Studies*, pp. 453–73.

142. For an empirical analysis, see Matteo Bassoli and Lara Monticelli, Precarious Voices? Types of 'Political Citizens' and Repertoires of Action among European Youth, *PArtecipazione e COnflitto*, 2015, 9 (3), pp. 824–56.

143. Anna Kern, Sofie Marien and Marc Hooghe, Economic Crisis and Levels of Political Participation in Europe (2002–2010): The Role of Resources and Grievances, *West European Politics*, 2015, 38, pp. 465–90; Wolfgang Rudig and Georgios Karyotis, Who Protests in Greece? Mass Opposition to Austerity, *British Journal of Political Science*, 2014, 44 (3), pp. 487–513.

144. Nikolai Huke, Mònica Clua-Losada and David J. Bailey, Disrupting the European Crisis: A Critical Political Economy of Contestation, Subversion and Escape, *New Political Economy*, 2015, 20 (5), pp. 725–51.

145. E.g., see the empirical analysis of Anders Hylmφ and Magnus Wennerhag, Does Class Matter in Anti-austerity Protests? Social Class, Attitudes towards Inequality, and Political Trust in European Demonstrations in a Time of Economic Crisis, in M. Giugni and M. Grasso (eds), *Austerity and Protest: Popular Contention in Times of Crisis* (London: Routledge, 2015), pp. 83–109.

146. Giugni and Grasso, *Do Issues Matter?*

147. Martin Upchurch, Graham Taylor and Andy Mathers, The Crisis of 'Social Democratic' Unionism: The 'Opening up' of Civil Society and the Prospects for Union Renewal in the United Kingdom, France, and Germany, *Labor Studies Journal*, 2009, 34 (4), pp. 519–42.

148. Melanie Simms, Dennis Eversberg, Camille Dupuy and Lena Hipp, Organizing Young Workers under Precarious Conditions: What Hinders or Facilitates Union Success, *Work and Occupation*, 2018, 45 (4), pp. 420–50.

149. James E. Côté, Towards a Political Economy of Youth, *Journal of Youth Studies*, 2014, 17 (4), p. 528.

150. Keir Milburn, *Generation Left* (London: Polity, 2019), pp. 8–12.

151. Ibid.

152. Eric Hobsbawm, *Revolutionaries* (London: Abacus, 2007), p. 332.

153. Goran Therborn, New Masses: Social Bases of Resistance, *New Left Review*, Janurary–February 2014, 85, p. 6.

154. Andrews, The Three New Lefts, p. 71; Perry Anderson, *Arguments within English Marxism* (London and New York: Verso, 1980), pp. 16–58.

155. Magri, *The May Events*, p. 47.

156. See Michel Foucault, Truth and Power: An Interview with Michel Foucault, in P. Rabinow (ed.), *The Foucault Reader* (New York: Pantheon Books, 1984), p. 68.

157. Ibid.

158. Jon D. Wisman and Quentin Duroy, The Proletarianization of the Professoriate and the Threat to Free Expression, Creativity, and Economic Dynamism, *Journal of Economic Issues*, 2020, 54 (3), pp. 876–94.

159. Saskia Sassen, The Middle Classes, *Juncture*, 2013, 20 (2), pp. 125–8.

CHAPTER 6

1. The process of dealignment refers to the decline of social cleavages in terms of their causal power, as growing numbers of voters become less partisan and

transitory issues rather than durable programmatic allegiances structure the vote. Realignment refers to shifting partisan loyalties. See Simon Bornschier, Cleavage Politics in Old and New Democracies: A Review of the Literature and Avenues for Further Research, *Living Reviews in Democracy*, 2009, https://ethz.ch/content/dam/ethz/special-interest/gess/cis/cis-dam/CIS_DAM_2015/WorkingPapers/Living_Reviews_Democracy/Bornschier.pdf.

2. The growth of Euroscepticism since the beginning of the 1990s suggested for many scholars a decline in public consensus on the EU, which has had a constraining impact on the process of integrating European countries. Lisbet Hooghe and Gary Marks, A Postnationalist Theory of European Integration, *British Journal of Political Science*, 2009, 39 (1), pp. 1–23.

3. Stefano Bartolini and Peter Mair, *Identity, Competition, and Electoral Availability: The Stabilisation of European Electorates 1885–1985* (Cambridge: Cambridge University Press, 1990).

4. Claus Offe, Competitive Party Democracy and the Keynesian Welfare State, *Policy Sciences*, 1983, 15, pp. 225–46.

5. See also, Eley, *Forging Democracy*, p. 384.

6. Eric Hobsbawm, French Communism, *New Left Review*, May–June 1965, I(31), p. 95.

7. The main issue emerging from the Russian Revolution was whether social groups should become integrated into the national polity or commit as a part of the revolutionary movement on a strictly anti-systemic basis.

8. Dimitri Almeida, *The Impact of European Integration on Political Parties: Beyond the Permissive Consensus* (London: Routledge, 2012), pp. 45–68.

9. Eley, *Forging Democracy*, p. 500.

10. Robert Rohrschneider, Impact of Social Movements on European Party Systems, *The Annals of the American Academy of Political and Social Science*, 1993, 528 (1), pp. 157–70.

11. Brian Doherty, The Fundi–Realo Controversy: An Analysis of Four European Green Parties, *Environmental Politics*, 1 (1), pp. 95–120.

12. For noteworthy analyses of Green party identities, see Wilhelm P. Burklin, The Grünen: Ecology and the New Left, in G. Wallach and G. Romoser (eds), *West German Politics 1982/83* (New York: Praeger, 1985). Ferdinand Müller-Rommel, New Social Movements and Smaller Parties: A Comparative Perspective, *West European Politics*, 1985, 8 (1), pp. 41–54.

13. Some examples were the Trotskyist Socialist Workers' Party in the UK; the Marxist-Leninist Autonomia Operaia and Lotta Continua in Italy mentioned earlier; the initially Maoist Communist Movement, the Maoist Revolutionary Workers' Organisation, Workers' Party of Spain and Espagna Bandiera Roja in Spain; the Marxist United, Popular Unity in Portugal; the Maoist Communist Party of Greece (Marxist-Leninist) and the Maoist Workers Party of Norway (Marxist-Leninist) which survived until 2007.

14. Robert H. McNeal, Demonology: The Orthodox Communist Image of Trotskyism, *International Journal*, 1976, 32 (1), p. 39.

15. For the 'Golden Age' of British Trotskyism (1965–85), see John Kelly, *Contemporary Trotskyism: Parties, Sects and Social Movements in Britain* (London: Routledge, 2018), Ch. 3.

16. McNeal, *Demonology*, p. 32.

17. Belden A. Fields, *Trotskyism and Maoism: Theory and Practice in France and the United States* (New York: Praeger, 1988), pp. 231–50.

18. Robert Gildea, James Mark and Niez Pas, as cited in Quinn Slobodian, The Meanings of Western Maoism in the Global Sixties, in C. Jian, Martin Klimke, Masha Kirasirova, Mary Nolan, Marilyn Young and Joanna Waley-Cohen (eds), *The Routledge Handbook of the Global Sixties: Between Protest and Nation-Building* (London and New York: Routledge, 2018), p. 76.

19. See, e.g., Julia Lovell, The Cultural Revolution and its Legacies in International Perspective, *The China Quarterly*, 2016, 227, p. 643.

20. Alex Callinicos, *Trotskyism* (Buckingham: Open University Press, 1990), p. 41.

21. Eric Hobsbawm, Intellectuals, Society and the Left, *New Statesman*, 16 April 2007 [1978], www.newstatesman.com/society/2007/04/marxist-intellectuals-social.

22. Noam Chomsky, David Barsamian and Arthur Neiman, *How the World Works* (Soft Skull Press, 2011), pp. 294–5, https://1motorcyclist.files.wordpress.com/2016/03/noam-chomsky-2011-how-the-world-works.pdf.

23. Lovell, *The Cultural Revolution*, pp. 647–8.

24. Kelly, *Contemporary Trotskyism*.

25. Christian Hagsbjerg, Trotskyology, *International Socialism*, 2018, 150, http://isj.org.uk/trotskyology/.

26. Ibid.

27. For an overview, see Philippe Raynaud, *To Mosaiko tis Akras Aristeras* (Athens: Politeia), pp. 78–81.

28. Vicenzo Emmanuele and Allessandro Chiaramonte, A Growing Impact of New Parties: Myth or Reality? Party System Innovation in Western Europe after 1945, *Party Politics*, 2018, 24 (5), pp. 475–87.

29. Charalambous, *European Integration*, chapter 2.

30. See, e.g., PCE General Secretary Santiago Carillo's book, *Eurocommunism and the State* (London: Lawrence and Wishart, 1977), which aimed at elaborating 'a solid conception of the possibility of democratising the apparatus of the capitalist state, transforming it into a valid tool for constructing a socialist society, without needing to destroy it radically by force'.

31. Ioannis Balampanidis, *Eurocommunism: From the Communist to the Radical European Left* (London: Routledge, 2019).

32. Gerd-Rainer Horn, as cited in Maeckelbergh, *The Road to Democracy*, p. 313.

33. Marc Lazar, Communism in Western Europe in the 1980s, *Journal of Communist Studies*, 1988, 4 (3), pp. 243–57.

34. Francis Fukuyama, The End of History? *The National Interest*, 1989, 16, pp. 3–18.

35. See further in Martin J. Bull, The West European Communist Movement in the late Twentieth Century, *West European Politics*, 1995, 18 (1), pp. 78–97.

36. Chiocchetti, *The Radical Left Party Family*, p. 62.

37. March, *Radical Left 'Success'*, pp. 28–29.

38. See, Chiocchetti, *The Radical Left Party Family*, p. 38.

39. Bailey, *Protest Movements*, p. 61.

40. Patrick Berkurt, *Pirate Politics: The New Information Policy Contests* (Cambridge, MA: MIT Press, 2014), p. 57.

41. Martin Fredrikkson, The Pirate Party and the Politics of Communication, *International Journal of Communication*, 2015, 9, pp. 909–24.

42. Björn Swierczek, 5 years of Liquid Democracy in Germany, *The Liquid Democracy Journal*, 7 August 2011, https://liquid-democracy-journal.org/issue/1/The_Liquid_Democracy_Journal-Issue001-02-Five_years_of_Liquid_Democracy_in_Germany.html.

43. Dmytro Khutkyy, Pirate Parties: The Social Movements of Electronic Democracy, *Journal of Comparative Politics*, 2019, 12, pp. 49–58.

44. Kirk, M. Winans, Direct E-democracy and Political Party Websites in the United States and Sweden, thesis, Rochester Institute of Technology, 2015.

45. See Berkurt, *Pirate Politics*.

46. Margret Archer, The Generative Mechanism of Reconfiguring Late Modernity, in Margret Archer (ed.), *Late Modernity* (Dondrecht: Springer, 2014), pp. 93–117.

47. Martin Frederiksson and James Arvanitakis, Piracy, Property and the Crisis of Democracy. *eJournal of eDemocracy*, 2015, 7(1), pp. 134–50.

48. See especially, Jens Rydgren (ed.), *Class Politics and the Radical Right* (London and New York: Routledge, 2013).

49. Luke March and Charlotte Rommerskirchen, Out of Left Field? Explaining the Variable Electoral Success of European Radical Left Parties, *Party Politics*, 2015, 21(1), pp. 40–53.

50. Giuseppe Morosini, The European Left and the Third World, *Contemporary Marxism*, 1980, 2, pp. 67–80.

51. Ibid.

52. For a comparative analysis of the PCF and PS, see Valentine Lomelini, *Les Relations Dangereuses: French Socialists, Communists and the Human Rights Issue in the Soviet Bloc* (Brussels: Peter Lange, 2012), pp. 60–6.

53. As cited in ibid., p. 78.

54. Martin Shaw, Social Democracy in the Unfinished Global Revolution, in L. Martell (ed.), *The Future of Social Democracy* (London: Macmillan, 2001), pp. 8–25.

55. For France, the UK and Germany, see Roger Karapin, The Politics of Immigration Control in Britain and Germany, *Comparative Politics*, 1999, 31(4), pp. 423–44.

56. See Alec G. Hargreaves, Multi-ethnic *France: Immigration: Politics, Culture and Society* (London: Routledge, 2007), p. 171. For TV coverage of the story, and statements by the protagonists, see INA France, Foyer malien à Vitry, 27 December 1980, www.ina.fr/video/CAA8001946101.

57. Hargreaves, Multi-ethnic France. For a polemical view, reflecting tension between students and communists at the time, see Mitchell Abidos, 1968: When the Communist Party Stopped a French Revolution, *Revista de Prensa*, 2018 (19), www.almendron.com/tribuna/1968-when-the-communist-party-stopped-a-french-revolution/.

58. Joost Van Spanje, Contagious Parties: Anti-immigration Parties and Their Impact on Other Parties' Immigration Stances in Contemporary Western Europe, *Party Politics*, 2010, 16 (5), pp. 563–86.

59. See Volker Schmitz, The Wagenknecht Question, *Jacobin*, 15 January 2017, www.jacobinmag.com/2017/02/die-linke-germany-sahra-wagenknecht-immigration-xenophobia-afd/.

60. David Adler, Meet Europe's New Nationalists, *The Nation*, 10 January 2019, www.thenation.com/article/archive/meet-europes-left-nationalists/.

61. Leandros Fischer and Mark Bergfeld, Challenges Ahead: Germany's Die Linke in Times of Polarization, *Transform: A Journal of the Radical Left*, 2, pp. 71–112.

62. Max Van Lingen, The Stagnation of the Dutch Socialist Party, *International Socialism*, 2016, 151, https://isj.org.uk/the-stagnation-of-the-dutch-socialist-party/.

63. Francis McGowan and Daniel Keith, The Radical Left and Immigration: Resilient or Acquiescent in the Face of the Radical Right, in March and Keith, *Europe's Radical Left*, pp. 106–7.

64. See, Robert Stuart, *Marxism and National Identity: Socialism, Nationalism, and National Socialism during the French Fin de Siecle* (New York: SUNY University Press, 2006).

65. McGown and Keith, *The Radical Left and Immigration*, pp. 106–7.

66. David Adler, Meet Europe's New Nationalists, *The Nation*, 10 January 2019, www.thenation.com/article/archive/meet-europes-left-nationalists/.

67. See Lorenzo Cicchi, The European Parliament's Political Groups: Between High Cohesion and Recurrent Breakdowns, Technical Report, PADEMIA Research Notes on Parliamentary Democracy, 2017/03, figures 2.5 and 2.11.

68. McInnes, *The Communist Parties*, pp. 82–3.

69. See R. Dunphy, *Contesting Capitalism: Left Parties and European Integration* (Manchester: Manchester University Press, 2004), chapter 2.

70. McInnes, *The Communist Parties*, p. 83.

71. John Foster Leich, Communist Parties in the European Parliament: The Quest for Legitimacy, doctoral dissertation, University of Massachusetts at Amherst, 1976, pp. 50–73.

72. Ibid.

73. Dunphy, *Contesting Capitalism*, chapter 2.

74. David Bell, Western Communist Parties and the European Union, in J. Gaffney (ed.), *Political Parties and the European Union* (London: Routledge, 1996), pp. 220–35.

75. The EP approves the funding of the Europarties and the ELP has received increasing funds, all of which it has absorbed. See Enrico Calossi, *Anti-austerity Left Parties in the European Union: Competition, Coordination and Integration* (Pisa: Pisa University Press, 2016), p. 185, figure 6.

76. Ibid., p. 184.

77. Coates acted as the chairman of the human rights sub-committee and his initiatives included an EU-wide Pensioners' Parliament and a Convention for Full Employment. As a Euro-Keynesian, Coates was also in favour of the single currency. His political persona figured frequently in the polemics between parties such as the PCP and the KKE on the anti side, and Rifondazione or the IU on the pro side.

78. Sweden and Finland joined the EU in 1995. Denmark had joined in 1973.

79. Fritz Scharpf, Negative and Positive Integration in the Political Economy of European Welfare States, in M. Rhodes and Y. Mény (eds), *The Future of European Welfare: A New Social Contract?* (Houndmills: Macmillan, 1998), pp. 155–77.

80. Gerard Strange, The Left against Europe? A Critical Engagement with New Constitutionalism and Structural Dependence Theory, *Government and Opposition*, 2006, 41 (2), p. 215.

81. See, Giorgos Charalambous, All the Shades of Red: Examining the Radical Left's Euroscepticism, *Contemporary Politics*, 2011, 17 (3), pp. 299–320.

82. See also the analysis in Richard Dunphy and Luke March, *The European Left Party* (Manchester: Manchester University Press, 2019), p. 221.

83. As developed in Costas Lapavitsas, *The Left Case against the EU* (London: Wiley, 2018).

84. Panagiotis Sotiris, Why SYRIZA's Defeat Still Haunts the Left, *Jacobin*, 18 February 2020, www.jacobinmag.com/2020/02/syriza-greece-left-troika-brexit-eu-gramsci.

85. Daniel Keith, Opposing Europe, Opposing Austerity: Radical Left Parties and the Eurosceptic Debate, in B. Leruth, N. Startin and S. Usherwood (eds), *The Routledge Handbook of Euroscepticism* (London: Routledge, 2016), pp. 95–6.

86. See, e.g., Andrew Burgin, Brexit Britain, *Transform Europe*, 18 February 2020, www.transform-network.net/en/blog/article/brexit-britain/.

87. Thomas Fazi and William Mitchell, Why the Left Should Embrace Brexit, *Jacobin*, 29 April 2018, www.jacobinmag.com/2018/04/brexit-labour-party-socialist-left-corbyn.

88. Chiocchetti, *The Radical Left Party Family*, p. 61.

CHAPTER 7

1. Giovanni Sartori, *Parties and Party Systems: A Framework for Analysis* (Cambridge: Cambridge University Press, 1976), p. 194.

2. For content and discourse analyses of CPs and communist governments, see Franco Andreucci, The Languages of the Italian Communists: Some Descriptive Remarks (1921–1964), in Giulia Bassi (ed.), *Words of Power, the Power of Words: The Twentieth-Century Communist Discourse in International Perspective* (Trieste: EUT Edizioni Università di Trieste, 2019), pp. 27–56. See also Giolia Bassi, Introduction: Why Should the Linguistic Turn Be Taken?, in Bassi, *Words of Power*, pp. ix–xxi.

3. Hobsbawm, *Revolutionaries*, pp. 86–9.

4. Ernest Mandel, The Debate on Workers Control, *International Socialist Review*, 1968, 30 (3), www.marxists.org/archive/mandel/1968/wcontrol/workontrol.htm.

5. For an overview, see Max Liebman and Ralph Miliband, Reflections on Anti-communism, *Jacobin*, 12 December 2017, www.jacobinmag.com/2017/12/anti-communism-soviet-union-united-states-miliband.

6. Sociologist Daniel Bell's work on Soviet totalitarianism is representative of established Western epistemic communities centred on Cold War dynamics and deconstructing the enemy through the language of freedom. For the intellectual history behind this claim, see Hugh Wilford, Playing the CIA's Tune? The 'New Leader' and the Cultural Cold War, *Diplomatic History*, 2003, 27 (1), pp. 15–34.

7. Kyril Postoutenko, Prolegomena in the Study of Totalitarian Ideology, in K. Postoutenko (ed.), *Totalitarian Communication: Hierarchies, Codes and Messages* (Bielfeld: Verlag, 2010), pp. 11-42.

8. Sassoon, *A Hundred Years*, pp. 263–4.

9. Uwe Backes, *Political Extremes: A Conceptual History from Antiquity to the Present* (London: Routledge, 2011), p. 134.

10. Ibid.

11. Ibid.

12. Cited in David Arter, 'Communists We Are No Longer, Social Democrats We Can Never Be': The Evolution of the Leftist Parties in Finland and Sweden, *Journal of Communist Studies and Transition Politics*, 2002, 18 (3), p. 1.

13. The party name was often a compromise between their communist or radical tendencies on the one hand and the green libertarian or democratic socialist

on the other side. One such example is the Dutch Groen Links, established in 1989, and the Swedish Left-Communists of 1969.

14. For an analysis of how New Labour used a very similar discourse to Thatcher, see Stuart Hall, The Neoliberal Revolution, Soundings, 2011, 28 (2), pp. 9–27.

15. See, foremost, Anthony Giddens, *The Third Way: The Renewal of Social Democracy* (Cambridge: Polity Press, 1998), pp. 37–46. See also Joel Krieger, *British Politics in the Global Age: Can Social Democracy Survive?* (Cambridge, Polity Press, 2009), p. 26.

16. Based on the data in Tables 6.1 and 6.2, the following, common labels were systematically chosen by the main parliamentary RLPs established since the 1960s either out of splits or not: 'Left Socialist', 'Socialist', 'Left', 'Alternative', 'Red-Green', 'Green Left', 'Democratic Socialism/st'. The case of GUE/NGL established in 1994 is also indicative – European United Left/Nordic Green Left.

17. Anthony Oberschall, Opportunities and Framing in the Eastern European Revolts of 1989, in D. McAdam, J. D. McCarthy and M. N. Zald (eds), *Comparative Perspectives on Social Movements: Political Opportunities, Mobilizing Structures, and Cultural Framings* (Cambridge: Cambridge University Press, 1996), p. 97.

18. March, *Radical Left Parties in Europe*.

19. Parties such as Lutte Ouvriere in France, which are strictly anti-capitalist, use more class-based language. Indicatively, the party's slogan for the 2019 national parliamentary elections was 'Against big capital'.

20. See Congcong Wang and Dan Keith, The Greening of European Radical Left Parties: Red and Green Politics, *Journal of Contemporary European Studies*, 2020, https://doi.org/10.1080/14782804.2020.1792280; Andreas Fagerholm, What Is Left for the Radical Left? A Comparative Examination of the Policies of Radical Left Parties in Western Europe before and after 1989, *Journal of Contemporary European Studies*, 2017, 25 (1), pp. 16–40.

21. Wang and Keith, The Greening.

22. John Gaffney, Rhetoric and the Left: Theoretical Consideration, in J. Gaffney and J. Atkins (eds), *Voices of the UK Left: Rhetoric, Ideology and the Performance of Politics* (London: Palgrave Macmillan, 2017), p. 15; Judi Atkins, Reflections on the UK Left, Narrative, Leadership, Performance, in Gaffney and Atkins, Voices of the UK Left, pp. 231–40.

23. Giles Scott-Smith, *Western Communism and the Inderdoc Network* (London: Palgrave Macmillan, 2012), pp. 1–2.

24. Luke March, *Contemporary Far Left Parties in Europe: From Marxism to the Mainstream?* (Berlin: Friedrich-Ebert-Stiftung, 2008), p. 4, https://library.fes.de/pdf-files/id/ipa/05818.pdf.

25. See Moschonas, *In the Name of Social Democracy*, chapter 2.

26. See Kenneth M. Roberts, Crises of Representation and Populist Challenges to Liberal Democracy, *Chinese Political Science Review*, 2019, 4, pp. 188–99.

27. Sassoon, *One Hundred Years*, p. 99.
28. Ibid.
29. Mao Zedong, *On the Correct Handling of the Contradictions among the People*, 1957, www.marxists.org/referencearchive/mao/selected-works/volume-5/mswv5_58.htm.
30. Ross, *May '68 and Its Afterlives*, p. 99.
31. Patrick H. Hutton, *The Cult of Revolutionary Tradition: The Blanquists in French Politics, 1864–1893* (Berkeley: University of California Press, 1981), pp. 35–39.
32. See Kevin Olson, Populism in the Socialist Imagination, in C. R. Kaltwasser, P. Taggard, P. Ochoa Espejo and P. Ostiguy (eds), *The Oxford Handbook of Populism* (Oxford: Oxford University Press, 2017), pp. 661–78.
33. Ibid.
34. Pauline Johnson, In Search of a Leftist Democratic Imaginary: What Can Theories of Populism Tell Us?, *Journal of Political Ideologies*, 2017, 22 (1), p. 74.
35. Ibid., p. 84.
36. Ibid.
37. Eric Fassin, *Populism, Left and Right* (Chicago: Prickly Paradigm Press, 2019).
38. Chantal Mouffe, *For a Left Populism* (London: Verso, 2017), pp. 22–24.
39. Fassin, *Populism, Left and Right*.
40. Laura Roth and Kate Shea Baird, Left-Wing Populism and the Feminization of Politics, *ROAR*, 13 January 2017, https://roarmag.org/essays/left-populism-feminization-politics.
41. The slogan of Labour's and Jeremy Corbyn's campaigns, 'For the many, not the few', can be found in various other countries across the whole of Europe.
42. See Juha Herkman, Articulations of Populism: The Nordic Case, *Cultural Studies*, 2017, 31 (4), pp. 470–88.
43. Cultural resonance theories have shown very clearly how framing affects the ability of movements to achieve changes in values, attitudes and identities. See Verta Taylor and Nella Van Dyke, The Cultural Outcomes of Social Movements, in D. A. Snow, S. A. Soule, H. Kriesi and H. J. McCammon (eds), *The Wiley Blackwell Companion to Social Movements* (Oxford: Wiley Blackwell, 2014), pp. 262–93.
44. Juan Rodríguez-Teruel, Astrid Barrio and Oscar Barberà, Fast and Furious: Podemos' Quest for Power in Multi-level Spain, *South European Society and Politics*, 2016, 21 (4), p. 580.
45. James Petras, The Rise and Decline of Southern European Socialism, *New Left Review*, July–August 1984, 146, p. 37.
46. Ibid., pp. 37–8.
47. Seraphim Seferiades, Populism as Deceptive Invocations of the Popular, in G. Charalambous and G. Ioannou (eds), *Left Radicalism and Populism in Europe* (London: Routledge, 2019), pp. 223–56.

48. Michael Bray, Rearticulating Contemporary Populism, *Historical Materialism*, 2015, 23 (3), pp. 14, 18.

49. Boris Frankel, Confronting Neoliberal Regimes: The Post-Marxist Embrace of Populism and Realpolitik, *New Left Review*, November–December 1997, I(266), pp. 57–92.

50. Francisco Panizza, Introduction: Populism and the Mirror of Democracy, in F. Panizza (ed.), *Populism and the Mirror of Democracy* (London: Verso, 2005), p. 4.

51. See Kernallegenn, Les Gauches, pp. 147–8.

52. Waldeck Rochet, PCF general secretary between 1964 and 1969, declared: 'We always have, and always will, fight unhesitatingly against the nihilistic attitude towards our nation preached by certain so-called "revolutionary" anarchist elements. The Communists love their country passionately.' See David Broder, Class Struggle in France, May–June 1968, *Workers' Liberty*, 22 July 2008, www.workersliberty.org/story/2008/07/04/class-struggle-france-may-june-1968/.

53. Marc Lazar, The French Communist Party, in N. Naimark, S. Pons and S. Quinn Judge (eds), *The Cambridge History of Communism* (Cambridge: Cambridge University Press, 2004), pp. 619–41.

54. See Sassoon, *One Hundred Years*, pp. 133, 273; and Judt, *Marxism and the French Left*, p. 186.

55. Broder, Class Struggle.

56. David Adler and Ben Ansell, Housing and Populism, *West European Politics*, 2020, 43 (2), pp. 344–65.

57. For instance, the PCP leadership in Portugal has identified a 'two-fold character' in the current crisis: class struggle and national sovereignty. Hence it presented itself as a party with 'a patriotic politics of the left' (see also Appendix 2).

58. Costas Eleftheriou, Greek Radical Left Responses to the Crisis: Three Types of Political Mobilisation, One Winner, in March and Keith, *Europe's Radical Left*, pp. 289–310.

59. Yiannis Mylonas, Crisis, Austerity and Opposition in Mainstream Media Discourses of Greece, *Critical Discourse Studies*, 2004, 11 (3), p. 311. The 22 February 2010 cover of the weekly German news magazine *Focus*, which caused outrage in Greece, showed the goddess Aphrodite pointing the finger. The story, titled 'Swindlers in the Euro Family', included a detailed description of Greek society and claimed that the country had experienced '2000 years of decline'.

60. Sophia Hatzisavvidou, Demanding the Alternative: The Rhetoric of the UK Anti-austerity Movement, in J. Atkins and J. Gaffney (eds), *Voices of the UK Left: Rhetoric, Ideology and the Performance of Politics* (London: Palgrave Macmillan, 2017), pp. 211–30.

61. Jonas Van Vossole, Framing PIGS: Patterns of Racism and Neocolonialism in the Euro crisis, *Patterns of Prejudice*, 2016, 50 (1), pp. 1–20.

62. E.g., John Milios and Dimitris P. Sotiropoulos, Crisis of Greece or Crisis of the Euro? A View from the European "Periphery", *Journal of Balkan and Near Eastern Studies*, 2010, 12 (3), pp. 223–40.

63. See Costas Eleftheriou, Greek Anti-imperialism: Contemporary Era, in Zak Cope and Immanuel Ness (eds), *The Palgrave Encyclopedia of Imperialism and Anti-imperialism* (Basingstoke: Palgrave Macmillan, 2021), pp. 341–6.

64. Immanuel Wallerstein, The Global Left: Past, Present, and Future, *Verso Blog*, 4 September 2019, www.versobooks.com/blogs/4429-the-global-left-past-present-and-future.

65. Connor Walker, *The National Question in Marxist-Leninist Theory and Strategy* (Princeton: Princeton University Press, 1984), pp. 554–5.

66. Rogers Brubaker, Populism and Nationalism, *Nations and Nationalism*, 2020, 26 (1), pp. 44–66.

67. Gordon Laxer, The Movement that Dare Not Speak Its Name: The Return of Left Nationalism/Internationalism, *Alternatives*, 2001, 26 (1), pp. 1–32.

68. George Souvlis and Neil Davidson, The National Question, Class and the European Union: An Interview with Neil Davidson, *Salvage*, 22 July 2017, https://salvage.zone/online-exclusive/the-national-question-class-and-the-european-union-neil-davidson/.

69. Ibid.

70. Yasmeen Yerhan, Ireland's Nationalist Past Breaks Through, *The Atlantic*, 10 Feb. 2020, www.theatlantic/international//2020/02/ireland-election-sinn-fein-brexit-nationalism/606328/.

71. See Jorge Sola and César Rendueles, Podemos, the Upheaval of Spanish Politics and the Challenge of Populism, *Journal of Contemporary European Studies*, 2018, 26 (1), pp. 99–116; Marc Bassets, Spain's New Patriots, *Dissent*, Summer 2015, www.dissentmagazine.org/article/marc-bassets-podemos-patriotism-spain.

72. According to Pablo Iglesias: 'Saying patria with pride is a question that goes beyond left and right ... This is about being patriotic and being decent, and in this country no government has been either patriotic or decent.' As cited in Bassets, Spain's New Patriots.

73. See Lorenzo Bossi, Explaining Pathways to Armed Activism in the Provisional Irish Republican Army, 1968–1972, *Social Science History*, 2012, 36(3), pp. 347–90.

74. Boaz Vilallonga, The Catalan Left: An Interview with Boaz Vilallonga, *Jacobin*, 18 October 2015, www.jacobinmag.com/2015/10/catalanreferendum-spain-podemos-independence/.

75. Gregoris Ioannou and Giorgos Charalambous, Conclusions: Populism and Left Radicalism in Europe across Time and Space, in G. Charalambous and G. Ioannou (eds), *Left Radicalism and Populism in Europe* (London: Routledge), p. 265.

CHAPTER 8

1. March and Keith, *Europe's Radical Left*.
2. In the 1910s, for example, the German SPD had more than a million members. Moschonas, *In the Name*, p. 25.
3. Jane Jenson and George Ross, *The View from Inside: A French Communist Cell in Crisis* (Berkeley: University of California Press, 1984), pp. 361–2.
4. Frank P. Belloni and Dennis C. Beller (eds), *Faction Politics: Political Parties and Factionalism in Comparative Perspective* (Santa Barbara, CA: Clio Press, 1978).
5. For a review, see McInnes, *The Communist Parties*, pp. 130–40.
6. Waller, *Democratic Centralism: An Historical Commentary* (Manchester: Manchester University Press, 1981), pp. 35–44.
7. Ibid.
8. Branko Pribicevic, Eurocommunism and the New Party, in R. Kindersley (ed.), *In Search of Eurocommunism* (London: Macmillan, 1981), p. 177.
9. As cited in ibid.
10. Waller, *Democratic Centralism*, p. 120.
11. Fields, *Trotskyism and Maoism*, p. 87.
12. Ibid.
13. See, e.g., the analyses of intellectuals and members of the PCF, Etienne Balibar and Louis Althusser, who led the front of criticism against the PCF's shift to Eurocommunism without changing its fusion with the working class. Althusser had accused democratic centralism of 'cementing' (homogenisation). Jörg Nowak, Louis Althusser's Critique of the Communist Party and the Question of the Postrevolutionary State, *Rethinking Marxism: A Journal of Economics, Culture and Society*, 2017, 29 (2), pp. 234–55.
14. See the treatment of Simon Tormey, After the Party's Over: The Horizontalist Critique of Representation and Majoritarian Democracy – Lessons from the Alter-globalisation Movement (AGM), paper prepared for presentation at the European Consortium of Political Research workshop on Democracy and Political Parties, Granada 2005.
15. Kevin Devlin, The Challenge of Eurocommunism, in David Albright (ed.), *Communism and Political Systems in Western Europe* (Boulder: Westview Press, 1979), pp. 289–324.
16. Pribicevic, *Eurocommunism*.
17. See Eley, *Forging Democracy*, p. 361.
18. See Giorgos Charalambous, Illiberal Organisation? Patterns of Internal Party Democracy on the European Radical Left, *PArtecipazione e COnflitto*, 2021, 14 (1), pp. 411–34.
19. Daniel Keith and Giorgos Charalambous, On the (Non) Distinctiveness of Marxism-Leninism: The Portuguese and Greek Communist Parties Compared, *Communist and Post-Communist Studies*, 2016, 49 (2), p. 157.

20. Manuela Caiani, Erica Padoan and Bruno Marino, Candidate Selection, Personalization and Different Logics of Centralization in New Southern European Populism: The Cases of Podemos and the M5S, *Government and Opposition*, 2021, pp. 1–24, https://doi.org/10.1017/gov.2021.9.

21. For the Dutch SP, see Amieke Bouma, The Socialist Party (SP) in the Netherlands, in C. Hildebrandt and L. Wagner (eds), *Radical Left in Europe* (Berlin: Rosa Luxemburg Stiftung, 2017), www.rosalux.de/fileadmin/rls_uploads/pdfs/transform/Radical_Left_in_Europe_2017.pdf.

22. Krowel, *Party Models*.

23. This is a widely documented tendency of the PCI, while for the PCF it was a more temporary affair.

24. Paolo Chiocchetti, *Radical Left Party Database*, 2017. The author thanks Chiocchetti for sharing data from the database.

25. See also Neil Tannahill, *The Communist Parties of Western Europe: A Comparative Study* (Westport, CT: Greenwood Press, 1978), pp. 249–64.

26. Chiocchetti, *The Radical Left Party Family*, p. 44. See also, Stedano Bartolini, *The Political Mobilisation of the European Left*, 1860–1980 (Cambridge: Cambridge University Press), p. 269.

27. Chiocchetti, *The Radical Left Party Family*, p. 44.

28. Loudovikos Kotsonopoulos, Strategic Difficulties of Organisational Experiments in European RLPs: The Case of SYRIZA, paper presented at the Radical Left and Crisis in the EU: From Marginality to the Mainstream? University of Edinburgh, Scotland, 17 May 2013.

29. Gerbaudo, *The Digital Party*, p. 5.

30. Ibid.

31. *Insider*, Τι φοβάται η Αριστερή Πτέρυγα του ΣΥΡΙΖΑ, 27 October 2019, www.insider.gr/eidiseis/politiki/124191/ti-fobatai-i-aristeri-pteryga-toy-syriza.

32. Gideon Rahat and Assaf Shapira, An Intra-party Democracy Index: Theory, Design and a Demonstration, *Parliamentary Affairs*, 2017, 70, pp. 84–110.

33. Dean, *Crowds and Party*, chapter 5.

34. Jodi Dean, *Comrades: An Essay on Political Belonging* (London: Verso, 2019).

35. Gerbaudo, *The Digital Party*.

36. Giorgos Katsambekis and Alexandros Kioupkiolis, *The Populist Radical Left in Europe* (London: Routledge, 2019), p. xi.

37. Peter Lange, C. Irvin and Sidney Tarrow, Mobilization, Social Movements and Party Recruitment: The Italian Communist Party since the 1960s, *British Journal of Political Science*, 1990, 20 (1), pp. 15–42.

38. Michael Waller, The Radical Sources of the Crisis in West European Communist Parties, *West European Politics*, 1988, 37 (1), pp. 39–61.

39. Marzio Barbagli and Piergiorgio Corbetta, The Italian Communist Party and the Social Movements, in M. Zeitlin (ed.), *Political Power and Social Theory: A Research Annual*, Volume 3 (Greenwich, CT: JAI, 1982), pp. 77–112.

40. As cited in Victor Strazzieri, Forging Socialism through Democracy: A Critical Review Survey of Literature on Eurocommunism, *Twentieth Century Communism*, 2019, 17, p. 53.

41. Picchio, *Party Responses to Social Movements*, pp. 67–91.

42. Strazzieri, Forging Socialism, p. 52.

43. Sven E. Olsson, Swedish Communism Poised between Old Reds and New Greens, *Journal of Communist Studies*, 1986, 4 (2), p. 366.

44. E.g., see Martin Thomas, Winning the Battle of Ideas: Methods and Contact Work in the Lutte Ouvriere, *Workers' Liberty*, 7 April 2020, www. workersliberty.org/story/2010-04-07/winning-battle-ideas-methods-contact-work-lutte-ouvriere.

45. John Kelly, *Contemporary Trotskyism: Parties, Sects and Social Movements in Britain* (London: Routledge, 2018).

46. Ben Criddle, The French Socialist Party, in W. P. Paterson and A. H. Thomas (eds), *The Future of Social Democratic Parties in Western Europe* (Oxford: Clarendon, 1986), pp. 223–41.

47. Carl Boggs, *Social Movements and Political Power: Emerging Forms of Radicalism in the West* (Philadelphia: Temple University Press, 1986), pp. 89–105.

48. Petras, *The Rise and Decline*.

49. Giorgos Charalambous, Between Realignment and Entrenchment: The Europeanisation of Rifondazione Communista, *Perspectives on European Politics and Society*, 2011, 12 (1), p. 42.

50. The ELP declared at its first congress in Athens in 2005: 'The European Left and its member parties are committed to fight together with social movements, trade unions, and political left forces for another Europe, which is possible.' As cited in Massimiliano Andretta and Herbert Reiter, Parties, Unions, and Movements: The European Left and the ESF, in Donatella della Porta (ed.), *Another Europe: Conceptions and Practices of Democracy in European Social Forums* (London: Routledge, 2009), p. 179.

51. Daniel Keith, Radical Left Parties and Left Movements in Northern Europe, in Magnus Wennerhag, Christian Fröhlich and Grzegorz Piotrowski (eds), *Radical Left Movements in Europe* (London and New York: Routledge, 2017).

52. Martin Bak Jørgensen and Oscar Garcia Agustin, Uplifting the Masses? Radical Left Parties and Social Movements after the Crisis, in March and Keith, *Europe's Radical Left*, p. 78.

53. Ibid., p. 88.

54. Kostas Kanelopoulos and Konstantinos Kostopoulos, The Major Organizations/ Groups behind the Greek Anti-austerity Campaign: Repertoires of Action and Political Claims, paper presented at 8th ECPR General Conference, 3–6 September 2014, University of Glasgow, http://ecpr.eu/Filestore/Paper Proposal/ff897920-1ba0-49c7- 947b-562c8ee29448.pdf.

55. As claimed, for example, by Jørgensen and Augustin, *Uplifting the Masses*.

56. Keith and Charalambous, *On the (Non) Distinctiveness*.

57. See, Charalambous, *European Integration*, p. 123.

58. Giorgos Charalambous and Iasonas Lamprianou, Societal Responses to the Post-2008 Economic Crisis among South European and Irish Radical Left Parties: Continuity or Change and Why? *Government and Opposition*, 2016, 51 (2), pp. 261–93.

59. Myrto Tsakatika and Marco Lisi, Zippin' up My Boots, Goin' Back to My Roots: Radical Left Parties in Southern Europe, *South European Society and Politics*, 2013, 18 (1), p. 6.

60. E.g., Jon Burchell, Evolving or Conforming? Assessing Organisational Reform within European Green Parties, *West European Politics*, 2001, 24 (3), pp. 113–34.

61. Lasse Thomassen and Marina Prentoulis, Movement Parties: A New Hybrid Form of Politics?, in C. Flesher Fominaya and R. Feenstra (eds), *The Routledge Handbook of Contemporary European Social Movements* (London: Routledge, 2020), p. 345.

62. Manuel Cervera Marzal, Podemos: A 'Party-Movement' in Government, *Jacobin*, 1 September 2020, www.jacobinmag.com/2020/01/podemos-party-social-movement-pablo-iglesias.

63. Jiri Valenta, Coalition Strategies and Tactics in Marxist Though, in Todd Gilbert (ed.), *Coalition Strategies of Marxist Parties* (Durham, NC: Duke University Press), p. 39.

64. Ibid., p. 41.

65. Chiocchetti, *The Radical Left Party* Family, p. 70.

66. Jonathan Olsen, Michael Koss and Dan Hough, Conclusions: Left Parties in National Government, in J. Olsen, M. Koss and D. Hough (eds), *Left Parties in National Governments* (Basingstoke: Palgrave Macmillan), p. 184.

67. Ibid., p. 184.

68. March, *Radical Left 'Success'*, p. 42.

69. Olsen et al., *Conclusions*, p. 184.

70. Bailey, *Protest Movements*, p. 206; Jonah Birch, The Many Lives of Francois Mitterand, *Jacobin*, 19 August 2005, www.jacobinmag.com/2015/08/francois-mitterrand-socialist-party-common-program-communist-pcf-1981-elections-austerity/.

71. Peter A. Hall, *Governing the Economy: The Politics of State Intervention in Britain and France* (New York: Oxford University Press, 1986).

72. Maria João Ferreira and Pedro Fonsesca, in I. David (ed.), *Crisis, Austerity and Transformation: How Neoliberalism Is Changing Portugal* (Lanham, MD: Lexington Books, 2018), pp. 133–56.

73. March, *Radical Left 'Success'*, p. 35.

74. See Bartolini, *The Political Mobilization*; Tannahill, *The Communist Parties*, p. 64.

75. Chiocchetti, *The Radical Left Party* Family, p. 71.

76. Olsen et al., *Conclusions*, pp. 84–6.

77. Ioannis Balampanidis, Ioannis Vlastaris, Giorgos Xanozakis and Magdalini Karagkiozoglou, Bridges over Troubled Waters? The Competitive Symbiosis of Social Democracy and Radical Left in Crisis-Ridden Southern Europe, *Government and Opposition*, 2019, 1–23, https://doi.org/10.1017/gov.2019.8.

78. Ralph Miliband, *The State in Capitalist Society* (London: Weidenfeld & Nicolson, 1969).

79. Adam Przeworski, Social Democracy as a Historical Phenomenon, *New Left Review*, July–August 1980, I(122), p. 35.

80. Florian Wilde, Winning Power, Not Just Government, *Jacobin*, 18 April 2017, www.jacobinmag.com/2017/04/left-parties-government-elections-socialist-politics/.

81. Catarina Principe, Introduction: Europe in Revolt, in C. Principe and B. Sunkara (eds), *Europe in Revolt* (Chicago: Haymarket Books, 2016), p. 3.

82. Ibid.

83. Birch, *The Many Lives*.

84. Boggs, *Social Movements and Political Power*, p. 237.

85. Ibid.

86. Maia Kirby, Instituting Momentum, in J. Ibrahim and M. Roberts (eds), *Contemporary Left-Wing Activism*, Volume 2 (London: Routledge, 2018), pp. 127–43.

87. Ibid.

88. This practice violated the party statute. See Giannis Mavris, *ΣΥΡΙΖΑ, Κόμμα, Κράτος, Μετά τη Διακυβέρνηση, τι*, www.mavris.gr/6019/syriza-party-state/.

89. Catarina Príncipe, *Anti-austerity and the Politics of Toleration in Portugal: A Way for the Radical Left to Develop a Transformative Project?* (Berlin: Rosa-Luxemburg-Stiftung, 2017), pp. 9, 19, www.rosalux.de/fileadmin/rls_uploads/pdfs/sonst_publikationen/Politics_of_Toleration_Portugal.pdf.

90. Richard Dunphy and Tim Bale, The Radical Left in Coalition Government: Towards a Comparative Measurement of Success and Failure, *Party Politics*, 2004, pp. 488–504.

91. Richard Katz and William Cross, The Challenges of Intra-party Democracy, in W. Cross and R. Katz (eds), *The Challenges of Intra-party Democracy* (Oxford: Oxford University Press, 2013). pp. 1–10.

92. Ibid.

93. Herbert Kitschelt, Movement Parties, in R. S. Katz and W. Crotty (eds), *Handbook of Party Politics* (London: SAGE, 2006), pp. 288.

94. The party was founded by Robert Linhart, a student of Louis Althusser.

95. Jeremy Tranmer, A Force to Be Reckoned with? The Radical Left in the 1970s, *Revue Française de Civilisation Britannique*, 2017, http://journals.openedition.org/rfcb/1728.

96. See ibid., esp. p. 45. In Cyprus, students with Trotskyist and Third Worldist attachments from France and the UK joined the socialist party at the time, Eniaia Dimokratiki Enosi Kentrou.

97. McInnes, *The Communist Parties*, pp. 75–78.

98. Tannahill, *The Communist Parties*, pp. 183–203.

99. Moschonas, *In the Name of Social Democracy*.

100. Tannahill, *The Communist Parties*.

101. Jane Gingrich, A New Progressive Coalition? The European Left at a Time of Change, *Political Quarterly*, 2017, 88 (1), p. 42.

102. For example, see Paul Nieuwbeerta and Nan De Graaf, Traditional Class Voting in Twenty Postwar Societies, in G. Evans (ed.), *The End of Class Politics? Class Voting in Comparative Context* (Oxford: Oxford University Press, 1999), pp. 23–56.

103. Gingrich, *A New Progressive Coalition?*, p. 42.

104. H. Mendras and Alistair M. Cole, *Social Change in Modern France: Towards a Cultural Anthropology of the Fifth Republic* (Cambridge: Cambridge University Press, 1991), pp. 75–6.

105. McInnes, *The Communist Parties*, p. 51.

106. Ibid., p. 58.

107. See Luis Ramiro, Support for Radical Left Parties in Western Europe: Social Background, Ideology and Political Orientations, *European Political Science Review*, 2016, 8 (1), pp. 1–23.

108. Daniel Oesch, *Redrawing the Class Map* (Basingstoke: Palgrave Macmillan, 2006).

109. Philip Manow, Bruno Pallier and Hanna Schwander, Conclusion, in Philip Manow, Bruno Pallier and Hanna Schwander (eds), *Welfare Democracies and Party Politics: Explaining Electoral Dynamics in Times of Changing Welfare* (Oxford: Oxford University Press, 2018).

110. See Raul Gomez, Luis Ramiro and Laura Morales, Varieties of Radicalism: Examining the Diversity of Radical Left Parties and Voters in Western Europe, *West European Politics*, 2016, 39 (2), pp. 351–79.

111. See also Herbert Kitschelt, *Diversification and Reconfiguration of Party Systems in Postindustrial Democracies* (Bonn: Friedrich-Ebert-Stiftung, 2004), p. 6, https://library.fes.de/pdf-files/id/02608.pdf.

112. Bruno Palier, Jan Rovny and Allision E. Rovny, The Dual Dualization of Europe: Economic Convergence, Divergence, and their Political Consequences, in Manow et al., *Welfare Democracies and Party Politics*, pp. 29–60.

113. Daniel Oesch, The Class Basis of the Cleavage between the New Left and the Radical Right: An Analysis for Austria, Denmark, Norway and Switzerland, in Jens Rydgren (ed.), *Class Politics and the Radical Right* (London: Routledge, 2015), 31–51.

114. Luis Ramiro Fernandez, The Crisis of Western Communist Parties: Reconsidering Socio-structural Explanations, Working Paper 10/2003, Departmento de Cienca Politica e Estudios Internacionals, University Autonoma de Madrid, 2013.

115. See Thomas Piketty, *Capital in the Twentieth Century* (Cambridge, MA: Belknap Press: 2017). For southern Europe, where the phenomenon has been more pronounced during the economic crisis there and where mobilisations were massive, see Gregoris Ioannou, *Employment, Trade Unionism, and Class: The Labour Market in Southern Europe since the Crisis* (London: Routledge, 2021).

116. Therborn, *New Masses*, p. 10.

117. Erik Olin Wright, *Classes* (London and New York: Verso, 1985); Erik Olin Wright, *Class Counts* (Cambridge: Cambridge University Press, 1997).

118. Therborn, *New Masses*, p. 16.

119. Rosalind Shorrocks, Cohort Change in Political Gender Gaps in Europe and Canada: The Role of Modernization, *Politics and Society*, 2018, 46 (2), pp. 135–75.

120. Kitschelt, *Diversification and Reconfiguration*, p. 9.

121. In reading the graphs, there are two caveats: first the lack of data between 1995 and 2002 might have shown a smoother drop; and second, measurement errors may overestimate the drop. Nevertheless, there is clearly a theoretical rationale for the drop and the two surveys used are highly correlated in terms of their left–right self-placement questions.

122. Anne Muxel, Youth and Politics in France: Democratic Deficit or New Model of Citizenship?, in M. Demossier, D. Lees, A. Mondon and N. Parish (eds), *The Routledge Handbook of French Politics and Culture* (Oxford and New York: Routledge, 2020), pp. 97–108.

123. Ramiro, *Support for Radical Left Parties*.

124. Miki Caul, Women's Representation in Parliament: The Role of Political Parties, *Party Politics*, 1999, 5 (1), pp. 79–98.

125. Oddbjørn Knutsen, *Social Structure and Party Choice in Western Europe: A Comparative Longitudinal Study* (Houndmills: Palgrave Macmillan, 2004), pp. 198–200.

126. Zoe Lefkofridi and Juan Casado-Asensio, European Vox Radicis: Representation and Policy Congruence on the Extremes, *Comparative European Politics*, 2013, 11, pp. 93–118.

127. Michael A. Hansen and Jonathan Olsen, Sibling Rivalry: Voters for Radical Left Parties and their Competitors in Germany, Sweden and the Netherlands, *Party Politics*, 2021, https://doi.org/10.1177/13540688211035027; Giorgos Charalambous and Iasonas Lamprianou, The (Non) Particularities of West European Radical Left Party Supporters: Comparing Left Party Families, *European Political Science Review*, 2015, 9(3), pp. 375–400.

128. Among many other sources, see Ronald Tiersky, Declining Fortunes of the French Communist Party, *Problems of Communism*, 1988, September–October, pp. 1–22; Balampanidis, *Eurocommunism*, p. 212; McInnes, *The Communist Parties*, pp. 83–95.

129. Herbert Marcuse, *Counter-revolution and Revolt* (Boston: Beacon Press, 1972), p. 45.

130. Fabien Escalona, The Heritage of Eurocommunism in the Contemporary Radical Left, *Socialist Register*, 2017, 53, p. 111.

CHAPTER 9

1. Carl Boggs, *Social Movements and Political Power*, p. 239.

Index

Index

Panhellenic Socialist Party (PASOK), xiii, 209, 229, 234
pacifist/m, 71–2, 81, 83, 136, 169, 230, 264
peace movements, 40, 70–6, 104, 153, 159, 214
  and movement structures, 122; and parties, 170, 228–9; and violence, 130; examples of peace movement organisations, 170; Campaign for Nuclear Disarmament (CND), 72; World Peace Council (WPC); 70, 169, 293
  see also, anti–war
people–centrism, 94, 97, 96–8, 200
People's Global Action, 118
peasants, 65, 103, 138, 214, 248
pirates/Pirate Parties, 36, 167–8, 184, 225, 266
Platform for People Affected by Mortgages (PAH) 39, 114, 231
political consumerism, 20–1, 122, 261
Popular Front, 35, 46, 197–8, 276
Portugal, 39, 54, 62, 145, 161, 162, 167, 170, 191, 193, 205, 215, 234–5, 239–40, 267, 317
  Portuguese Communist Party (PCP), 165, 175, 192, 194, 200, 215, 222–3, 232, 239, 273–4, 313, 317; Bloco, 160, 174, 191, 222, 224, 230, 239, 244
post–communist 166, 191
post–modern(ism), 50, 99, 260
post–structural(ism) 50, 100, 290
  see also post–democracy
Poulatzas, Nicos, 95
precariat, 141–2
prefigure/ation/ative, 17, 24, 40, 55, 62, 81, 87, 107, 108, 116, 120, 124–6, 126, 149, 230, 254
proletariat/n, 146, 158, 186. 190–1, 194, 231, 246–7, 258
  dictatorship of the proletariat, 186, 189–90, 195, 197, 218; internation-alism, 64, 166; proletarianisation 146, 168

Radical Right (Parties)
  and RLPs, 169–72; and voters, 199–200, 248; Populist Radical Right, 4; Alt Right, 4; New Right, 4; extreme right, 15, 49, 75, 83, 168, 169 172–3, 184, 201, 253, 282; far(-)right, xv, 131, 134–5, 169, 172, 199, 207, 270
Reagan, Ronald, 51
realignment, 18, 21, 145, 153, 157, 231, 255, 264, 270, 309, 321
red–green, 183–93, 214, 258, 266, 315
refugee(s), 67–8, 118, 119, 134, 258
  'refugee crisis', 118; asylum seekers, 134 ; and the French Socialist Party (PS), 173
  asylum policy, 79; refugeehood, 68, 70
  see also, immigrants/ation
reformism/ist, 35, 45, 49–50, 54–6, 60, 80–1, 86, 88, 166, 176, 183–4, 188, 201–3, 211, 229, 238, 241, 258, 261, 267
regionalism, 103, 105, 203–4, 212, 262, 264, 270
  regionalist parties, 104
revisionism/st, 100, 108, 158, 169, 186–8, 190
revolution(s), 5, 11, 24, 35–6, 40
  cultural revolution, 103, 260; everyday, 86; French Revolution, 98, 198, 260; Pots and Pans Revolution, 44; Russian revolution 155, 309; 'silent revolution', 50; revolutionary subject(s), 138, 233, 254, 258, 260
riot(s/ing), 128, 133, 135–7, 231–2
Ritzer, George, 97
Rosa Luxemburg Stiftung, 168, 230
  see also, Luxemburg, Rosa

ruling class, 83, 86, 90, 95, 164, 203,
210
Capitalist class, 262
see also, bourgeoisie

Sassoon, Donald, 280
Sanders, Bernie, 144
Sassen, Saskia, 83, 111
Schwartzmantel, John, 22
Scotland, 84, 106, 204, 207–8, 270, 306
Scottish National Party (SNP), 183,
208; Scottish Socialist Party, 224
Seferiades, Seraphim, 202
Sino–Soviet conflict/Split, 103, 187, 270
sloganeering, 96, 194, 196, 210, 258
'Beauty is in the Streets', 111; 'For
the many, not the few', 316;
'Everything, now', 48; 'No one is
illegal', 67; 'People before Profit',
97; 'All power to the 99%'; '(All)
Power to the People', 95; 'Occupy
Everything', 111; 'Don't vote,
occupy, 111; 'System Change,
Not Climate Change, 56;; 'We are
all immmigrants', 67; 'We want
everything', 48; 'Your wars, our
dead', 293; 'Solidarity against your
Fortress Europe', 293
slogans and Parties, 271–7 (Appendix
II)
Social Democratic Parties (SDPs), 8, 32,
34–6, 69–70, 155, 157, 161, 170,
178, 186, 193, 214, 216–7, 229, 231,
235–6, 240, 243, 246, 251–4, 260–1
socialism, 58–9, 100, 108, 114, 139, 158,
164–5, 173, 175, 197–8, 221, 229,
232–3, 238, 239, 241, 246, 254, 268
Albanian socialism 159; and anti-
capitalism, 58; and definitional
issues, 34–6, 41; and nationalism,
103, 185, 203–10; and populism,
101–2, 206–7; ecosocialism, 57;
humanistic, 187; in party slogans,

275; pseudo–socialism, 169;
scientific, 59, 186, 197; authoritarian 81, actually, existing socialism,
'peace and socialism', 193, 81,
165–6, 192, 197, the parliamentary
road to, 154; theory of socialism in
one country, 173
see also, democratic socialism
solidarity economy/ies, 55, 118–21
sovereign(ty), 23, 317
economic sovereignty, 202, 212;
national sovereignty 102, 104–5,
107, 177, 196, 209, 317; popular
sovereignty, 94, 96, 98, 102, 106,
17, 186, 200; sovereignty and
movements 45, 55, 57, 73–4, 80,
89–90, 94, 96, 98, 102–6, 107; and
parties, 172, 176–7, 179, 182, 186,
196, 200, 202–4, 207, 209, 212, 267;
shared sovereignty, 106
Spain, 39, 43–4, 55, 60–2, 84, 101, 104,
106, 112, 119, 126, 128, 144–5, 156,
160–2, 164–5, 167, 170, 172, 174,
191, 193, 200–1, 205–6, 208, 215,
229–31, 233–4, 240, 264–5
Spanish Civil War, 86; Spanish
Communist Party (PCE), 164–5,
170, 175, 215, 275–6, 311; United
Left (IU), 62 171, 174, 176, 177,
191, 201, 215, 222, 224, 230–1,
275–6; Socialist Workers' Party
(PSOE), 215, 229; Podemos, 61–2,
84, 93, 114, 117, 126, 144, 149, 160,
174, 178, 193, 200–1, 204, 208, 215,
222, 225, 231, 233–4, 243, 275–6
squat(ting/s), 43, 11, 114, 122, 136, 260
Stalin, Joseph, 156, 183–4, 187, 191,
246, 259
death of Stalin, 81, 270; stalinism and
totalitarianism, 46; totalitarian
communism, 193; totalitarianism
and the USSR, 189, 314; Stalin and
Trotskyism, 157; anti–Stalinism,

Thanks to our Patreon Subscribers:

Lia Lilith de Oliveira
Andrew Perry

Who have shown generosity and
comradeship in support of our publishing.

Check out the other perks you get by subscribing
to our Patreon – visit patreon.com/plutopress.

Subscriptions start from £3 a month.